10630692

MARY PICKFORD
From Here to
Hollywood

Mary Pickford

From Here to Hollywood

By

SCOTT EYMAN

Harper Collins
TORONTO

Copyright © 1990 by Scott Eyman

All rights reserved, including the right of reproduction in whole or in part in any form. Published in Canada by Harper Collins Publishers Ltd., Suite 2900, 55 Avenue Road, Toronto, Ontario, M5R 3L2. Published in the United States of America by Donald I. Fine, Inc.

Canadian Cataloging-in-Publication Data
Eyman, Scott, 1951–
Mary Pickford, From Here to Hollywood/Scott Eyman.
p. cm.
ISBN 0-00-215684-9
1. Pickford, Mary, 1893–1979. 2. Motion picture actors and actresses—Canada/United States—Biography. 3. Motion picture producers and directors—Canada/United States—Biography.
I. Title.
PN2287.P5E96 1990
791.43′028′092—c90-093431-x

Manufactured in the United States of America

10 9 8 7 6 5 4 3 2 1

Designed by Irving Perkins Associates

This book is for
Lynn Robin Kalber Eyman
<u>my</u> sweetheart

"I think a biography is much more interesting than an autobiography. [In my own book] I couldn't tell the worst and the best. And to round out a character, it has to be three-dimensional, if possible four-dimensional. It makes for interesting reading."

—*Mary Pickford, 1957*

Contents

Introduction

*A*T night, she dreamed of Douglas. He seemed so real that she would call out for him, her small voice draining away in the hushed halls of Pickfair. Other times she would see Charlotte, her mother, who had controlled her so rigidly. Dreaming of Charlotte was the worst, for it was Charlotte as she had been in the last months of her life, when the cancer had eaten away at her. Then, Mary would cry out that she wanted to be dead, too, so she could be with her mother.

When the dreams were not about Douglas or Charlotte, they were about her childhood: She was on her bicycle, the one she had gotten on her eighth birthday, cruising up and down Toronto's University Street in front of her old house, a little girl with long golden curls whose name was Gladys Smith.

Once, it seemed as if she was making a movie again. She imagined herself being photographed in a long shot, wondering if the camera was close enough so she would have to fix her hair.

She had not been well for a long time now, and almost never got out of her bed. In the parlance of the people that served her, she "had her good days and her bad days." But the carefully guarded truth was that now, at the age of eighty-four, even Mary Pickford's good days weren't very good.

Nevertheless, she was not yet prepared to go gently into that good night. Four years before, she had been greatly irritated when Charlie Chaplin had come back to America to receive an honorary Oscar. Unlike Chaplin, Mary had actually won a competitive Oscar, for her performance in 1929's *Coquette,* but that had been nearly fifty years ago.

She had refused to see him during his brief stay in California, for Mary had been fiercely competitive with Chaplin ever since 1915, when he, a "cheap" comedian not two years out of the music halls, had signed with Essanay for $1,250 a week, while she, a woman who had acted for David Belasco, *for D. W. Griffith for God's sake,* was earning only slightly more. It had been the beginning of a long, stormy relationship, and now Mary Pickford knew one thing: If Chaplin deserved an honorary Oscar, then so did she. Hints were dropped; quiet inquiries were made.

And so it was that on March 29, 1976, Gene Kelly strode to a podium and began to speak to the millions of people watching the Academy Awards. "For more than three generations of movie goers," he said, *"this* was the face of the most popular woman in the world." Then the stills came up and began dissolving into one another, images of an ineffable, glowing beauty, a perfect innocence.

These radiant scenes were soon replaced by a film showing a plush room and a tiny figure huddled in the corner of a couch. Producer Howard W. Koch handed the figure the gold statuette known as the Oscar. The woman the audience saw in medium close-up was old, very old, with bright, shiny eyes and an ill-fitting blonde wig laying uneasily on her head.

This was the woman Cecil B. deMille called the easiest person on the screen to direct, as pliable and responsive as a fine Stradivarius. This was the woman Chaplin regarded as the best head for business in the movies. This was the woman who, in March 1917, had polled 1,147,550 votes, nearly twice the number of her nearest competitor, in a popularity contest run by a popular movie magazine. This was the woman known as America's Sweetheart, who achieved full control over her career, including the contractual right of final cut of her films, by the time she was twenty-five-years-old.

She touched the statuette gingerly, her hands betraying a slight shakiness. Finally, she looked at Koch and said "I will treasure it always. I'm overcome. I'm amazed. I didn't know that people remembered me." The camera then cut to Charles "Buddy" Rogers, her third husband, a handsome man with white hair sitting in the audience, brushing away a tear.

People who had known Mary stared transfixed at their television sets, appalled that Buddy had allowed her to appear in so transparently fragile a state. "I was angry," said Joan Marsh Morrill, the daughter of Mary's cameraman Charles Rosher and a former child actress in her pictures. "It was obvious that she wasn't right." James Kirkwood Jr., a friend and the son of one of Mary's directors, thought she looked "like a little monkey, all dressed up, with her little eyes. It made her look like something from a circus."

There had never been any possibility of her appearing in person for the presentation; just getting her ready for her brief appearance on film had taken weeks. Up until the presentation itself, no one knew if she would be able to go through with it—in that case Buddy would have accepted the award for her—but Mary had been determined to go through with it.

Kemp Niver, an old friend, had been called to shoot some stills of the presentation ceremony. Because he had not seen her for ten years—hardly anybody but Lillian Gish, Douglas Fairbanks Jr. and Buddy had—Niver entered the room cautiously, not knowing what to expect, fully prepared to have to introduce himself as if they had never met.

Mary looked up at him and gave a little half-smile. "Remember, don't you cross-light me," she snapped, "The hump in my nose will show up." Niver relaxed and began snapping pictures. Somehow, Mary had managed to pull herself together for what she must have known would be her last public appearance. Smart, tough and sassy, she was the same Mary Pickford he used to know.

———— ————

We are, nowadays, used to strong, dominant women who mold their own show business careers. Stars like Jane Fonda, Barbra Streisand or Jessica Lange produce their own pictures, officially or *de facto.* We admire them; from the heavy, sighing interviews in which they talk about the burden of it all, that admiration is obviously important to them.

Yet the fact is that Mary Pickford was doing all this more than seventy years ago. In addition to managing her own career, she was married to the most famous male star of his generation, and she was instrumental in setting up and running United Artists, a major movie distribution company. Mary Pickford, in fact, was the first female movie mogul. On the scale on which she worked, she was, perhaps, the *only* female movie mogul. Yet today she is remembered, if at all, either dimly or incorrectly. Partially, this is a function of time; Mary Pickford defined her era, roughly 1910–1925, as surely as Marilyn Monroe defined hers, yet, as the twenties moved on, her era belonged more and more to the past, and her professional identity became ever more anachronistic. Her films increasingly relied on recaptured associations—the mutual bonds of memory and cumulative emotion between a star and her audience, of the times when they and the cinema had been young.

In addition, she was penalized by the highbrows for her extraordinary popularity with the mass audience. Sensing all this, she began constructing an emotional escape hatch, a scenario of inherent obsolescence.

"Sometimes . . . it depresses me when I realize that our pictures, in which we strive so hard for real artistic achievement, may not last very long," she wrote in 1923. "I feel confident that the whole method of picture making will change so much in the next ten to fifteen years that the ones we are doing now will be hopelessly antiquated."

To fulfill this fantasy of transience, of her abiding aesthetic unimportance, for years Mary Pickford did little to save her body of work from the chemical instability of the early nitrate film stock. Unlike her beloved second husband Douglas Fairbanks, who donated all of his films to the Museum of Modern Art shortly before his death, or her compatriot and one-time intimate friend Chaplin, who preserved his prints and negatives in immaculate condition, Mary was uncomfortable with the idea of herself as an artist. Those films that were preserved were rarely shown.

The result is that the reputations of both Fairbanks and Chaplin have survived, indeed flourished, while Mary Pickford, the only woman ever to have been the focal point of an entire industry, has been slowly forgotten.

Admittedly, she never made her *Thief of Bagdad,* her *City Lights,* never performed that feat of simultaneously defining herself and surpassing herself, the prerequisite of all mythic stars.

"[My father] was by nature an extrovert," said Douglas Fairbanks Jr., Pickford's stepson. "He was like a painter or a sculptor; his personality went into his work. Mary was much more conservative, and she worked on a smaller scale. She was a miniaturist; she was the girl next door or the sweetheart. She was not a maker of spectaculars and her screen character was not a spectacular personality."

This is as far as her stepson would go, but then he elaborated on the basic problem, and one of the central conundrums of this fascinating career, this sad life. "Mary was capable of doing more than her business sense allowed her to do. She could have been more versatile, as in *Little Lord Fauntleroy* where she played both mother and son. She didn't go too far afield because she knew what the audience wanted of her. She knew what her public wanted to buy. She was not what I would call an inspired artist, but a thoughtful, analytic artist."

Caution. Always caution.

If all this is true, why does this tiny, insecure, cloistered, ultimately tragic woman compel our attention? Why is her life worthy of examination?

Partially because her films, while lacking a single, towering masterpiece, are considerably more interesting than the prevailing image of a relentlessly one-note, sunny optimism suggested by her reputation. Cumulatively, they add up to a fascinating portrait of an audience, an era and the woman who caused them to be made.

Mary Pickford's films invariably revolve around poverty, adversity and social humiliation. As Andrew Sarris wrote in palpably pleased surprise after seeing her films for the first time in 1967, "If her toughness and resiliency prevailed over all obstacles by the end of a movie, the obstacles themselves made grim going through most of the footage." Good may have prevailed in Mary Pickford's movies, but the set of her tough little jaw told you that it damn well better.

In addition, she had a very broad acting range; while she always felt that her forte was comedy, and her public clearly preferred her that way, she was perfectly capable of dramatic performances of shattering impact, and her comments about those performances make it clear that she was very much a Method actress long before that acting technique became popular.

As the eminent film historian William K. Everson has noted, "The charm of Pickford is that there really is no 'typical' Pickford film . . . Pickford could don the mantle of Doug Fairbanks or Charlie Chaplin as readily as that of 'America's Sweetheart' and there was poignancy and melodrama as well as sentiment in her work. Aware of the need to avoid being just the little girl with golden curls, Mary strove for variety from the very first, and her best films . . . had a happy mixture of quantity, quality, variety and spontaneity."

For two generations, Mary Pickford played, not so much a sweetheart, but an odd combination of child and Madonna. She did so effortlessly because of an acting personality of a nearly unalloyed—there is no other word—purity.

However pristine she was on-screen, she was quite sensual off-screen. Personally shy and reclusive, she seized and held more power for a longer period of time than any other woman in the history of the movies. Contradiction upon contradiction, a mystery worth investigating.

And that, finally, is the reason I have written this book: In her life, if not always on the screen, Mary Pickford was far more of our time than of her time. Like so many modern women, she molded her life with a fierce determination to approximate the woman she seemed to be, wanted to be, not the woman she actually was.

Mary Pickford's screen character sprang from a social matrix whose components are almost completely obscured by the passing of generations; she was acclaimed as the feminine ideal by an age that prided itself on its innocence the way more recent generations have prided themselves on their cynicism.

Although the matrix may change, human motives and needs don't. Although the screen character may seem simplistic to us today, all vibrance and never-say-die pluck, the life behind it wasn't. At times, she seemed ignorant of the rules of the game she was playing but, before Pickford, the game hadn't existed. Her life and career were helping to formulate the rules and the game.

While Mary Pickford was not the very first movie star, she was certainly the first movie star to achieve more than a transient fame, the first movie star to use the intimacy of the medium to codify the rules of stardom: An apparently quick, meteoric rise, an arc of triumphant success that promises immortality, and then a sudden, mystifying fall, not through scandal, but through age and the weird, indefinable beast called change in public tastes.

It can hardly be a surprise that, when her screen career ended with very little warning, her personal troubles increased in near-geometric ratio; a personality constructed out of the refracted light of a career can be counted on to deteriorate when the light of that career dims, then switches off altogether. In short, Mary Pickford compels our attention because she was among the first women to try to have it all, and to seem to attain it all . . . with the inevitable result being that she lost it all.

Yet, to imply ultimate failure is harsh and unfair. The fact remains that Mary Pickford's life was utterly singular because she had the mingled fortune and misfortune to live in a day when films were a true, universal folk art. Her public—indeed, the whole world—loved her as no actress will ever be loved again. This was the story I wanted to tell.

Chapter One

"Mary Pickford was the best known woman who has ever
lived. The picture business, when it made great money, really
came in first with Mary Pickford . . ."

—*Adela Rogers St. Johns*

O N the night that her sister Lottie died, one memory, one
image flashed through Mary Pickford's mind. They were
children—little Gladys Smith, her sister Lottie (short for
Charlotte, after their mother) and Jack, the baby of the
family, whom Mary usually called Johnny because he was named
for their father.

Gladys might have been four or five, no more. She and Lottie
were sledding through the snowbound Toronto streets, occasionally hooking on to one of the big horse-drawn sleighs that would
come by in a sea of hoofs, bells and frozen breath. Suddenly, the
sled was yanked aside and Lottie was thrown from it, arcing
through the air and landing in a snowbank. A horrified Gladys
rushed over and found her sister unhurt.

"I saw her brightly colored, tasseled stocking cap and I became
dizzy with the wave of love that swept over me," she remembered
more than a half-century later. "I gave my unspoken thanks to
God that Lottie was safe. I thought to myself 'This is my very own
little sister.' That was my first realization of what . . . love
was . . ."

It was a defining moment, a crystallization of family relation-
ships that would never change: Gladys would be the protector;

Gladys would be the provider; Gladys would have the responsibility. Since the role of unquestioning nurturer was a role she filled for nearly ninety years, it clearly was one she felt comfortable with. Yet, there was a part of her that rebelled at it and at much else besides, a hint of the duality that would mark her life. One day, Charlotte, Gladys's mother, saw her mumbling to herself. The devout woman assumed that her sweet, blonde daughter was reciting a rosary or imploring a favor from a saint.

"What are you doing, darling?" asked Charlotte.

The reply was decisive. "I'm hating God."

The woman the world would come to know as Mary Pickford always claimed to have been born Gladys Marie Smith at 175 University Avenue, Toronto, Canada on April 8, 1893. In fact, and despite her frequent denials, her birth certificate shows that she was born Gladys Louise Smith on April 8, 1892. Two small but typical evasions, the one probably devised to make her seem an even more precocious child actress than she was, the other a replacement of a name she found ugly with a name close to the one she eventually chose for herself. Mary Pickford would only rarely engage in the fantasies that can come with the actor's territory, but she did construct a slightly skewed reality that invariably put her in the right, that made her and her background seem more genteel, more gracious than they really were.

The house on University Avenue was a tiny building, with two windows on either side of the front door and a dormer window set into the second floor below the roof. As the city of Toronto expanded, and University Avenue was extended southward, the number of the house became 211, then 561. All her life, in the way that many people have of worshipping quite ordinary things that are relics of their childhood, Mary revered the memory of that modest house; when it was torn down in 1943, she had twenty bricks saved and sent to her in California as souvenirs.

Both sets of Gladys's grandparents had come to Toronto via the St. Lawrence River around the middle of the nineteenth century. Her father's parents were English Methodists named Sarah Keyes and Joseph Smith. Grandmother Smith lived to be ninety-one and was remembered by her granddaughter as a bulky, forbidding Victorian who couldn't abide seeing people enjoying themselves on a Sunday. Neighborhood children were afraid of her and were forbidden to play in the house.

Her mother's parents, John Pickford Hennessey and Catherine Faeley, had both emigrated from County Kerry but did not meet until they arrived in Canada. This union resulted in Charlotte Hennessey, Mary's mother, who was said to have been born on Toronto's Queen Street.

Although the Hennessey's were ardent Catholics, John Pickford Hennessey, like many of his countrymen, was a good man with a bottle. His drinking compelled his wife to be a rabid teetotaller. One of the more charming traits of this good Catholic woman was to barge into various Canadian whorehouses and harangue the girls about the necessity of saving their immortal souls, a tactic that was to be accomplished by going back to their mothers. This Valkyrie's temperament was to be passed on to Charlotte as well as to her daughter.

The Hennesseys were shanty Irish, with a strong strain of Celtic mysticism, which is to say a kind of poetic ignorance. Grandmother Hennessey's own mother went to her grave convinced that the sewing machine was an invention of the Devil. Both sets of grandparents had only one thing in common: they had no use for the theater.

Following in her family's footsteps, Charlotte was also a devout Catholic until her marriage to John Charles Smith, who was probably born in 1868. In addition to having the requisite amount of charm, and possessing the gold/brown hair he bequeathed to his eldest daughter, Smith followed his mother's lead and was a staunch Methodist. Charlotte, being a dutiful wife, went along with the prevailing tide. Both Lottie and Gladys were sent to the Methodist Sunday School on Adelaide Street.

John Smith was, apparently, a gentle man. Surviving photographs show a delicate face and a passive demeanor, which, together with a diminutive build, must have made him an unprepossessing package. At the time of Gladys's birth, he was working as a printer. Charlotte was apparently a doting mother, except for one blunder when she briefly left Gladys, aged nine months, in a carriage beside Eaton's Department Store. Gladys worked out from under her blankets and developed a bad case of bronchitis. In later years, whenever she was troubled by a cold or a cough, Mary would say, "There's that Eaton cough."

"In those days," remembered Mary, "it was my father I loved. I didn't really care so much about my mother. She was always too busy to play with me." Apparently, John Smith was a warm and loving father. Once, he told Gladys to open her hands and into them he dropped seventy-five cents that he had earned from a part-time job lugging scenery at a local theater. It seemed a great deal of money, and Gladys was proud of her father's seeming wealth.

But he was also an indifferent provider and capable of acting like a blowhard. Neighbors of the Smiths remembered with particular disdain a time when he went to western Canada for a brief visit and came back wearing a ten-gallon hat and talking about the cattle business as if he'd been punching cows for years. Mostly, he just scraped by. For some years, he worked for the Niagara Navigation Company as a steward; he had the fruit and candy concession on the *Corona,* one of the boats that went back and forth across Lake Ontario.

Despite Gladys's stronger bonding with her father, Charlotte's feelings about her other children were less ardent than they were for Gladys. On the day Charlotte gave birth to Lottie, she apologized to her husband for giving him "just another girl." Perhaps to compensate for his wife's indifference, John Smith adored Lottie and always considered her his favorite. Indeed, the first time Gladys ever felt jealousy was when her father would get off a streetcar and Lottie would run into his arms. The already austere Gladys would usually stand still and wait for him to approach her.

In 1897, when he was working on the *Corona,* John Smith was in a hurry to go ashore. Running toward the gangplank, he jumped over a shaft and smashed his head on an iron pulley. At first, the only damage was a fairly ugly scalp wound, but things started to go wrong inside the young man's head, and, within a year, he was dead at the age of twenty-seven.

That, at least, was Mary's official version of her father's death. John Smith's death certificate shows that, at the time of his death at home, at 17 Walton Street, on February 11, 1898, he was thirty years old and employed as a bartender. The actual cause of death is unlisted, and the death announcements in the Toronto papers do not mention it. It is, of course, possible that he was working as a bartender because the shipping lanes were closed during the long Canadian winter, but there are those with close ties to what became the Pickford family who insist that his death had a good deal to do with his persistent consumption of alcohol; that, in fact, he was at least mildly drunk at the time of his fatal accident.

Whether he was drunk or sober, the fact was that he left a twenty-four-year-old wife and three children. Gladys, the oldest, was about to turn six; Lottie was not yet three, and John Jr. the youngest, was still in diapers. (Birth certificates for Lottie and Jack do not exist.) Virtually the only tangible proof that John Charles Smith had existed, aside from his three children, was a silver wedding ring. All Lottie Smith would ever remember of her father was that he had soft, white hands; after John Smith died, nobody ever loved Lottie quite as intensely again.

Charlotte did her best to keep her children's minds off their father's death. Gladys would fondly recall riding her bike down University Avenue, not having to peddle at all because of the grade of the hill. For a long time she had to ride a rented bicycle, which cost ten cents an hour, but in 1900, on Gladys's eighth birthday, Charlotte gave her a bike of her own, and she enjoyed riding for hours up and down the bridle path in front of their house. Other special treats involved taking the old trolley cars on Yonge Street, or the Belt Line around the city, or riding the merry-go-round and picnicking at Hanlan's Point.

Gladys's favorite place, though, was Queen's Park, where she liked to skip amongst the tulip beds. Among the charms of Queen's Park was a drinking fountain with a copper cup on a chain. Charlotte was none too sure about letting Gladys drink from a public fountain—tiny bugs called germs seemed to be transmitted that way, according to stories in the papers—but Gladys insisted. The water was always so sweet and cold.

"We loved the beautiful crisp winters," she wrote seventy years later, "But even more we loved the spring that brought us the lilacs. Every year, my memory is refreshed and my heart warmed by filling my room with lilacs as long as the season lasts." Her love of flowers was a constant; whenever Gladys got an extra penny, she would go to the local florist and buy a rose. One day, the florist asked her what she did with all the flowers. "I eat them," Gladys told him, and it was true. The little girl believed that if she ate the flowers, the beauty and color and the delicate scent that she loved so much would gradually come to be embodied in her as surely as they were embodied in the flower.

It was around this time that Charlotte visited a fortune-teller. "You have three children," she was told. "One of them will be so rich some day that you can't even imagine it now. Her name and face will be known and loved in countries where she will never set foot." For a sentimental Irish woman like Charlotte Smith, this seemed a delightful, if dubious forecast, although, if it came true, there was never any doubt in her mind which child would fulfill the prophecy.

Shortly after her husband died, Charlotte moved her family up the street to 81 Walton Street, while she tried to keep the concession on the *Corona* going. Charlotte had to give that up, however. Next, she tried running a fruit store on Queen Street, moving her children yet again, this time to 9 Orde Street, next door to her sister Lizzie.

Charlotte was at this point, verging on destitution, yet, on their first Christmas without their father, Gladys and the other children awoke to find the two doll carriages (one for each of the girls) and the dancing bear that had been their primary requests. On top of each stocking was a candy man, and inside the stockings were oranges, raisins and hard candy.

It was not until Gladys was older that her mother told her how that comparatively bountiful Christmas had been achieved. Four weeks before December 25, Charlotte had seen a doll carriage in a shop window and offered to embroider a scarf in exchange for two of them. Every night for the next four weeks, after a day of housekeeping and dressmaking, she worked on the scarf. By Christmas Eve, she had the two doll carriages but nothing else. It would be all right for the girls, but what about Jack?

Then the doorbell rang. Two men from the Knights of Pythias, her late husband's lodge, handed her ten dollars, the lodge's (belated) death benefit. With that, she ran to the grocer for food and to the toy store for Jack's dancing bear.

At night, in the small, mean house, Gladys would occasionally awaken and hear the steady whir of Charlotte's sewing machine, the only means the family had of surviving. Getting out of bed, she would hold a light over her mother's head, sharing Charlotte's burden as well as her solitude. While she could not help feeling abandoned by her father, the memory of waking up in the middle of the night to hear Charlotte working to keep the family together instilled in Gladys a slavish loyalty and love for her mother.

———— ————

Even before her father's death made her aware of her family's straightened circumstances, Gladys had a serious frame of mind. When she was about three, she had her picture taken; the resulting image is notable for the lack of the usual smile, and for a sternness in the little girl's eyes. It wasn't that she didn't like to have her picture taken; it was that the photographer had said to her, "Look into the hole in this little black box and you'll see a little bird."

Gladys thought he must be crazy to think that a bird could live in such an unlikely place. She decided she did not like the foolish man, or much else besides.

"I have a distinct memory of not liking the world," she remembered, "of thinking, 'If I could only get back there.' I had some sort of a vague memory of another existence. I'd like to know why that little child was so depressed and unhappy about the world, because at that age I didn't have anything to make me unhappy. My father was still alive."

Another time, in Sunday school, Gladys marched up to her teacher and demanded to know which was stronger, God or the Devil.

"Why God, of course," said the teacher. "He is all-powerful."

"Well," replied Gladys, "why doesn't he kill the Devil so I wouldn't be a bad little girl any more and have to go to the hot place?"

It is possible that a strong streak of religiosity combined with a genetic fondness for alcohol predisposed the Smith family to intense, self-flagellating guilt, with the notable exception of Jack, who, insofar as it can be determined, never felt guilty about anything in his life.

After John Smith's death, his family lived close to poverty. "I remember times we had to feed them," said Gertie Clegg, a neighbor of the Smiths, in 1934. "There's more than one family in Toronto that has given a meal to the Smiths."

At one point, in order to get a brass clock as a present for her Aunt Lizzie, Gladys saved coupons from Sweet Caporal cigarettes, even picking them out of the gutter. She would use the experience as fodder for her acting years later, during the filming of *Rebecca of Sunnybrook Farm,* when the character of Rebecca has to do the same thing. It was during this period that Gladys attended the McCaul Street School, for, she said, no more than six months; it was, according to her doubtful recollection, the only formal education she would ever have.

Charlotte's problem was a familiar one for women of that era: There weren't many jobs for a woman outside the home. Given the times and the circumstances, a reasonable tactic for survival might have been for Charlotte to snare another man, but a stout widow with three children was not considered a great catch; besides, Charlotte apparently never had much use for men after her husband died. Douglas Fairbanks Jr., who knew her at the end of her life, remembered that "she was more interested in her own children than anybody else, and she didn't mix with anybody but her own family."

Mary always remembered that her entry into show business came about through a stage manager who worked at a Toronto theater and who was renting Charlotte's spare room. Since it is far more likely that Charlotte was herself a renter rather than an owner, the odds are that the stage manager was actually a fellow boarder.

At any rate, noting the young widow working long hours at her sewing machine, the stage manager idly suggested that putting her children on the stage might make things a little easier for all of them. Being a properly brought-up Irish Catholic, Charlotte was horrified at the thought of her children being on the stage "where actresses smoke and curse." She had, of course, never actually attended such an establishment.

But the urgings of the stage manager—and her own depressing predicament—wore Charlotte down; one day, she sat in the wings and, to her surprise, observed that there was nothing taking place that could possibly corrupt her family.

Although Charlotte always told the story so that it seemed to be necessity that drove Gladys to embark upon an acting career, at least one friend of Gladys's remembered otherwise. Ethel Clegg, the sister of Gertie, told a story about picking up Gladys, who was about five at the time, to take her to the Clegg's home for dinner. She found the little girl pricking her cheeks with a hairpin.

"What in the world are you doing?" Ethel asked.

"I'm trying to make my cheeks red like Nellie Marshall's" (the leading lady of Toronto's Valentine Stock Company).

Whether she was stagestruck—Toronto was a sophisticated theater town that was regularly visited by the *A* touring companies of hit shows—or desperate or both, on September 19, 1898, little Gladys Smith made her first appearance on stage at the Princess Theater, Toronto, with the Cummings Stock Company, which, with typical professional acuity, she would remember as being "second rate." For a one week run stretching from Monday, September 19 to Saturday September 24, she played two parts, a little boy and a mean little girl, in Henry Arthur Jones's *The Silver King*. She had one line: "Don't speak to her, girls; her father killed a man." She felt sufficiently at home to ad lib some business, using some prop blocks and a hobby horse to construct a wall, which fell with a noticeable clatter when she rammed a toy horse into it. For six evening performances and two matinees, Gladys was payed eight dollars.

Some time later, the Valentine Stock Company presented the same play. Knowing a possible meal ticket when she saw it, Charlotte, already well on her way to being among the most cooly aggressive stage mothers of the century—any century—hustled Gladys down to the theater. Charlotte explained that this was the little girl that had played Ned Denver earlier in the year.

"In that case, I think that she can play Cissy Denver this time," said the producer. "Oh, you couldn't trust her with lines," protested Charlotte, but Gladys quieted them both with a simple "I can do it." By the next day's rehearsal, Charlotte had Gladys letter-perfect in the part.

Sixty years later, Mary Pickford told an interviewer a story about those days and the terrible weight she felt oppressing her even then. She had been walking down a street near her house when she passed a ragged old man and felt a wave of pity. At the end of the street, she saw a small patch of dandelions on an incline. It was late afternoon, and the wildflowers were silhouetted in the evening sun. Gladys made a move to go up the slight incline to play with them, but she stopped, for she heard an interior voice.

"You must think about that old man," the voice told her. "If you expect to be an actress one day, you must feel sorry for people. You must think about it. And you're not going to play." And she didn't.

Remembering that episode later in life, Mary exclaimed wonderingly, "Now, as I hope for heaven, that is the absolute truth. That's a strange experience for a six-year-old child, isn't it?"

From the beginning, the child took to the theater, loved the lights, the smell of the rope riggings, the feeling of clannishness among the actors, the way the audience fell quiet when the curtain rose. And, being a child, a quintessentially narcissistic being, she also loved being the focus of attention. A beautiful blonde child like little Gladys was a target for all the unused paternal and maternal love of the other actors and actresses in the company. In later years, she would always make a determined effort to maintain the same sense of warmth and camaraderie within her own company.

All her life, she would remember the response an actor got on stage, remembering it as "an electric impulse, a definite vibration, a palpable bond. Nothing takes the place of the theater, the presence of an audience. Great personalities like D. W. Griffith or Cecil B. deMille try to supply it, but they can't. The curtain goes up and whatever happens, happens! I've always missed the presence of the audience."

It may not have been the loving caress of a father, but it was a kind of love; maybe not the best kind but a reasonable substitute.

There were some other plays around Toronto that season and the next, but Gladys did not become immersed in the theater as a way of life until two years after her debut. From February to May 1901, the Valentine Stock Company presented plays as various as *Kidnapped, Uncle Tom's Cabin, East Lynne, The Merchant of Venice,* and, for the week of April 1–6, *The Little Red Schoolhouse,* by a man named Hal Reid, whose friendship was to change the world for the Smith family.

Hal Reid was a prolific author of melodramas that had a solid following out in what the tradepapers called "the sticks." He was also the father of future screen idol Wallace Reid. Although Hal Reid's career had already reached its peak, he was the right man in the right place for the Smith family. Had Reid not tried out his play in Toronto in April, he would never have hired Gladys for the tour that began that November and she might not have begun her gradual rise from the ranks of lowly stock actress.

By 1901, Gladys was a known quantity in the world of Toronto theater; the program for *East Lynne* announced that "the souvenirs tonight will be of Gladys Smith, the little tot whose work has been so much admired." Reid liked the way Gladys played the part of Mabel Payne, so, in November 1901, he took her out on the road for the first time in *The Little Red Schoolhouse.*

The tour began in nearby Hamilton, played a few other dates in Ontario, then moved across the Canadian border to Grand Rapids and through the midwest. Everything seemed fine, but the production closed in January, after Reid, according to the tradepapers, "got convivial" with some friends in Columbus, Ohio. A few days later, the show bowed out with a week's stand in Chicago. For Gladys, it was back to Toronto and stock.

But Reid was loyal; that fall, from September 1902 to May 1903, Gladys was on the road with another of his melodramas, *In Convict Stripes,* playing mostly one-night stands. By the fall of 1903, the Smiths were making a name for themselves out of the narrow realm of Hal Reid's influence, as the entire family managed to get jobs in the *D* company of Theodore Kremer's hit play *The Fatal Wedding.* The tour began in Pennsylvania and was mostly routed through the south.

In *The Fatal Wedding,* "Baby Gladys Smith" played the lead of the Little Mother—a prophetic role. Lottie understudied Gladys, Jack had a small part and Charlotte made her stage debut as an Irish maid named Bridget. On opening night, in Pottsville, Pennsylvania, Gladys and Lottie got down on their knees and prayed: "Oh Lord, please don't let Mama forget her lines." The Lord must have been listening, for the terrified, amateurish Charlotte came through unscathed.

In August 1904, Gladys went back to work on a tour that lasted through most of February 1905, in something called *The Child Wife*. After only two weeks down-time, she was back on the road for Hal Reid in *The Gypsy Girl,* which played through April.

For a small child, the touring life verged on the brutal. During several of these seasons, Gladys endured nineteen weeks of one-night stands, never spending two nights in the same town. The hotels were always the cheapest, costing about a dollar a day, with a bathroom at the end of the hall. (A bath usually cost twenty-five cents, and you had to be sure to scour the tin tub before you filled it.) The mattresses were thin and hard and the windows almost never opened. If clothes needed to be washed, the quickest way of doing it was filling the chipped porcelain basin in the room with cold water and scrubbing the laundry with soap made out of boiled granite and lye.

Trains had to be caught at the most outlandish hours, and, to save money, the Smith clan usually traveled sitting up in day coach. For years, even after she attained worldwide fame, Gladys slept with her arms over her head because she had grown so used to sleeping in chairs. She grew to loathe cerise, the particular red material that covered most of the railroad cushions of the day.

On rare occasions, Gladys would be hired *sans* family, but Charlotte made every effort to keep the family together. Charlotte was a good cook; at home, she would store the water from cooked vegetables or the juice from canned vegetables, add flour and water, some basic spices and some cream and come up with something that Mary always insisted tasted wonderful. Even on the road, Charlotte could take a tough piece of cheap round steak and pound it with a rolling pin until it was as tender as filet mignon.

Mary remembered only one time when Charlotte lost control. It was early in the morning and Jack didn't want to get out of his warm bed to catch the train to their next one-night stand. They managed to get him up and dressed, but, once he got outside into the snow, Jack put his foot down, literally. He refused to budge. Charlotte dropped her bags, went over to her son, picked him up and threw him over the railing. Luckily, there was a snowbank underneath him. They made the train.

Continually on the run, it was difficult for Charlotte to teach manners, but she did her best. "No lady ever goes out without gloves," was one dictum, which had several addenda: "A lady isn't much of a lady when she puts gloves on on the stoop of her house. And a lady is no lady at all when she puts them on in the street."

The shows themselves failed to provide any nourishment for their actors beyond that of a fairly meager meal ticket; Mary remembered that the entire family's savings from a year on the road were barely sufficient to buy a new theatrical trunk.

In later years, Mary tended to refer to the generic melodramas as "dreadful," and the surviving evidence confirms her opinion. The April 8, 1905 edition of The New York *Clipper* gave the following synopsis of Hal Reid's *The Gypsy Girl:* "The play is in four acts, Gypsy Jack and Meg Merritt, his fortune-telling wife, are expecting a visitor, one Irving Thorwald, who years before had left in their keeping a little girl, his stepdaughter. He is anxious to get rid of her, as he is acting as the executor of her mother's estate and is robbing her. Her baby brother has been sent to Ireland.

"The gypsy couple have a son, Rollo, who idolizes the waif, Daisy. Ben Bolton, a tramp, visits the camp, discovers that Thorwald has ruined his daughter, Annie, and he takes an oath to avenge her. Thorwald appears and the gypsy thinks it is to claim the child, but instead it is Thorwald's object to get Gypsy Jack to kill her. Later poor Freckles [Gladys], the brother sent to Ireland, comes to camp, and is fed and cared for by his sister, without knowing of their relationship. Daisy defends him and saves his life. The children are pursued by Thorwald and Jack, but they finally escape, and Ben Bolton makes good his oath and kills Thorwald."

However ghastly these shows may have been, they were reliable. "Serious" plays had even less of an audience than they do now, but the old melodramas were hearty and could sustain long tours on what was called "the kerosene circuit" (because that was what fueled the footlights).

In those days, people *needed* the theater; it was, reading aside, the sole entertainment medium within the reach of the common person. The theater responded nobly; in the 1901–02 season, the first time the Pickford clan came to New York, there were 314 plays produced in New York City alone and around twice that number were on tour and being cast from New York.

New York offered better shows and better audiences. It also offered better food. There was all the difference in the world between the thirty-cent dinners Gladys grew accustomed to on the road—a pork chop, some soggy fried potatoes, a dab of corn and some bread—and the fare at luxurious restaurants like Lucho's or Child's where five-cent butter cakes were made right in the front window and there was a big slab of sweet butter on every marble-topped table.

In addition to the overwhelming banality of the plays and the physically arduous traveling, the audiences were often noisy, rude and contemptuous. Gladys was never fazed by them, though, for if the audience was boisterous or unruly, Gladys would turn her back and refuse to continue with her lines. To emphasize the point, she might glare over her shoulder. The audience, curious and more than a little amused by the tiny girl's spirit and pluck, would usually calm down and the performance would continue.

Gladys early on developed an imaginative gift that co-existed with a bear-trap pragmatism. She learned to read by observing billboards and signs from railroad and automobile windows, figuring out one word, then waiting for the same sign to flicker past again a few miles down the road so she could parse the next one. Eventually, she would have a whole sentence. During a long wait on a train platform, she learned to spell Schenectady.

She read, although probably nowhere near as much as she later claimed she did. Her supposed favorites were Dickens, Emerson and James M. Barrie, although she admitted that half the time she didn't know what on earth Barrie was talking about. And, like all the other actors and actresses on the road who hadn't given up, she dreamed of a day when she would no longer have to work in such demoralizing, even degrading, conditions.

Living from week to week in a succession of boardinghouses, Gladys grew wary, and learned the tricks of the theatrical trade, its liking for sharp dealing. She also observed the way the actors tried to protect each other. Theater dressing rooms had stickers advertising local boardinghouses, and actors would write their opinions of a given establishment on the wall, or the Call Board. "You get pork Monday and every day thereafter until Friday, then you get fish and soup, and pork goes on the bill again Saturday!" was one typical piece of information; another was "Keep out of Jim Fat's laundry; the s.o.b. ruins your stuff."

Not that the world of the theater was a bastion of Jeffersonian democracy; Gladys always indignantly remembered the theater's caste system: The leading lady of the *A* touring company of a play rarely deigned to speak to the leading lady of the *B* touring company. It was a way of creating and maintaining a pecking order, an interior status that was a defense against an outside world that granted actors no status at all. Years later, when she became a star, she made a point of being friendly and accessible to all the members of the cast and crew.

Although Gladys's own memories were remarkably imprecise regarding the actors she worked with and the plays she was in, she did remember following a vaudeville act called "The Three Keatons" into a Brooklyn boardinghouse, and being fascinated by stories about the roughhouse antics the young Buster and his father Joe would enact to amuse themselves and others.

In September 1905, Charlotte scored a coup when she landed jobs for the entire brood in a Chauncey Olcott production of *Edmund Burke.* They were clearly moving up the ladder and the reviews ("The three Smith youngsters . . . made a clever trio of children for Mr. Olcott, and their work was most praiseworthy"— New York *Clipper,* October 7, 1905) indicated as much.

Rising from the amorphous ranks of stock actors to supporting a major star like Olcott in only five years was quite an accomplishment. The Smiths felt their plain name needed a little embellishment if it was to keep such august company, so, for the engagement with Olcott, which lasted until May 1906, each of them used the entirely imaginary but highly dignified middle name of "Millbourne."

After *Edmund Burke* closed in the spring, the Smiths opened in November 1906, with their old friend Hal Reid, in something called *For a Human Life,* on a successful tour that lasted through May 1907. Despite the improvement in the caliber of the companies, exhaustion was rapidly overtaking Gladys and eroding whatever feeble store of optimism she had been able to horde. She was filled with a sense of desperation and futility; futility from the treadmill of bad plays presented to ignorant audiences, desperation from her need to get out of a deepening rut.

She began to have nightmares, which generally came in two varieties. There was the one where she made an entrance only to discover an empty theater, and there was the one where she went dry, forgot her lines, and trooped off stage knowing she would be fired. Both are anxiety dreams so common among actors and actresses as to be generic, but both are somewhat extreme for a teenager.

She kept grinding on, telling herself that at the end of the stock season, she would go back to New York and get a good part in a prestigious company. Because she was, in every meaningful sense, the family breadwinner, and knew it, she had long-since developed a feeling of responsibility, of dignity, that prevented her from ever taking part in childhood give and take.

"When I was not in the rooms or the house," she remembered late in her life, "[Lottie and Jack] would put on wrestling matches and tumble around, with Charlotte joining in. The minute I'd come in, Mother would straighten herself out and say 'That's enough of that nonsense,' because she knew that I was worried about her [Charlotte] being hurt."

Or maybe it was just that Gladys was so obviously for work and Lottie and Jack were, equally obviously, for play. Whichever, Gladys would always compensate for these lost years by insisting that her duties as an adult gave her a closer bond with her mother: "I was her confidante; I was her beloved." Charlotte would often say that Gladys was the light of her life, although even she was nonplussed by the small child's habit of talking as if she were the adult and her mother the child, Gladys, for instance, would often promise her mother that she would always care for and look after her.

This perverse lurch toward a premature adulthood meant that, in a very real sense, Gladys never lived her own childhood. For years, she drew upon this hidden storehouse of playfulness, of dependency, of unexpressed primary emotions of joy and sorrow that existed under an umbrella of youthful innocence, to create indelible, vital acting images of an unmatched vivacity and charm. She did this even when she personally had long since ceased to be innocent. The emotional backlog also enabled her to countenance playing adolescents well into her thirties, even though the objective side of her knew that this was, in some way, unhealthy, if for no other reason than she could become hopelessly typed.

These, then, were the things that young Gladys Smith learned: how to make do without the toys and games of other children; how to make out a weekly budget that would keep her just inside her meager salary; how to use cardboard to attempt to cover the holes in her shoes, albeit unsuccessfully, how to keep herself warm by covering herself with newspapers during long night train rides and how that that didn't work either; how to use a simple gas ring in a dressing room to heat up water to do her laundry; how to travel as cheaply as possible from one part of the country to another. She also learned the kinds of plays and characters that the simple, largely rural audiences liked, and she became a savvy negotiator with theater managers and boardinghouse keepers. She learned to hate the tawdry, low-life aspects of life on the road. And she developed a ferocious desire to better herself and her family.

The child-woman never became bitter about all this premature psychological aging so much as she stolidly ignored the alternatives. These mean years left their mark on her in small but telling ways; she would, for instance, become difficult in money matters, slightly penurious and always putting off paying expenses like legal fees, which, because of her combative nature, she easily ran up. Mostly, she would be susceptible to paranoia in business, a sense that people were always trying to take advantage of her.

And, deep down, she would always be afraid, terribly afraid. From her mother's intense, if stifled Catholicism, Gladys had been inculcated with a fear of death. Just saying her prayers at night, the ones that go "If I should die before I wake," filled her with terror. Dying meant you might go to that place she had seen in the Doré engravings that were in every Victorian family's Bible. That would be awful. But what if Charlotte was the one that died? As the theatrical equivalent of a migrant worker, Gladys's only real security was in Charlotte. Without her, Gladys would truly be cast into a deep, everlasting darkness.

Gladys never told her mother of these fears, even though many nights she cried herself to sleep, afraid that she wouldn't wake up. Years later, wealthy and living on top of a Hollywood hill in a house known as Pickfair, she would say that "I am glad I was a poor girl, that we had those early struggles . . . They seem much more real to me than my life since."

There was only one person she felt she could trust. "No matter how bad times got," she remembered, "how empty the larder, or how complicated our personal problems, we knew that our mother was always there with the answer. We knew that she would take care of everything, and she always did." Mary went on to add, in a burst of improbable hyperbole, that "we kids had no worry, no concern, no anxiety," but then she made a central point.

"It was through my mother that I first learned what the term 'love' really means. She diffused love in all directions as a flower diffuses perfume . . ."

For Mary Pickford, "love" came to mean a fount of uncritical blessings, a never-ending source of benevolence. Because she gave unswerving support, she would come to expect unswerving support, a virtual *La Ronde* of emotionally extreme expectations and dependencies.

Although she would invariably be outwardly pleasant and charming, Gladys's inner self was always carefully guarded and she would permit only a few people to be truly close to her. But for those few, nothing would be too much.

Gladys and Lillian Gish had met glancingly during their touring days, when Lillian played the part in *The Little Red Schoolhouse* that Gladys had created in Toronto. Soon afterwards, and for a few years thereafter, the Smith family and the Gish family threw in their lot with each other during the summer, down-time for those in the theater, and lived together in a flat on 8th Avenue and 39th Street in Manhattan.

While Charlotte and Mary Gish sewed costumes for the coming season (in those days, actors and actresses had to furnish their own costumes), Gladys, Lillian and her sister Dorothy would sit on the front steps during the evening, looking across the street at nothing in particular, talking of their plans to conquer the world of the theater. "It was the first time that Lillian and I ever had any other children to play with," remembered Dorothy Gish, while Lillian would simply say, "I don't remember the world without Mary."

Lillian and Dorothy's mother Mary learned to respect Gladys's sense of economy, of management. Even though she was only ten, it was Gladys who did the budget, sitting at the kitchen table and figuring out how much could be spent on food, how much on entertainment. It was also Gladys who served as a surrogate mother when Charlotte or Mary Gish was out looking for theater jobs.

"There was never any question when [Gladys] told us to do something," remembered Lillian Gish. "We did it. She had one of those cute little Irish tempers. She'd get mad and everybody would adore her for it. And she always had the most perfect natural blonde hair."

"She was constantly looking after our needs, though she was only [a bit] older than I," remembered Lottie Pickford of these days. "I always used to think that she imagined Jack and I were just her big dolls."

The small-ish flat contained two mothers, four girls and one boy. There could not help but be times when things got a bit hectic. Charlotte was taken with little Lillian's pre-Raphaelite beauty, and told her children that Lillian "looked like an angel dropped out of heaven." But Gladys remembered her mother talking about an old Irish superstition that the good die young, so she didn't like to be left alone with Lillian, for fear that Lillian might drop dead at any time.

In an attempt to broaden the financial base for the hardy little band of troupers, Mary Gish opened a candy and popcorn stand one summer on the grounds of the Fort George amusement park. At peak season, Gladys, Lottie and Jack would show up to help, and take their pay out of the stock. Unfortunately, they soon grew tired of eating candy, and grew fond of another food stall that served German fried potatoes for a nickel a dish. They all thought it would be much more fun to work at the potato stand than Mary Gish's candy stand.

Because most of the time was spent ekeing out a living, there was no time for cooking; mostly, the five children would buy their dinner in the delicatessen on the way home, usually pickles and some sliced turkey.

Entertainment costs were kept to a minimum because Gladys was adept at getting all the children in to see every worthwhile play then on the boards. Gladys, Lottie, Jack, Lillian and Dorothy would troop up to a box office, where Gladys would present her card, asking if the management recognized fellow professionals. The card read:

GLADYS SMITH
Little Red Schoolhouse Company

"We hear you have a very fine play with good actors," Gladys would say. "Perhaps we could learn from them." If the house was sold out, the five children would be waved away; otherwise, few could resist such a gently comic presentation. After climbing up into the gallery, Gladys would tell her charges, "Now, you children listen carefully to the way they speak, and watch everything they do; maybe someday we will play on Broadway."

But Broadway never seemed to get any closer. "Next year" it was back on the road, in endless tours that ranged from tank towns (Altoona, Owensboro, Keokuk) to cities with appetites for prime theater (Chicago, Detroit, Philadelphia). It was around this time that Mary threw what she always recalled as her most profound display of star temperment. They had been touring in *The Fatal Wedding,* and Gladys was being billed as "Gladys Smith, the Baby Wonder" (she kept the magenta-colored handbills to the end of her life). Being human, she began to believe her own billing. When Gladys was shown her dressing room, she first noticed the lack of a star on the door, then noticed its sty-like condition. Charlotte, wearing a hat and pinning a bath towel around her waist, busied herself in cleaning it up. Gladys put her hands on her hips and said, "Do they expect me, the star of the company, to dress in here? I'm not going on tonight."

Charlotte didn't even turn around, just looked at Gladys's reflection in the dressing room mirror. "What was that?" she said. "I want that repeated." Charlotte peremptorily played her ace: She threatened to bench Gladys and have sister Lottie play the part. "You are not the star," she charged. "You are just the little girl of the company, and a nasty, spoiled little girl. I'm grateful that the ladies and the gentlemen of the company didn't hear that disgusting, revolting speech. You're right; you're not going on tonight. *Remember, Gladys, a child has charm only when she is sweet.*"

It was the most severe tongue-lashing Charlotte had ever given her and to top it off, Charlotte made her clean up the dressing room herself. Gladys panicked; she may have hated the dinginess of it all, but she was earning the money for her family, and she reveled in the attention she got as the family "star," whether Charlotte was willing to acknowledge it or not. She also loved the applause at the end of the performance, something that people who lived in Toronto brownstones seldom heard.

Gladys begged to be allowed to go on with her performance that night. "I cried so bitterly that she let me go on," remembered Mary. "She shouldn't have. She should have let Lottie go on and play that part."

Some summers, or during occasional gaps between shows, Charlotte would take her brood back to Toronto to visit friends and family. Even then, work had to be attended to; for a free-lance, down-time is dead-time, inevitably leading to an empty wallet the next month. Gladys, along with Gertie Clegg, would try to get small parts or even extra work at one of the larger Toronto theaters.

Because there were few plays that could accommodate all four Smiths, Charlotte resigned herself to having the family split up more than she would have liked. In 1904–05, while Lottie and Gladys went on tour with *The Child Wife,* Charlotte and Jack stayed in New York. Gladys's salary was twenty-five dollars a week; she would have it changed into dollar bills to make it seem like more than it was.

By 1905–06, when Gladys was fourteen and touring with Chauncey Olcott, she had already reconciled herself to a primary cornerstone of her life: Making It. "I decided that if I was to be a success by the time I was twenty, I had best be stirring . . . when I saw the things other girls had, I determined to have them, but I would not get them from my family; I'd work for them. I'd have a fur coat one day, and it would be warmer because I had known what it was like to have insufficient wraps."

On May 18, 1907, Gladys closed out her last play for Hal Reid when *For a Human Life* played its final performance in Brooklyn.

Charlotte trooped back to Toronto but Gladys decided to stay in New York, where she moved in with a family she had stayed with once before. At night, she slept in a Morris chair, paying her rent by doing the shopping and cleaning the house. She had twenty dollars to her name.

Her plan was to get a job with one of the leading producers of theater in the country or get out of the business. If the latter, she was going to become a clothes designer. She began making inquiries about low-level jobs in the garment industry. She found that she could make five dollars a week pulling out threads and planned to use that to go to night school to learn design with an eye on becoming a dress manufacturer.

And she began laying serious siege to the man who, she was convinced, was going to lift Gladys and her family out of the dreary, degrading circumstances they found themselves in. She may have been only fifteen-years-old, but she was an actress looking for work, and not just any actress and not just any work. She was going to meet David Belasco and get hired. Gladys Smith might have been common clay, but she would, by God, be a star.

Chapter Two

"I'd have made a great actor."

—*David Belasco*

N E W York in the first decade of this century was still redolent of the Gilded Age. In the prosperous parts of town, the streets were wide, and most of them were lined with trees. Hansom cabs, their drivers perched high on the rear seats, filled the streets. Off the main thoroughfares, traffic was light.

From 23rd to 34th streets, the theater district ran through the dicey neighborhood known as the Tenderloin. Past 34th Street, Broadway transformed itself into what a later generation would call the Great White Way.

Although Gladys Smith, mired as she was in unsophisticated road companies, could not have known it, she was living through a primary transition in the American theater; the established order of barnstorming melodramas—of a leading man (or woman) discovering one meal-ticket play and flogging it around the country for the next quarter of a century, of Joseph Jefferson and James O'Neill—was approaching extinction. The only question was, what would replace it?

One of the holdouts of the era was David Belasco, a native of San Francisco who had, over the last twenty-five years, achieved an eminence in the American theater to which he felt fully entitled. A genial egomaniac who referred to the theater as "my adored profession," Belasco was a Jew who nevertheless habitually wore a reversed stand-up collar to give himself the unassailable dignity of a cleric. Short and stocky, Belasco challenged his dark clothing with his flourishing silver hair, the front of which was teased till a lock hung over his forehead.

He was a gorgeous ham who prided himself on presenting rip-roaring melodramas like *The Girl I Left Behind Me,* plays full of a surface realism and utter emotional hysteria. He was also a brutal taskmaster, rehearsing until all about him were collapsing. Once, he supposedly jabbed a hatpin into an actress to achieve the desired shriek of anguish, an act which, along with Belasco's richly absurd, oratorical personality, would be hilariously parodied in the superb Ben Hecht-Charles MacArthur play *Twentieth Century.*

Yet, for all his success, "Belasco's finest production was always himself," as the theater historian Allen Churchill put it. For The Maestro—as he liked to be called—specialized in superb productions of atrocious plays.

In a career spanning over fifty years, Belasco produced only one classic, *The Merchant of Venice,* starring David Warfield. It lost a lot of money. According to Belasco the sum was $250,000, a ridiculously inflated figure. Even if true, however, $250,000 was a paltry sum beside the profits of Belasco warhorses like *The Return of Peter Grimm, Seven Chances, The Girl of the Golden West* and *Tiger Rose.*

More than building sets of breathtaking verisimilitude (he once precisely reproduced the popular Child's restaurant on stage) or coaxing an actor into giving a brilliant performance, what Belasco really lusted after were poor scripts that he could re-work to such an extent that he could claim co-authorship, hence, a share of the royalties.

That was not all he lusted after, though. Within the Broadway community, it was well-known that Belasco ran one of the more active casting couches in the business. What's more, he made sure that that fact was known. Toward the end of his life, Jeanne Eagels successfully resisted his advances, whereupon Belasco excused himself and retired alone to his bedroom. Looking through the keyhole, Eagels saw The Maestro tearing his bed apart, in a fair simulation of the effects of passion, for the benefit of some soon-to-arrive guests. Eagels threw open the door and demanded he make the bed. He did, and the two sat eyeing each other suspiciously until the guests arrived, whereupon Eagels left.

Gladys Smith was ready-made for the world of Belasco; as Belasco's chief rival Charles Frohman, had cunningly observed, "In all my experience, I have seldom known of a very rich girl who made a finished actress on the stage . . . The daughters of the rich are taught to repress emotion . . . Give me the common clay, the kind that has suffered and even hungered. She makes the best star material."

By 1906, Gladys Smith was fourteen years old. She had been working in the theater for nearly eight years, six of them spent in non-stop touring. She, like hundreds of other actors and actresses, hungered for stardom on Broadway. The difference was that the hundreds of other actors and actresses didn't have Gladys's particularly devastating combination of ambition and talent.

Gladys's favorite fantasy was that Belasco would discover her as she fell into a dead faint—whether from hunger, overwork or a combination of both was unspecified—whereupon the Great Man would pick her up and take her into his office. He would be dazzled by a death scene beyond the reach of Duse, but then Gladys would snap out of it, Belasco would realize it had all been a performance and hire her on the spot.

It didn't quite work out that way. Gladys's visit to Belasco's office didn't get her anywhere; neither did a long series of letters she sent The Maestro. According to Mary, Belasco kept her waiting for nearly an entire summer; according to Belasco, it was just "a long time." In one of the letters she sent him, she said that she would never appear in New York except under his management. "With each of her letters she enclosed a photograph," remembered Belasco, "[and] in nearly every picture there was such variety of facial expression."

When he finally consented to see her, it was either eleven o'clock at night (Gladys's version) or during a Thursday matinee of *The Rose of the Rancho* (Belasco's version). A child wished to see him, the doorman told Belasco. He refused. The child insisted, saying she had come a long way to see him and had to leave town at noon the next day to resume a theatrical tour. "I simply must see him," Belasco remembered her saying. Very well, the Great Man consented with matchless *noblesse oblige.*

She was, he thought, "an image of girlish beauty . . . with long golden-brown curls." He said to her gravely, "You want to become an actress?" "I am an actress," Gladys answered proudly. "But I want to become a *good* one." Belasco remembered that she looked straight into his eyes, never blinking, never wavering.

Her audition piece for Belasco was a part she knew well, Patsy

Poor, from *For a Human Life.* "The ordeal was terrible, and the electric chair would have seemed preferable to me," she remembered. It's easy to believe her, for there was not merely her own future at stake, but that of three other people. Her audition was played to a chair that was supposed to be a policeman. Belasco's only immediate response was that she might want to consider modulating her performance somewhat; given the producer's preference for outsized acting, Gladys must have played a scene of awesome, tattering passion. He then strongly hinted that she was "in" when he suggested that she might want to get a book on southern accents. With that he curtly ordered the electrician to turn off the lights.

Belasco had been looking for a child actress to play the part of Betty Warren in William deMille's new drama *The Warrens of Virginia.* A few days later, he sent for her, and hired her (Belasco's version was that he hired her at once, but that seems out of character for his Napoleonic ego; making actors sweat and crawl was part of the game, for the entire world existed to serve the ego of David Belasco). He again cautioned her that she would be required to speak and act in a much more naturalistic fashion.

The pay would be twenty-five dollars a week; she had made more than that in stock, but the value of appearing in a Belasco production far outweighed the modest salary. There was only one problem: her name. Gladys Smith was too, too . . . flat; it sounded like one of the lily-white pansy heroines with which Belasco peopled his plays. Something else—anything else—was called for.

Gladys ran through her other family names, among them Pickford, from Elizabeth Denny Pickford, Charlotte's paternal grandmother. Belasco thought that was different, and then Gladys mentioned Marie, which she had always wished had been her name instead of the ugly "Louise." It was at that moment that Gladys Smith ceased to be, and Mary Pickford was born. That night, Mary sent a telegram to her mother in Toronto: GLADYS SMITH NOW MARY PICKFORD ENGAGED BY DAVID BELASCO TO APPEAR ON BROADWAY THIS FALL.

At the first rehearsal for *The Warrens of Virginia,* Mary arrived having memorized the entire script. Soon afterwards, Belasco threw one of his patented tantrums, administered as shock therapy to bored actors (one of whom was the author's brother, Cecil B. deMille, playing Mary's older brother). A jar that the script indicated should be full of molasses was found to be full of maple syrup. Intolerable! A screaming Belasco smashed the jar on the stage, then began jumping on the remains, grinding the maple syrup into an expensive Oriental carpet.

He sidled over to where Mary was sitting and casually asked her what she thought of his performance. When she sputtered something about ruining such a beautiful rug, he explained that it only cost fifteen dollars or so, and that the tantrum he had thrown at the dress rehearsal of *The Girl of the Golden West* had caused damage adding up to $150. "Don't you think I missed my vocation?" he finally asked. "I'd have made a great actor." Lost in rapt self-admiration, he strolled away to pick up the pieces of the rehearsal.

To the emotionally—and financially—frugal Mary, this *outre* behavior was fascinating, horrifying and exciting. Such a cavalier disregard of money was plush velvet on her parched, weathered skin.

"To me, David Belasco [was] like the King of England, Julius Caesar and Napoleon all rolled into one," she wrote. For his part, Belasco enjoyed the child's intensity about the theater, which was nearly as great as his own. "She was . . . the first at rehearsals and the last to go," he remembered. "She would read and re-read her lines to find out which was the best way to speak them . . . She was very creative and a highly imaginative little body."

When Mary asked Belasco for dialogue directions, he would ask her which reading she felt most comfortable with. After she demonstrated, he would invariably respond with "That is the best way." If she thought of a piece of business, she would demonstrate. "Invariably, she was right," said Belasco, "and I always let her do as she suggested." Mostly, Belasco confined his directions to her with one recurring refrain: "Remember, always keep it natural."

The Warrens of Virginia opened on December 3, 1907, at the Belasco Theater, after trying out at the Lyric in Philadelphia beginning November 19. The opening night went well, with Mary's only regrets centering on the costumes; she hated the pantalettes and skirts the period of the play required. An amused Belasco remembered that she was by far the most relaxed member of the company; to the end of her life, Mary wistfully recalled the elegant perfumes that the actors had been able to smell as the curtain rose, and contrasted it with the dank, grimy smells she had gotten used to in her barnstorming days. The eminent theater critic William Winter called the production "A memorable example of taste and excellence."

After the first night, she went to Belasco and told him that she thought she'd feel more relaxed on stage if she had a doll to play with. "Betty"—Belasco always referred to her by the name of the first character she played for him—"what kind of doll do you want?"

Charlotte had once mentioned that when she was a little girl she had had a doll whose entire head was made of china. Mary requested that kind of doll; she had it for the next day's performance and it became another of the keepsakes that Mary would cherish for the rest of her life.

The Warrens of Virginia was a hit of sufficient size to play for two seasons, one in New York (it ran until May 16, 1908) and one on the more-lucrative (in those days) road. In a day when 100 performances was a considerable hit, *The Warrens of Virginia* officially amassed 190. ("Officially" because Burns Mantle, the notable critic and theater historian who was doing the counting, figured eight performances a week, even though in those pre-Equity days shows regularly gave nine, and sometimes ten, performances a week.)

For the tour, Mary got a five dollar a week raise. She remembered that, for the first time, the Belasco production gave her the appreciative response of a sophisticated audience. "I could feel that they liked to see me play—that it was giving them some genuine pleasure." The little child actress, this newly christened Mary Pickford, was finding the first buyers for her emerging product of happiness.

Although the Belasco name promised Actor's Heaven, one-nighters were not completely a thing of the past. The tour of *The Warrens of Virginia* was oddly routed, opening on September 21, 1908, at the Majestic Theater in Boston, moving to New Haven, Providence, back to New York, then to Brooklyn, then through engagements in Philadelphia, Baltimore, Washington, Pittsburgh, Cincinnati, Indianapolis, Bloomington (a one-nighter), Vincennes (also a one-nighter), Belleville (another one-nighter), and St. Louis.

After a one-week Christmas layoff, the troupe was back in Manhattan, then up to Toronto (at the still-standing Royal Alexander Theater), then down to Buffalo, Cleveland, Racine (a one-nighter), Omaha, Kansas City, Chicago, Toledo, finally finishing up with a five-day engagement ending March 20, 1909, at the West End Theater in Harlem, Manhattan.

Mary's roommate on the road was a young tyro named Blanche Yurka, who would go on to achieve a measure of fame on stage and as Madame DeFarge in Selznick's 1935 film of *A Tale of Two Cities*. During the tour, Mary taught Blanche how to save even more money by doubling up in hotel rooms. The two girls breakfasted daily on bananas and milk, a dish served frequently at Child's restaurant and which Mary had taught herself to like because it cost only five cents.

In Cleveland, during the last week of January, Mary and her roommate were walking to the hotel after a performance at the Colonial Theater when they were accosted by two men, who thought they were working girls in another profession entirely. Mary and Blanche speeded up, ignoring the lewd remarks. Under her breath, Mary told Yurka, "Don't answer yet; wait until we get to the hotel. I'll tell them what's what."

As they reached the hotel doors, Mary turned on them, loosing a flow of invective worthy of an Irish fishwife. "I felt a little like a St. Bernard being protected by a barking poodle," remembered Yurka.

During the tour, Mary accompanied Yurka and some of the other actors and actresses in the company to a matinee of one of the old barnstorming melodramas on which Mary had cut her performer's baby teeth and which were gradually petering out. The other actors sniggered at the extravagant melodrama of the writing and the sweepings and posturings of the actors, but Mary sat quietly.

When she and Yurka returned to their hotel room, she exploded into tears of rage. "You were all just awful," she charged. "Those actors were working just as hard to be convincing as any of you snobbish Broadway actors. I think you all behaved dreadfully." This suspicion of intellectual arrogance, the sense of bonding with the mass audience, would serve her well in the very near future.

During the entire run, Mary lived on five dollars a week, turning the rest over to Charlotte for the family. At the end of the two-year run, they were $240 ahead; more importantly, Belasco had drilled one of his favorite maxims into her brain: "There must be heart, heart, heart. Soul is only a glow. The definite thing is the heart, the capacity to feel. Intelligence is secondary, but it is desirable."

Desirable, but not absolutely necessary. In all of her pictures, Mary would stress "heart." As for intelligence, the world of business would be room enough for that.

The tour of *The Warrens of Virginia* ended and Belasco had nothing for her. "Before she left me," Belasco remembered, "Miss Pickford said, 'Mr. Belasco, remember, no matter where I am or what I am doing, when you want me just let me know and I'll come.' " It was a promise the canny showman would hold her to.

Still, two seasons with Belasco had validated Mary as an actress, at least in her own mind, as well as leapfrogging her over most of her peers. Working in the big time, getting a chance to see and compare other major actresses, had also allowed Charlotte and Mary to stumble across a role model: Maude Adams. Like Mary, Maude Adams had had a strenuous childhood without a father but with the theater, playing in *Uncle Tom's Cabin, The Octaroon,* and other plays. Although Adams had been born in Salt Lake City in 1872, it was not until maturity that her luminous skin and what contemporaries called an "enchanting" voice helped make her a star in 1897's *The Little Minister.* In 1905 she created *Peter Pan* and achieved apotheosis.

The necessity of survival gave Adams the personality of a classic workaholic; like Mary, she made it a pious virtue. Like Mary, she countered increasing fame by withdrawal; and, like Mary, Maude Adams played child characters when she herself was long past the age of thirty.

Her stage character was one that was invariably described as "elfin" or "ethereal," i.e. pre-sexual. A winsome, feminine charm that was ever-so-slightly sexless was her stock in trade. Mary would modify that quality and shape it to her own uses; there would never be any doubt about her femininity, on screen or in life, but it was leavened by a sweet, questioning seriousness that gave her screen character a rare gravity.

Adams had a closeted, apparently cloistered private life and was so devoted to her art that her private railroad car had a small stage so she could rehearse her company when they were en route. She possessed a certain ambition—in 1909, she played Shaw's Saint Joan in an outdoor production at Harvard—but her greatest successes invariably came in more modest vehicles. William Winter described her 1892 Juliet as that of "an intellectual young lady from Boston, competent in the mathematics and intent on teaching pedagogy." Brooks Atkinson said that Adams had "a soft, elusive charm that could not be analyzed or resisted."

Adams had the foresight to retire in 1918, after her final triumph in Barrie's *A Kiss for Cinderella.* When she made a comeback in 1931, playing Portia to Otis Skinner's Shylock, the production was generally termed regrettable and never made it to New York.

Yet, there was an undoubted magic there; stills show her to have possessed deep blue-gray eyes that exude a sense of tranquility, and a kind of asexual attractiveness; one can see why she made an excellent Peter Pan.

Mary studied her model carefully. In a 1917 article in *Vanity Fair,* she wrote a thoughtful article about the technique of portraying children that owed much to her predecessor. "The facial muscles of the grown-up are controlled, while those of the child spontaneously reflect passing moods," wrote Mary. "A child pouts when it is displeased. When children are awed or surprised or frightened, their eyes open wide and their mouths droop, but their foreheads remain unwrinkled—and just there is another difficulty, for when we older people are under the influence of similar emotions, our brows have a tendency to become lined. Then there are the muscles about the mouth; those of the child, unlike those of the grown-up, are relaxed."

Maude Adams's success, and the indifference that greeted her return to the stage in a different era, were eerie simulacrums of Mary's period of greatest success . . . and greatest failure. As both of them were to learn, in art as in life, timing is everything.

Chapter Three

"You're too little and too fat, but I may give you a chance."
—D.W. Griffith to Mary Pickford, April 1909.

T HE building that housed the American Mutoscope and Biograph Company was a typical four-floor brick structure at 11 East 14th Street, in New York. Its basement peeped out over the street; to get to the studio proper you ascended ten steps between ornamental cast-iron railings. On either side of the top step were windows, under which hung inconspicuous signs announcing the company's name in gold lettering. Just below the window on the right was a tailor shop, the door of which was often used by nervous actors who didn't want to be seen entering what everybody knew was a movie studio. At that time, working in the flickers was considered only a step away from entertaining in the parlor of a whorehouse.

At the top of the stairs, there was a set of double doors behind which was a marble-floored foyer; another short flight of stairs led to the main floor. A long hallway ran nearly the length of the building; on either side of the hallway were the front offices; at the hallway's end was the studio's production center, a converted ballroom. The ballroom measured 50 feet by 35 feet, and rolls of canvas, paint, and spare 2 by 4's were piled up just out of camera range on either side. In one corner was a 5 foot by 5 foot platform on rollers, which held the camera.

The studio was surrounded by two dozen arc lights that were hung on pulleys. A dozen Cooper-Hewitt mercury-vapor lamps were mounted on ceiling banks or on floor rollers. The Cooper-Hewitts had a way of clicking when in use, a castanet-like beat that seemed to give the actors a sense of rhythm. Wardrobe, props and dressing rooms were jammed together in the cellar. Here, in the summer of 1908, had come David Wark Griffith, a refugee from a marginal career in the theater.

He had been born on January 22, 1875, the son of a Civil War veteran. Young David's primary—and, probably, permanent—ambition had been to be a playwright, but his single produced effort, *A Fool and A Girl,* had been a failure. Unable to make any more money in the theater as an actor than as a writer, he edged his way into the movie business in 1907 at the Edison studio, where he played the lead in a film called *Rescued From an Eagle's Nest.* The film has survived, and it clearly shows why Griffith had such a perilous time making a living in the theater: He was as bad an actor as he was a writer.

But at the Biograph company, Griffith not only picked up some acting jobs, he sold some stories. When a director fell sick, Griffith was asked to replace him. Accustomed as he was to failure, Griffith accepted, with the proviso that, if his efforts were inadequate, he would still have a job at Biograph as an actor/writer. But he did not fail; indeed, he had at last found the one job he was perfectly suited by nature to perform.

Griffith's films were quickly perceived as the best being made in motion pictures, at the time a largely despised offshoot of peep-show amusement. By the latter part of 1909, the demand for Biograph films was so great that the company had to add another unit.

It was a hard life, grinding out two and three films a week in the cavernous ballroom, so hot from the mercury-vapor lamps and flaming arcs, so dark just outside the range of the camera manned by Billy Bitzer. Location trips to Fort Lee or Cuddebackville were regarded as paid vacations.

Like nearly every business decision Mary Pickford ever made, her decision to go into the movies was a matter of harsh economics. *The Warrens of Virginia* tour had ended, and Charlotte was eking out a living in a Chauncey Olcott show. In the theater of that time, with far more shows needing far more actors, two weeks out of work was a long time. While Mary had been out of work less than a month, summer wasn't far off, and there was usually very little work in that season, meaning she might not get a job until the fall. Charlotte began to panic. There seemed to be few prospects except a return to barnstorming in stock, and, after the prestige of Belasco, that was intolerable.

"Mary, what about those motion picture studios?" Charlotte said one day in April 1909. She got the idea from a couple of actors she was working with in the Olcott production who had worked for Biograph the previous summer. (Mary appraised Charlotte's act-ing talent thusly: "She was far from being a professional; it was a means to an end.") Mary was mortified; this was worse than a comedown, it was a complete disgrace. She had, after all, gone through a great deal to secure her position as a Belasco actress; to work in movies would be quite a step down professionally.

Charlotte listened to all this, then pointed out that a job in the movies meant that the four of them could stay together that sum-mer rather than be separated into different stock companies. "I hear they pay as much as five dollars a day," Charlotte pointed out with crushing finality. "That's worth lowering your pride a little bit, isn't it?"

Mary was a dutiful daughter accustomed to obedience. "Yes, mother," she said, although she hated the idea.

The trolley fare to the studio from their boarding house on West 17th Street was a nickel. Combined with the fare back, the outlay came to ten cents, which Mary regarded as too much to spend on such a speculative venture. Mary took a five-cent transfer, which meant that she could get a cross-town car, do her duty at the film studio, then (illegally) change to an up-town car and check out the various theatrical agencies on Broadway . . . assuming that the conductor didn't notice that the stamp wasn't in order.

She walked to West 14th, took a cross-town trolley, and got off the streetcar near the ugly brownstone on East 14th. She walked in, hoping and praying that the casters wouldn't want her. After what she later described as "the usual business"— "There's no work. Have you registered with us before?"—she was on her way out the door when a fairly tall, lean, deep-voiced man with an imposing aquiline nose stepped out of a side door.

Mary introduced herself. "I thought I wouldn't mind acting in pictures for a while," she said. "That is, if the salary is satisfactory."

"Have you had any stage experience?" D.W. Griffith inquired in his deep, courtly voice. "Ten years," she replied, mentioning her seasons with Belasco, trying hard not to sound boastful and un-doubtedly failing. Griffith looked her over. "It so happens that we need a type like you in our next picture. About salary—we pay five dollars a day when you work."

"I must have at least ten. You realize I'm a stage actress and an artist. I've had important parts on the real stage. I must have twenty-five dollars a week guaranteed."

Intrigued by her brashness, Griffith said that he would submit her proposal to the front office. Later, he would remember that Mary was hired "on her own terms." It was Mary's recollection that she worked in front of the cameras on that very first day; Griffith must have been satisfied, but others weren't. Some of the front office thought she was just another ingenue, and a plump one at that.

According to the Biograph records, Mary Pickford made her first appearance before a movie camera on April 20, 1909. Griffith himself applied Mary's first makeup. With the heavy whiteface, darkened eyebrows and eyeliner necessary to register on the slow film of the day, Mary thought the makeup "made me look like Pancho Villa." She was photographed milling around in the background of a film oddly—if deliciously—titled *Her First Biscuits*, starring Dorothy Bernard. The trade advertisement went:

BIOGRAPH COMPANY, U.S.A.
Biograph Films—You Can See Them Think.
The following subjects will be released on the 28th July:
Was Justice Served? Length, 962 feet.
Showing what might result from circumstantial evidence.
Her First Biscuits. Length, 514 feet.
A comedy subject.
Faded Lilies. Length, 481 feet.
Bulletin fully describing the above will be sent on application.

That first day ran late, till nearly 8:00 P.M., but she was paid for her troubles and she promised to be back the next day. "When I got outside, it was raining very hard," she remembered. "Mr. Griffith walked me to the subway under his umbrella." When Mary arrived at the theater where Charlotte was working, the heater was on and Jack was curled up in a corner, asleep. Not only was Mary's new hat ruined but even the money she had clutched in her hand was wet. She was, in fact, soaked through. No matter; Charlotte put Mary's clothes and the dollar bills on the radiator to dry. Charlotte thought this movie business sounded quite promising.

It was a beginning.

By April 1909, when Mary walked into the Biograph studio for the first time, there were over 5,000 nickelodeons in America, each showing multiple subjects amounting to between a half hour and an hour of film that was changed daily. (Eighteen months later, there were 9,480.)

Mary's time with David Belasco had tipped the salary scales in her favor. "Griffith paid me ten dollars a day [when he was only paying everybody else five dollars] because I was a Belasco actress," she insisted years later, pride giving her voice a steely ring. A variant version was that Griffith did some hard haggling, agreeing to pay her twenty-five dollars for the first three day's work, then five dollars a day thereafter. (The Biograph pay vouchers that would confirm or deny Mary's story no longer exist, but her version is possible; Griffith was not above playing favorites when it came to money.)

There was, of course, a down-side: the fall from the stage to the "flickers" was a mighty one, nearly approaching that of the angel Lucifer. To the end of her days, Mary proclaimed her pride at being a Belasco actress, as well as accompanying feelings of condescension toward the movies. "I was steeped in the tradition of the theater and I didn't want my stage friends to know that I was working in what they all called those awful flickers! I just longed for a beard and a wig to crawl into the Biograph studio so no one would recognize me."

And yet, as much as she loved it, Mary knew that there was something sad about the theater. Every night, as the great curtain came down at the end of a performance, she had felt as if something was dying. And then, after the makeup was scrubbed off and it was time to go home, the walk through the dark, empty theater, bereft of all the emotion and excitement of the performance, always depressed her.

Mary Pickford had not realized it, but she was only, truly alive when she was acting; all else was a waiting, a gray half-life. The great bonus of working at Biograph was that there was a great deal of acting to do, for Griffith instantly recognized a usable, malleable talent. In the weeks that followed her April debut, Griffith used Mary frequently, in films like *The Violin Maker of Cremona* and *The Lonely Villa*. Griffith must have been pleased; for her part, Mary was most uneasy.

For one thing, there was the unfamiliarity of it all; Mary remembered that during one of her first appearances before the Biograph camera, she was struck by a severe, unfamiliar attack of stage fright, to the extent that the floor began rising and falling in waves.

For another, she was horrified at the way she photographed. Mary then carried 115 pounds on her 5-foot-1-inch frame and she did appear to be carrying some leftover baby-fat. (Her weight in later years was around 95 pounds, distributed on a 33$^{1/4}$-25-36 figure.) Then as now, the camera tended to add a good 10 pounds; if the actor was not trim and lithe to begin with, the results could be blimpish. "I had no idea I was so stocky," Mary said later. This was a common reaction; Lionel Barrymore went to work at Biograph in 1911, and was appalled at the way he photographed. "Little girl," he said, poking Mary with his index finger, "little girl, tell me: Am I really that fat?" Mary had no alternative but to confront him with the truth: "I'm terribly sorry, Mr. Barrymore, but you are." "Then that does it," said Barrymore, "no more beer for me."

She also missed the continuity of the theater; "The scenes were cut so quickly that we did not have time to act. We could never really get into an emotion; revenge, great joy, grief had to be shown in about ten feet [of film]."

In addition, having grown up poor, Mary clung to the thin aura of dignity conferred by having worked for Belasco; she was offended by the informality of the Biograph players, the way they addressed each other by their first names . . . except for "Mr. Griffith," and, behind his back, they even called him "D.W."!

There were, nevertheless, compensations. For one thing, it was different. Griffith and his cameraman Billy Bitzer were able to pull settings of amazing variety out of the old ballroom. For another, there was a definite air of the exotic about Biograph; when the mercury lights were turned on, the actors looked ghastly, as if they'd been dead for days, complete with purple lips. On film, however, they appeared to be normal. Once in a while, one of the lights would shatter, and the mercury inside would spill to the ground. Mary was still enough of a little girl to gather up the mercury and play with it, breaking it up into particles and then running them together into a seamless mass.

The studio had beautiful circular staircases as well as lavish marble mantelpieces. The dailies were shown in one of the master bedrooms, and, between the every day grind of making the films, followed by the free and open appraisal that Mary gave her own acting and that of the others in the company, she slowly began to feel at home.

The Biograph actors formed a classic repertory company; because of their youth, they had a maximum of adaptability and a minimum of star ego. To increase her paycheck, Mary made some tentative forays into writing, selling a few scenarios to Biograph. Stories for split-reelers brought fifteen dollars while stories for one-reelers brought twenty-five dollars. Mack Sennett, at that time a (bad) small-part actor who specialized in country oafs, still some years from becoming the producer whose name was synonymous with comedy, was frankly envious, and not just of the extra money Mary was making. Sennett liked his women plainspoken and hearty, and as far as he was concerned, Mary was "affected." Nevertheless, she seemed friendly enough. After some conversation, Mary agreed to front for Sennett's own literary endeavors.

A few days later, Sennett presented her with three scenarios. Mary in turn presented them to the scenario editor, who looked at them and tossed them into the wastebasket.

"My dear girl," he told her, "don't you know that O. Henry has been writing quite a while?" It was the last time Sennett asked her for any favors.

With several raises, overtime work and writing scenarios, Mary always claimed that she was able to save $1,200 in her first six months at Biograph, far more money than she'd ever been able to save in the theater. The figure seems high, especially when one of the few surviving pieces of correspondence from this period is taken into account. On November 2, 1909, she wrote a hotelier with whom the Biograph company regularly stayed and who had evidently lent her some money that "I thank you kindly for the check. I was worried to know how to make up for the loss of five dollars. You are very kind, Mr. Predmore, to trust me and take my word, but I asure [sic] you, your trust has not been misplaced."

In addition, Mary found work for others in the family; Jack picked up some small acting jobs and Donald Crisp, who began working at Biograph the same year as Mary, distinctly remembered that Charlotte would occasionally serve as the janitor, cleaning up the one toilet in the building. Things were indeed looking up.

It was not a place totally without the usual tensions of actors and actresses, however. When Mary was still a newcomer to Biograph, a young actor named Owen Moore thought she was dawdling in a scene and muttered "Get on with it, dame." Mary broke character and turned on Moore. "I'll have you understand, sir, that I am no dame. I'm a respectable young girl."

Griffith was furious. *"Never,* as long as you live, do a thing like that again," he admonished her. "Film costs two cents a foot and you just ruined ten feet." Realizing her mistake, she apologized. It was the beginning of a pattern of adversarial respect, an element of push/pull over status and power intensified by Mary's resentment of Griffith's manipulation of his actresses that would be repeated between Mary and Griffith for years to come.

"He always had four or five ingenues," remembered Marshall Neilan, later to be the director of most of Mary's best films. "He'd pump them all day and give the synthesis of what he got to the one he preferred."

Not unnaturally, the teen-aged girls were often entranced by their lordly, commanding director. "D.W. had [Mae] Marsh, [Blanche] Sweet, [Lillian] Gish and other young girls fall in love with him," remembered James Kirkwood Sr., "but Mary had perception. She was a little old lady; Griffith couldn't get anywhere with Mary."

Despite the fact that they would invariably bump heads, Mary, to the end of her life, spoke of Griffith with the highest respect. "I'm so very, very grateful to him," she once said. Mostly, she seemed to appreciate his genuine concern for his actors, the way, for instance, he would designate a few people to watch over the gentle, gifted Henry B. Walthall, a periodic alcoholic who would disappear for days at a time. "He was like a father to us," she said. "If we looked pale he'd worry or do something. 'My dear child, you must be allowed to [get your rest].' "

Griffith's attitude towards his (mostly) youthful charges was, with rare exceptions, studiously paternal; he considered himself their mentor as well as their director. Location trips to New Jersey —the subway to the 129th Street ferry, then over to New Jersey— were eagerly awaited. Particularly sought after were spots on the roster that Griffith would take to Cuddebackville, a little town in the Orange Mountains, near the New York–New Jersey border, with scenic views of the Hudson River and Delaware Canal. In 1909 alone, Griffith took his charges, including Mary and Lottie, to Cuddebackville three times. Although Mary had been using her new name for two years, and everybody in the company called her "Mary," she was still not entirely comfortable with it; on at least one occasion, she signed the register at the hotel in Cuddebackville as "G. Pickford."

It didn't seem to matter whether the location was Greenwich, Connecticut, Fort Lee, Edgewater, or Englewood, all in New Jersey. The Biograph locations were invariably sylvan fields separated by running brooks and beautiful, wooded hillsides. Even when Griffith might ask for multiple takes of someone falling into the water, these were good, innocent times, somewhere between a school outing and a Sunday picnic.

When the company was on location in Cuddebackville, the actors and crew stayed at the Caudebec Inn; if the day's work had gone particularly smoothly, Griffith would usually stand for a round of drinks, while Billy Bitzer would buy the second round. After that, Griffith often retired to his room to figure out what he was going to shoot the next day, so the actors were free to drink at the bar in the front of the hotel, play cards or games.

At one time or another, one of the older actors might declaim Shakespeare, but most of the men occupied themselves with a poker game that took place in a small building across the road, next to an icehouse. (Once, someone got up a crap game, but Griffith wandered by, saw what was going on, and put a stop to it.) There would also have been time for some lighthearted "sparking," although Griffith kept a weather eye out for any illicit goings-on in the bushes; he was particularly protective of Mary and, on her first trip to Cuddebackville, made sure that she and Lottie had the room directly across from him. It was not a foolproof plan, for it was the romantic summer evenings in Cuddebackville that firmly cemented Mary's attraction to Owen Moore.

Back in the studio, the Biograph routine seldom varied. Mondays would usually be for rehearsal. Griffith would gather the company around the camera platform, explain the story and ask for suggestions, giving them all a chance to feel a personal interest in the picture. After accepting or rejecting the ideas, he'd go around the circle of players, asking "How do you like that, Pickford?" or "How do you like that, Gish?"

Tuesdays would be for interiors and Wednesday for exteriors. "He was your audience," Claire McDowell told the historian Barnett Bravermann. "He'd cry, laugh, he'd simply draw it out of you. His enthusiasm was infectious. 'That's fine, that's dandy, do it some more!' And when a scene was over, he'd come and put his arms around you. He was magnetic." Griffith's chimerical, emotional direction heavily influenced Mary's ideas of acting. She grew to distrust any style that depended on the technical. "I don't believe in gestures," she would say. "[With Mr. Griffith] we just listened to his voice to get his feeling," for Griffith "devised ways and means of bringing actors out of themselves . . . he could make an actor surpass himself . . ."

In rainy weather, the interiors for several pictures would be completed, and Griffith and his young actors would have to wait for the sun, then charge out to complete exteriors pell-mell so as not to fall behind in the releasing schedule, which, as of January 1909, demanded two films a week.

Although Griffith was, in 1909, only thirty-four years old, he adopted the lordly remoteness of a country schoolmaster. He didn't always realize that the youth of his actors and actresses meant they were highly impressionable; once, enthralled with a recent spate of French films, he showed his actors Coquelin's adaptation of *Tosca,* running it for the Biograph players as if it were a model of the pantomimists' art. The next day, Griffith found himself saddled with a repertory company that was doing their studious best to imitate French actors, with horrifying results. Griffith never showed them another French film.

He was manipulative when he had to be. Unhappy with a Pickford (as Griffith always called her) performance, he suddenly tore into Owen Moore, who was also in the film, humiliating and belittling him in front of the entire cast and crew. Mary's surprise quickly turned to rage. Griffith suddenly yelled "camera" and began instructing Pickford what to do.

But Mary was still a girl, and Griffith wanted—*needed*—more of a woman. "Do you know anything about lovemaking?" he asked her soon after she started at Biograph. Of course, the seventeen-year-old who had never had a date assured him that she did. At that moment, a carpenter walked by carrying a papier-mâché pillar. Griffith instructed the carpenter to put the pillar down and for Mary to make love to it. Mary protested; all that kept her from walking away from the entire lurid business was the ten dollars a day. At that point, Owen Moore walked out of the dressing room.

"Come here, Moore. Stand there. Miss Pickford doesn't like to make love to a lifeless pillar. See if she can do any better with you."

"I shall never forget that moment when Owen Moore put his arms around me," remembered Mary. "My heart was pounding so fast from shame and embarrassment that I thought I would die. If I had known that less than two years later I would be Mrs. Owen Moore, I probably would have died."

The hours at Biograph were grueling, from 9:00 A.M. to 8:00P.M. (after 8:00 P.M. entitled them to overtime), and the surroundings were a considerable come-down from Belasco's; the women's dressing area was a long room divided down the middle by a shelf-like dressing table. One side was for the lesser actresses, bit and non-featured players; the other side was for veterans or the putative stars. It was on this side that the only two individual dressing tables were located, and it became Mary's ambition to earn one of them.

For a long time, however, Mary, being the smallest of the Biograph actresses, had to endure the humiliation of being pinned into old dresses that had been fitted for larger actresses like Marion Leonard or Florence Lawrence. This trial had the favorable effect of forcing her to keep her face toward the camera at all times, so the safety pins holding up the dresses wouldn't show. Only once, in her first few weeks at Biograph, did Griffith authorize a costume especially for Mary to wear, in *The Lonely Villa.* Linda Arvidson, Griffith's wife, got twenty dollars from petty cash and took Mary to Best's, on 23rd Street, where she was outfitted in a pale blue linen frock, matching silk stockings and patent leather pumps.

Mary's star quality did not take long to manifest itself. After only three months at Biograph, the New York *Dramatic Mirror* reviewed the company's *They Would Elope* by saying, "This delicious little comedy introduced again an ingenue whose work in Biograph pictures is attracting attention."

The location for the film had been Little Falls, New Jersey, and Mary had to do a scene in which the canoe she was in overturned. It seemed like as good a time as any to ask Griffith for a raise. Wet and shivering, she was rushed back to Griffith's car, where she looked up into his face and sweetly reminded him that he placed a high value on actors and actresses being good sports and doing minor stunts when they came up. She got her raise.

Around July 1, 1909, Florence Lawrence, who was so popular with the public that she was known by the appellation "The Biograph Girl," left the company to work for Carl Laemmle's Independent Motion Picture Company, or, for short, IMP. Griffith told Mary to take over her dressing table. It was official; she was a star

By her eleventh month at Biograph, Mary had appeared in about forty-five films, and the April 15, 1910 issue of *The Nickelodeon* paid fulsome tribute to her anonymously, this time for her performance in *A Romance of the Western Hills,* in which she played an Indian maiden. "The acting of the Indian girl, especially when she appears as a civilized member of the household, is particularly charming. In fact, it is undoubtedly true that the popularity of the Biograph film is in a great measure due to this actress, and this is a particularly fine example of her art." Mary's rapid rise to the front of the Biograph ranks was made all the more remarkable by the fact that she was competing on a fast track, with actors such as Blanche Sweet, Harry Carey, Mabel Normand and Florence Lawrence, most of whom had a year or two of movie experience behind them.

After Mary started at Biograph, Belasco hunted around for her, unsuccessfully. In his loftiness, he never stopped to think she might be working in the movies; in her shame, she could not bear to tell him. What she didn't know was that he eventually became aware of the sad state to which she had fallen. William deMille had run into Mary and promptly sat down to write Belasco.

"Do you remember that little girl, Mary Pickford, who played Betty in *The Warrens of Virginia?*" deMille wrote. "I met her again a few weeks ago and the poor kid is actually thinking of taking up motion pictures seriously. She says she can make a fairly good living at it, but it does seem a shame. After all, she can't be more than seventeen, and I remember what faith you had in her future, that appealing personality of hers would go a long way in the theater, and now she's throwing her whole career in the ash-can and burying herself in a cheap form of amusement which hasn't a single point that I can see to recommend it . . . I pleaded with her not to waste her professional life and the opportunity the stage gives her to be known to thousands of people, but she's rather a stubborn little thing for such a youngster and she says she knows what she's doing.

"So I suppose we'll have to say goodbye to little Mary Pickford. She'll never be heard from again, and I feel terribly sorry for her . . ."

Shortly after starting at Biograph, Mary made what she retroactively realized was a momentous discovery. She had, she admitted later, labored under the "delusion" that she could be a great actress. "I was sorely tempted to abandon my childish parts and to try to become like some of the other actresses I admired. Either consciously or unconsciously I began imitating them."

While she never specified the moment of this epiphany, it nevertheless came. "I was not and and never would be a great tragedienne," she said. "It was a shock, but a very sanitary and wholesome one. In stature, temperament and general appearance, I was not fitted for great emotional roles."

"I decided . . . [that] if I were only to be a semiprecious gem, to be frankly that rather than a paste imitation of something more glittering and gorgeous." (italics added)

It is entirely possible that this realization was a wise and rational adjustment to the talent at hand. Certainly, Mary was a coldly objective observer of her own career ("Of all the elements of character, I think self-analysis is the most important," she said years later), as would be proven when, after nearly a quarter-century of unprecedented success, she walked away from her film career after only two failures.

But her newfound attitude could also have been a justification for the seeking of security, the only security Mary would ever know: that of playing children, adolescents and girl/women with such endearing expertness that any possible criticism of her as a person or an actress would be disarmed. Mary may have sensed what we now know, that an audience seldom demands more of a star than the star; the audience will, in fact, submissively fall in behind . . . until the vehicles get sub-standard, or the audience gets bored.

But there wasn't much chance of anyone getting bored at or by Biograph; it was a true repertory company, and they made too many pictures, with too wide a group of settings and stories. In nearly three years at Biograph, Mary averaged nearly one film a week and not all of them leading parts. A lead in a film made one week called *The Renunciation* could easily be followed the next week by a virtual walk-on as a maid. That was the way Griffith liked it; it kept his charges malleable. It also kept the labor cheap. If nobody could be sure of star status, then nobody could demand star wages.

For Griffith, the hectic Biograph production schedule forced him to rely on his energy and his instincts. There was never time for more than two takes of a given scene, and the general rush occasionally resulted in horrendous tripe released hard on the heels of a gem. *The Violin Maker of Cremona*, made in June 1909, is a virtual textbook example of what the ignorant presume typical of early cinema, with everyone from the stars to the bit players mugging and gesticulating so broadly it's a good thing the camera was ten feet away or it would have been knocked over. Yet, just a few months later, Griffith would send out *A Corner in Wheat*, one of the most perfect films ever made.

Mary had quickly found that the discipline imparted by hundreds of weeks of trouping and working with Belasco was a godsend, for working at Biograph—or in the movies at all—demanded intense concentration. An audience was not attentively watching, but often walking by. Although Biograph had only one indoor stage, other movie companies habitually built sets for different movies adjacent to each other. Nothing was enclosed, and actors had to block out the sounds of the carpenters hammering, and learn to react only to what *their* director was yelling at *them,* not what the director next door was yelling at *his* actors.

In the eighty-one films Mary made in her first stint at Biograph from 1909 to 1911, she played, besides young girls, young wives, mothers (at the age of seventeen, she played the mother of a ten-year-old!), prostitutes, virgins, Mexicans, secretaries and, because her hazel eyes photographed dark, an Indian squaw in a rather good film called *Iola's Promise.* She did not enjoy playing Indians, because it meant you had to get up an hour early, at 5:00 A.M., and rub in a makeup of clay mixed with water, put on a horse-hair wig, alligator necklaces, a heavy, beaded horsehide gown, and then stay out in the sun all day long. Still, that didn't stop her from trying; nothing did.

"One thing set Mary apart from all the other girls I was engaging at Biograph at the same time," said Griffith. "Work. I soon began to notice that instead of running off as soon as her set was over, she'd stay to watch the others on theirs. She never stopped listening and looking. She was determined to learn everything she could about the business." Billy Bitzer, echoed his boss about Mary's unceasing appetite for work, but he also noted her attention to detail.

"[The] business of makeup for instance—none of us gave it much thought," Bitzer wrote, "but Mary first used one makeup and, when she saw herself on screen, would reblend it and come to me. 'Do you think this is better, Billy?' she would ask . . . 'Do you think I should put in a little more yellow? More pink?' " Bitzer's final word on Mary was that she "would have succeeded in any career she wished to follow."

One episode clearly indicates the respect Griffith had for Mary. On September 26, 1910, Mary sold Biograph a story entitled *The Goose Girl,* for which she received the usual twenty-five dollars. Shortly thereafter, she left Biograph for more money elsewhere, but Griffith did not schedule the film for production with another actress. The story was not filmed (as *Lena and the Geese)* until September 1912, after Mary had returned to the company. Griffith was right to wait for her return; *Lena and the Geese* is among the most enchanting of the movies Mary made for Biograph.

At Biograph, Mary held herself somewhat aloof. Possessed of an innate dignity that kept her from mixing too freely—her only nickname appears to have been "The Little Dumpling," a reference to her plumpish appearance, although she also remembered being called "The Great Unkissed"—Mary's habit was to sit on one side of a set, often accompanied by Charlotte, until she was called. The company wasn't entirely sure what to make of this relationship, and a rumor went around that Charlotte often sat by Mary's bedside just watching her sleep, raptly worshiping the beauty of her daughter.

Although just turning out the films was a large enough task, Griffith also had the duty of managing a large company of youthful, spirited actors and actresses.

There was Arthur Johnson, the resident matinee idol, one of seven sons of a minister and the only one who hadn't followed in his father's footsteps, a good actor who would die of alcoholism at the age of forty.

There was the young Lionel Barrymore, who really wanted to be an artist, but who was gradually getting used to the more comfortable living that he could make as an actor. He found doors opened immediately because of the theatrical reputations of his father, Maurice Barrymore, and his uncle, the eminent John Drew.

And there was Owen Moore. Moore was born in December 1886, in County Meath, Ireland. His father, John, brought the family over to America in 1898, where he landed a job as a laborer in, unaccountably, Toledo, Ohio.

Tom and Owen, respectively the eldest and next-eldest of the six children, got restless in Toledo and left home while still in their teens, drifting into traveling shows, road companies and vaudeville. (Four of the six Moore children would eventually work in the movies.) In December 1908, five months before Mary arrived, Owen Moore went to work at Biograph.

Although Owen was a good enough actor, there was something about him that put a lot of people off. For one thing, he had a bad temper; shooting *Resurrection* during an unseasonable April heat wave, Owen grew querulous and began heaving tables and chairs at the other actors. Although the scene called for the action, there was an uncomfortable lack of artifice about Owen's rage, and some of the actors objected to the realism.

In truth, Owen was an alcoholic-in-training. "Owen Moore was especially apt in hiding himself," euphemistically remembered Linda Arvidson, Griffith's wife. "He had an unfriendly way of disappearing . . . At times we had quite a job locating him."

About this time, Mary's salary was raised to thirty-five dollars a week but that still seemed insufficient; she wrote George Spoor at the Essanay Company in Chicago to inquire if he might be interested in her at fifty dollars a week. As far as Spoor was concerned, forty-five dollars was the limit, so Mary stayed on with Griffith.

In January 1910, Griffith got permission from the budget-conscious owners to take selected members of the company to California for a winter's worth of filmmaking. Although Mary had only been with the company slightly more than eight months, she was included in the trip. The roster that left New York included Griffith and his wife, Kate Bruce, Marion Leonard, Florence Barker, Billy Quirk, Henry B. Walthall, Mack Sennett, Eleanor Hicks, Dorothy West, Del Henderson and wife, George Nicholls and wife, Arthur Johnson, Alfred Paget, and Mary. In addition, Biograph sent along two cameramen, three prop boys, a man from the front office and a manager who doubled as a second-unit director.

It must have been quite a leave-taking. The anointed members of the company took a ferry to Jersey City and boarded the Lehigh Valley Black Diamond Express to Chicago, where they caught the California Limited. When the time came for the train to pull out, Jack Pickford, angry at being left behind, threw a fit, which led Billy Bitzer to begin regarding him as "spoiled." Griffith relented, and allowed Jack to make the trip too.

Arthur Johnson, very much the worse for wear, barely made the train, while Owen tried to parlay his newly-begun relationship with Mary into a ten-dollar raise. Griffith refused and Owen threatened to leave Biograph, but he showed up at the train station anyway, hoping that some carefully placed tears from Mary might turn the tide in his favor. They didn't, and Owen never made another picture for Griffith.

What Mary did not know was that an alarmed Charlotte had made a private deal with Griffith. The price for allowing Mary to make the trip to California was Owen Moore's absence. At the same time, Charlotte tried to up the ante by making a pitch for a raise for Mary and threatening to keep her in New York unless she got it. Griffith had been around stage mothers all his adult life and had been prepared for just such a gambit; he told Charlotte that he had brought Gertrude Robinson to the station to take Mary's place . . . just in case she had been indisposed. Charlotte backed down.

The trip across the country to San Bernardino took four days; Mary and the rest of the actors got three dollars a day meal allowance. After arriving at the Alexandria Hotel in Los Angeles on January 20, 1910, Griffith and company set up a makeshift office in a loft on Spring Street, and a studio in a lot on the corner of Grand Avenue and Washington Boulevard. The "studio" was on a fenced-in acre next to a lumberyard and a small baseball diamond. For a stage, Griffith's carpenters built a 50 feet by 50 feet wooden plat-form, then hung cotton shades overhead to diffuse the sunlight. Since there were no dressing rooms, the actors got into their costumes every morning at the hotel.

Mary decided to save as much money as possible, and rented rooms for herself, Jack, Dorothy West and Effie Johnson at a board-ing house on South Olive and Fifth streets, paying $3.50 per week per person. That seemed too spartan, so they relocated to the New Broadway Hotel, on North Broadway and Second Street, which charged them $5.50 per week per person for two rooms and a connecting bath.

The Hollywood that Mary Pickford came to in 1910 was more like a little Spanish town than an entertainment megalopolis. Trails that were not wide enough to be roads led up to the moun-tains or down to the ocean. Orange and lemon groves dotted the town, and their fragrance perfumed the night air. The heart of the town consisted of the six blocks or so around Hollywood Boule-vard, the center of which was approximately where the Egyptian theater now stands. Buildings were mostly one-or two-story struc-tures painted yellow and white. Vine Street was cobblestoned, there were hardly any buildings on Wilshire and Melrose barely existed.

By the time the Biograph company arrived in California, the actors and actresses had virtually adopted Jack, who had begun working in small parts or as a stunt man for the actresses. They would give him liquor after work, or even take the fourteen-year-old to Los Angeles whorehouses. The first time at least, Jack was scared to go, for he had no pubic hair and was afraid of being laughed at. One of the actors grabbed a makeup kit and outfitted the boy with a merkin, a pubic wig, and off they went. The girls at the whorehouse thought this was hilarious; by the age of fourteen, then, Jack Pickford had already been introduced to the two activi-ties that became the central preoccupations of his life.

Six days a week, the cast would meet at the studio. Since Griffith was the only one with a car, his favorites would hitch a ride while everybody else rode a trolley to the location. Once in a while, Mary and Jack would get off the streetcar to pick some of the poppies that grew wild on the boulevard and take them back to the hotel. They didn't last long, but it was a joy to have fresh flowers in your room. Besides, it was one of the few perks that

Biograph offered, for Mr. Griffith was a serious-minded man and Biograph got its money's worth.

Still, to Mary's way of thinking, the discipline was a good thing. "Mr. Griffith was perfectly right; in fact, as I look back . . . I think that he was a paragon of patience."

If there were no cars for the actors, no dressing rooms, no conveniences whatever, there was, increasingly, a kind of nominal recognition; the Biograph films were regularly shown at fairly prestigious New York theaters like the Crystal Palace on 14th Street and the Herald Square. Unfortunately, the Biograph management was still afraid that giving actors individual publicity would cause them to demand more money, so everybody remained anonymous. Because the English were used to the more formal traditions of the theater, they demanded names, so the English distributor of the Biographs obliged . . . with a notable lack of invention. James Kirkwood was "Walter Scott," Mabel Normand was "Muriel Fortescue," Mack Sennett was "Walter Terry," and Mary was "Dorothy Nicholson."

Inevitably, the hypnotic power of an image in the dark was already being felt all over the world. In June 1910, an article in the *Citizen,* the newspaper of the small English town of Letchworth, stated that "each film-making firm has its own special favorites, and one of the most known at our own Picture Palace is she who takes the leading part in all the films of the American Biograph Company. From gay to grave, the quick flash of her eyes transports us, and many a lesson has she taught us by means of the characters she portrays."

Because Biograph shielded its actors from these kinds of notices, recognition for Mary came in sudden, unexpected bursts. One day, Arthur Johnson walked into a drug store and was recognized. The clerk demanded to know whether "the girl with the pout" was also in town. As a tribute to Mary's growing renown, it was a compliment; as a slur on a mannerism, it was appalling but somewhat accurate; for days, she made a conscious effort both on-screen and off-screen not to do anything that could remotely be described as pouting.

Another time, on her way home from the Biograph studio, Mary was amazed at being recognized by three different people. The next day she rushed in and tried to negotiate a five dollar raise on that basis. Griffith's response was a wistful "I'd give my whole week's salary if I'd be recognized." (Mary got raises for more concrete accomplishments than being noticed on the street; when *Willful Peggy* was released in August 1910, it sold an unprecedented 250 copies, which was worth an extra ten dollars a week. Clearly, Mary's face sold movies.)

If, with hindsight, this first era of Hollywood filmmaking seems impossibly *al fresco* and romantic to us, it seemed the same way to the people creating the legend of Hollywood. From the lofty vantage point of 1916, Griffith said that "Those early Biograph days were the most picturesque since the time of Moliere and Villon . . . there [was] the freedom, the change of scene, and the coursing about the country as Romans, pirates, royalty, great lovers and great villains."

"Nobody was a great star then," reminisced Chaplin in 1966. "There were no great moguls. [We] liked the freedom of it . . . the simplicity of it. We all did our job. If there was no sun, [or] we were tired, we were all very happy to think it was a nice dull day and we didn't have to work. It was very romantic."

But not to Mary; to her puritan spirit, it seemed too much a Lotus land. At least there was the money, forty-five dollars every week, plus fourteen dollars expense money. Aside from that, however, for much of that first trip to Los Angeles, she was mopingly dreaming about Owen. One day, the eastbound Santa Fe Limited roared by the company's location, and Mary sighed, "God bless all the trains going East and speed the one we go on."

For nearly five months, Griffith and his cast and crew roamed over Southern California, to the Sierra Madre mountains, to Pasadena, the beach at Santa Monica, to San Juan Capistrano and various spots in the San Fernando Valley. By the time they got back to New York, in the second week of April 1910, Griffith was already trying to schedule a few week's shooting in Cuddebackville in the summer to break up the dreaded monotonous heat of New York City.

Mack Sennett always assigned the blame for Mary's first marriage to a prankish collective lark. "I don't think they ever once thought of each other in any sentimental light," he said, "not until the rest of us put it into their heads. But . . . she was such a sweet-looking girl and he was such a sweet-looking boy—Owen Moore used to make you think of a kid whose mother had scrubbed his face and brushed his hair and got him all tidy for school—well, altogether they seemed to the rest of us so exactly suited that we got to teasing them about each other. We'd go up to Mary and say, 'Why don't you and Owen get more friendly?' and then we'd go after Moore in the same way about her."

Fifty years later, Mary confided to a friend what had led to the precipitous marriage. "We were necking behind a set and Mr. Griffith came around the corner. 'Not on company time,' he said. Then he took Owen aside and said, 'Don't you *dare* do anything to hurt that girl!' "

Caught between Mary's obvious innocence and his employer's thinly veiled disapproval, Owen was so terrified that, according to Mary's recollection, he quickly hustled her to the altar. The place was Jersey City, the date was January 7, 1911. Owen gave his address as 601 West 137th Street, while Mary was living at 560 West 148th Street. "That night," Mary told a friend years later, "I was deflowered." If so, it must have happened in a hurried interlude on the way home from the county courthouse, because Mary couldn't work up the nerve to tell her mother what she had done. Owen said goodnight at Charlotte's front door, just like he always did, and Mary slept with Lottie in a double bed . . . just as she always did. The next morning, Mary went to work with Owen's ring on a string around her neck.

Mary kept her marriage a secret from her mother, probably because she knew precisely what Charlotte's reaction would be. The marriage was largely the result of Charlotte's stonewalling the matter. She did not consider Owen suitable material for her darling and told her so; in fact, she had forbidden Mary to see Owen. Mary would always recall Charlotte's maternal bullheadedness as one of the few mistakes her mother ever made. "I think that if she had used different tactics I might have avoided a lot of unhappiness for everybody concerned," she would recall in the mid-1950's.

Charlotte, of course, didn't see it that way. After Mary finally broke down and told her what she had done, Charlotte was in a daze for weeks, endlessly repeating to anyone that would listen, "He must have bewitched her that she'd do such a thing and not tell me."

——— ———

Once, when Mary was asked why she left Biograph, she quickly replied "Because Owen was working with IMP and I wanted to be with him." Although that was undoubtedly a factor, another major cause was the anonymity endemic to acting for Biograph. Besides tearing up all the fan mail that came to the studio, the Biograph management instructed their players never to speak to actors in other companies, so they could not discover what other companies were paying their actors.

Mary had been a trifle restless for some time. One day in July 1910, on location at Cuddebackville, Mary turned to Linda Arvidson and said "You know, Mrs. Griffith, I used to think this canal was the most beautiful place I'd ever seen, and now it just seems to me like a dirty, muddy stream."

By the latter part of 1910 Mary had received an offer of $175 weekly from the IMP Company. Both parties thought they needed each other; IMP founder Carl Laemmle needed a new leading lady to replace the defecting Florence Lawrence (Mary was once again following in her footsteps) and Mary thought the money was just too good to pass up even though she knew Griffith was making the best pictures in America. Mary signed and Laemmle flooded the trade papers with ads crowing "Little Mary is an IMP now!"

In December 1910, a few weeks before she and Owen were married, Mary and the rest of the family left Biograph. Charlotte cried crocodile tears to Linda Arvidson, saying "What's to become of Mary . . . with no one to direct her? What good will the [extra] money do with her career ruined?" But Griffith knew it would have been inconceivable for Mary to make such an important business decision without Charlotte's active participation.

Laemmle wanted to place his newly recruited company in California, but discreet inquiries revealed that General Film Company, the official trust of which Biograph was a member but IMP was not, would promptly enjoin any non-trust company that attempted to locate in California. A brief survey of alternatives impelled Laemmle to opt for Cuba. Very shortly after her marriage, Mary, Owen, Lottie, Jack and Charlotte sailed on the S.S. *Havana.* It was while on board the ship that Mary told her mother that she and Owen were man and wife. Charlotte's response was wounded grief and tears; Mary's was pain at having caused pain.

———— ————

The IMP Company, under the direction of Thomas Ince, set up operations at the Palacio del Carneado, on the outskirts of Havana, which had once been a jail but was presently deserted. Ince supervised the construction of a stage in the courtyard, and the cast and crew were able to shoot all their interiors just a few yards from their breakfast tables.

That, however, was as convenient as things got. Looking back on her experience with IMP from the vantage point of 1927, Mary would say that "those were strange days, and we were strange folks," and she was right.

The company prop man had shipped a large vat of cold cream from New York for use in removing makeup and had placed it in a large ice chest to keep it from liquefying in the Havana heat. At one of the first company dinners, nine people became deathly ill. It was ascertained that all nine had eaten pie at dinner. Further investigation revealed that the Cuban cook had mistaken the cold cream for lard. Things like this never happened with Mr. Griffith. It was an inauspicious beginning to Mary's sojourn with IMP, but an entirely typical one.

"The pictures taken by IMP were not good," Mary freely confessed. The stories were ordinary, the handling of them less than that, and, for an image-conscious actress like Mary, the photography was quite inferior. The IMP cameramen made her prized hair look darker than it was, and her fair coloring was transmogrified into that of an Indian. She placed the blame for this state of affairs on none other than her husband, Owen Moore, who was arguing with Ince about his direction.

"I exonerate Carl Laemmle, who had nothing to do with it," said Mary in 1958. "It had to do with one person who I forgave a long time ago. I realize now it all started because of envy and resentment. I was getting seventy-five dollars a week more than this individual and it wasn't fair. This person should have been getting as much as I." Although Mary claimed to have forgiven him, she couldn't bring herself to mention Owen's name.

Few of Mary's IMP films have survived, but those that do make clear the reasons for her displeasure. *Artful Kate*, released in February 1911, her second month at IMP, features silent film plot 4-A: hero's fiancée masquerades as a flirtatious girl to see if her boyfriend is faithful. Ince gives the story a lackluster treatment fully commensurate with the story, which had been around since the earliest Edison kinetescope rolls.

Griffith's Biograph films invariably had something—a shot, a story, a performance, the director's masterly sense of gracious landscape, *something*—that set them above and beyond the conventional films of the time. But the Cuban locations of *Artful Kate* are limited to some quick views of Havana harbor and some palm trees.

Although Tom Ince would later prove to have a remarkable gift for setting, for milieu, for action, those gifts couldn't be expressed with such trivial material. *Artful Kate* is of its time, not beyond it, and Mary quickly sensed the difference.

"I didn't like the direction," Mary recalled. "I missed all of the Biograph family. Then there was the friction between my husband and my family. I lost eighteen pounds . . . I only had three more months to go on my contract, but I thought that if I worked there three more days I'd die."

From Laemmle's point of view, the Cuban films were doing just fine; he would tell his biographer John Drinkwater that, at the time, they were the sensation of the business because the tropical scenes Ince captured were being exhibited to large, envious audiences hopelessly entrapped by an unusually harsh Northeastern winter.

But as far as Mary was concerned, she would rather have been in New York. With three months to go on her IMP contract, Mary was "taken ill" and took advantage of the fact that she had been a minor when she signed the contract with Laemmle to break it. She signed a contract with Harry Aitken's Majestic Company at $225 per week. But Majestic made their films in Chicago, which was cold, and, although Owen was finally getting his wish and directing his wife, she didn't like the results. After only five films at Majestic, she realized that there was only one thing to do: See if Mr. Griffith would take her back. She called; he would.

It made sense for Griffith as well as for Mary. Biograph had been hurt by actors defecting to the independents. When an opus entitled *His Daughter* was released in February 1911, one critic said that "the picture has something of the spirit and character of the old Biograph stock company's work."

Mary rejoined Biograph in December 1911, a year after she had left, at $150 a week. She had learned, the hard way, that a few extra dollars could not compensate for a loss of quality or for sympathetic working conditions. It was a lesson she never forgot.

Yet, Mary's sojourn away from Griffith proved, in the long run, worthwhile. For it was Laemmle's crowing publicity touting Mary as America's greatest film star that truly began the Mary Pickford myth. For the first time, audiences could attach a name to the radiant face and the golden curls; now that they knew who she was, they would not forget it.

———— ————

Griffith's Biograph films are a particular treasure; the compression that made Mary so uncomfortable, vast narratives and oceans of emotion being crammed into ten or twenty minutes, lends a sense of activity, of teeming ambition that gives the films a startling intensity.

Instinctively, Griffith understood that Mary was not, for instance, Lillian Gish. In a Griffith/Gish collaboration like *The Mothering Heart* (1933), there is a scene involving Gish as a young wife whose child has just died because of her husband's neglect. Stunned to the point of catatonia, she wanders alone in a garden. Suddenly, she picks up a dead branch and begins madly thrashing at the foliage around her, an explosion of motion betraying a sublimated, seething emotion, a woman overcome by death trying to destroy the strong green life around her.

In comparison to this kind of ferocious austerity, Griffith initially saw Mary as decorative, placid; her part was often that of the heroine who didn't have that much to do. In the early Biographs, Griffith plugs her into nominal heroine parts simply because she was blonde, his other leading ladies were mostly brunettes, and the variety appealed to him. In *The Light That Came,* (1909), a variation on the Cinderella theme, he cast another actress as the homely plug, while giving Mary little to do as a nasty stepsister. For a man with the profoundly Victorian sensibilities of Griffith, nobody with Mary's face could possibly play homely, although she later proved she could, and brilliantly.

For the first few months of her return to Biograph, Mary is demure and pleasant, but there are no startling displays of talent. What does set her apart from the other leading ladies is her sense of inner life, her star quality; she invariably draws the eye, and does it without seeming to act. Although all about her are usually emoting furiously, Mary does *less,* radiates a sympathetic restraint mixed with her particular quality of a spirited sadness, and therefore achieves more.

Nor was she afraid of looking silly. In *A Romance of the Western Hills* (April 1910) one of the films in which Griffith cast her as the world's most unlikely Indian, she wears a dark wig with the hair pulled back to reveal more of her face than audiences usually saw. She's not exactly convincing, but she does get away with it, which is more than any other actress on the lot could have done.

By October 1909, with a film called *The Mountaineers Honor,* Griffith had devised the essential Pickford persona, a backwoods scamp betrayed by those of less loyalty or kindness. Except that Griffith has her hopping around, skipping behind trees and indulging in all the bizarre, hyperactive behavior that Griffith was wont to impose on actresses (and which Mary always insisted she was too strong-willed to allow), it is a virtual blueprint for the Pickford roles of 1914–1919 that established her world-wide fame.

By 1912, and Mary's second tour of duty with Biograph, Griffith's films with her have a perfect, flowing, easy charm that is augmented by the director's increasing technical sophistication. Griffith's very first Biograph film, *The Adventures of Dollie,* has thirteen scenes photographed from twelve different camera positions; *A Girl and Her Trust,* made four years later, has one hundred thirty scenes photographed from thirty-five camera positions. Both films have approximately the same running time. (This increasing reliance on the principles of montage did not come without a good deal of critical resistance; in particular, *Moving Picture World* complained that, by mid-1912, Griffith's films were "bitten by the lightning bug," and that long-shots and close-ups were out of order because "on the vaudeville and talking stage, figures of human beings do not expand or contract irrationally or eccentrically.")

Despite its unpromising title, a late Griffith/Pickford collaboration like *The Schoolteacher and the Waif,* (June 1912) is typical. It's a delightful little film about a tough little hoyden who won't have her face scrubbed and doesn't want to go to school. Finally making it to class, the other children make fun of her. Only the schoolteacher sees her special qualities; indeed, he falls in love with her. The part gives Mary a chance to display coquettishness, petulance, rage and insecurity, and it likewise foretells the dispossessed characters she would play in later successes like *Tess of the Storm Country* and *Daddy Long-Legs.*

Friends (September 1912), is a quietly audacious little movie about an orphan who lives up above a western bar. Although some later viewers have refused to believe that Mary's character is what she appears to be, what else could she be but a prostitute? Griffith's intentions could scarcely be made more explicit than in a scene where Mary pretties herself up and comes down to the foot of the stairs and beckons the bar's inhabitants to come up for a visit. Torn between two suitors, Mary agrees to go away with one, but Griffith ends with a tentative, Lady-or-the-Tiger closeup that leaves Mary's decision in some doubt.

The New York Hat (December 1912), her last film for Biograph, shows clearly how Griffith had become attuned to her particular gifts. Mary's character has been dreaming of the hat in the title, awakens and instinctively feels for it. As her hands touch air, her face falls into perfectly judged it-was-only-a-dream disappointment. Griffith keeps the moment in medium shot, but he knew that he didn't need to cut to a close-up; Mary had already mastered the art of projecting emotion through the lens directly to the audience—the true art of screen acting.

———— ■ ————

Despite Mary's perceptible success, she had a sense of aggrievement that wouldn't go away. Griffith claimed that he invariably assigned Mary the best parts, but she remembered otherwise. "I got what no one else wanted, and I took anything that came my way because I . . . early decided that if I could get into as many pictures as possible I'd become known and there would be a demand for my work."

In later years, Mary would be as embarrassed by the Biographs as she was by her great silent features, feeling that temporal things like changes of style rendered invalid the emotional truth contained in these often superb little films, halfway houses between the primitives of Melies and the total, commanding sophistication of the great Hollywood films of the '20s. "We never changed our costumes in a picture," she would complain. "Ten years might elapse and the leading man would be wearing the same checked shirt. Anytime a person was supposed to have money, it was indicated by putting potted palms in their living room or dining room, always the same potted palms."

She was perturbed by the smallest things; in *Friends,* Mary wore an old dress of her mother's with balloon sleeves that made it nearer 1894 than the 1849 called for in the story. She promptly complained that "our costumes were left to us, and so was the checking up of what we wore from one scene to another." For an actress who would never get over her insecurity, or an abiding feeling that her work could amuse the audiences of the moment but wasn't quite deep enough to please posterity, Biograph seemed entirely too slapdash, which, in turn, placed entirely too much pressure on Mary.

———— ■ ————

In June 1912, Dorothy and Lillian Gish were living in east St. Louis, where their mother had opened a candy shop. Next door was a nickelodeon where the children would often wile away an hour during the long afternoons. One day they began watching a charming little Biograph called *Lena and the Geese.* There, playing the title character, was the unmistakeable blonde countenance of their friend Gladys Smith. After the movie was over, they rushed home to tell their mother. Her reaction, remembered Lillian, was "What terrible misfortune has happened to the Smith family that Gladys has had to go into films?" They resolved that when they returned to New York, they would look Gladys up.

A month later, while visiting an old friend in Connecticut, the sisters decided to call on her. Looking up the address in the phone book, they found their way to 11 East 14th Street and asked for Gladys Smith. The man at the front desk told them there was no one there by that name.

"Oh yes," Dorothy said. "We saw her in one of your pictures called *Lena and the Geese.*"

"Oh, you mean Little Mary." In a minute the girls were reunited, and Mary told them of her stint with Belasco, the changing of her name, and of how valuable she had found the movies.

"They're great between stage jobs," she said. "I've been making films for three years and all that time our family's been together. I'm earning more than I ever have before—much more!

"You should try films. You can always work in them while you're looking for a play. Now wait here, I'll find our director." As Lillian remembered it, it was at that point that Griffith came down the stairs. He was singing snatches of opera to himself in a good baritone.

"Oh, Mr. Griffith."

"Yes, Pickford."

"I'd like you to meet my old friends, Mrs. Gish and her daughters, Lillian and Dorothy."

Griffith put the Gish sisters right to work, despite the fact that Dorothy, an even spikier personality than Mary, had, out of earshot, called him a "hook-nosed kike." He was lucky that he did, for he was about to lose his leading lady.

———

"We had this great argument," remembered Mary in old age. Actually, she and Griffith had several. As usual, Griffith had taken the company to California in January 1912, where they worked for slightly more than four months. The chemistry was slightly different now; Mary was the primary star of the company, and she inspired mixed feelings from young, up-and-coming ingenues. "I . . . noticed some resentment when I returned," Mary noted, "especially among the girls who had stepped up during my absence."

In May, Mary and Griffith had an argument over the issue of

baring her legs in a caveman film entitled *Man's Genesis.* Mary refused to do it, as did Blanche Sweet, Dorothy Bernard and every other established actress on the lot. Griffith promptly gave the part to Mae Marsh. Then, "as a reward for her graciousness,"—and for her obedience—he also cast Marsh in *The Sands of Dee,* which called for covered legs and which had been intended for Mary; indeed, the part Marsh was to play was even named "Mary." Mary was thunderstruck; both she and Charlotte began to cry. Their outrage was shared by others in the company; character actor Edwin August protested at being forced to act with such a rank amateur and threatened to quit. Griffith called his bluff, and August appeared as cast.

And that wasn't the worst of it. "[Mae Marsh] was magnificent," Mary told Kevin Brownlow with perceptible chagrin. "She had had no experience; she had previously worked in a department store. And I thought, 'This does it. I've spent ten years in the theater, and if she can do that without any experience, I don't belong in pictures.'"

Shortly after that, Griffith began irritating Mary by telling her that Lillian Gish's appearance was far more attractive than her own, so much so that Lillian might make a better lead for a new film. The obvious attempt at fomenting jealousy between two old friends, and at putting Mary on her acting mettle, greatly irritated her. There may also have been an element of anger at Griffith's being so obviously smitten by Lillian, when he had always been able to hide any vague, romantic feelings he might have had about Mary. Mary told Griffith that it was a shame "you can't get a good performance without trying to come between two friends."

"I'll have none of your lip. I'll run my company as I see fit without the insolent criticism of a baby."

"I won't be treated like a baby."

"Well, that's all you are and you know it."

According to Mary's unlikely account, Griffith then shoved her out of his way, causing her to fall to the floor, which occassioned threats of quitting, which occassioned a major effort at placation by Griffith, leading to an uneasy truce.

The proverbial last straw came just a few months later, when Mary and Griffith got into a wrangle about Billie Burke, the inspired stage comedienne and wife of Florenz Ziegfeld. "I was too young to realize what an splendid actress she was," remembered Mary. "I was completely wrong. I thought she was insincere and I said so."

Griffith lashed out at her insolence, telling her she wasn't entitled to criticize as fine a talent as Burke's. It was more than Mary could take. "And you're not privileged to criticize me," she retorted. "You can take these amateurs. I'm going back where I learned my *métier,* my profession. One year from tonight, I will be on Broadway." Griffith pooh-poohed such idle boasting; for one thing, she had soiled herself by working in the movies.

Again, her sense of grievance, of the treadmill speeding up to such an extent that she would not be able to keep up, was tormenting her. If an inexperienced girl could give the performance Marsh gave, it was time to go back to the theater, where experience bred technique and technique mattered.

And, underneath the bruised ego, the cash register was toting up numbers. "If experience was to count for nothing, salaries would be lowered, and . . . I would be wasting my time to stay in the pictures," she later admitted. "I wanted to go where I was protected."

So, in September 1912, she called Belasco. Where have you been? inquired one of the Great Man's minions. "I've been hiding in the pictures," replied Mary.

Belasco told her of a part he had for her, a blind girl named Juliet, in a Rostand play called *A Good Little Devil.* It was precisely the reaction she had been hoping for, but she played it cool. "I promised I would come whenever you wanted me. If you want me now I'll keep my word."

"Mary," said Belasco, "I not only want you—I need you."

"Then I'll come back to you."

After Griffith's impugning of her chances at getting another job with Belasco, Mary felt a surge of triumph. But by the time she arrived back at 14th Street, there was a lump in her throat, for however much she and Griffith wrangled, Biograph was still her professional home. She walked into the studio and found Griffith rehearsing. Very meekly she said, "Mr. Griffith . . ."

Without looking around, he snapped, "Don't interrupt. You know that's a rule."

"It's important."

Nothing.

She turned to go, when an exasperated Griffith finally turned around. "Pickford, why do you bedevil me like this?"

"I'm sorry, Mr. Griffith, but I'm leaving."

"Oh, Pickford, it's a hot day and I'm tired."

"No, it's the truth, Mr. Griffith. I'm going with Belasco; here's the part. I start Monday morning . . . with your permission."

According to Mary's recollection, Griffith got tears in his eyes and promptly dismissed the company. "I'm going to miss you terribly," he told her. "But that's where you belong. But I'm very pleased and proud. Today's Thursday; we still have Friday and Saturday. Let's make a last picture together." They did, and they called it *The New York Hat*, a charming story submitted, as the Biograph story register attests, by one "Anita Loos, 2915 F. Street, San Diego, California." (Mary's last Biograph film to be released, *The Unwelcome Guest*, had actually been shot before *The New York Hat*.)

Finally, on October 25, 1912, she threw a party for the entire Biograph company in her apartment on Riverside Drive. As far as Mary was concerned, it was her farewell to sunlit summer days at Cuddebackville, to the strange light of the mercury-vapor lamps. As far as Mary was concerned, she was going back to the world she felt safest in, and she was doing it for good.

Chapter Four

"Miss Pickford is the greatest drawing card in the film world today according to the exhibitors."

—*Rochester Times*, July 8, 1914

*M*ARY'S salary for the Austin Strong adaptation of Rostand's *A Good Little Devil* was set at $175 a week. The first few rehearsals were extremely difficult. Mary had been away from the stage for three years. Her natural insecurity exacerbated the perfectly normal fear that she would be unable to recover her stage technique. As she put it, "I've never been sanguine before a camera, before an audience, before a microphone. [When I went back to Belasco] I was scared to death." Griffith tried to jolly her over it, bringing a group of the Biograph players to the play's out-of-town tryouts in Philadelphia, where it opened on December 12, and Baltimore, where it opened on December 23.

Adding to Mary's uncertainty was the fact that the blind girl in *A Good Little Devil* was a difficult part. It all had to be worked out in minute detail. Mary had to memorize the geography of the stage, because she couldn't focus her eyes on anything. Thus, she not only had to know her lines, she had to know every object on stage. So many steps to a bench, so many steps to a door.

"I can't describe how nerve-wracking it was not to look into people's eyes, to stare blankly over their heads or just beyond their faces . . . When I left for home after the performance I was aching in every nerve, bone and muscle of my body." To take the edge off her nervousness, she arranged a part in the play for Lillian Gish.

Although she was back with Belasco, many associated her with the movies, which did not seem to carry a negative connotation to anyone but Mary. In Baltimore, one of actors in the cast knocked on Mary's dressing room and told her that "There are hundreds of people waiting in the alley to see Little Mary, Queen of the Movies, leave the theater." He wasn't kidding; surviving photographs show the crowd, bundled against the cold, with Belasco leading Mary out of the stage door. It was a trenchant demonstration of the power of the movies. It was the kind of selfless devotion that always meant a great deal to Mary, and that, years later, would make it impossible for her to risk disappointing those people displaying it.

After one last tryout engagement in Washington, *A Good Little Devil* opened on January 8, 1913, at the Republic Theater. Belasco was a theatrical traditionalist; after the lights went down and before the curtain rose, the stage manager hit the stage three times with a stick, then rang a little bell. Before her entrance in the second act, Mary was suddenly seized by a fear that she would open her mouth and nothing would come out. Standing in the wings just before her entrance, she was about to test her voice when she noticed an electrician putting a scrim over a light. She was too embarrassed to reveal her insecurity. All she could do was say her prayers. She walked out to the center of the stage, opened her mouth and out came her small, but entirely appropriate voice. She was safe; she was back in the theater.

The New York *Dramatic Mirror* acclaimed her "silvery, vibrant voice" while the Brooklyn *Eagle* said "Mary Pickford, as the blind girl Juliet, lived the part. Such an utter absence of apparent playing for effect . . . is not often witnessed." The New York critics were only repeating what the critics had said during the tryout. Belasco read the notices and raised Mary's salary to $200 a week.

But Mary's continual feeling of dissatisfaction was already working on her; she did not care for the part of the sweet blind girl. It seemed stilted and unnatural. Then there were the conventions of the stage. "The scenery looked so fakey, so unreal, after the open air and the woods in which we usually pose," she complained in a December 1914, interview with Alan Dale. "I couldn't get used to it. Also the fact that I could never see myself from the front rather disconcerted me." Already, the actress was achieving a stoney objectivity about herself, becoming her own favorite object of contemplation.

Nevertheless, business was as good as the reviews. Lillian Gish got out of the play quickly in time to hook up with Biograph for their annual winter season of filming in California, but Mary stayed with the show until it closed on May 3, giving 152 performances. *A Good Little Devil* was a hit of sufficient size that a man named Adolph Zukor, putting Mary's theatrical success together with her previous picture success, decided to make a move that would be the decisive factor in both their careers.

Zukor had been born in Risce, Hungary, in the Tokay wine district, in 1873. His father died when Adolph was just a year old; his mother remarried, but died when Adolph was eight. His stepfather refused to have anything to do with him, so Adolph went to live with an uncle in a nearby village. His uncle apprenticed him to a large dry goods store, but the now teen-aged Zukor looked around the barren Hungarian countryside and began to ask himself, "What future can I look forward to here?"

An Orphans Board, charged with the guardianship of the parentless, advanced him the equivalent of forty dollars, and the sixteen-year-old Adolph Zukor set out for America. As a young man in America, he learned to box, which left him with a slightly cauliflowered left ear. Mostly, though, he worked, starting in the upholstery business, quickly graduating to the fur trade, taking the raw skins and turning them into neckwear for a dollar or two per piece. There were no unions; if you did the work better than the next man, you received better pay. This wonderful country with its new history paid you what you earned, what you deserved. It seemed eminently sensible to Zukor, eminently fair, and he would conduct business along those lines all his life.

By the mid-1890's, Zukor was operating a fur business out of Chicago; a man named Marcus Loew was operating a fur business out of New York. They met in 1898, and consolidated their operations in 1901. As Zukor remembered it, his getting into the movies was purely accidental. In 1903, he and Loew began operating penny arcades, which grew in importance until they attained the rarified name of nickelodeons. Zukor became the treasurer of Marcus Loew Enterprises, but in 1912 he went out on his own. His idea was to make films starring actors from the legitimate stage, usually in roles with which they were associated. He called it Famous Players in Famous Plays.

He could not do this alone; he needed a partner who could give him credibility and class. With a remarkable gift for making all the

right moves that would rarely fail him, Zukor sold himself to Daniel Frohman, the brother of the eminent producer Charles Frohman (who thought his brother's sudden enthusiasm for the movies
was futile lunacy) and a considerable Broadway presence in his
own right. Actors like James O'Neill and James Hackett might not
know or care who Adolph Zukor was, but they would certainly
listen raptly to anything Daniel Frohman suggested. Frohman
would get them through the door, and then Zukor would sell
them; for a tough, flinty character, he could wax surprisingly romantic, a quality guaranteed to appeal to most actors.

Zukor was a polite, correct man of considerable probity, scrupu-
lous about paying his debts. In the early, up-and-down days of
Famous Players, Zukor thought nothing of yanking his family to a
five-story walk-up in Washington Heights in order to save money,
but he always made the payroll even if he had to issue stock
certificates in lieu of salary.

But people who didn't like the life-long Republican ("because I
like protection") regarded him as cold. Behind his back, some
called him "Creepy." Once, he made a fur piece for his bride-to-
be, whose mother would not allow her to accept it. Rather than
save it till after their wedding, Zukor promptly sold it, and for a
good price. "It was very good workmanship," he dryly noted.

Certainly, he was not a raucous good time. Once, when his son
Eugene was dragooned into a movie scene by a director who
didn't know who he was, Adolph allowed his son to finish his chore,
then, on the way home, told him why he must never allow anything like that to happen again. The studio, he explained, is a
factory; the people in the studio are there to work and to earn
their money. It was unwise to allow any intimacy to get in the way
of a simple business transaction.

On the surface, Zukor would seem to have been spare, sandy soil
for an organism in need of as much nurturing as Mary, but he was
strong, he was not a hypocrite, and he was direct. He was a man
she could feel comfortable with.

——— ———

"The main reason I was tempted to make a deal with Belasco at
that time was because he had Mary Pickford under contract,"
Zukor remembered. "Belasco agreed to take the play that she
appeared in and have a picture made of it, with her playing the
lead . . . During the time we made this picture, Belasco had no

play planned for her the following year, so we made a contract with her for Famous Players, and she stayed in pictures."

Zukor made it all sound simpler than it really was. With nothing in the offing for the summer, Mary was perfectly amenable to a picture offer, but the deal to bring her into features nearly fell apart over her financial obstinence. By a complicated—and essentially nonsensical—formula, the cast of *A Good Little Devil* was to make the movie on days when they didn't have matinees and were to be paid on a per diem basis of an amount equal to one-ninth of the weekly pay received for stage performances. Mary held out for one-eighth.

The difference, over the duration of the shoot, would have amounted to about forty dollars. "It wasn't the fact of the money alone, it was the principle of the thing," said Mary with a notable lack of originality. In truth, it was precisely about money; movies were rapidly becoming big business and Mary wanted her share. Why, Biograph had been paying Griffith as much as $3,000 a month in 1912, and Mary saw no reason why she shouldn't be making at least as much. This was the woman who once observed that "I was the father of my family; I wanted security for my people . . ." Nevertheless, and for what may have been the last time, she yielded on a matter of money.

A Good Little Devil was filmed in May 1913, at the Famous Players studio—a glorified loft, really—on 26th Street, between 10th and 11th avenues. It was a slavish imitation of the play; Mary found, to her horror, that the stage manager even held the script, while the cast was forced to mouth their lines. It was clear that the picture was not going to turn out well. "It was not according to Mr. Griffith's methods," said Mary, noting primly that she had written thirty movies (an exaggeration), appeared in about 150 and knew whereof she spoke.

Zukor and company knew that the film was ineffective; Mary later called it "one of the worst pictures, if not the worst picture, I ever made." Although it was Mary's first feature, it was the fourth to be released, and then only in March 1914, nearly a year after it was shot. It didn't matter; Zukor and company knew what they had. After *A Good Little Devil* was finished, Zukor offered her $500 a week for fourteen weeks, during which she was to make three pictures back to back. Belasco's original production of *A Good Little Devil* was due to go out on tour in the fall, so Zukor's offer was a summer windfall; this time, there was no dickering over money. It was impossible for Mary to believe this gravy train wasn't going to come to a dead stop, and soon.

"I was always so amazed," she said. "It never occurred to me that my career would continue. I just thought it was for the moment and that I had to make the best of it." Her acting ambition took second place to getting all the money she could for her and her family. Years later she would accurately, but with a perceptible touch of disapproval, refer to herself in this period as "the ambitious one."

Mary also took the offer because she would no longer have to fulfill the burdensome expectations that had been so oppressive at IMP, where she was the *raison d'être* of the entire program. At Famous Players, she could not be expected to compete with Minnie Maddern Fisk and James O'Neill. "I thought it would be better to be a small fish in a large pond than a large fish in a small pond," was the way she put it.

The first Famous Players film to be released was *In the Bishop's Carriage,* which was also the last Pickford picture to be seen by her English grandmother. That redoubtable lady had only been in a theater once before, to see her granddaughter play Little Eva in *Uncle Tom's Cabin.* That, however, had had a religious theme, hence it was a valid experience, and Grandmother Smith had not been shocked. *In the Bishop's Carriage,* however, put Mary into a ballet costume, and Mrs. Smith nearly fainted at the amount of her granddaughter's flesh that was being exposed.

She was in for another shock when she found out what Mary was being paid. "For a year's work, you mean," she said. "No, a week." "My son John's child is making $500 a week? She's not worth it!" Recalling the story more than forty years later, Mary chuckled and said, "I think she was right."

After *In the Bishop's Carriage* came *Caprice,* but then Mary, as she recalled years later, was taken "violently ill, went to the hospital for surgery and nearly passed on." According to Mary, the illness derived from an abdominal condition that had resulted from lifting another actress during a scene.

Although Mary was still supposed to tour in *A Good Little Devil* that fall, she was not fully recovered from the aftereffects of her "illness," so Belasco kindly released her from her contract. Shortly thereafter, Zukor signed her to a one year contract, at $500 a week.

She said goodbye to Belasco and remained on good terms with him. For a number of years, "The Governor" was always invited to previews of Mary's new pictures. "No one takes more pride and pleasure in her success than I," he wrote. "No one knows better than I that it is due, not to mere circumstances, but to the artistry and charm by means of which Mary Pickford has become known in every city, town and hamlet in the land and beloved by all our people."

Zukor sent Mary, Edwin S. Porter, his secretary, and Charlotte out to California so his star could recuperate and, in the process, make some more pictures. On the train, Mary told Porter of a story she had read in a magazine a few years earlier that seemed like a good bet for a movie. Mary couldn't remember the name of the magazine, so Porter offered her $100 to write it out anyway. "I told him it wasn't original and the author would come after us," Mary explained years later, but Porter insisted. After *Hearts Adrift* was released, the author of the original did indeed come after them, and was generously paid off.

After carefully observing Mary for less than a year, Zukor began to know his woman, know that what Mary craved after so many years of ceaseless, grinding trouping was, in addition to money, something beyond money, something comparatively easy to give. When Mary returned to New York after shooting on the West Coast, she asked for and received a raise; her salary was doubled, to $1000 a week. To celebrate, Zukor and his wife took Mary to afternoon tea on Broadway. Across the street, *Hearts Adrift* was playing. They lingered while dusk drew on. Then, Zukor led her to the mezzanine overlooking Broadway and pointed.

"Suddenly I saw it," Mary recalled, "one of the most thrilling sights of my whole career, my name blazing on the marquee in electric lights. The dear sweet man had planned his surprise with such loving care and I had repaid him by asking for a raise." That was Mary's reaction in retrospect; at the time, her first remark had been, "Oh, what will my mother say when she hears this?"

This gesture of appreciation and caring cemented Mary's relationship with Zukor, and with his company. She treasured what she believed were Zukor's qualities of dignity and charm, compared to what she felt to be the hurly-burly tackiness of the closely allied Lasky company, and its flamboyant director-general (as he liked to bill himself) Cecil B. DeMille, who had capitalized the first letter of his name as soon as he entered the movies.

Samuel Goldfish, who later modified his unfortunate name to the more euphonious "Goldwyn," and who was Jesse Lasky's brother-in-law as well as general manager of the Lasky company and, later, chairman of the board, recalled at least one time when

Mary had ever-so-subtly broached the idea of transferring to the Lasky side of the partnership. "I can't tell you how I admire your photography," she had told him. "It must be a wonderful pleasure to work in such a studio." Class was one thing, business, i.e. money, quite another. Goldfish didn't pursue the matter, however, probably because it would have provoked civil war in the partnership.

After finally unloading *A Good Little Devil* in March 1914, Zukor quickly recouped the disappointment bred by that stage-bound adaptation by releasing in that same month *Tess of the Storm Country*, which became Mary's biggest hit to date. Ironically, Mary hadn't wanted to do the picture. "I flatly refused," she remembered. "Why they put up with me in my youth I don't know. [Porter] pleaded with me and almost wept, but I had played a barefoot girl in *Hearts Adrift* and I didn't want to play another ragged urchin. I was tired of that kind of role. Porter asked me to take it home and read it. I went home and I couldn't put the book down. When I was halfway through it, I called him at the hotel and told him he was so right."

Although *Tess of the Storm Country*, her fifth Famous Players feature, was her biggest success, it only served as confirmation of what the critics and box-office returns had already indicated: Mary Pickford was a great movie star. It was right there in the credits, just as it had been on Broadway: "Daniel Frohman presents America's Foremost Film Actress Mary Pickford . . ." The credits were followed by a pre-film curtain call in which Mary comes out from behind a velvet curtain carrying a large bouquet, and decorously arranges the flowers in a large, conveniently located vase.

Although the bold credits belong to the brassy fanfares of a later era, *Tess of the Storm Country* itself seems to belong to the pre-Biograph era. As dramatized, the plot of Grace Miller White's 1909 novel has the narrative abruptness of the early one-reelers and eventually deteriorates into complete incomprehensibility, as if everybody in the audience knew the plot anyway, so all that was necessary was a hurried series of illustrations of the novel's most famous scenes. Most of the actors wear makeup better suited to a Mack Sennett burlesque than a putative drama, while director Edwin S. Porter never uses anything closer than a medium shot. Except for Mary's long curls, Tess could be played by practically anybody.

Despite attractive Del Mar locations, the film is cumulatively stultifying. At one point, Porter even gets his screen directions wrong; a dog exits frame left, then, in the next cut, enters from frame left, an egregious violation of what was even then basic screen technique. Despite its manifest inadequacies, *Tess of the Storm Country* was an enormous hit; despite its financial triumph, Mary knew it wasn't well done. In 1922, she bought the story and the film (for $50,000, five times the entire negative cost of the original) from Zukor and remade it the next year, with greater narrative clarity if nothing else.

It was obvious that, if Mary could pull along a shabby piece of work like *Tess of the Storm Country*, any talk of going back to the stage or Belasco was hyperbole meant only for salary negotiations. Mary Pickford was in the movies to stay. "I don't regret that I am out of [the stage]," she told Alan Dale in December 1914. "It is a very hard life." She defended her decision to leave the stage and finally bluntly exclaimed that "I'm in the movies for money. In the three years and eight months I was in motion picture work, I was laid off only four weeks." She went on to confide that she went to see each of her movies only once, "because I want to see how an audience takes them. After that, I never go. I am a very severe critic."

Although she was making a great deal of money by the standards of the theater, it didn't seem to have any meaning for her. "They hand me the checks . . . and I don't feel one bit rich. I've worked since I was five years old, and I work all the time, so I don't really seem to be anything different to what I once was."

The perceptive, sensitive Dale was nonplussed. She was, he noted, "pensive," even "doleful." But why?

——— ———

By 1915, Adolph Zukor's Famous Players and Jesse Lasky's Lasky Company were part of a combine called Paramount Pictures, which was nothing more or less than an umbrella organization for a group of independent producers. But Paramount was only advancing $35,000 (against 65 percent of the gross) for each of the Famous Players pictures, which for sense amounted to about half of the Paramount product. With production costs rising, largely because of the salary being paid to Mary, which in turn bumped up the salary structure of the entire industry, and with Paramount refusing to up their advances, both Zukor and Lasky were caught in a cash squeeze.

It was Adolph Zukor who suggested a merger between his company and Lasky's, pooling all their star contracts, which would in turn enable them to get sufficient bank backing to continue production. What the Lasky company had were the remarkably successful films of Cecil B. deMille, which were grossing a minimum of three times their cost, and often as much as six to eight times their cost. What Zukor had to offer was, in essence, Mary Pickford, who, according to Jesse Lasky, "was a property of inestimable value."

The merger was accomplished in December 1916; the new company was called Famous Players-Lasky and was indisputably the largest producer/distributor in the movie business. Although Zukor's company got top billing, stock was split on a 50–50 basis. Zukor was president, Lasky vice president in charge of production, and Sam Goldfish, Lasky's brother-in-law, was chairman of the board.

The first time Goldfish met Mary she was talking over an endorsement with Zukor, saying, "They've offered me $500 for the use of my name, but do you really think that's enough? After all, it means a lot to those cold-cream people." Goldfish was struck by her wide-eyed tone, "which made you think of a child asking whether it ought to give up its stick of candy for one marble or whether perhaps it could get two."

By early 1915, Mary was receiving 500 fan letters every day and was dividing her time between New York and Los Angeles. Her New York apartment on upper Broadway, past Central Park, had eight rooms with a predominantly rose color scheme and mahogany furnishings in the slightly heavy style of that period. That, at least, was the story according to Zukor's publicity. Yet, when Sam Goldfish visited the apartment to take Mary and Charlotte out to dinner, he was shocked to find a few unprepossessing pieces of furniture and an inexpensive trunk out of which Charlotte lifted Mary's evening gown. When photographers weren't around, Spartan severity was the watchword.

Nevertheless, there could be no doubt that Mary was rapidly achieving something no other actress in motion pictures had, and for very specific reasons. Mary was inhabiting an American myth at almost the last historical moment she could have. The career of Mary Pickford was a fortuitous coming together of the person and the moment. To a great extent, her screen character was derived from popular literary taste of the turn of the century, now largely unreadable confluences that placed nearly equal stress on Christian morality, patriotism and virginity. Writers like Theodore Dreiser and Frank Norris were lone wolves in the literary fraternity. They sold reality, which everybody knew meant pessimism. The accepted rule was Life As It Ought To Be, not Life As It Was, a cultural conspiracy that even the highbrows of the time were involved in.

Willa Cather's *One of Ours* was awarded the Pulitzer Prize for literature in 1923 because, according to the award citation, it "best represented the wholesome atmosphere of American life and the highest standard of American manners and manhood." Similarly, Owen Davis's forgotten play *Icebound* got the Pulitzer for representing "the educational value and power of the stage in raising the standards of good . . . taste and good manners."

It was in this moralistic atmosphere that, for two generations, Mary Pickford and her image of femininity were accepted. As Edward Wagenknecht has written, "without question or analysis . . . [her] own personality cast a Madonna-like exaltation . . . and the roles [she] often played made her our mischievous child."

At the same time, Mary's screen character was one she was particularly suited to play with conviction. The sole support of her family from the time she was five, deprived of any kind of childhood or fantasy life, Mary walked right into a mythic American archetype that, as she played it, fed her own needs: the child who never played could play; the child whose only ambition was to provide food and clothing for her mother and siblings could wear the finest velvet; the child who was always prey to the most morbid imaginings and fears of death could compensate by playing predominantly optimistic characters; the child who could never quite bring herself to believe in happiness could provide it for others.

In the wake of the success of *Tess of the Storm Country*, Zukor kept Mary running on a furious treadmill. In 1914 she made seven features; in 1915, eight. She did not resent the long hours, and Zukor's respect for the hard-driving little actress increased almost daily. "She taught me a great deal," he said. "I was only an apprentice then; she was an expert workman."

When working on a picture, Mary would be up by 7:00 A.M., have a simple breakfast of an orange, toast and tea, then be off to the studio. Lunch occupied less than half an hour, with correspondence and letters filling up the time between camera set-ups. Returning home at 7:00 P.M., the exiled Owen being nowhere in evidence, there was dinner and the ritual evening talk with Charlotte about the events of the day.

Once a week, there would be a dinner meeting at Daniel Frohman's office atop the Lyceum Theater, where story ideas would be discussed. It was Frohman's exhaustive memory for nineteenth century theatrical evergreens still remembered by the public that supplied Mary with early Zukor efforts like *Esmerelda.* "She used to make suggestions that usually were adopted before the picture was put into production," remembered Frohman. "She was an expert critic." Frohman also noted that Zukor resisted anything that tended to stray from what had already proved successful. "Many of the things we wanted to do, he opposed, and held us in check by saying, 'We are not quite ready for that.'"

Interviewers regularly commented on Charlotte and Mary's mutual devotion. "Her children were her life," was how Adela Rogers St. Johns appraised Charlotte's character, while another journalist referred to her, with a nice touch of acid understatement as "a very compelling personality." There was no question that Charlotte loved Mary with that grinding, obsessive adoration that can only accompany a meal ticket; Mary's co-workers began thinking long and hard about outwitting Charlotte's strict guidelines for Mary's behavior on- and off-screen.

In 1915, when Mary was making *A Girl of Yesterday* for director Allan Dwan, the script called for the villain to abduct Mary in an airplane. The stunt pilot was none other than Glenn Martin, who would go on to found his own aviation company, but Charlotte was still terrified. She allowed the scene to be shot providing that the plane never got more than one hundred feet off the ground. Dwan knew very well that it is much more dangerous for an airplane at one hundred feet than at ten thousand feet, but Charlotte was the boss.

Dwan, however, gave Charlotte's dictum an unexpected spin. He had Martin fly the plane parallel to a road atop the Griffith Park mountains, with the camera car following them around the contour of the mountain roads. Although the plane was a good deal more than a hundred feet off the ground, it was never more than a hundred feet from the mountain, which Dwan loosely defined as "the ground."

At one point during the shot, Martin turned to the actor playing the villain and said, "Look, I don't even have to hold on," only to have the already nervous actor faint dead away. "We could see him flop right over," remembered Dwan, "with Mary trying to support him and shaking him, trying to get him back." With the sequence shot, Dwan had kept his word to Charlotte . . . sort of.

On September 11, 1915, the Famous Players studio on 26th Street burned down. Mary narrowly missed being trapped; leaving the studio that night, she had been in the car when she realized she had left a pin in her dressing room. She was about to go back for it when her mother told her not to bother.

Mary and Charlotte went on to a dinner date at the Knicker-bocker Hotel with Zukor, his son Eugene and James Kirkwood, her director. Afterwards, when Zukor and his son left to attend a boxing match, they heard the fire engines. Kirkwood got up to see what was going on and returned to tell them the studio was on fire.

Mary and Charlotte took a cab to the burning studio. "Mother and I were standing outside watching this fire when he [Zukor] came. I was crying. Mr. Zukor said, 'Sweetheart honey, don't cry. Just be grateful to the Lord that nobody's in there.' As it turned out, all we lost was a little dog."

Although the fire would have caused a good deal of trouble to the concerned under any circumstances, if only by disrupting the production schedule, what made it particularly problematic was the fact that the studio's entire store of unreleased negatives was stored in a safe that was hanging onto a charred wall.

Observing the smoking ruins, Zukor came upon Edwin S. Porter, the director who was also a partner in the concern. "You don't look very well," said Zukor. "Everything I've ever done is gone," responded a morose Porter. "Well, we'll start over again," said the indomitable Zukor. "I mean, we know how. We'll just do it in a different place."

The fire had been on a Saturday, but the safe was too hot to be opened until Tuesday. Although Zukor always said that the company's negatives came through unscathed, the fact of the matter is that at least one of them, *The Foundling*, directed by Allan Dwan and starring Mary, was destroyed. (Mary also remembered that a picture called *The Dawn of Tomorrow* had burned up; no such picture was ever released by Famous Players, although it is possible that it was a temporary title for a film that was released with a different name.) Zukor's luck was holding fast; had the fire happened a year earlier, he would probably have been wiped out, but the accelerating success of Mary's pictures that had begun with *Tess of the Storm Country* made it possible to recoup. *The Foundling* went back into production under another director at a new studio converted from a riding academy on 56th Street, and was released in January 1916.

——— ———

As one reporter observed about Mary, "her greatest interest in life is her mother." Somewhere in those words lies the pit into which Owen Moore had vanished without a trace. He never had a chance. "I cannot recall that I ever invited Owen Moore to join the entourage," remembered Adolph Zukor of Mary's public appearances. "If the public did not recollect that Mary was a wife, no harm was done."

At the same time, Moore was denied his full status at home. There was a story that, during the early days of the marriage, Moore rented a suite at the Biltmore. Charlotte and Mary followed Moore into the rooms. Charlotte surveyed the suite, nodded and said, "Very fine, Owen. You take that room in there and Mary and I will sleep in here."

It must have been a maddening situation for a brooding Irishman like Moore, a good enough actor but a small man with a small man's disease. Moreover, Moore desperately wanted to be accepted as a good actor, but he had rapidly been relegated to the status of a spare piece of his wife's contractual luggage. The more obvious his humiliation, the more he drank; the more he drank, the easier it became for Charlotte to humiliate him.

As the marriage evolved, it seemed more and more as if Owen Moore couldn't do anything; he was coasting on his wife's apron strings, just like her sister, just like her mother, just like her brother. Eventually, it would prove to be the only kind of relationship with which Mary was entirely comfortable. Moore's drinking got progressively worse, which made his eventual replacement all the more inevitable, if no less maddening.

Mary ardently collaborated in the public relations chicanery. A 1913 profile in *Cosmopolitan* said that Mary was "still in her teens and [was] an unsophisticated believer in fairies . . ." while she was quoted as ruminating wistfully, "If I were married and had children . . ." A 1914 article in *Moving Picture World* mentioned offers of marriage in her fan mail, and Mary acknowledged that, yes, she did get some, "but these letters are very few."

But Mary would never have children. Over the years, a great deal of disinformation was spread about that inability. At various times, her sterility was ascribed to a fall from a horse, or the aforementioned internal injuries.

Passing over the gynecological improbabilities of either, the truth, according to family members, was a good deal simpler. Early in her marriage with Owen Moore, Mary had an abortion that rendered her sterile. It was generally known within the confines of the Pickford clan, but Mary almost never referred to it and never with any specifics.

But she may have inadvertently hinted at the period of the abortion in her 1920 divorce trial. Referring to the fall of 1912, when she and Owen had separated for a time, Mary said that "from unhappiness and overwork, I was taken sick and went to a hospital, and he came to see me under the influence of liquor, which disturbed me that night, and I was just coming out of the ether, and four times he came there and made me cry and the doctor told my nurse that he was not allowed to come into the room, and until my temperature was normal he was not permitted in the room."

In 1912 or any other time, people hospitalized for exhaustion were not given anesthesia. There is, moreover, a touch of breathless hysteria in Mary's relating of the events, an emotional intensity far removed from the cool, cogent summaries in the rest of her testimony.

Whether the operation took place in 1912, or the late summer of 1913, it is hard to imagine Mary, no matter how badly the marriage was going, volunteering for an abortion; it is considerably easier to imagine Charlotte, who never wanted her daughter married in the first place, and certainly not to—in her mind—an inappropriate lightweight such as Owen Moore, devising and executing the scheme.

It would not do for a girl who was supporting Charlotte in the manner to which she had rapidly become accustomed to be in the papers giving birth when nobody knew that she was married in the first place. Charlotte Pickford instinctively understood that, in the movies, illusion is everything; once that is destroyed, careers—and fortunes—can be lost.

And so Mary's marriage to Owen Moore ceased to be anything except a legality, although, in her later years, she would often speak of how much she had wanted to have a baby of her own. There were, always, whispers that she actually had. Years later, after Charlotte died, and Mary took over her guardianship of Lottie's daughter Gwynne, there were whispered discussions to the effect that Gwynne had actually been Mary's child all along—Douglas Fairbanks and his first wife had planned that their first child, if it was a girl, would be named Gwen—and that Lottie had merely been the beard for Gwynne's birth in 1917 as an issue of the then-torrid affair between Mary and Douglas Fairbanks.

An equally interesting—although only slightly more likely—possibility involves Arthur Loew, Jr., the grandson of Adolph Zukor and a sort of nephew by adoption of Mary's. "Mary once told me that I was really her son," remembered Loew. "Your grandfather wanted to keep me in curls," she told him, "and the public wanted to think I was younger and your grandfather took the baby away from me and gave it to Mickey [Mildred Zukor Loew,

Adolph's daughter]. The public would never believe I was old enough to have a baby."

Loew Jr. was amused, but didn't put much credence in the story. "Then, one day," he remembered, "I was with my father and we were eating some chocolate mousse, when I started sneezing. 'Are you getting a cold?' he asked me. 'No,' I said, 'I always sneeze when I eat rich chocolate.' And he said, 'That's interesting. The only other man I ever knew that did that was Douglas Fairbanks.' So I've always wondered . . .'"

Even though her marriage was on the rocks, Mary did not necessarily lack for sexual companionship. By the early part of 1914, she was engaged in an occasional affair with James Kirkwood, an old acquaintance from Biograph days whom she had requested as a director despite the fact that he had little previous experience. Kirkwood was ten years older than Mary, and a boon drinking companion of Jack's. Like a later generation's Leslie Howard, he was an unlikely ladykiller who was nevertheless devastating to women.

"Oh God, he had them all," exclaimed James Kirkwood Jr. with a note of pride. Kirkwood Jr., the product of his father's marriage to Lila Lee, Valentino's leading lady in *Blood and Sand,* grew up to become a successful novelist and playwright, with the co-authorship of *A Chorus Line* among his credits. "Mary Miles Minter, Anna Q. Nilson . . . Everybody slept with my father, except for Lillian Gish, and that includes Dorothy."

What made it particularly interesting was that Owen was her occasional co-star in the pictures Kirkwood was directing. "My father always said that he adored her, that he was very much in love with her and they had a lovely relationship," said Kirkwood Jr. "He even spoke about a time when they were very close to being married." (A possible reference to the relationship predating her marriage to Owen?)

"My dad liked Owen Moore and he liked Owen's brother Matt, too. He liked Douglas Fairbanks as well. These men were all very strange about cuckolding each other. They seemed glad to bed each other's wives and girlfriends. There was no animosity or one-upmanship; if you could spirit her off to bed, it was fine. No hard feelings."

Kirkwood Sr. thought Mary had that certain quality that makes stars, a chemistry with the camera, an ease, without a lot of the eye work that hammier actresses resorted to to express emotion. "The lovely thing about working with her," Kirkwood Sr. told his son, "was that you didn't have to fight a lot of stilted, heightened acting she was trying to drop over the screen. It was all natural."

———— ————

By 1916, Mary was twenty-four, a married woman with at least one lover, making considerably more money than the President of the United States, yet as far as the public was concerned, she was somewhere between the ages of twelve and sixteen. It was an illusion everybody conspired to maintain, one whose psychic cost to Mary can only be guessed at.

The problem was both practical and metaphoric. For the former, there was the endless trouble caused by Mary's baby-fine long hair and the curls ("a miserable nuisance") that were as unvarying a part of her screen character as Chaplin's mustache, bowler hat and cane. Very quietly, Mary commissioned George Westmore, progenitor of the Westmore makeup clan, to make fake curls to supplement her own.

Westmore fashioned the hairpieces by wrapping the gold hair around a smooth stick to the length of the curl he wanted to fabricate. On top of that, he layered damp toilet paper. The paper dried out, the curl was taken off the stick, and voila!

One strategically placed hairpin located the fake curl undetectably among Mary's own. Westmore even constructed a leather carrying case to carry dozens of Mary's hairpieces when she traveled. Westmore charged Mary fifty dollars a curl, and one can assume that very little of the money got back to the women from whom he bought the hair: prostitutes at Big Suzy's French Whorehouse in Los Angeles.

Even with fake curls, there were tactical problems. Once, shooting a scene at the Pasadena railroad station, a little girl who was watching turned to her mother and said, "Mama, she's not a real little girl. She's got long fingernails." Mary immediately cut off the long nails.

The symbolic problems were harder to manage. "Smoking was . . . taboo," recalled Zukor. "In public—for example in a box at the theater—she could not be permitted to toy with a lipstick, a pencil or a bit of paper. From a distance it might be taken for a cigarette. Occasionally, she did so thoughtlessly, and I have seen her mother or my wife take the object gently from her fingers. "If you are to be the queen of motion pictures," Zukor warned her, "you must pay the penalties of royalty." It seemed like a fair exchange.

If Zukor wasn't watching, Charlotte was. She was always there, in story conferences or sitting quietly on the set, making sure that Mary didn't do anything untoward. Occasionally, the raffish Kirkwood would convince Mary to tweak Charlotte's nose and do a scene in which she came off second-best or, worse, threw away completely. Charlotte would launch herself out of her chair, raise hell and Mary and Kirkwood would back down with a great show of reluctance, although they had never intended the scene to go into the picture in the first place.

Mary was learning how to survive among the smiling carnivores very nicely indeed. Every six months or so, vociferous complaints from Mary and Charlotte would begin to arrive on Adolph Zukor's desk. Her shoes were incorrectly fitted; her costumes were sloppily made and bagged in all the wrong places; the directors were incompetent; the stories offered her were intolerably dim. Zukor would adopt a peculiarly harried expression and Sam Goldfish would immediately ask, "How much does she want now?"

"This was not [her] true nature," said Zukor wryly. "It was Mary's way of opening salary negotiations." At these times, Mary and Charlotte would become a classic Good Cop/Bad Cop team; in fact, Zukor could never recall a negotiating session with Mary. That was Charlotte's domain. By this time, Mary and Zukor had equal billing in a sort of father-daughter relationship—assuming that the father and daughter in question were in direct, cut-throat competition for the same pile of dollar bills. Still, there was a loyalty there; Zukor remembered her as the studio favorite, writing, arguing with directors, "suggesting" performance strategies to other actors. Zukor became convinced that Mary, had her business been manufacturing instead of movies, would have risen to the top of United States Steel.

Although Mary loved him, she had no illusions about his abilities. Once, in an interview, Zukor was referred to as a "producer." "He wasn't a producer," she interjected, "he was a businessman." Film happened to be what Zukor sold, and he was unquestionably a brilliant entrepreneur, but he lacked that mixture of narrative gift and motivational football coach that makes a producer. Irving Thalberg he wasn't. To the end of her life, Mary would always refer to him as "Papa Zukor" and, when asked about the strange bond between them, reply that "I always liked his ideas."

That loyalty came into play very soon after Famous Players merged with Lasky, when Sam Goldfish walked into a story meeting between Lasky and Mary and blurted out, "Jesse, don't let Zukor butt in on this picture. He's OK as an executive but . . ."

Mary promptly informed Zukor of the conversation. The next day, the steely little Hungarian gave Lasky a "him or me" ultimatum. Despite the fact that Goldfish was his brother-in-law, Lasky chose Zukor; Goldfish was given $900,000 for his stock and sent on his way; he was also given the basis for a veiled animosity that would always exist between him and Mary.

Mary's act must have confirmed to Zukor that she had a genuinely protective feeling toward him and the company, but business was still business, and negotiations between Mary, Charlotte and Zukor for a new contract took months. Although it was generally known that Mary's old contract paid her $2,000 a week, there was also a secret clause giving her a $10,000 bonus for every finished picture. Thus, in a typical year she would bring home in the vicinity of $150,000.

It was an unprecedented amount of money for an actress; in a nicely ironic touch, *Photoplay* magazine reported that "her earning capacity and tremendous following can only be compared with that of Maude Adams. For she is indeed the Maude Adams of film."

No woman since Cleopatra had achieved the kind of power and control that Mary Pickford had; back in Toronto, tours of the city began to include her birthplace. Tourists gazed in wonder at the plain brick row-house where it had all begun.

Yet, the fact of the matter was that she was worth practically anything she asked. In those days of block booking, when exhibitors were obligated to take the entire product line of a studio or nothing, the promise of six or so Pickford productions yearly was all the nudge any exhibitor needed. Sight unseen, he could book the six or eight Pickford films and, even at the jacked-up rental rates imposed by Famous Players, know that his theater would be full. "He [Zukor] can sell his entire program of pictures by hanging them around Mary's neck," was the contemporary crack and Jesse Lasky admitted years later that Mary was "worth very much more to us than her own pictures brought in."

Why was Mary more important than, say, Chaplin? Because she offered more leverage for a sales organization. Mary made six or eight features a year; Chaplin was making only two-reel shorts. To exhibitors, Pickford films were meat and potatoes, while Chaplin was the seasoning.

"There has never been anything just like the public adulation showered on Mary," remembered Zukor. But, locked up in the studio six days a week, with little chance to come into contact with the public that adored her, the public's expression of its affection became a spasmodic, sometimes terrifying thing. For an appearance in Chicago, a dozen policeman were required just to clear a path for Mary when she left a train. She gradually saw her already limited horizons contracting. The only tangible measure of her success thus became money.

But no matter what Papa Zukor was paying her, it was not enough, for now Mary had become obsessed by the fact that Charlie Chaplin was making more; in February 1916, Chaplin had signed a contract with Mutual that would pay him $10,000 a week, plus a $150,000 bonus, while he made twelve two-reel comedies. The total was $670,000 for, theoretically, a year's work. (Due to illness and Chaplin's endemic delays in quest of perfection, the twelve two-reelers actually took nearly two years.)

"Just think of it," she complained to Goldfish, "there he is getting all that money, and here I am, after all my hard work, not making one half as much." Again, she struck Goldfish as a child, with a child's hurt and sense of injustice at the wretched unfairness of a world that would pay Charlie Chaplin more than Mary Pickford. There was only one thing to do: Put the screws to Papa Zukor.

Mary's feelings had been intensified by an incident occurring in that same year. She had been on her way home from the studio when she passed the Strand Theater, where a double line of patrons was lined up to see one of her pictures. The following week, she again passed the Strand, where another picture had replaced hers, and there was nobody at the box office. On a whim, she parked her car, bought a ticket and went in. "You could have shot a cannon off on the main floor and not hit anybody," she noted.

The next day she marched into Zukor's office and, quite nicely, asked how much money the Strand had paid for the picture of hers they had played last week. "Why, sweetheart honey?" he asked. "Why, I just want to know. I've got to learn business sometime."

Zukor brought out the books. The Strand had paid $3,000 in rentals for Mary's film. And then she sprang the trap, asking, while the books were there, just what the Strand happened to be paying for this week's picture. Zukor gave her a funny look, but told her. "$2,600." Mary nodded her head, thanked him very much and went home to Charlotte. "The next time around," she told her mother, "this is going to stop."

The contract Mary finally signed on June 24, 1916, is a small masterpiece of employee demand and employer humiliation. The contract was to run for two years; it paid Mary 50 percent of the net profits from her films. That 50 percent was guaranteed by Zukor and Lasky to be not less than $1,040,000, payable at the rate of $10,000 weekly over the life of the contract. This sum was guaranteed for services rendered, "and in no event to be returned by said Miss Pickford."

After the film's negative cost, and a sum equal to however much Mary's salary for the picture came to was recouped, the overage, up to $150,000, was to be directly payable to Mary; the next $150,000 in overage went to the corporation, and anything beyond that was to be split down the middle.

In addition, Mary had approval over directors and all other actors in her pictures. Zukor and Lasky also had to pay for a secretary, a press agent, and transportation for commutes from New York to California ("including parlor car accommodation"). In addition, Famous Players-Lasky had to provide a fully equipped, private movie studio, in which no other movies could be made without Mary's consent.

In one clause Mary gave clear indication as to the reasons for her continual drift towards independence: "All leases for 'Mary Pickford' films pursuant to this agreement shall be separate and apart from the so-called program method of marketing motion pictures and separate and apart from leases or sales of other motion picture films, and in no way used to influence the sale or lease of other motion picture films . . ." Clearly, Mary was at least as concerned with eliminating the possibility of block booking as she was in achieving security for herself and her family.

Finally, and most brutally, Mary inserted a clause stating that "inasmuch as Miss Pickford has consumed four weeks from the 29th day of May 1916 to this 24th day of June 1916 in examining scenarios suitable for motion picture productions . . . and inasmuch as the corporation desires to compensate her for this time . . . it is agreed as further consideration for the making of this contract, Miss Pickford shall receive the sum of Forty Thousand dollars . . ." In other words, Mary was to be paid for the time she and Charlotte had been negotiating her contract.

With this contract, Mary began a habit that would continue throughout the better part of the 20s, that of living on her expense account and perquisites, while banking and investing the vast bulk of her salary. (Charlotte handled Mary's money; a financial conservative, for years her main mode of investment was United States bonds; later, real estate became the preferred investment.) To be precise, Mary received $560,000 in salary in 1917 and saved $420,000 of it.

Taken all in all, Zukor and Lasky must have counted themselves proud that they had managed to hold onto their wives' jewelry.

The most astonishing thing about Mary's career at Famous Players up to this point was that she had achieved her unique position of power without ever making a truly superior picture. As nearly as can be gauged from the surviving titles, Mary's early Famous Players movies are programmers, nothing more, whose only notable feature is her presence; Zukor didn't even bother to surround her with other good actors. Most of the time, Mary is playing opposite nonentities like David Powell.

Fanchon the Cricket, one of eight films Mary made in 1915—and one that has apparently been lost—has for years been listed as providing the first film appearance of Fred Astaire as well as the only film of his sister Adele. These references all stem from Astaire's autobiography, where he casually mentions that he and Adele visited the film's location at the Delaware Water Gap. Years later, asked point-blank by historian Kevin Brownlow if she appeared in the film, Adele Astaire replied, "No." As the film is apparently lost, we must assume that Zukor's talent-hunting machinery had no momentary bright spots where Mary's supporting casts were concerned.

Of the early Famous Players films that survive, the best is probably *The Eagle's Mate,* a mountaineer story directed by James Kirkwood in 1914 with commendable style. Kirkwood uses the same deep-focused interiors that brought William Wyler such acclaim in *The Little Foxes,* but he also utilizes some stunningly framed exterior long-shots that clearly recall Griffith. Kirkwood instinctively understood—as Edwin S. Porter did not—the importance of presentation. There is no question who is the star of the picture; Mary is showcased with entrances, exits, closeups and believably solid, naturalistic settings.

But *The Eagle's Mate* is a comparative rarity. As an example of the fact that Mary could carry any story Zukor slung at her, no matter how ludicrous, consider *Poor Little Peppina,* from 1915.

As a small child, Peppina is kidnapped by a Mafia chief who doubles as the family butler. After she grows up, and to escape from an unwanted suitor, Peppina cuts her hair, hides her female sexual characteristics under a voluminous blouse, and stows away on a boat to America, where, in due time, she is re-united with her parents. (Although set in Italy, *Poor Little Peppina* was actually shot in and around Peapack, New Jersey. Daniel Frohman, visiting the location site, the mountain home of Mr. and Mrs. James Blair, noted that Mrs. Blair watched the scene of Peppina's abduction being shot. When she saw with what ease the actor playing the villain gained entrance, she "became frightened and at once gave orders that her sleeping quarters were to be made impregnable.")

Likewise, Mary always remembered *Less than the Dust* as a particularly bad example of the period, usually calling it "Cheaper than the Dirt," the name a confused fan gave it. Although her retrospective feelings about her films were notoriously subjective, she was certainly right in this case. In *Less than the Dust*, Mary plays Rahda, "a waif of the bazaars," a half-caste Indian scamp, her racial characteristics being indicated by a slight application of Fuller's Earth. The plot is a variation on *Madame Butterfly*, with Mary in love with an English officer and helping to quell a native revolt. It might have just about passed muster as a mediocre Biograph; stretched out to five reels, it's insupportable, and probably the worst picture she ever made.

In most of the pictures of this period, the acting style is still the predominantly presentational style of 1910–1912, not the quieter, more modulated technique that would be the norm by 1920. Although any great star must be able to carry indifferent pictures on his or her personal recognizance, the career pictures, the ones that are hauled out for obituaries, were yet to come. Zukor was giving Mary the sort of material that, although typical of his studio at the time, ought to have been reserved for the glorified personal appearances of stars who are coasting on the fame and goodwill of years gone by.

That, however, would change; with the signing of her last contract with Zukor, and for years thereafter, Mary achieved creative freedom. Perhaps it was the security wrought by her munificent salary, or the torrential public acclaim that enabled her to, for the first time in her life, attain a feeling of security. Whatever, it was during 1916–1920 that Mary would make most of her best pictures, and prove to the critics that the public enthusiasm for her had been completely correct. For that breakthrough, she would forge alliances with two of the most remarkable directors of their time.

Now that the ultimate deal had been signed with Zukor, its terms headlined throughout the world, the money had to be earned. Mary called a meeting with her favorite writer, Frances Marion, and the director she instinctively felt was right for her, Marshall Neilan. "I will be good," she said simply; "I will make good pictures."

She was; she did.

Chapter Five

"I do not believe anybody can understand America in the years during and after the first World War who does not understand the vogue of Mary Pickford."

—*Edward Wagenknecht*

*M*AURICE Tourneur was born in Paris, in 1878. He had been studying sculpture (Rodin was one of his teachers) when he was seduced by the cinema. A bulky, strong-featured man who had a gift for exquisite composition and *mise-en-scène*, Tourneur believed that a film, to be any good, had to have a unity.

"I shall always assert that the play is *not* the thing," he said. "If the play were the thing, the lack of acting, the good interpretation and ensemble, would not spoil it. To me, neither the play, the acting, the star, the director, nor the presentation is the thing. It takes all of them."

Mary's first collaboration with Tourneur was *The Pride of the Clan,* a mediocre story shot at the end of 1916 with many visual hints of the richness of their next film. A story of fishing folk off the coast of Scotland, *The Pride of the Clan* is of interest for the splendid design of the sets (by Ben Carré) and the luminously beautiful, silhouetted compositions that Tourneur uses throughout the picture, which give the film a sense of atmosphere so intense you can almost feel the rushing wind.

Nor are the interesting angles limited to the windswept exteriors; in the cramped interiors of the fishing cottages, Tourneur frames low, getting looming ceilings into the shots, and keeps the illumination dark, with a single light source, usually a window. These visual gambits are far more sophisticated than the flat, slightly rushed, interchangeable house style used by less distinctive Pickford directors like Sidney Olcott and John O'Brien. Tourneur gives his film an oppressive sense of enclosure that contrasts beautifully with the vast, stormy, open spaces of the exteriors.

With a compositional gift as strong as Tourneur's, less plot was needed, and that of *Pride of the Clan* doesn't even kick in until the film is more than half over. Until then, it's all character and atmosphere, with Mary giving a performance of quiet authority and intensity. As interesting as it is, however, *The Pride of the Clan* is an apprentice work compared to its immediate successor.

Released in March 1917, *Poor Little Rich Girl* was a landmark film for Mary, one that exercised a major influence over the rest of her career. Mary plays Gwendolyn, a child of wealth isolated from her Wall Street-obsessed father and social-climbing mother. She is a playful, loving child—Frances Marion's script makes the character a good deal less lofty than the original source material does—and Tourneur captures some charming moments with location footage of an auto ride through Central Park, with Gwen first breathing on a window, then drawing pictures on the fogged surface until being reprimanded by her governess.

Her parents promise to spend time with her soon, tomorrow maybe, but those tomorrows never come. "Haven't you time to love me a little?" she plaintively asks her father. What nurturing Gwen gets comes from brief, surreptitious encounters with kindly plumbers, etc.

Essentially a series of episodes, the film is more than half over by the time Gwen is accidentally poisoned by an hostile, officious nurse. She staggers down from the second-floor bedroom, with Tourneur's camera tilted off-center àla *The Third Man*, until she collapses.

Hovering between life and death, Gwen imagines an alternate world with places like the Garden of Lonely Children (someone had obviously read Maeterlinck's "The Blue Bird" probably Tourneur, who directed a film version of it in 1918). Like most children, Gwen takes things literally. She half-hears her governess being called two-faced and, in her delirium, imagines the woman's head spinning like Linda Blair's, with faces on either side. Likewise, when she hears the phrase "the bears are loose on Wall

Street," she imagines her father beset by a half-dozen or so delightfully fake bears.

As she is about to be gathered into the waiting arms of the rather lovely woman who plays the Angel of Death, Gwen opts for life. Her near-demise brings her parents to their senses and the requisite happy ending ensues.

The Poor Little Rich Girl is stylistically subtle but cumulatively stunning. Ben Carré's sets are oversized, and create a true child's view of the world, which, typically, seems much bigger than it really is. Likewise, Mary is not really playing a child—eleven-year-old children do not, as a general rule, wear lipstick and mascara—but, rather, an idealized simulacrum, a projection of what the audience, from the standpoint of adulthood, thinks and wishes they might have been as children: tough, resilient, and put-upon by insensitive adults.

The Pickford molded by Maurice Tourneur is a gentler girl than the one Marshall Neilan would mold; more winsome, more fragile, less resourceful. Mary's two films for Tourneur have a whimsical, fairy-tale quality her others lack.

That this is the way Tourneur saw Mary's screen character can't be doubted; neither can the growing gap between what she played and what she really was. During the production of this, her first truly fine film, Mary and Tourneur clashed. Mary's recollection was that Tourneur's aestheticism was strangling the spirit out of the picture, that it needed more life, more gags. "I am a dignified director and my pictures should be dignified," Tourneur said.

Nevertheless, Mary and Frances Marion kept on improvising, leading Tourneur to protest "Where, exactly, ladies, do you see that in the script? *Mais non, c'est une horreur!*"

In one sequence, Gwendolyn throws all her beautiful clothes out the window rather than have them given to a disgusting little rich snot as punishment for a prank. The neighborhood urchins grab the fine clothing and run off, in a scene that eerily prefigures the famous scene in Preston Sturges's script for the 1937 screwball comedy *Easy Living,* in which a fur coat tossed out a window instigates the plot.

The major disagreement between Mary and Tourneur involved a scene of a mud fight, with the spunky Gwen vigorously giving as good as she gets. Tourneur was horrified. "I have had a dignified career," he told Mary. "French children are not permitted to behave like that. I'll have nothing to do with it."

Mary explained that this picture was about an *American* child; Frances Marion tried charming the director, as did Mary. Nothing helped. Finally, Mary said that Tourneur should shoot it, and if he didn't like it, they would cut it out. But the fact of the matter was that, once the film was "in the can," it didn't matter whether Tourneur liked it or not, as, Zukor aside, it was Mary who controlled the finished product. The scene remained in the picture, as Mary always knew it would, but Tourneur never directed another picture for her.

A very sophisticated primitive imbued with remarkable charm, *A Poor Little Rich Girl* was the immediate success it deserved to be. Mary took it and ran with it. "I climbed on my high horse and rode off in all directions," she acknowledged years later. "I'm going to say what I'm going to do. I'm going to do *Rebecca* . . . and I want Mickey Neilan and Frances Marion and I don't want anybody from the Lasky Company on the set." Forty years later, remembering her naked power grab, Mary sighed and referred to "the ambitious one that I used to be."

All that, however, came after the film was released. At the exhibitor and trade screenings, reactions were dangerously tepid —one can easily imagine the film looking narratively vague and dangerously arty. Since Mary had run roughshod over her director, and everybody at Paramount knew it, a good deal of her personal coin was on the line. The indifferent response was the worst-case scenario. Mary went home in tears, as did Frances Marion. This is the story agreed upon with some unanimity by both Pickford and Marion in old age. The astonishing thing is the breadth of Mary's innate insecurity; a woman who had years of strong successes behind her feared for her career after only one (apparent) failure.

Zukor was sufficiently chagrined about the film's prospects to force Mary to write a placating letter to Cecil B. deMille, the company's leading director. "I have no desire to interfere in the choice of stories," she wrote, "in the casting of the different actors, including myself, and in the final editing. I am placing myself unreservedly in your most capable hands. Obediently yours . . ." It was a subtle, carefully calibrated act of revenge on Zukor's part, and Mary never forgot the implicit humiliation.

As for Maurice Tourneur, he got his revenge three years later, when, in a magazine article about the banality of the public's demands upon filmmakers, he broke down the conventional idiocies of silent movie storytelling into various categories. Second from the top was "a cute, curly-headed . . . smiling and pouting ingenue . . . She runs through beautiful gardens (always with the same nice backlighting effects) or the poor little thing is working under dreadful factory conditions that have not been known for at least forty years. Torn between the sheer idiocy of the hero and the inexplicable hate of the heavy, is it any wonder that her sole communion is with the dear dumb animals, pigs, cows, ducks, goats—anything so long as it can't talk."

The message—and the target—were both unmistakable, but, if she noticed at all, Mary gave no sign.

———— ————

Mary and deMille did two successive pictures together that were commercial successes but not particularly felicitous experiences for either star or director, both of whom were used to more submissive temperaments in their co-workers. *The Little American*, released in the summer of 1917 as the second of the two collaborations, is a World War I propaganda piece that posits Mary as Angela More, in love with Jack Holt's Karl von Austreim, an apparently nice young man of German descent. But, when the war breaks out, Karl is revealed to be just another beastly German, a product of genetics mixing with peer pressure.

Except for deMille's customarily brusque, fast-forward narrative, *The Little American* is a film of little distinction, filled with the rape fantasies that were *de rigeur* for these sort of films. There is an effective recreation (shot in San Pedro Bay) of the sinking of the Lusitania, and deMille achieves a lurid, if unlikely, melodramatic splendor when he has his beastly Huns say things like "Where are the pretty girls, Fritz?" Worse, the Germans force Mary to undergo the second-worst degradation: taking the muddy boots off a German general sporting a Kaiser Wilhelm mustache.

Except for random flashes, *The Little American* is a film of no importance, demonstrably inferior to the results that had been obtained when Zukor had given Mary her head. In any case, the success of *The Poor Little Rich Girl* done Mary's way, far outstripped that of *The Little American* or *Romance of the Redwoods*, done Zukor's way. After the highly successful release of *The Poor Little Rich Girl* in March 1917, Zukor, in effect, let Mary serve as her own producer.

Although there were no banner headlines in the trade papers, it was still a momentous event in terms of Hollywood history: The first time a major Hollywood studio abdicated its supervisory role and functioned simply as a funding entity.

Jesse Lasky made the decision to send Mary to the West Coast, while Zukor decided to start Artcraft Pictures, a special division of

Famous Players-Lasky that would handle films too expensive to be block-booked.

When Mary arrived in California, Lottie, Jack and Charlotte trailed dutifully behind. Lottie and Jack shared a temperament that was far more carefree than that of their older sister. Lottie had grown up to be taller, thinner, homelier than Mary, with dark brown hair that was much straighter than Mary's. Jack and Lottie's relationship with their sister was mostly affectionate, but, on a deeper level, ambivalent; among their nicknames for Mary were "The Big Stick," "The Policewoman," and, at especially imperious times, "The Czarina."

Mary had always felt threatened by Lottie; even in the Biograph days, she had been hesitant to bring Lottie to the studio and had confided in Linda Arvidson Griffith that she didn't think Lottie was either pretty or likely to be any good in the movies. Mrs. Griffith remembered, that "No one was especially interested in Lottie."

But, as she would always point out, Lottie had a talent of her own. At the very beginning of their careers, touring with the Chauncey Olcott company, Lottie had understudied Mary, although, whenever she got a part of her own, she "got perfectly splendid notices, quite eclipsing Mary," she would proudly recall in 1915. She was enough of a realist to know that she had to get out from under her sister's shadow if she was to achieve any public image of her own. "I like the work in Los Angeles," she said, "but I knew there was no chance of getting very far with [Famous Players-Lasky] as long as they were featuring Mary. One Pickford at a time is enough for any company to feature."

Lottie took an offer from the American Film Company, located in Santa Barbara, where she had a brief vogue as a serial star. But Lottie's career flamed out early, at least partially because her mind seemed to be occupied by less rigorous pursuits than building and maintaining a career. There were numerous instances of wild parties at which fights had a odd way of breaking out. When reporters would ask about this unseemly habit, she would smile and laugh and say, "Oh, the boys just raised a little whoopee, but they're good friends now."

In March 1923, Lottie and Jack were summoned before a federal grand jury investigating "a coastwide conspiracy to violate the Volstead Act" after numerous checks from the two of them were found in the possession of prominent bootleggers. Since three quarters of the nation seemed to be violating the Volstead Act, if not quite so vigorously as Jack and Lottie, nobody paid much attention. Shortly thereafter, Lottie's last two pictures, 1924's *Dorothy Vernon of Haddon Hall* and 1925's *Don Q, Son of Zorro* were made for her sister and brother-in-law, respectively.

A far more serious situation made the papers five years later. More than $100,000 in I.O.U.'s from Lottie were found when a federal narcotics squad raided the headquarters of gambling kingpin Arnold Rothstein, the man who fixed the 1919 World Series.

On November 9, 1928, three days after Rothstein was murdered, Lottie was abducted, beaten and robbed by four men. Lottie's companion of the moment, Jack Daugherty, formerly married to Barbara LaMarr and Virginia Brown Faire, was knocked unconscious in the attack. After that misadventure, Lottie retired to the bottle.

Jack lacked both Lottie's gumption and Mary's looks. Jack's aquiline features and narrow face gave him a strong resemblance to Will Hays, the rat-faced Republican Postmaster General during the Harding administration who later became the czar of the movies. Given Jack's features, weaselly heavies were a better idea than heroes. Unfortunately, his name was Pickford, and no one named Pickford played heavies. So Jack was forced into playing country-boy heroes like Charles Ray for which he was physically and temperamentally unsuited.

As one reporter for *Photoplay* noted in a rare burst of candor in 1917, "when [Jack] went out he was picked on as Mary's brother and when he came home Mary bossed him around and told him what was good for him in maternal fashion that was most exasperating."

Jack happily fell into the role of scapegrace. "Jack was always a problem in the Pickford family," said editor Stuart Heisler, who worked on Mary's films in the early '20s. "He was always getting into trouble with girls; he'd get them pregnant." "Jack was *always* pleasant and *always* loaded," remembered William Bakewell, who knew him in the late '20s and early '30s.

For years, Jack was a member in good standing of a sort of alcoholic's version of The Four Musketeers, as he, Norman Kerry, Lew Cody and Marshall Neilan regularly closed night spots like Vernon's, the Hotel Alexandria, the Sunset Inn and every bar and whorehouse in Tijuana.

When James Kirkwood married Lila Lee, Jack and his friends conspired to get Kirkwood so blind drunk that he passed out. They then dragged him out on the lawn of the Beverly Hills Hotel, removed all his clothes, and covered him with a sheet.

"Lila, you better come quickly," one of them told the new bride.

"There's been a terrible accident." They led her out to the lawn where they sadly removed the sheet from Kirkwood's prone, apparently lifeless body; when Lila let out a crazed shriek, they all broke up into hysterics and dragged Kirkwood inside to sober up.

Until 1917, Jack was considered no worse than most of his scapegrace friends, but that year, even though the newspapers reported he was below draft age (in fact, he was twenty-one), he enlisted in the aviation section of the Navy, only to get caught in one of his usual schemes. Soon after his induction, Jack began serving as a go-between for a Lieutenant Benjamin Davis and worried bluebloods who were willing to pay for berths in the Naval Reserve that were guaranteed to be far away from shot and shell.

Davis and Jack were both caught; Davis was court-martialed and found guilty, while Jack quickly turned state's evidence and testified for the prosecution. Nevertheless, he was recommended for a dishonorable discharge by the Navy's lawyer in the case, who, in his official report, noted that Jack "had willfully and deliberately made a false statement in regard to his use of intoxicants" and concluded by saying "it is apparent that he is not a fit person to be retained in the naval service . . ."

At the last minute, a letter was received from Joseph Tumulty, President Wilson's personal secretary. The letter asked that Jack be given a conventional, honorable discharge so that he could appear in a movie called *The Brood of the Bald Eagle,* which was expected to be effective war propaganda for aviation.

Jack was given the conventional discharge; no movie entitled *The Brood of the Bald Eagle* was ever made. Asked about the strange coincidence in the timing of his request, Tumulty said that he had not known about the charges against Jack, that his letter asking for an honorable discharge just seemed like a good idea at the time, "after an inquiry . . . on behalf of Pickford's mother."

Soon after his discharge, Jack married Olive Thomas, an exceedingly beautiful Ziegfeld Follies star, cover girl and sometime actress. The marriage had the usual ups and downs associated with Jack, but on what was billed as a second honeymoon in Paris in 1920, things took a disastrous turn.

Jack and Olive were staying at the Ritz Hotel and, after the usual round of nightclubs, got in about 3:00 A.M. According to Jack, "We both had been drinking a little . . . I went to bed immediately; Olive fussed around and wrote a note to her mother. She was in the bathroom. Suddenly, she shrieked, 'Oh, my God!'

"I jumped out of bed, rushed towards her and caught her in my arms." Olive had ingested a lethal dose of mercury bichloride, even though the bottle had been clearly marked with a skull and crossbones. For four days she lingered. On September 10, 1920, she died. As the investigation got under way, the Paris authorities announced that "the theory of suicide has been definitely abandoned." Shortly thereafter, the same authorities did a ninety degree turn and announced that Olive Thomas had died accidentally after taking the mercury thinking it was a sleeping potion.

The "inside" version of what had really happened was that Thomas had committed suicide after finding out that Jack had infected her with syphilis. After Thomas died, Jack left for London in the company of Owen Moore, an interesting choice of companion.

Jack—and undoubtedly Mary—tried to recoup the public relations disaster by renouncing any share of Thomas's small $36,875 estate, but it was too late. Jack may not have been culpable of anything but self-indulgence, but Jack took self-indulgence to felony proportions. The truth was that Jack was soft; after Olive's death, Jack existed almost totally on his sister's never-ending indulgence.

He married another Ziegfeld girl, the great star Marilyn Miller, who, like Olive Thomas, had been one of Ziegfeld's mistresses. Mary recalled that Miller "was the most ambitious woman I ever met," a revealing remark in the it-takes-one-to-know-one sweepstakes. That marriage, too, had its rocky moments and a few years later Jack was trying to date Norma Shearer. Jack's easy charm was initially attractive but Shearer also detected something sinister about him and backed off when Lilyan Tashman told her Jack's private nickname was "Mr. Syphilis." Miller divorced Jack in 1927, shortly after a newspaper account of the couple's troubles ended with these dryly brutal sentences: "Miss Miller is Pickford's second wife. His first, Olive Thomas, killed herself in Paris several years ago." Mary regularly paid Jack's legal bills, although, to the disgust of William Hayward, one of his attorneys, Jack purposely underreported the extent of his bills. "(Jack) is not man enough to tell his sister about it," Hayward wrote to his brother Leland. A final marriage in 1930 was also unsuccessful, lasting only two years.

Mary spent years bailing Jack out of various scrapes, even going to the extent of producing pictures for him, and, on two memorable occasions, hiring him to co-direct pictures of hers, so he'd at least have something to do with his days. Mostly, it was all for nothing.

In January 1927, she proposed selling two story properties she owned to Universal, one called *Her Son,* priced at $5,000, another entitled *The Land Just Over Yonder* for $10,000. The prices were entirely reasonable for properties of the period—in and of itself unusual with Mary, who priced everything on the high end—but Universal passed, saying they weren't interested if the properties came with the proviso that Jack had to star in them. The proposed deal promptly collapsed.

Yet, there was also a sense of thwarted ambition about Jack. Preserved in the Pickford Company files is a story written by Jack in 1927 entitled "Burnt Fingers." Briefly, it's the story of a bored wife of a preoccupied Wall Street wolf. To try to make him jealous, she pretends to get involved with, then actually does get involved with, a lounge lizard about town, then is horrified to find out all he wants is her money. She wakes up and returns to her now attentive husband.

It's a competently plotted, if very silent–movie-ish scenario, and it bespeaks a desire to do other things. As with Lottie, however, Mary's success seemed to act as a drain on Jack's own ambitions; after 1925, his appearances in pictures grew infrequent, for Jack was far more enamored of women and alcohol than he was of work.

Jack's last picture was *Gang War,* a 1928 quickie made for FBO Pictures, an independent studio that was later reconstituted into RKO. By that time, Jack had been dabbling in narcotics for some time, which, in addition to his alcoholism, explains his increasingly frequent hospital stays for vaguely defined complaints like "breakdowns" and "severe colds" that somehow metastasized into near-death close-calls, as well as "heart attacks" that only necessitated hospital stays of a week or so.

At least Jack wasn't pretentious. Leaving for Paris to get his divorce from Marilyn Miller, he told reporters to "Call me Jack, and not Mr. Pickford. I'm one of the boys, you know."

———— — ————

Still, the problems with Jack, the problems with Lottie, all seemed manageable to Mary. There was nothing wrong with her world that good pictures couldn't cure, and, for the first time, they spilled out of the Artcraft studio in profusion.

By this time, the Pickford image—and technique—had solidified. In a film like *Rags* she is piquant, adorable and, in the very best sense of the word, cute. She is not "being" in the accepted manner of later movie stars like Gary Cooper; she is almost always acting, giving a performance. Compared to the later screen acting of a Garbo or a Menjou, where the lift of an eyebrow can connote either irony or devastating emotional import, she seems too big. But Cooper or Menjou or Garbo would have been incomprehensibly minimalist on a stage, and that is the key. What Mary is actually giving, and, for the most part, continued to give, were expert, emphatic stage performances that were slightly scaled down for the camera.

The audience—and the critics—responded with rapturous praise. Underneath the treacly, stardusted prose of the fan magazines, the *New Republic*'s occasional film critic Vachel Lindsay characterized the Pickford phenomenon for what it was. In an approving review of deMille's *A Romance of the Redwoods*, Lindsay warmed up by calling her the "Little Eva" of her generation, and then noted her odd ability to shapeshift in a picture; "Sometimes . . . she is innocent eight, sometimes dangerous sixteen, with no notice given of change in time." He protested that Mae Marsh was a better actress and overall artist, if only because she had the advantage of Griffith's direction.

Then, approvingly quoting Yeats's dictum about "Rhetoric being heard, poetry overheard," Lindsay caught the essence of the remarkable achievements of Mary in her last several films. "For the first time in my knowledge, the acting of Mary Pickford is permitted by her directors to have divine accident in it, poetry overheard . . . It begins to appear that the higher the imagination of Mary Pickford's scenario writer and director, the more sensitive is her response. If there is anything in a film at all, it is worth seeing three times. I went to see this one six times because I was glad Mary was beginning to emerge . . ."

Lindsay closed his review with a stentorian cry: "To repudiate this girl in haste is high treason to the national heart." He was right about one thing: the better her collaborators, the better Mary would be.

——————— ——————

By 1917, when he began to direct Mary, Marshall Neilan had been her leading man in more features than any other actor. During the production of 1915's *Madame Butterfly*, with Neilan playing Pinkerton to Mary's Cio-Cio-San, Neilan made some suggestions to director Sidney Olcott that Mary thought excellent. This in turn encouraged Mary to get into the act. "My idea was to have the first scenes showing Pinkerton teaching the Japanese girl some American game like baseball. But would the director listen to me? Not a bit of it."

Mary loved the quality of Neilan's ideas. "I knew that he was a potentially great director," said Mary. "I went to Zukor and asked that he be engaged. It would only cost us $150 a week. But Mr. Zukor said, 'Sweetheart honey, let someone else discover him and we'll pay him double that. It'll be cheaper in the long run.'" So Mary remained stuck with Sidney Olcott, who ignored both Mary and Neilan's suggestions, and quarreled with Mary. The finished film struck Mary as so lifelessly plodding that she suggested it be re-titled "Madame Snail." In fact, Olcott's direction does stress the decorative, ceremonial aspects of the story; the pace is slow, but the final film has a dramatic power missing from many of the Pickford films of the period, while Mary's performance is subtle and effective.

In 1917, Neilan was just twenty-six years old. One of the delights of the silent movies, and a possible explanation for their undiminished, enchanting vigor, was the youth of many of the creators. The son of a civil engineer, Neilan was born in San Bernadino and become an actor at six; like Mary, he had worked for Belasco as a child.

Landing a job with Kalem studios, Neilan progressed from driver to assistant cameraman, to writer, on up the ladder to actor. From Kalem he went to Biograph, then American, Universal, Lasky and Famous Players. He had begun directing at Selig and, by the time he arrived at Lasky, was a rising star among directors. He was rambunctiously charming and iconoclastic, loud and constant in his dislike of the men for whom he was working; since the men he was working for were Jewish, some took this as anti-Semitism. "You must remember that lots of people were anti-Semitic in those days," remembered Lina Basquette, who acted for Neilan in the 20s. "They just didn't say so the way Mickey Neilan did. The same thing hurt Jack Gilbert."

But, as a director, Neilan was both good and fast; at Selig, he had won the attention of the industry by making 112 shots in one day, and completing and shipping the picture in seven working days, something of a record for a feature. Neilan was an irrepressible Irishman who was particularly vocal when directing a scene. "Irishmen like Mickey or Jack Conway or Tay Garnett had a great deal of ham in them," remembered Lina Basquette. "With them talking you through a scene, and with the music playing in the background, why, they could get a performance out of a turnip."

With Neilan, Mary felt free, unencumbered, and was at her most forbearing. "He could wrap Mary Pickford around his finger," remembered Blanche Sweet, Neilan's wife for a time. Mary's comments about him seem to confirm Sweet's analysis. "Mickey was one of the most delightful, aggravating, gifted and charming human beings I have ever known," she remembered. "There were times when I could cheerfully have throttled him—especially at his frequent failures to make an appearance on the set until after luncheon, keeping a large company waiting at considerable expense.

"I would use the most insulting Irish language I could think of, telling him he was nothing but a bogtrotter, far-down Shanty Irish and a dirty scut! Mickey, who was a good actor, pretended to be shocked, and, to shame me said 'Tad (the endearing Irish name he always called me), what would The Public think of their darling using such language?' And then he would pacify me with one of his creative gags that my fans still remember forty years later."

Neilan's particular gift was an improvisational ability to stimulate the precisely right response in an actor. "He would dream up running gags long in advance and then at the psychological moment unexpectedly blast them at me," Mary said. On *The Little Princess,* Neilan wanted a close-up reaction shot of Mary exploding into laughter. He inveigled Charlie Chaplin and Jack Pickford into dressing up in outlandish drag and dancing while Neilan whistled the "Spring Song." It worked. One of Neilan's technicians put it another way. "Mickey just kids 'em along," he said.

A script girl on *Rebecca of Sunnybrook Farm,* Lucita Squier, met Mary on the first day of production. "I'm pleased to meet you, Miss Squier," Mary said. "I hope you won't mind, Miss Pickford," said Squier, "if I stare at you to watch details?"

"Go ahead," she replied, "I'll stare right back at you to check before the camera starts to grind."

"It seemed to me that the public was often cheated out of the best of Mary's talents," Squier remembered. "The banter, the mimicry, and the happy fellowship that went on behind the scenes. [Mary and Mickey] liked to clown and tell stories in an Irish brogue. Mickey could play the piano well and enthusiastically. He used to make fun of D.W. Griffith, whom he considered an old fogey."

Squier noticed that Mary always learned lines and spoke them, even though they wouldn't be heard. But as the successful collaborations between Pickford and Neilan added up, Neilan's Irish temperament began to get the better of him. "Things came too easily to him," was the way Squier put it. By the time of *Daddy Long-*

Legs, probably the finest result of their collaboration, he often showed up for work without having been to bed, and from there it was only a short step to not showing up at all.

One day, when Neilan hadn't arrived at the studio by lunch, Mary announced that she was closing down the picture. On her way out of the studio, she met Neilan on his way in.

"Hello, Tad!" he said, smiling. "Go away," she snapped. "I'm not going to speak to you again. You ought to be ashamed of yourself, keeping us waiting like this. I've made up my mind to call off the picture."

Neilan dredged up all his charm. "Oh come on, Tad. Just wait until you hear my story." He put his hands firmly around her neck and guided her back into the studio, whereupon Mary burst out laughing. Neilan could manipulate her in ways that the men she married could not. The only other man who would ever be able to claim a similar hold on her moods and affections was Jack, her equally alcoholic brother.

She could at least hold her own in the battle of wits with Neilan. "Mickey's greatest failing is his inability to sustain interest throughout a long production," she accurately observed; on their last picture together, *Dorothy Vernon of Haddon Hall,* she schemed her way around this by beginning production with the dramatically meaty middle of the story, so that, if he went off on a bat or got bored toward the end of production, the drama would still hold.

The last picture Lucita Squier worked on with Mary was *M'Liss,* and, on the final day of shooting, Mary told her "Remember, Lucita, we're friends for life." It is the sort of promise usually made at the end of a film, but one that is rarely kept, especially between a star and a script girl in the caste-conscious world of Hollywood.

But Mary kept her promises. She and Squier always kept in touch, occasionally visited each other and Mary always closed her letters with "Friend for life, Mary."

——— ———

The Pickford of these years was self-assured without being oppressively pretentious. Like most actors, there was a duality about her; on the one hand, she liked the adulation. On the other, she was nervous about whether it could get out of hand or, catastrophically, stop altogether. She would eagerly peruse the movie magazines for mentions of herself, and be delighted when an article or photo appeared, or be disappointed when they didn't. "People are always disappointed in me," she declared at this time. "Once . . . I had on a little gingham frock and garden hat . . . and as I came along I heard one small boy exclaim, 'Gee, is that Mary? Ain't she dinky?' "

She was already bridling at the tight vise of public expectations; "this dramatic rut keeps me eternally playing the curly-headed girl," she said in September 1917. "And I hate curls. I loathe them —loathe them!" Then, with a straight face, and in the same conversation, she would run for comforting cover: "Of course, I never want to play a role that would ever offend the little girls that love me."

Of one thing she was determined. "Now that I have enough money to buy bread and, now and then, cake for the rest of my life, I will have happiness in my studio." A Pickford set was invariably a pleasant set; Frances Marion, her favorite writer, recalled their working methods: "I dashed off the stories. Those were the days before conferences, before associate producers . . . We wrote off the cuff. All the scenarists and directors worked hand in hand, not fist against fist as it is today."

The work was hard and, for Mary, seldom ended before seven or eight at night, but temperament, even her own, was frowned upon. She was particularly pleasant to the child actors on a picture; Wesley Barry, a successful juvenile whose career began with Mary's *Daddy Long-Legs*, remembered her sharing her picnic basket lunch with him every day on location.

At the end of production of *Pollyanna*, late in 1919, there was a cast party, with all the men dressing in female drag and vice versa. Except for Mary. "She went home early," remembered Howard Ralston, a child actor on the picture.

She was unfailingly gracious and playful with Ralston. When she found out that he was worried about his sick dog, she made it a point to begin each day by asking after the dog's health. "Once, I asked her what kind of coat she was wearing," remembered Ralston. "I told her the dog was better and she said her coat was sable."

They would talk about her French lessons, and she would admit to the child actor that she had trouble with proper pronunciation, saying *"sur la train"* (on top of the train) instead of *"à la train"* (in the train). When an actor fell into the river, she sent everybody home for the day so the actor could get into some dry clothing and not catch cold.

While events off-screen were giving her a sense of her own

potential as a woman, she was discovering a concurrent freedom on-screen.

A central part of the Pickford persona of these years was a strong working-class orientation. She told tales of the Victorian poor that would have been considered Dickensian if they didn't so closely resemble the observed reality of her own barnstorming youth. In films like *Suds* and *Amarilly of Clothes-Line Alley,* Pickford regularly ascribed honor and authenticity to the working class, and arrogance and phoniness to society's upper strata. Very consciously, Mary played roles that the predominantly working-class audiences of the silent era could immediately relate to: in *Hearts Adrift* (1913), she bears an illegitimate child; in *The Eternal Grind* (1916) she's working in a sweatshop; in *Tess of the Storm Country* (1914 and 1922) she fakes a pregnancy to save someone else's life.

Before 1914, the movies had often catered to the working classes, at least partially because they were the movies' principal patrons. But as the teens wore on, the movies increasingly broadened their audience. Although Chaplin devoted even more time to the doings of the underclass, equally popular stars like Douglas Fairbanks (at least until he devoted his career to swashbucklers) played predominantly middle-class characters. Popular actresses like Alice Joyce and Clara Kimball Young specialized almost exclusively in "Ladies." Yet, problems of the working class were a motif that Mary continued to weave into her films. She always imbued her pictures with humor and optimism, usually avoiding overt moralizing. Her zesty performances provided the main fillip of primary pleasure.

At the same time, she was interspersing these neo-realist depictions of grim grime with more conventional stories like *Rebecca of Sunnybrook Farm* (1917) and *Pollyanna* (1920). She attempted to cut the treacle of these Victorian artifacts by the unregenerate spunk of her own personality, sometimes more successfully than others. She may have been playing characters ten or fifteen years younger than she was, but she didn't do them to the exclusion of everything else—1920's *Pollyanna* was her first child part in three years—and when she did play them, she gave them a mischievous fighting spirit and an occasional streak of perversity that only a mature actress would have thought of.

In one scene in *Pollyanna,* for instance, Mary catches a fly. "Do you want to go to heaven?" she solicitously inquires. She promptly smashes it and calmly notes, "Well, you have." These malevolent grace notes justify and make bearable some of the tiresome plot contrivances of the surrounding material.

In *Rebecca of Sunnybrook Farm,* from 1917, that year of ingenuity, invention and ambition, Mary and Neilan attempt to compensate for the story, which dates from 1903, by trying to turn the film into an idyllic, nostalgic voyage into the values and mores of late nineteenth century rural America.

The story is of Rebecca Randall, who leaves her impoverished family and goes to live with her two aunts in a nearby town. The aunts are mean, moralistic scolds who look down on everybody, including Rebecca. There is some adept comedy, as Rebecca attempts to navigate on the tiny runners the aunts have placed over their perennially virgin carpets, and there is the usual sickbed scene—two actually—at which first Rebecca's aunt, then later Rebecca, learn the error of their judgmental ways.

The only interesting aspect of the story is its suggestion, rare in 1903, that rural values were not somehow inherently superior to those of the (supposedly) corrupting city. In *Rebecca,* there is every bit as much bigotry and small-mindedness as most novels and movies of the period imputed to the urban landscape.

None of this fazes Rebecca, played by Mary on the single, relentless note of an adorably scampish little hoyden. Here, Mary again works bigger, heavier than she needs to, and her characterization is too treacly and cute by half. The performance is just that, a performance obviously aimed at pleasing the crowd, with every wink and joke italicized so nobody could possibly miss them.

Nothing in the film suggests New England (the milieu seems closer to Riverside) and the picture as a whole seems notably cruder, less distinctive and certainly less polished than *Poor Little Rich Girl,* even though it was made several months later. In particular, Walter Stradling's lighting is rudimentary; attempts to make Mary look younger by pouring light on her face from a low angle and washing out everything but her eyes seem appallingly crude, more like a film of 1912 than of 1917.

In this, his first film with Mary, Marshall Neilan fills the film with a certain irritating busyness, even when inappropriate. To indicate the shiftlessness of the town's poor white trash, Neilan shows them gathered desultorily around a small crate, on which sits a spoon they are trying to flip into an empty glass. Both Neilan and Mary knew poverty first-hand more acutely than did author Kate Douglas Wiggin, and the idiotically condescending characterization is aimed at the lowest level of yahoo non-sophistication.

The film flares briefly to life on a couple of occasions. There is the famous scene where Rebecca, after having been denied dinner, is about to sneak a piece of pie when she spots a sign: "Thou

Shalt Not Steal." With an appropriate expression denoting piety, she backs off and is about to leave the room when she sees another needlepoint maxim: "God Helps Those Who Help Themselves." She quickly reconsiders and promptly begins gobbling down a piece of pie.

The other scene involves Rebecca listening to a long-winded clergyman. Suddenly, Mary flashes a startlingly contemporary look of boredom and disgust. For one flashing moment, the original, modern woman playing the part shoulders the stock character aside.

In the latter part of the film, after three years have passed and the pre–adolescent Rebecca is now the teen-age Rebecca, Mary throws away her posing and makes the transition to young womanhood with a becoming calm and sense of assurance. (To be fair, in the earlier sections of the film, the twenty-four-year-old Mary, playing an eleven- or twelve-year-old girl, acts with real eleven-year-olds and blends in perfectly.)

Unfortunately, the coyness that permeates the film's earlier portions returns at the end. Rather than close with a kiss between Rebecca and the nominal hero, Mary has Rebecca run off, little-girl like, into the sunset; Eugene O'Brien, one of the innocuous, sexless leading men that the great female stars of silents invariably worked with, has to chase her as the scene slowly fades out.

Rebecca of Sunnybrook Farm is nowhere near as good a film as its reputation would indicate, and seems to validate the notion of Mary's limited range, and, indeed, the range of all silent screen ingenues. Yet, even as *Rebecca of Sunnybrook Farm* was being released in September 1917, Mary was engaged in giving one of her most extraordinary screen performances.

——— ———

Mary had come across the novel *Stella Maris* while waiting for a train to Del Mar. She bought the book to read on the way and became fascinated by a character called Unity Blake, an ugly little orphan cockney slavey who lives a miserable life and gets beaten to death, but possesses a wonderful sense of humor without self-pity. Mary felt an immediate kinship with the character, calling her "a little mutt dog."

Essentially, *Stella Maris* tells two parallel stories; there is Stella, an invalid and another one of Mary's poor little rich girls, and there is Unity Blake, a homely servant girl for the alcoholic wife of the man who loves Stella. As Unity, Mary is unrecognizable, her hair darkened and slicked straight back, her mouth a thin, twisted line, her shoulders hunched over in the manner of someone who expects a beating, whether or not she's done anything wrong.

Adolph Zukor arrived on the set one day while Mary was shooting the scene of Unity in the hospital after she has been savagely brutalized by her alcoholic employer. He was, predictably, horrified by the realistically brutal makeup.

As Mary recalled the conversation, Zukor was interested only in seeing that Mary did nothing to deviate from the accepted image that kept the money flowing in.

"Sweetheart honey, what is this? You look awful."

"Well, I'm supposed to look awful."

"Wait till the exhibitors see this . . ."

"But I play another character with curls. You'll like it when you see it. Besides, this character dies."

"She does? When?"

"She dies next week."

"Well, she can't die soon enough."

Stella regains the use of her legs, but is disillusioned by the cruelty and poverty that surround her leisurely life, as well as by the discovery that the man she loves is married.

When Unity realizes that the only thing standing in the way of John Risca's happiness is his alcoholic wife, she shoots her, then kills herself.

On one level, the characters of *Stella Maris* are metaphors in the familiar manner of Victorian novelists like Marie Corelli, but the specificity of Mary's dual performances transform the schematic plot. In one scene, the homely Unity looks at a picture of the glowing Stella, then studies herself in the mirror, her face slowly crumpling in grief at the hopeless gap between the two images. That the same actress plays both parts, and without benefit of anything approaching heavy makeup, is a remarkable testament to a talent that made too few demands on itself.

Stella Maris is Mary's *Broken Blossoms,* her portrayal of a tragic innocent slaughtered by a cruel world. Unity Blake has to die so that Stella might find happiness, and Unity's self-sacrifice was ultimately the same as Mary's: Uncompromising characters would die —or never be born at all—so that the Little Girl with the Curls might live.

———— ————

Some idea of Mary's primary importance to Famous Players-Lasky, and to the industry as a whole, can be gauged by the financial returns of her films. *The Little American,* the unremark-able Beware-the-Hun programmer she dashed off for deMille just after *The Poor Little Rich Girl,* had a negative cost of $166,949, including Mary's salary of $86,666.66. It had a worldwide gross of $446,236.88, meaning that net profits were in the vicinity of $130,000–$150,000.

Taking that as an average profit on a Pickford picture, and multiplying by six (the number of films she appeared in during 1917), it is clear that Famous Players-Lasky was netting close to a million dollars a year off Mary's pictures alone. When you factor in that those pictures were the locomotive pulling the train of the less commercially potent Famous Players releases, it becomes clear that Mary was worth whatever she happened to cost.

By 1917, though, Zukor was less concerned about Mary's next round of salary negotiations than he was about Mary's private life destroying her public image. For Mary was having an affair; worse, Mary was obviously in love.

He was a small man in an era of small men. John Gilbert was about five feet nine inches tall, John Barrymore was a little over five feet eight inches, but Douglas Fairbanks was only about five feet seven inches. People who did not know Douglas were invariably sur-prised at his modest height, for on the screen, he looked to be about six feet tall. His compact size, combined with his habit of taking regular nude sunbaths to keep him very dark, led one wag to claim that, hollowed out, he would have come in handy as a golf bag.

He did rather witty imitations, a special favorite being the for-mer Sam Goldfish, now Sam Goldwyn, which the actor keyed around barging in and out of doors while screaming in a high-pitched, Hungarian-accented gabble. A radiant extrovert most of the time— "At a party, when he left the room, there was no one left," said Mary—he was also capable of the blackest depressions.

For most of his life, he was a serious teetotaler and authorized a long series of Boy-Scoutish books under his name. Yet, he was not above a casual, extramarital dalliance from time to time.

Always mercurial, he was the sort of man who, his son noted in 1930, "never reads a long book through. When he is unprepared to answer a question he evades it in a breezy manner . . . He is bored with flatterers but loves flattery . . . He is a man of great ego but little conceit . . . He cannot endure being crossed and it is hard for him to forgive a direct or personal slight. He can never quite concentrate on other people's troubles, although he is sincerely sorry for them and always ready with consolation . . . he is a mild authority on almost everything . . . he is a series of masks . . ."

Over fifty years later, his son's reading of the father had changed only in wording. "[He had] such a persuasive gift of projecting his ideal self-portrait that he came to believe in it himself," wrote his son. "He designed the living of his life, almost from the start, coloring it as he went along. He did it so successfully that his best friends and biographers were seldom able to see him accurately."

In short, Douglas Fairbanks was an actor.

He had been born Douglas Elton Ulman in Denver in May 1883. His Jewish father, an alcoholic, abandoned the family when Douglas was six, which helped make him a devoted Mama's Boy. A natural performer, something of a ham, he took the name he would make famous from his mother's first husband who had died. By the time he went out on tour for two years with the noted Shakespearean Frederick Warde, he was known as Douglas Fairbanks. After the usual amounts of hills and valleys—one valley was so low that Douglas quit acting to become a Wall Street broker—by 1906 he was under contract to producer William A. Brady as a light leading man, albeit an increasingly successful one.

Douglas—for that was how she always referred to him—and Mary met in the fall of 1914 at a Sunday party at the Tarrytown home of Elsie Janis, a musical comedy star on Broadway. Janis had made a tentative venture into the movies and had used Owen Moore, whom she regarded as handsome but lazy, as her leading man. When he arrived in Hollywood, Moore confessed to Janis that he and Mary had not been getting along and he was "on the loose." In her autobiography, Janis wrote, with remarkable candor, that, while "there was no doubt about his devotion to Mary . . . we had a lot of love scenes in the picture and when I saw Owen I wrote in a few more!"

Moore and Janis went on to make two more pictures together, when Mary appeared without warning one day on the set to find Moore holding Janis's hand. "Mary and I often laugh over it now, but at the moment it was a situation not in my scenario," wrote Janis.

At the time of their initial meeting, Douglas had just agreed to appear in films for Triangle. Mary was politely encouraging, while his wife, Beth Fairbanks, was sure that her husband would triumph because everything Douglas did was wonderful. Janis, who had been nursing something of a lech for Douglas, invited him to go for a walk, only to have everyone else think that it was a wonderful idea as well.

With Janis and Fairbanks in the lead, and Mary, wearing white Russian boots, bringing up the rear with Owen, the procession took off. Across the Pocantico River, up a rocky hill, Janis led the troupe, hoping that Mary would drop back and give her a few moments alone with Fairbanks. Unhappily, Fairbanks followed Janis, Mary followed Fairbanks and Owen followed Mary. By the time they got back to Janis's house, Mary's boots were ruined, but Mr. Fairbanks and Miss Pickford had become Douglas and Mary.

It was clear to Mary that Fairbanks was interested in her. Mary was amused and slightly attracted, but that was all. The nascent relationship may have been complicated by the fact that Mary had previously seen Douglas on stage and had been resolutely unimpressed.

They did not meet again for another year, until October 1915. Douglas' first film *The Lamb*, had opened the month before. Mary was then living at the Knickerbocker Hotel, while Douglas, Beth and Douglas Jr. were living at the Algonquin. Frank Case, the proprietor of the Algonquin, threw a party. Although Douglas was there with his wife Beth, he nevertheless paid serious court to "dear Mary." "Do you know who are the two outstanding artists in pantomime?" he said. "You and Charlie Chaplin. You do less apparent acting than anyone else I know, and because of that you express more."

Douglas spent most of the evening dancing with Mary, while Beth, a pleasant, plumpish *hausfrau,* albeit a *hausfrau* with a rich father, was thrilled to be in the same room with such a glowing female star and didn't mind at all. Mary, insecure to begin with and accustomed to the churlish criticism from Owen that is *de rigeur* for alcoholics, lit up at Douglas's fulsome praise. "I had been living in half-shadows," she wrote, "and now this light was cast on me, this sunlight of Douglas's approval."

A few days later, Fairbanks visited his mother, Ella, and told her he was in love with Mary Pickford and wanted to bring her and Charlotte over to meet Ella.

Some time later, Mary and Charlotte visited Ella's apartment, with Ella afterward warning Douglas that "everyone must be held responsible for his actions . . . Only you and Mary can decide . . . but be careful. Sometimes we pay dearly for the unhappiness of others."

Spurred on by his passion, Fairbanks took the prideful, arrogant, dangerous step of bringing Mary to his family's hotel suite so she could meet his young son, Douglas Jr.

Although Mary was "apprehensive," she was also a skilled actress and carried it off smoothly. "Are those your toys?" she asked the six-year-old Douglas Jr. "I nodded," he remembered. Mary smiled. "May I play with them, too?" she said. Douglas Jr. then recalled that "To my delight, she knelt down to the floor and joined me. Mary had made another conquest."

And, quite obviously, so had Douglas. In a daily newspaper column that Frances Marion was ghosting for Mary in 1916, she made public her rapt fascination with this leaping, mercurial, profoundly original personality. "No one has ever had or could have had just such a smile as Douglas Fairbanks," she dictated in July of that year. She recalled the meeting at Elsie Janis's house and said coquettishly that "the only reason he asked us [to go for a walk] was because he knew we had qualms about ruining our footwear."

She finished the column by urging her readers to give his movies a try. "I know after you have seen him once you will watch and wait for him just as we of the profession do when we really expect a merry evening." Overall, the column is little short of a mash note.

At the end of 1916, Douglas's mother Ella died suddenly. Mother and son had been estranged because of tension between Ella and Beth, and Douglas's anguish at the lack of closure with his only parent must have been considerable. Some days after the funeral, Douglas and Mary were driving through Central Park when Douglas, who had maintained a steely self-control, began to cry uncontrollably. As she comforted him, Mary noticed that the dashboard clock in the car had stopped at the hour of Ella's death. Mary and Douglas took this as a sign from beyond, a justification and sanctification of their growing love for each other. In years to come, whenever their love needed to be stressed to one another, either verbally or in letters or telegrams, they would say "by the clock."

Mary went to Los Angeles in February 1917, staying there for a full year. She made six pictures in that year, working very fast indeed; she had precisely one week off between finishing *Amarilly of Clothes-Line Alley* and starting *M'Liss*. For the most part, however, the pictures could just as easily have been made in the East; the move had been made to accommodate Mary's relationship with Douglas. Years later, on their honeymoon, Mary hinted at the difficulties of this period when she told Frances Marion, "You can't imagine the luxury of a comfortable bed after the hurly-burly of the couch."

According to Marion, Douglas's passion worked a remarkable transformation in Mary. "You never thought of Mary as being sexy until Doug," Marion said. "He was so physical. Other actors looked sexy, like Owen Moore, but Doug was the only one with that physique and drive to back it up. Another thing, he'd listen to Mary. He treated her like an intelligent person. Any woman goes for that."

The evidence is clear even on the screen. *Amarilly of Clothes-Line Alley* is an unremarkable programmer, albeit one with Mary's only homage to Chaplin. Amarilly, in long shot, with her back to the camera, seems temporarily defeated after getting fired from her job. But then, in long shot, back to the camera, she pauses, throws her shoulders back and moves briskly off into the horizon, full of new, never-say-die resolve in precisely the manner that Chaplin had already patented. What makes the film interesting is the profusion of undiffused, razor-sharp, unself-conscious close-ups of Mary that show her to be absolutely radiant with love.

By the middle of 1917, Mary and Doug were having regular trysts in a little house in Franklin Canyon that Fairbanks's brother Robert had rented. The affair was common knowledge in the Hollywood community. When Beth would visit the West Coast, a place she frankly disliked, she would often spend time with her friend Hedda Hopper, then the bored young actress wife of De-Wolf Hopper.

Once, Beth insisted on going for a walk with Hedda, who lived near the trysting place. "Beth was curious about it; the place was so beautifully kept," Hopper remembered. "One day my heart nearly stopped when she insisted on peering through a window. After that I saw to it that we walked in a different canyon. I told her the other one was full of rattlesnakes."

It was just a short while later, after she was back East, that Beth began to grow suspicious and suspected something was up, if not the someone with whom it was up. On August 3, 1917, Douglas wired his wife from Hollywood: TERRIBLY IIOT TRIP. SORRY I DID NOT TELL YOU MORE THAT I LOVE YOU BEFORE I LEFT. CHEER UP DEAR . . .

By the latter part of the year, "I couldn't hold a conversation with Mary but that Fairbanks interrupted it with a call," remembered Adolph Zukor. At the studio, a young property man named Howard Hawks had to fetch Mary so many times from bungalow *tête-à-têtes* with Douglas that it became virtually a part of his job description.

Mary still felt constrained to act as if Doug was just a friend, which undoubtedly made for some interesting sessions at home with Charlotte, for Mary was already attempting to mediate between her lover and her mother.

"She [Mary] did not light up at the sight of him," remembered Howard Ralston, who was acting in some of Mary's films when Douglas was around. "You couldn't tell if she was in love with him or just liked him." Part of this was undoubtedly her innate reserve, but part of it was also the fact that her mother was standing by glowering, inwardly furious that her talented daughter, the family meal ticket, seemed perfectly willing to risk throwing her career away for another actor . . . again! To Charlotte, Mary's short-sightedness was maddening; didn't she remember what had happened the last time she had gone against her mother's wishes?

"In New York, they sometimes donned motorist's linen dusters and goggles and drove about, believing themselves disguised," wrote Adolph Zukor. "It was the sort of thing that appealed especially to Doug's romanticism." Chaplin agreed with Zukor's assessment of the man he called his "best friend"; the comedian recalled staying overnight at Douglas's house, only to be awakened at three in the morning by a Hawaiian orchestra serenading Mary through the mist from the Pacific.

Nevertheless, Douglas was still afraid to confront his wife and reacted to her suspicions with the desperate hypocrisy of a guilty husband. YOU HAVE MISJUDGED ME TERRIBLY, he wired her on October 9. THERE NEVER WAS ANYTHING WRONG. WILL FINISH PICTURE AND LEAVE FRIDAY FOR EAST. CAN YOU MEET ME IN CHICAGO. WANT TO SEE YOU ALONE. AM WORRIED ABOUT YOUR CONDITION . . .

Although a woman whose career was as important to her as Mary's must have been terrified at the possible repercussions, she chose to continue the affair. For three long years, she and Fairbanks continued their relationship under what they thought was deep cover. "They both acted like frightened rabbits about it," wrote Chaplin in his autobiography. With the characteristically blunt sexual candor of the cockney, Chaplin advised them not to marry, but to live together and get it out of their systems. They did not agree.

After more than a year of sleeping with each other, the affair had failed to burn itself out; if anything, they only wanted each other more. In 1918, besotted with passion, Mary called on her reliable friend Frances Marion, who brought along Adela Rogers, St. Johns. "If I get a divorce and marry Douglas," she asked her friends, "will anyone ever go to see my pictures again?"

The women conferred; the consensus was that if the procedure was carefully handled, the chances were better than even.

Better than even?

One can practically hear Mary's stomach constricting in panic. The first decision she had made without Charlotte was her marriage to Owen, and that had been an unmitigated disaster. Douglas would be the second decision. All that she and her family had they owed to Mary's career and her public; now she was in a position where, if she was going to be true to herself, her chances of maintaining all that she had slaved for were only a little better than even. And in addition, she knew full well what a pair of divorces would mean to her devoutly Catholic mother.

Charlotte was panicked. According to a 1934 breach of contract lawsuit against Mary filed by a professional middleman named Edward Hemmer, Charlotte retained Hemmer and asked him to talk to Owen and have him "refrain from giving Mary a divorce" until Mary "should have had an opportunity to overcome her infatuation for Fairbanks."

It sounds like something Charlotte might do. What is certain is that there was never much rapport between Charlotte and Douglas. Although Douglas was certainly preferable to Owen—even if he was half-Jewish—and he obviously made Mary happy, they were both married to other people and Douglas's ardent pursuit had put the livelihood of the Pickford clan in jeopardy. For that, Charlotte would never forgive Douglas. From the testimony of Douglas Fairbanks Jr. and Buddy Rogers, Mary's last husband, about the most that would ever be able to be said for the relationship between Charlotte and Douglas was that it was one of wary mutual tolerance.

The Third Liberty Loan campaign was scheduled to begin on April 6, 1918, and the most prominent movie stars had been enlisted to sell the war bonds. Mary's previous contribution to the tidal wave of patriotism that marked the outbreak of World War I had been her support of the Lasky Home Guard, a group made up of studio employees who drilled with prop rifles and costumes donated by the studio.

"Mary . . . presented them with their colors," remembered Agnes de Mille, "and I remember Mrs. Pickford saying she'd had it all made out of silk, the finest silk, and all the stars were hand embroidered. Mary had a special couturier's outfit of patriotic grey, with a little veil down the back. She looked splendid." It wasn't all playacting, however, for the unit did serve overseas and suffer casualties.

Mary threw herself into the Liberty Loan drive; William S. Hart was assigned to tour the west, Douglas the midwest, Chaplin the south and Mary the northeast. Although Douglas was supposed to go on to Baltimore, he had his schedule changed so he and Mary could be together in New York. In Washington, they stayed at the New Willard Hotel in adjoining suites. Charlotte, of course, was beside herself.

In New York, Mary and Douglas had a fine opportunity to do their civic duty and at the same time enjoy the titillation of trysting right under the noses of the press, their fans, and Beth Fairbanks. Although Beth and Douglas Jr. were staying at the Algonquin, Douglas couldn't bring himself to visit them. It was then that whatever suspicions Beth had crystallized. She went to the newspapers.

"He told me that he and the woman love each other," she said on April 11, 1918. "They felt that theirs was the one big love of their lives and that nothing mattered in comparison." To another reporter, Beth declared that "When he reached the point where his wife and son no longer mattered in comparison, then I knew there was only one thing to be done—that he must go his way while I went mine."

The report went on to say that "Fairbanks came to New York a few days ago with Charlie Chaplin and Miss Mary Pickford to help in the Liberty Bond campaign," then spelled it all out with "Miss Pickford declared that if Mr. and Mrs. Fairbanks had separated it concerned no one but themselves." The accompanying headline reiterated what the story was hinting at: "Mary Pickford Abjuring Worry Over Domestic Row of the Fairbanks Family."

In New York, from her suite at the Plaza, Mary issued a bald-faced lie: "I have not the remotest idea that my name has been brought into any difference between any man and his wife."

Beth leaped on the statement. "I am sorry the woman who has caused all this unhappiness in our home is not willing to acknowledge to the world, as she has acknowledged to her friends and her family, her love for Mr. Fairbanks."

Douglas saw the stories and panicked. He stupidly told reporters that reports of marital difficulties were the result of German propaganda. Beth shot back "It is much to have a husband with a thorough-going sense of humor . . . His 'German propaganda' reply . . . was not quite playing the game. I did not speak until matters had passed the point of endurance. I am ready to prove every assertion I have made . . .

"If no statement is made within the next few days either by the woman I can name as the party responsible for my separation from my husband, or by my husband, I shall verify my own statements by proofs."

Owen Moore helpfully gave out a statement saying that he sympathized with Beth. Beyond the genteel facade, the cuck-olded, alcoholic Moore began threatening to kill Fairbanks. At one point, Douglas met Allan Dwan on a train. "I had to get out of Los Angeles for a while," he told Dwan. "Your friend Owen Moore says he's going to shoot me, if he's sober enough to point the gun." Concurrently with Douglas's escalating marital disaster, Mary's contract with Famous Players-Lasky had expired. *Stella Maris* had been released in January, but after two more efforts with Mickey Neilan, the rest of the year's output—*How Could You Jean, Johanna Enlists* and *Captain Kidd, Jr.*—had all been directed by the ill-fated William Desmond Taylor, whom Mary described as "a very charming man who directed me in three very bad pictures."

In addition, Artcraft, the production company Zukor had formed to make Mary's pictures, had not worked out to her satis-faction; good pictures like *Rebecca of Sunnybrook Farm* had done only marginally more business than bad pictures like *Romance of the Redwoods* (Mary remembered only a $20,000 difference in their world gross). It was obvious to her that, one way or another, Zukor's sales force was still block-booking her pictures. It seemed to Mary as though the association had reached the point of dimin-ishing returns. Mary expediently blamed others for her failures, this time saying that "I was being very obedient to Lasky and Zukor and I was really slipping. *How Could You Jean* should have been called *How Could You Mary?*"

Mary leaves unanswered the basic question of why she should suddenly have turned passive after nearly five years of hammer-and-tongs battle; it would seem obvious that her attention had been seriously distracted by the affair with Douglas.

At any rate, she determined to regain the ground she felt she'd lost. Her mother went to New York and came back with the rights to *Pollyanna* and *Daddy Long-Legs*. This time, Mary wanted com-plete control, with Zukor and company to act only as a releasing organization. Zukor balked, saying that there had to be *some* su-pervision. And then there was the question of money. Zukor's offer was $225,000 a picture and a share of the profits, comparable to the offer of the newly organized First National exhibitor's circuit except for one, vital clause: the newspapers reported that First National was offering Mary a $250,000 guarantee, a share of the profits and what later filmmakers would call "final cut," i.e. complete creative control.

Finally, Mary and Zukor reached a point at which no accommodation was possible. It was, simply, a point of principle between two disparate mentalities: Zukor's were the principles of the businessman/manager, who demands input as to how his money is spent and who could never really believe that any actor knew more than he did. (When he was a hundred years old, Zukor referred to the turbulent period when stars, led by Mary, began to gain power: "It wasn't a healthy situation," was his final, unalterable opinion.)

Mary's principles were those of the commercial artist, determined to make better pictures that were worthy of her own ambitions and her respect for her audience.

On November 9, 1918, Mary, or rather, "Gladys Mary Moore, known as Mary Pickford," signed the contract with First National, and went back to the Knickerbocker Hotel to call Zukor. "Mr. Zukor, I've done it," she said. There was a long silence, broken finally by Zukor's quiet voice saying, "God bless you, Sweetheart honey." Mary started to cry and broke off the conversation.

After thirty-four films, Mary and Zukor parted on good terms. Mary remembered her years with Zukor as "the happiest years of my screen life." Beyond the undoubted sentimentality, each was probably glad that they no longer had to go through their grueling annual negotiations. In any case, there was by no means a universal feeling that Mary would thrive away from the Paramount story and production apparatus. "Let her go," Adolph Zukor had been advised. "It'll serve two purposes: It'll cure her swelled head and it'll ruin First National."

For two people who were at loggerheads so often, they remained close, at least partially because of Mary's friendship with Zukor's daughter Mildred. Throughout the '20s, whenever Mary was in New York, she would often drive up to Zukor's Mountainview farm near Nyack, nearly one hundred acres of woods and ravines, where she would charm Zukor grandchildren like Arthur Loew Jr. and Stewart Stern (who grew up to be the writer of, among other screenplays, *Rebel Without a Cause* and *Rachel, Rachel*).

The quiet little Hungarian did not pause to grieve about losing Mary, nor did her loss impel him to forsake the star system, as he had once vowed it would. Instead he went out and signed the

Gladys Smith, circa 1896, looking notably stern in spite of the
photographer's pleadings.

Gladys Smith in "The Fatal
Wedding," 1903.

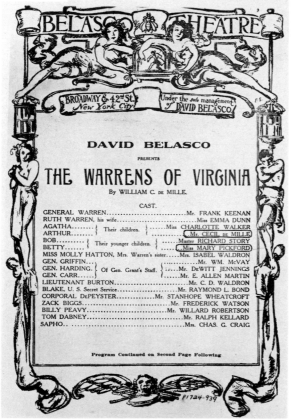

BELASCO THEATRE

BROADWAY & 42nd St.
New York City

Under the sole management
of DAVID BELASCO

DAVID BELASCO

PRESENTS

THE WARRENS OF VIRGINIA

By WILLIAM C. DE MILLE.

CAST.

GENERAL WARREN	Mr. FRANK KEENAN
RUTH WARREN, his wife	Miss EMMA DUNN
AGATHA	Their children.	Miss CHARLOTTE WALKER
ARTHUR	Mr. CECIL DE MILLE
BOB	Their younger children.	Master RICHARD STORY
BETTY	Miss MARY PICKFORD
MISS MOLLY HATTON, Mrs. Warren's sister	Mrs. ISABEL WALDRON
GEN. GRIFFIN	Mr. WM. McVAY
GEN. HARDING	Of Gen. Grant's Staff.	Mr. DeWITT JENNINGS
GEN. CARR	Mr. E. ALLEN MARTIN
LIEUTENANT BURTON	Mr. C. D. WALDRON
BLAKE, U. S. Secret Service	Mr. RAYMOND L. BOND
CORPORAL DePEYSTER	Mr. STANHOPE WHEATCROFT
ZACK BIGGS	Mr. FREDERICK WATSON
BILLY PEAVY	Mr. WILLARD ROBERTSON
TOM DABNEY	Mr. RALPH KELLARD
SAPHO	Mrs. CHAS. G. CRAIG

Program Continued on Second Page Following

P1724-939

The playbill for "The Warrens of Virginia," which
opened in New York on
December 3, 1907.

David Belasco was already
creating the proper context
for the career of his protege
when this photograph was
taken in 1913.

Mary happy, Mary sad. The woman the world was falling in love with in 1914.

Douglas Fairbanks Sr. with his son in 1914.

A plumpish Mary in one of her better films for Zukor (1914).

The Famous Players-Lasky brain trust in 1916. From left, Jesse
Lasky, Adolph Zukor, Sam Goldfish (later Goldwyn), C.B.
DeMille and Al Kaufman.

Maurice Tourneur (left) prepares Mary for a close-up in "Poor Little
Rich Girl," (1917), with John Van Der Broek at the camera.

Mary gagging it up with Marshall Neilan on location. *(Robert S. Birchard Collection)*

A scene from the Tourneur film, one of her best pictures.

Mary with her pal and frequent scenarist Frances Marion. *(Robert S. Birchard Collection)*

America's Sweetheart—1917.

Mary and Charlotte in Hollywood, 1918.

Mary with her beloved niece Gwynne.

In "Daddy Long-Legs,"
(1919) Mary played an un-
happy orphan who was
not eager to spread the
misery around.

Mary with Albert Austin in
the superb "Suds," (1920).

Mary in "Pollyanna" (1920) with Katherine Griffith.

The wedding party at Pickfair. From left, Charlie Chaplin,
Edward Knoblock, Marjorie Daw, Robert Fairbanks,
Jack Pickford, Charlotte Pickford, Mary and Douglas,
Mrs. Robert Fairbanks and Benny Zeidman.

Mary in the dress in which
she married Douglas.
Photograph by Baron de
Meyer.

The Mary Pickford the public never saw: pensive, womanly. This was also the Mary Pickford she didn't want the public to see.

Another shot of Mary the public never saw. In her handwriting on the back is the notation "n.g." for "no good."

Mary as "Little Lord Fauntleroy," (1921) the best of her costume pictures.

While Charles Rosher cranks the camera, co-directors Alfred E. Green and Jack Pickford (still in mourning for Olive Thomas) guide Mary through a close-up on "Through the Back Door" (1921).

1922: Douglas and Mary posing by their newly-christened studio on the corner of Santa Monica and Formosa in Hollyood.

Charlotte Pickford projecting her particular brand of warmth and charm towards Ernst Lubitsch as he signs his contract for "Rosita." *(Robert S. Birchard Collection)*

Ernst Lubitsch directing "Rosita," (1923).

A continuing feature of Mary's films was her insistence on the finest in production values and lighting. Here, a scene from "Rosita," (1923), design by Svend Gade, lighting by Charles Rosher.

Lottie (far left) and Mary receive a visit from Lottie's daughter Gwynne and Charlotte on the set of "Dorothy Vernon of Haddon Hall."

Quintessential Pickford, a curly-haired member of the underclass. A portrait by James Abbé on the set of the second "Tess of the Storm Country" (1922).

sixteen-year-old Mary Miles Minter, whom he hoped to groom into a reasonable facsimile of Mary Pickford. As it happened, Mary Miles Minter was also a strong-willed little woman with a ferocious stage mother. Minter's career proceeded at a reasonable, if unspectacular pace, with films like 1920's *A Cumberland Romance,* which reveals the Pickford imitator to have the same long, ash-blonde hair, but with sharper features and a more knowing, frankly sexual appeal. In the few Minter pictures that have survived, it can be seen that she lacked the easy intimacy with the camera that Mary possessed, relied far too much on stock gestures, was more of a passive "poser" than a real actress in front of a camera, and, in fact, didn't bring much to the party at all.

The difference between the two actresses is obvious in the plot development of *A Cumberland Romance,* in which Minter plays a sharpshooting little hillbilly who falls in love with an "outsider." At their wedding, his mother and sister are appalled at their boy marrying such poor white trash. Had *A Cumberland Romance* been a Pickford picture, her fiancé's relatives would have clearly seen and been impressed by the Pickford beauty, gentility and, for lack of a better word, class. Nor would it have been mere scenario shifting, but a valid difference between Mary's more refined appeal and Minter's personality as revealed by the camera.

When Minter's career was derailed by scandal, Zukor bought out her contract for $350,000, said good-bye to innocent blondes, and began concentrating on brunettes like Gloria Swanson and Pola Negri, whose more sardonic, knowing personalities wouldn't leave them so vulnerable to every wafting breeze of scandal.

Years later, when Zukor and Mary ran into each other in New York, Zukor pointed to the Paramount Building on Times Square that had been built in 1926. "Mary, darling," he said, "you built that building." Zukor was not a man given to hyperbole; it was true and they both knew it.

Chapter Six

"I spent my honeymoon on a balcony waving to crowds."

—*Mary Pickford Fairbanks*

ARY'S contract with First National mandated three pictures be delivered within nine months, beginning December 1, 1918. The pictures were "to be of the same high class as to photography, acting and direction as the photoplays Mary Pickford has appeared in during the past two years, and to unfold an entertaining story, and to consist of between four thousand and six thousand lineal feet long . . ." The films were to be jointly copyrighted by Mary and First National, but at the end of the five- or six-year distribution period (depending on the territory) both the films and their copyrights were to revert to Mary.

For making the three pictures called for under the deal (there was an option for three more, but the option was at Mary's discretion and was destined to go unexercised), First National agreed to pay Mary $750,000, with a $150,000 advance. First National sweetened the deal slightly when it agreed to pay any costs of story purchases over $20,000 per picture.

Mostly, however, the deal was simplicity itself, and far more basic than Mary's last contract with Zukor. Out of Mary's allocation of $250,000 per picture, she had to pay her own production costs. Since Mary's pictures of this period, exclusive of her own salary, usually cost between $50,000 and $75,000 apiece, she was making about $200,000 per picture.

Nearly as important as the issue of compensation was Clause *E* under Advertising: "The corporation agrees that all leases of . . . said photoplays shall be made separate and apart from the leases or sales of other motion pictures or photoplays." Mary might as well have called it "The Zukor clause."

There was one noticeable omission: In return for what amounted to complete control over each film, from story selection to final cut, and the assurance that her films would be independently brokered to the market, Mary gave up any percentage agreement. Although publicity claimed otherwise, the actual contract, as preserved in the Warner Brothers Archives, noticeably omits any such arrangement. In return for ultimate ownership of the product, Mary was back to working for a straight salary. Like Chaplin, who had signed a very similar deal with First National rather than take a contract extension with Mutual that would actually have put more money in his pocket, Mary had opted for less money in exchange for greater control, at least partially, one suspects, because she needed to get away from Papa Zukor.

At the same time, in November 1918, Mary and Charlotte formally set up the Mary Pickford Company. It was a 50-50 deal, with Mary having charge of the actual making of the pictures and Charlotte "having charge of all matters pertaining to the business of the co-partnership and all matters pertaining to the finances and investments." All productions of the company would be copyrighted either by Mary personally, or by her company. The contracts were signed "Gladys Mary Moore, known as Mary Pickford" and "Charlotte Smith, known as Charlotte Pickford."

Mary now owned her own company—which was renting space at the Brunton studios—hired her own directors, and chose her own stories and supporting casts. Yet her sense of enslavement to the public had only strengthened. She told Karl Kitchen that "I'd like to appear in *real* plays—I'd much rather have a . . . play by D'Annunzio or Anatole France, but I have to consider my audiences."

In the frantic year of 1919, Mary negotiated the formation of United Artists, arranged her divorce from a grudging, recalcitrant Owen Moore, continued the delicate deceit of her affair with

Douglas, and made three pictures for First National. It is doubtful that she spent much time at her home at 56 Fremont Place in the Wilshire district, but her concentration seemed to be unhindered. *Daddy Long-Legs,* the first film under the First National contract, is one of the finest pictures she ever made.

Under the more delicate than usual direction of Marshall Neilan, Mary creates the entire emotional arc of a life. When the film opens, she is being named Jerusha (Judy for short), the name being picked off a tombstone. Jerusha is an orphan, a cheerfully tough, slightly bratty kid of thirteen or fourteen with the gumption to fight back in the drab, repressed, benighted world of the orphanage. When the orphanage trustees come to inspect the place, Jerusha dresses up and tries a spit curl on her forehead. Met with a grumpy reaction, she says, "I was only trying to make a depression on someone."

When one of the other little girls is dying, Jerusha steals a doll from a visiting (rich) brat and rushes it to the dying girl with a dozen or so people in hot pursuit. "Love it quick," she tells the little girl, "you ain't going to have it long." She is punished for her temerity by having her hand forced onto a hot stove.

Four or five years later, a kind trustee whom she has never met sends Jerusha to college. She writes him once a month; because the only reference point she has is his shadow that she once saw through a door, she always addresses him as "Daddy Long-Legs." While in college, she writes a novel that goes unpublished, then tries a book about her experiences at the orphanage, about the damage that "charity without kindness" can do to the human spirit. The book is a success.

Nevertheless, Jerusha is still a woman alone. She asks Daddy Long-Legs to attend her college graduation, but no one comes. In one shot, of Jerusha alone on a hill under a tree while below her classmates and their families celebrate, Neilan creates an image of isolation worthy of Chaplin.

The plot winds up most satisfactorily; Jerusha finds that an older suitor is really her Daddy Long-Legs, while an empty-headed society swell (played by Neilan himself) takes his rejection lightly because "Where there's no sense there's no feeling."

Daddy Long-Legs is a peculiarly modern movie in that it's not so much a blunt collection of dramatic highlights bundled together to form a narrative, as so many early silent films are, but a carefully structured plot with gradually growing, altering characterizations. (In essence, Agnes Johnson's script splices *Oliver Twist* and *David Copperfield* together and substitutes a female lead, but the film is so well-done that its hodgepodge nature is not immediately apparent.)

Although it's only seven reels long, *Daddy Long-Legs* has a spacious narrative and a sense of life as it's really lived. Mary's performance—natural, unforced, relaxed, almost literally glowing —scarcely seems to be acting at all. She effortlessly creates the unforced evolution of a child into a woman, and gives the audience the heartening emotional satisfaction of seeing an orphan's dreams realized.

———— ————

Realizing that Douglas's relationship with Mary was a *fait accompli,* Beth Fairbanks accepted the inevitable with a winning, if rare, sense of sportsmanship. "Mary is a great and tender woman, and neither of them could help falling in love," she told her son. "She has always loved and been kind to you, so you must always be sweet and love her as well." Douglas Fairbanks Jr. always would. Douglas's divorce was granted in New Rochelle on November 30, 1919; named as correspondent was "an unknown woman."

When reporters pressed for Douglas's reaction, his brother Robert said "How could he say anything about the divorce? Why, he hardly knows anything about it himself." The price for Beth's gentle equanimity was every dime her husband had: $600,000 (Doug Jr.'s memory was of $500,000) in cash and securities.

Now, clearly, the ball was in Mary's court, but she hesitated. Against her basically cautious temperament was the fact that Douglas was pressing hard. "Dad wanted all of Mary," wrote his son, "herself and her talent and her fame and her exclusive devotion. And he longed to be able to display their union to the world like a double trophy."

In Chicago, for an appearance promoting *Pollyanna,* Mary received a call from Douglas. Frances Marion, who was in the room, heard Mary utter a little cry. "Douglas is going away," she cried. "He says he's waited long enough for me to decide about my divorce. It's now or never, this very night, or he'll be on his way tomorrow and I'll never see him again."

Charlotte again tried to talk her daughter out of marriage to Douglas. "Remember, Mary, you're America's Sweetheart," she told her. "I only want to be one man's sweetheart," Mary screamed, "and I'm not going to let him go!" Douglas' ultimatum worked; Mary called him and told him she would divorce Owen.

Owen Moore finally agreed to appear at, ironically, Douglas

County, Nevada, at the same time as Mary, so that the divorce papers could be served with dispatch. Robert Fairbanks and Frances Marion, Mary's best friend, both remembered the money paid to Moore for his cooperation and silence as being $100,000. In light of what Owen knew Mary's income to be, $100,000 sounds too low.

With the deal finally cut, and arrangements with Moore made to everybody's satisfaction, Mary entrained for Minden, Nevada, where court was convened on Monday, March 1, 1920; the next day, Mary testified for about a half hour. By sundown, she was again a single woman. It was all very simple.

Mary's divorce testimony is a fairly consistent portrayal of male brutishness and alcoholism, with Owen as Simon Legree and Mary as Little Eva. According to Mary, Owen got drunk within a day or two of their wedding night and, for the most part, stayed that way. After the lawyer asked a few questions to establish the chronology of this matrimonial disaster and brought the story up to 1912, Mary couldn't allow her emotions to be pent up any longer.

"Well, if I may be permitted to tell the court, from the time of my marriage, I was forced to support myself, my mother, my brother and sister, and I was forced to work and my husband said that a wife was a luxury and that he did not intend buying my clothes and we had been in Chicago, and it was necessary for me to seek employment with a company and that company was going west to California and I asked my husband to go along, and I offered to pay his fare but he said that he wanted to stay in New York."

Mary testified that, after a few years of an off-and-on marriage, in 1914 Owen had told her that "I was the cause of his failure in life and that I caused him to drink and [he] was sorry that he ever had a wife." She went on to assert that they had been living together as man and wife as recently as the late summer of 1917—highly improbable—and that she had been writing, telegraphing and sending him presents in an effort to induce him to return to her.

There is no mention of Mary's studious public avoidance of the fact of her marriage, nor is there any mention of her long affair with Douglas Fairbanks. There is, on the other hand, a fair amount of glad-handing perjury.

"State whether or not it is your intention to make this your permanent residence," asked P.A. McCarran, Mary's attorney, later to become a powerful United States senator.

"It is."

"Mrs. Moore, did you by any means know of the coming of your husband into this state?"

"No, sir."

"When did you first learn that he was in this state?"

"My manager told me Mr. Moore was coming to Nevada to look for a coal mine for one of his pictures."

Such enviable coincidences were passed over by the presiding judge, who appears to have been a starstruck Mary Pickford fan. Nevertheless, the judge couldn't restrain himself from asking if she, Mary Pickford, was *actually* going to relocate to Douglas County.

"Well, if I can find a place to suit me I will," was the reply.

"[Do I understand] that you have not come into the State of Nevada for the [sole] purpose of instituting divorce proceedings?"

"No, sir."

"That is absolutely so?"

"Absolutely so."

The divorce petition was granted that same day, March 2, 1920. Two days later, Mary left the state where she had been planning to live. Three weeks later, on Sunday, March 28, Douglas gave a dinner party at his house. Mary arrived with Charlotte, while the other guests included Douglas's brother Robert and his wife; Chaplin; Marjorie Daw, an occasional leading lady and ex-girlfriend of Douglas's, who served as maid of honor; Jack; playwright and friend Edward Knoblock; and Bennie Zeidman, Douglas's press agent.

Most importantly, the Rev. J. Whitcombe Brougher, the pastor of the Temple Baptist Church, was there. The party had been planned for a Sunday night because there would be less possibility of the story leaking to reporters.

The marriage license had been issued to Gladys Mary Smith Moore, twenty-six (Mary shaved a year off her age) and Douglas Elton Fairbanks, thirty-six. Finally, at 10:30, it was time. "I'd like you to read the passage about husbands and wives from St. Paul to the Ephesians," said Douglas, handing his mother's Bible to the pastor.

"Nevertheless let every one of you in particular so love his wife even as himself; and the wife see that she reverence her husband" read Brougher, as he married Douglas and Mary. After the ceremony, Douglas announced that he was giving Mary the new hunting lodge that he had just bought. It was done; now they had to wait and see what the reaction would be.

It was not long in coming, at least not from the direction of Nevada. The attorney general of Nevada took the marriage amiss and seemed to feel that his state had been misled. He filed suit to set aside the divorce decree on the grounds that Mary had not been a *bona fide* resident of the state. His complaint stated that Mary's testimony had been "wrongfully, willfully and fraudulently false, fabricated and untrue." Mary and Douglas ignored the possibility that they would be adjudicated bigamists and sat tight while the suit worked its way through the Nevada courts. In 1922, the Nevada Supreme Court sustained the original divorce.

In later years, Owen Moore seldom entered into Mary's conversation, but when he did, it was clear from her tone that, so far as she was concerned, the marriage belonged to the category of Youthful Indiscretions, with no particular emotional trauma involved. As for Owen Moore, he passed out of Mary's life for the last time. His later career consisted mostly of small parts in important films. For example, he appeared in *San Francisco,* and played the director of Janet Gaynor's screen test in Selznick's *A Star is Born.*

Originally, Douglas and Mary had only planned their honeymoon to encompass a trip to New York, but at the eleventh hour they took off for Europe aboard the S.S. *Lapland,* accompanied by Charlotte, which must have irritated Douglas greatly. Except for the unhappy time spent in Cuba with IMP, Mary had never been outside North America. They arrived in England on Monday, June 21, 1920, for the first leg of the honeymoon that would last four weeks. The first three days of it, in London, went well and truly started what Alexander Woollcott would call "the most exhausting and conspicuous honeymoon in the history of the marriage institution."

Newsreels of their reception in England resemble impromptu shots of a revolution, mobs of clamoring humanity surrounding the honeymooners' cars and trains with an emotive intensity that wouldn't be equalled until the advent of the Beatles forty years later. They are startling images; World War I had left all western civilization with a sense of horror and disillusionment, but the romanticism that remained was largely invested in these two people, as millions willfully forgot Douglas and Mary's rather public adulteries. For the first time, the public, on a large scale, was choosing to believe that actors were what they played on the screen. (The resulting emotional outpourings could never have greeted stage performers because not enough people saw them.) Mary and Douglas were even received by royalty because, also for the first time, the world of commoners had birthed the equivalent of blue-bloods.

"You see, we'd seen their films," Lord Mountbatten told Kevin Brownlow, "and it was the first time people had a chance of seeing and hearing in real life people they had only seen in silent films."

The rival English press lords vied in their approach about how to handle the honeymoon. The Northcliffe journals applauded the "Heroine Worship" and gave the general impression that, in some vague way, international relations were being cemented. Beaverbrook, on the other hand, made dark mutterings about the reception being "arranged" and harrumphed that there were far more important and worthy people in the world than two movie stars.

In London, Douglas and Mary hooked up with Frances Marion and her new husband, Fred Thomson. Mary was happy, but plagued by the constant attention of the masses. "Can't we just go away somewhere, just we four?" she asked rhetorically. "Can't we fly to Holland and have a wonderful quiet time away from everyone else in the world?" Three days in London seemed quite enough.

Douglas tried making arrangements in Holland, but word leaked out and they were met by civic delegations and committees and more cheering throngs. There was no escape. From Holland they went to Switzerland, then to Italy, where Douglas found that he was known as "Lampo" ("Lightning"). On July 4 they were in Coblenz, Germany, where they had their first fight as a married couple. The commander of the occupying American forces gave a dance in their honor and led Mary out to the floor. Douglas was on fire with jealousy, but managed to control it for the evening.

When it was all over, however, he took her back to the house where they were staying and left her at the door while he stormed off . . . alone. When he returned, he apologized and reminded her of a promise he had extracted from her on their wedding night, to avoid "twosing" with anybody else. Up to that point, Mary had not interpreted dancing as "twosing" but from that moment on, she did. "He was not only jealous of any man who looked at Mary," remembered Frances Marion, "he was even jealous of me. He was jealous of her mother! It was so silly; there wasn't any reason for it."

Then, on July 14, came France. All the border guards were engaged in uproarious celebration, and Douglas and Mary, although accustomed to cheering throngs, were startled at the intensity of their reception by the French people. The man in charge recognized them and explained that the celebration wasn't for them but for Bastille Day.

One night they had dinner at the *Tour d'Argent* in Paris and, like everyone else in the restaurant, Mary marveled at the great view of the floodlit Cathedral of Notre Dame. Fairbanks studied the view for a minute, then turned to his wife. "You know, I think I see enough handholds to climb all the way up that right-hand tower." Although Douglas had his gifts, aesthetic appreciation was not among them.

Finally, on July 21, they boarded the *Olympic* at Cherbourg and sailed for home. After the tumultuous throngs of the previous month, they elected to, for the most part, stay in their stateroom, usually coming out only at sundown for a quick half-hour walk around the promenade.

Both Douglas and Mary had alternated between the factory town enclave of Hollywood and blasé New York ever since their careers in the movies had begun; neither had had any real sense of what their stardom really meant beyond the dry confines of their bank accounts. For the first time, their worldwide fame was no longer the abstraction of a check or a bag of fan mail, but *real*. Their honeymoon trip must have made clear to them that they had attained a level of stardom that had never existed before, that Gladys Smith and Douglas Ulman's invention of their lives had succeeded far beyond their ability to control them. The honeymoon trip was something they never forgot; for the rest of the decade, they strove to relive the experience with more European and Asian trips.

It also confirmed that Mary and Douglas's gamble had succeeded. There was no question of recrimination for their divorces. *Photoplay* magazine spoke for the whole world when it printed a full page picture of the beaming, beautiful couple. Underneath was a facsimile *Western Union* telegram, addressed to Mr. and Mrs. Douglas Fairbanks, Honeymoon Lane, Happiness Always. COME HOME, the message on the telegram read, ALL IS FORGIVEN.

Chapter Seven

"Forming United Artists in 1919 was my idea. I brought in
Mr. Griffith and Chaplin. The latter was a mistake."

—*Mary Pickford, 1975*

YEARS later, with the inestimable advantage of hindsight, Mary claimed that she never wanted Charlie Chaplin in United Artists, that inviting him to join was a by-product of his intimate friendship with Douglas. This was almost surely displaced disgruntlement over the deterioration of their friendship. Chaplin's films, although already infrequent, were critical and commercial smashes; he was by far the most famous comedian in the world, and his agreeing to join United Artists was a considerable coup. Griffith, too, was still regarded as the premier director of the screen and one, moreover, for whom Mary still had warm feelings.

They had kept in touch over the years. While in production with *M'Liss*, Mary's leading man, Thomas Meighan, had recommended a book by Thomas Burke called *Limehouse Nights*. Mary read it and liked it, especially a story called "The Chink and the Child," which was full of that fascination with poverty and melodrama that Mary and Griffith had in common, although its tragic ending was too uncompromising for one of Mary's own pictures.

A year later, while Mary was shooting *Daddy Long-Legs* at the old Triangle studio where Griffith was also headquartered, Griffith idly asked if she had any story ideas for him. "I read a great story, but it would take a lot of courage to do it," she told him, directing him to *Limehouse Nights*. Griffith read "The Chink and the Child," liked it, and adapted it into *Broken Blossoms*, his last supremely great picture.

———   ——

Early in 1919, rumors swept through the industry of a forthcoming merger between Famous Players-Lasky and First National. Ironically, First National had been formed as an alternative to Zukor's arrogant hegemony. Mary, Douglas and Chaplin were naturally perturbed, for, if hundreds more theaters and the single most attractive, viable outlet for independent production fell under Zukor's long shadow, it would mean they would be forced to work for whatever terms Zukor deemed appropriate. Equally as important, their long struggle for control over their films would be nullified.

The merger scenario seemed to confirm Chaplin's paranoia about moneymen. First National had been most unsympathetic to his own requests, hadn't they? Suddenly, a variety of vague thoughts and dreams coalesced. As early as the 1918 Liberty Loan drives, Secretary of the Treasury William Gibbs McAdoo had suggested to Douglas that he should consider distributing his own pictures. Later that same year, B.P. Schulberg had, coincidentally, outlined a similar idea to Hiram Abrams, whom Zukor had just purged as president of Paramount. It was Schulberg's memory that the idea was first broached to Chaplin, who thought enough of it to take it to Mary and Douglas.

Sydney Chaplin called a meeting at his house on Tuesday, January 14, 1919. Attending were Chaplin, Douglas, Griffith, William S. Hart, and Charlotte, standing in for Mary, who had the flu. By Wednesday, news of the meeting had become general knowledge throughout Hollywood. That same day, all five people signed articles of agreement to what was initially called the United Artists Association. (Hart would soon drop out.)

The original contract, signed on February 5, 1919, called for each of the principals to buy 1,000 shares of common stock at $100 per share, with the company having the right to require that 20 percent of the total price be paid every thirty days for the first five months to finance start-up costs. In order to guarantee that the new company would have movies to distribute, the shares of each principal were divided into nine blocks and held in escrow; as each film was turned over for distribution, a block of stock was released from escrow to the producer/owner. In other words, the principals would not receive their full complement of shares until they produced the agreed upon number of pictures.

Mary was to deliver three pictures a year for three years, all produced at her own expense. She was to receive 77$1/2$ percent of the gross; of the remainder, 2$1/2$ percent, was to be held by United Artists in escrow to pay any deficits caused by the company's start-up and operating costs. Should United Artists function on a profitable basis, the 2$1/2$ percent was to be given to Mary, making her total remuneration 80 percent of the gross. United Artists was allowed to distribute the pictures for five years, after which the distribution rights reverted to Mary.

In most respects, it is a standard contract for the period, except for an unconcealed idealism:

"WHEREAS, they have heretofore acted together because of a threatened combination of motion picture stars and producers being formed which, in their opinion, would tend to force upon the theatre-going public, mediocre productions and machine-made entertainment and would defeat competition in the motion picture industry; and

"WHEREAS they desire, in furtherance of the artistic welfare of the moving picture industry and to better serve the great and growing interest in motion picture productions, to become associated in the distribution of . . . motion pictures . . ."

The standard provisions come to a sudden stop in Clause *E* of Section Three: "The corporation agrees that all leases or licenses to use . . . copies of said photoplays shall be made separate and apart from the leases or sales of other motion pictures or photoplays, and used in no way to influence the license, lease or sale of other motion pictures or photoplays . . ."

Although this clause prohibiting block-booking is buried in the middle of a twenty page contract, it is the heart of the deal; it is why Mary, Douglas, Chaplin and Griffith were risking their own financial security to embark on an experiment for which there was no precedent. No longer would their films serve as powerful engines powering a string of dreary, second-rate cabooses. Mary, Douglas, Charlie and Griffith felt so strongly about their abilities that they were willing to stand alone, without the financial umbrella of a major studio.

Their feelings about the integrity of their films were not just P.R. In December 1922, just a few years after the formation of United Artists, Douglas would be in court trying to prevent the distribution of bowdlerized re-issues of the early pictures he had made for Triangle. The attorney for the owners of the films said that Douglas had only been an employee, and that the producers had the legal right to change the commodity Douglas had been hired to help produce.

Douglas's position was that his contact with Triangle stated that the pictures were to be supervised by D.W. Griffith and that, should they be re-edited or re-titled by someone else, they would not be the same films and would, therefore, be a violation of his contract.

New York Supreme Court Judge Robert Wagner rejected Douglas's contentions, holding that he had no property rights in his early films. It was no accident that that same year, Mary purchased fifty of her original Biograph shorts to prevent the same thing happening to her.

Douglas's losing battle was a textbook case of why he, Mary, Chaplin and Griffith formed United Artists. Before the company was formed, the three had all been, each in their various ways, artists, but their films had been treated as, and had the legal status of, piecework sewn by craftsmen for hire.

By creating United Artists, they told the whole world that they were going to own and take responsibility for their own movies and were prepared to risk the embarrassment that would come if they failed to live up to their lofty ideals. The pride that Mary felt in finally achieving the independence she had long believed to be her due is clear from the opening frames of her first United Artists releases. Her name over the title is written out, in her own handwriting. By signing her pictures, she was telling the world who was responsible for them.

"The satisfaction was in one word," she said years later. "Freedom. It's a heady wine, and having tasted it, you find it impossible to go back to working for someone else."

Now, truly, they were United Artists.

——— ———

It was vital that Mary do something for her first United Artists release that would get cash flowing into the United Artists coffers. She chose *Pollyanna,* the dramatically obvious but commercially surefire staple about the little girl who's everybody's two-legged ray of sunshine. But before she could begin fulfilling her United Artists contract, she still had an obligation to First National for the last two of the three pictures she had promised to them.

Shooting on *Pollyanna* finally began in September 1919. Under the impersonal direction of the mediocre Paul Powell, filming went smoothly and the picture was released in January 1920. "Miss Pickford . . . has the supreme gift of the artist," wrote Burns Mantle in *Photoplay*, "The gift of compelling your belief in her." Mantle wrote that Mary had produced a film that was "sweet, but not drippy," an appraisal more generous than most modern audiences would be able to muster.

Mary is Pollyanna, the irrepressibly enthusiastic, orphaned daughter of Ozark missionaries, who is sent to a dyspeptic aunt in New England. Pollyanna's "glad game" reflects the belief in the perfectability of man that was prevalent in the earlier Victorian era. Pollyanna's aunt doesn't share the optimism, however. "I'm tired of this glad business, glad, glad, glad," she snarls. "Just for that you stay home."

Like most of Mary's children, Pollyanna desires only to be wanted, to be loved, and there is an effective moment of melodramatic poignancy when Pollyanna, having been crippled by a car, looks at her now grief-stricken aunt and says, "It's good to have you love me, Aunt Polly—I'm really glad I was hurt." But the happy ending—Pollyanna walking again—seems rushed and dramatically ineffective. Overall, Mary had made much better pictures than *Pollyanna* before and would again. She had gauged her public correctly, but personally she found the film "sickening." She would rarely make a picture that made greater profits.

The worldwide gross of *Pollyanna* was an astonishing $1,160,962.45. Mary's contributions to United Artists were off to a roaring start.

With the basic stories being fairly cut-and-dried, much of the creativity on a Pickford production was the province of the art director and the cinematographer. Mary always hired the best talent, as in the case of her cinematographer, Charles Rosher. Born in 1885, Rosher was a peppery, egocentric Englishman who had found his way to America as a cameraman for the Horsley company in 1911. For six years, Rosher worked for Universal and Lasky, until Mary hired him to replace Walter Stradling in 1917. He soon became the highest paid cameraman in the world and provided Mary with photography of a glistening perfection.

Directors came and went, but Rosher stayed with Mary for twelve years; she came to rely greatly on his expertise and devotion. "She was one of the finest characters I ever knew," Rosher told Kevin Brownlow. "She did a lot of her own directing. The director would often just direct the crowd. At the end of a scene, whoever was directing, she would always ask me for my opinion. I often chose the set-ups; I'd get her to play a scene where I could light her favorably."

With Mary's long hair, lighting was especially important, as was the camera angle; Rosher discovered that Mary's left side was her best, that her right side seemed slightly scrunched up by comparison, hence his nickname for her of "Old Monkeyface."

Rosher was not merely a glamour photographer, but a brilliant innovator as well; he faked a particularly convincing auto accident in *Pollyanna* by shooting in reverse. That is, the shot began with Mary in front of the camera holding a child out of the frame. Directly behind her, a car, with the driver half-standing, quickly drove away from her in reverse, with the driver sitting down. At the same time, Mary brought the child back from out of the frame and set it down in front of her. When the film was reversed, it appeared that Mary was tossing the child out of the way of a car that was bearing down on her; the illusion of Pollyanna being run down was well-nigh perfect.

A few years later, with *Little Lord Fauntleroy* Rosher achieved double-exposure effects that remain astonishing for an era without optical printers or computer-operated cameras. In one scene, Mary, as Little Lord Fauntleroy, kisses Mary, as her own mother. Rosher made the shot even more difficult by staging it so that Mary was kissing the far cheek, forcing her to move slightly behind her own image. To achieve the shot, Rosher first photographed Mary as the mother against a black background, then had the image blown up and painted as a silhouette on glass, in effect matteing out the original shot of Mary. The pane was mounted in front of the camera lens, with the entire structure tied down with steel girders so it could not move even a fraction of an inch. The film was then rewound, and Mary, as Fauntleroy, leaned over to kiss a pre-arranged spot of empty air. When the film was developed, the illusion was perfect.

Mary's second United Artists picture had less camera trickery but was considerably riskier and considerably better than *Polly-anna*. Although *Suds* was directed by an uninteresting minor talent named John Francis Dillon, it emerged as one of Mary's best pictures of the '20s, proving that a good director was not always vital on a picture where the primary creative force was the actress/producer.

Suds harkens back to the Neilan-Tourneur era of four years before, as it tells the story of a cockney slavey in a London laundry. The setting, London in the hansom cab era, gave Charles Rosher a chance to capture some lovely, mistily evocative model shots of the London docks.

In *Suds*, Mary seems to be encoring Unity Blake, except in a gentler, more loving vehicle. Certainly, her physical transformation is nearly as complete; hair straight and slicked back, mouth drawn in and twisted, shoulders hunched.

The central relationship of the film is between Suds and a pathetic, broken-down nag called Lavender, both regarded as hopeless outcasts fit only for the glue factory. "Who would love us?" she rhetorically asks Lavender. "Who could?"

The production of *Suds* was one of the few times that Mary's usual kindness interfered with her work. The company needed a spavined, emaciated horse to play Lavender. One was found but he seemed almost too far gone, not comic so much as pathetically unhealthy. The horse's name really was Lavender, and he was quartered on Douglas's side of the studio, where there were stabling facilities.

Feeling sorry for him, Douglas's company began a concerted effort to get him healthy, until, on the first day of production, he looked practically sleek. There was no time to go out and find another horse, so Mary recalled the old theatrical trick of having aging actors slap rouge under their chins so that, under the lights, the rouge gave the effect of a trim jaw and neckline. Ribs were painted on Lavender's no-longer emaciated sides; false hollows were applied over rolls of new-found fat. Production began only a few hours late.

Suds lavishes all her pent-up affection on the horse. At the same time, she develops a mad crush on a customer named Horace whom she imagines to be an incognito prince (played by Albert Austin, Chaplin's longtime foil). She finally works up the courage to confess to him that she's told her co-workers at the laundry that he loves her. When he laughs, Mary responds with an exquisite, bittersweet moment of mime, a delicate, slow little wave of her hand that clearly says that this is no laughing matter. Austin/Horace slowly stops his humiliating roar.

In one particularly charming sequence, the camera irises in on the Pickford curls and ringlets, then slowly opens out to reveal that Suds has placed them, not on her own head, but on Lavender's mane. The film is full of whimsical little in-jokes like that; Suds's fantasy life involves her being a child of royal birth, and her imaginary mother is the only glimpse we get of the traditional Mary Pickford. In another scene, the horses talk amongst themselves, exchanging snobbish, class-oriented remarks they've picked up from their owners.

At the end, Lavender is adopted by a rich lady who takes Suds along as a maid. There, on the rich woman's estate, she discovers that Horace is not a prince, but a groom, and they all, as the saying goes, live happily ever after. It is a perfectly enchanting little movie.

Despite its high quality, *Suds* grossed only $772,155, a quarter million dollars less than *Pollyanna*.

For her next picture, *The Love Light*, Mary made the mistake of allowing Frances Marion, who was to direct, talk her into letting Marion's new husband, Fred Thomson, co-star. "Fred . . . was not a good actor," remembered Stuart Heisler, the film's editor. "There were quite a number of retakes that had to be made. Then there were quite a few places in the picture where I, as a film editor, had to play off somebody else when Fred couldn't do something."

Thomson, a beefy, handsome sort, would later go on to be a successful cowboy star for FBO and Paramount, before dying of tetanus contracted by stepping on a rake in 1928.

Even coping with an inexperienced leading man didn't make a Pickford set unpleasant. While on location in Monterey for ten days, one of the musicians hired to put the actors in the proper mood during filming regularly waded into the ocean to catch mussels. A tasty sauce whipped up by another crew member provided a bountiful lunch and dinner from the sea for the entire crew.

Despite this atmosphere of collegiality, *The Love Light* continued the temporary downward trend of Mary's popularity at the boxoffice, grossing $690,965.

In 1922, Mary remade her 1914 hit *Tess of the Storm Country*, feeling that Edwin S. Porter, the director of the paralytic original, had failed to take full advantage of the material. The original had cost $10,000 and been shot in four weeks. Mary had used some of her own toilet articles to dress a bedroom set, while Famous Players-Lasky had borrowed a Japanese fishing village in Santa Monica. The remake took three times as long to shoot. Mary's company erected an entire village at Chatsworth, and the final cost of the film went over $400,000. One generator alone, used to power the lights for a night shoot, cost three times what the entire original picture had cost. Still, it was worth it; the remake grossed $927,953, more than double its cost.

The film business was changing, and Mary's films began changing too, not always for the better. Religious elements that were always present began to get more prominent play. And the producer-half of Pickford began to exploit the actress-half. She had always said that her image of a customer for a Pickford picture was "a tired businessman who gets home, settles down when his wife says, 'Ben, it's Mary Pickford tonight. Let's take the children.' "

She began to play to this imagined audience. Her mannerisms began to seem calculated; the little "moues," the glances to heaven to ask for divine understanding, all began to verge on mugging.

With the re-make of *Tess,* Mary's films began to show an increased emphasis on production values. In many respects, films like *Little Lord Fauntleroy* (1921) and *Dorothy Vernon of Haddon Hall* (1924) are the same historical romances that Hearst was making for his adored Marion Davies—remote, saga-esque epics top-heavy with architecture and costumes. Mary was undoubtedly falling under the influence of her husband, for Douglas was a firm believer in elaboration.

The difference was that Fairbanks's exuberant personality could animate a ten- or eleven-reel picture; Mary's could not. "She had a good sense of what the public would like about her stuff," remembered Stuart Heisler. "It was [more] a matter of pacing a picture. She liked to let things run a little bit longer than they should."

Early in 1919, Douglas purchased what had previously been a rambling weekend retreat on Benedict Canyon in Beverly Hills. The price was $35,000; almost immediately, he hired Wallace Neff to begin remodeling it as a wedding present for Mary. By the time he was through, the rustic lodge had been transformed into an attractive, surprisingly intimate twenty-two-room Tudor mansion situated on eighteen acres, with a view that went all the way to the ocean. There were frescoed ceilings, parquet floors, beautiful inlaid wood paneling and equally exquisite leaded windows. It was christened Pickfair, although no one ever seemed to know precisely by whom.

This house on a hill became the social center of Hollywood, its invitations among the most coveted in the world. But Pickfair was more than just a ceremonial place, it was also a working household, a conference center for filmmakers. Here, Mary, Douglas and Charlie Chaplin convened almost nightly to show their respective rushes to each other. "They'd get into real heated arguments sometimes," recalled Stuart Heisler, who brought the rough assemblies of material to Pickfair. "Actually, they were all trying to help each other. They [just] weren't pulling any punches."

One night, after everybody's rushes had been viewed and dissected, Chaplin went over to the piano, sat down and began to play. After a while, he moved over to the violin. Chaplin started to tell stories of his life in the English music halls, and then it was back to the piano for more of the elegant, slightly melancholy music that he liked. Heisler staggered out of Pickfair at 3:00 *a.m.*. At the very end of his life he recalled it as "one of the most interesting evenings I ever spent."

Another on-looker at the Pickford-Fairbanks *ménage* at this time was Mitchell Leisen, later a director but at the time the costume designer for *Robin Hood, Thief of Bagdad, Rosita* and *Dorothy Vernon of Haddon Hall.*

"Charlie Chaplin, [Ken] Davenport, and myself were up there almost every night for dinner," Leisen told Kevin Brownlow. "Mary would go to bed and we'd run a picture. Douglas would go sound asleep during the picture and would wake up and say, 'Best picture I've ever seen in my life.' And everybody would go up and go to bed and climb in the Rolls-Royce the next morning and go to the studio.

"I [would say] 'Douglas, I've got to go back home and get some clean clothes.' And he said, 'I've got plenty of clothes here. What the hell do you need?' I had more underwear and shirts of Douglas' . . ."

Everybody who knew Mary and Douglas in this period remembered an elemental aura of sunshine and happiness around them. In particular, Mary flowered. "Despite my success, I had been a very lonely person," Mary remembered. "More than anything else I had wanted desperately to be approved of, and that approval Douglas gave me. I had never believed anybody would speak of me and to me as he did."

This atmosphere of warmth and caring flowed over casual acquaintances and perfect strangers alike. One day in 1922, while Douglas was shooting *Robin Hood,* Mary noticed a little girl patiently waiting across the street from the studio. "This pretty lady with the most beautiful parasol in the world came over to me," remembered the little girl, who grew up to be the character actress Ann Doran. "I remember that it was lace and flowed in the breeze. She wanted to know where my Mama was. I said she was working up the street—she was working wardrobe on some two-reel comedies, but Mary knew what I meant. Then she asked me when she'd be back.

"That night, as my mother and I were going home on the steetcar, she told me that I was going to be playing with the kids that were working next door. The next day I started playing one of the pages in *Robin Hood*. Mary had found my mother and said, 'That child can't be by herself; why don't I put her to work in Douglas's picture so she'll have someone to look after her?' "

Despite the warmth of the Fairbanks personality, Pickfair could be a somewhat chilly place to sleep; ever since her trouping days, and the profusion of small rooms in cramped boarding houses, Mary had had an aversion to steam heat, regarding it as "tiring and dangerous." Even on chilly winter nights, Pickfair was kept very cool, with warm clothes being the preferred alternative to central heating.

Jack had recently returned to Hollywood in a deep depression over the death of Olive Thomas, so Mary tried to jog him out of it by hiring him to co-direct her next picture with Alfred E. Green, who had himself directed Jack and was a good friend. The resulting film, *Through the Back Door*, was a convoluted tale of a Belgian child given up for adoption by her rich, selfish mother. When World War I breaks out, she escapes to America and ends up working, conveniently enough, as a servant in her natural mother's house. The plot evolves—or, more accurately degenerates—into something about seduction and blackmail among the idle, corrupt rich, all thwarted by plucky Mary.

Although the script is attributed to Marion Fairfax, Mary later claimed credit for the original story. If true, she wasn't doing herself any favors; thematically, *Through the Back Door* is regressive. Mary tries to compensate for the banality of the material by laying stress on the artful production: the lavish, big sets, the glistening photography, etc. It doesn't help. *Through the Back Door* grossed a profitable, but unspectacular $774,064.

Yet, the making of *Through the Back Door* provided a revealing look at the real controlling factor on a Pickford set. It seemed that Mary had a long-standing custom of remaining off the set when other actresses were performing. "I was the producer as well [as the star] and, seemingly, I frightened them," she recalled. One day, Al Green came to Mary and said that they were having an impossible time with a scene featuring Gertrude Astor. They'd started on it at 9:00 A.M. and were still flailing away just before lunch.

Mary walked on the stage and noted the terrified look Astor gave her. Mary conferred with Green, told him to alert the cameraman and the electricians. She walked over and put a comforting arm around Astor's shoulder.

"I just can't cry, Miss Pickford," explained Astor, "I just can't." Mary patted her on the shoulder, saying she'd been in the same position herself and knew just how Astor felt. Operating on the presumption that self-pity is always a good prerequisite to tears, Mary proceeded to tell Astor that, while it would be tragic to replace her in the film, they had to do it. She would, of course, be protected, in terms of the press and the rest of the industry, in every way possible. No blame would be attached to her banishment. Rather, a sudden illness, or something else mutually agreeable could be devised. It was all too, too sad.

Astor, an ambitious actress, saw her career crumbling around her and began to cry. The cameras started grinding, Mary edged away from her. "The director was pleased and I was, too," remembered Mary. "When it was over, [Astor] came over and gave me a tearful, very wet embrace and kiss. 'Thank you for helping me,' she said. 'I couldn't have done it without you.' "

Next, Mary embarked on her production of Francis Hodgson Burnett's perennially popular 1886 novel, *Little Lord Fauntleroy.* Although not, on the surface, any more felicitous a choice of material than *Pollyanna, Little Lord Fauntleroy* involves timeless themes of class distinction and the bridging of a gap between generations that date it far less than most other Victorian stories.

Mary elected to play another dual role, assaying both Cedric, the little boy who becomes Lord Fauntleroy, as well as Dearest, his mother. While giving her public two Pickfords for the price of one, dual roles also enabled Mary to play someone besides the ubiquitous, imprisoning little girl (or, in this case, boy) with curls. Although Mary's inherent femininity prevents her from being particularly convincing as a boy, she does fulfill the primary demand made upon any actor in a dual role: create two distinct characterizations.

The plot of *Little Lord Fauntleroy* co-exists with layers of confused autobiography. In the first scene of the picture, Mary, playing a long-haired boy, looks wistfully through a window at a little girl getting her curls chopped off. When he/she broaches the subject to the mother, Mary, playing his/her own mother sighs and says, "Cedric, I cannot bear to have you grow up." This Gordian knot of Freudian implications appears again at the end, with Cedric happily sitting down to get a haircut.

Mary is playing both a mother and child, two people distressed at being separated from each other. It was a perfect metaphor for her daily situation: wealth, success and power as Mrs. Douglas Fairbanks/Mary Pickford, while, never far away were the memories of mean poverty that had been the daily lot of Gladys Smith. It is no accident that she would always say that the early days of poverty, of being a wayfaring trouper, were more real to her than any life she had lived since.

Little Lord Fauntleroy easily establishes itself as the best of Mary's costume pictures, largely because of its steady pace, with effective contrast made between the crowded hurly-burly of nineteenth century New York and the vast, austere, cold sets for Fauntleroy manor. As always when Mary played a child, the sets are oversized, but the castle sets are *really* oversized; doorways are ten feet high, dwarfing the other actors as well as Mary. This outsize scale gives *Fauntleroy* the quality of a fable told by a child, not merely one about a child.

Mary again asked Jack to co-direct with Alfred E. Green. "It was understood from the start that Al Green was the senior director," said Mary, "and I never overruled him in the few instances when he and Johnny [Jack] disagreed. They were both on the set at all times. Johnny thought more in terms of gags and business, while Al was better with the acting and camera angles."

The noticeably tougher-minded Charles Rosher had a less indulgent view of Jack's duties: "Al Green did the directing. Jack would show up at the studio when he felt like it. He seldom took any active part other than suggesting a few gags."

The response to *Little Lord Fauntleroy* proved that the public liked Mary in Victoriana; *Fauntleroy* grossed $1,108,882.66, only slightly less than her all-time hit *Pollyanna*.

Mary then re-made *Tess of the Storm Country*, which improves on the original by virtue of telling a coherent story. *Tess* features one of her most energetic performances, knocking unwanted swains into the river with a tomboy-ish gusto reminiscent of Mabel Normand. While the 1914 original was incoherent, the 1922 remake makes perfect sense but is too long.

Once again, Mary goes through a transformation, beginning the

film as an unbathed child of the rough seas. The transforming
agent is not a dream this time, but a bath, and she emerges looking
like . . . Mary, complete with ringlets of curls. As in *Through the
Back Door* and *Sparrows*, Mary selflessly takes care of babies that
aren't hers. (In other, later films, like *My Best Girl* and *Rosita*, she's
the sole support of adults who might as well be babies.) In her
films, as well as in her life, it all seemed to depend on Mary.

The trouble it took to remake *Tess* turned out to be worth it, at
least financially. The second *Tess* grossed $927,953.68. Clearly,
Mary had climbed out of the slight commercial trough of *Suds* and
The Love Light and was resting securely upon a lucrative plateau.
At the same time, Douglas had been making adventurous choices
of material like *The Three Musketeers* and *Robin Hood*, and was
thinking of embarking on his most lavish picture of all, *The Thief
of Bagdad*. By comparison, Mary felt slightly retrograde; something different seemed to be called for.

Mary had long felt that she had taken the little girl character
about as far as was tenable. She decided that she wanted to do an
adult role, a *real* adult role, with no fantasy sequences or dual roles
to serve as a sop to her public. At the same time, she had been
looking at some of the German films that had reached America in
the wake of the critical success of *The Cabinet of Dr. Caligari*,
some of the best of them directed by a man named Ernst Lubitsch,
who, to judge from the performances he extracted from Pola
Negri, had a genuine touch with women. After some fairly simple
negotiations, Mary signed Lubitsch to a contract, the announcement of which prompted a wave of anti-German sentiment left
over from World War I.

Lubitsch left Germany in October 1922. Nathan Burkan, Chaplin's attorney, quietly met him in New York in an effort to defuse
any bad press. Lubitsch's appearance did not jibe with the image
of a director who had "humanized history" and whose sly sensuality would come to be memorialized by the misleading term "the
Lubitsch touch." He wore egg-top trousers, banana yellow boots
and had several gold teeth in the front of his mouth. He looked, in
short, not like the suave continental seducer his films implied, but
a lower-class Jewish burgher, which, in fact, he was. (The secret of
Lubitsch's films was that they were fantasies of blithe sexuality and
emotional non-involvement, not just for the audience, but for him
as well.)

After considerable struggle, Burkan outfitted Lubitsch with a
new wardrobe and had his own dentist replace the gold teeth with
porcelain ones. By early December, Lubitsch was ensconced at

the Pickford-Fairbanks studio fighting for his life. As Mary remembered, "Poor Ernst Lubitsch arrived not knowing what kind of demon I was."

They were introduced by Edward Knoblock, a scriptwriter friend of Mary and Douglas' who spoke fluent German. Lubitsch, a small, lively, gregarious man, took her hand, then threw it away as if it was a dead thing. "My God," he told Knoblock in German, "she is cold. Yeah, she is cold. How can she be an actress and be so cold?" Two days later, Mary noticed Lubitsch walking through the wheatfield where Douglas had built his enormous castle set for *Robin Hood.* He was talking to himself and gesticulating. "There goes trouble," she told Charlotte.

Later that day, he told Mary he didn't want to direct the project Mary had offered him, *Dorothy Vernon of Haddon Hall,* a costume romance set in the court of Elizabeth I. "Der are too many qveens and not enough qveens," he said by way of explanation, meaning that the story, which involved Elizabeth I and Mary, Queen of Scots, was so grand that there was no room for Dorothy Vernon. According to her own recollections, Mary was disappointed ("It was [like] a blow to the face") but she could understand his point of view and said, "Let's try to find another story." Lubitsch went out and buttonholed Knoblock. "My God, now I know she is cold. She took it standing up. She is cold. She can't act."

"Well," said Knoblock, "wait until you get her before the cameras and then you'll see."

Lubitsch counteroffered *Faust,* which Mary was considering until Charlotte found out that the story called for America's Sweetheart to have a child out of wedlock (bad) and then strangle it (worse). Divorcing Owen Moore and marrying Douglas Fairbanks was one thing; on-screen infanticide was quite another. Charlotte forbade *Faust;* Lubitsch was furious. Years later, Mary said that she regretted not doing it.

Despite some disagreement within the Pickford unit ("I didn't think it the right kind of thing for Mary to do, either period-wise or anything else," said Mitchell Leisen), they finally agreed on a script tentatively titled *The Street Singer,* adapted by Knoblock from a minor French play called *Don Cesar de Bazan.* Just before production began, there was an argument when Lubitsch found out that Mary, not he, would have the final authority in any disagreement. "I told him [Lubitsch] that I would never interfere with him on the set, never gainsay him," remembered Mary. "But if it comes to an issue, I have to put the money up. I will be glad to arbitrate it, bring in a person we both respect, but you are not the person of last appeal."

Despite Edward Knoblock's telling him that Mary would not be unreasonable, that Lubitsch was being foolish to make such an issue out of something that would probably never even happen, Lubitsch lost his temper and tore all the buttons off his clothing, then pounced on Knoblock's papers, throwing them in the air. Most of this untypical behavior was nothing more than displaced nerves, for Lubitsch later confessed to a newly arrived Victor Seastrom that he had been continually on edge during his first few months in Hollywood.

Despite these obvious intimations of a fatal misalliance, shooting of *The Street Singer* began on March 5, 1923, and lurched on until May 31. Mary would claim that the battles became so pitched that the only way the film was finished was that she simply gave up and put herself in Lubitsch's hands.

Simple things like Lubitsch's thick German accent seemed to offend Mary's sense of decorum. Preparing a camera position, Lubitsch would turn to Charles Rosher and say "All right, upset your camera," which was good for a few giggles. In a scene involving Holbrook Blinn and a dagger, Lubitsch gave Blinn the line reading: "You should say to her, 'Rosita, ver is da dagger mit da yools.'" Blinn promptly turned to Mary with the cameras running and said, "Rosita, ver is da dagger mit da yools?" resulting in helpless laughter from the actors and confusion from Lubitsch.

There's an ugly, xenophobic edge to such stories of the actors having sport with a stranger in a strange land. Mary's side of the story was simple: Lubitsch was personally vulgar— "He ate German fried potatoes three times a day," which is probably what led to Lubitsch leaving greasy fingerprints all over Mary's newly painted dove-gray dressing room—and he was a manipulator of plots, press and settings, more than a director of actresses.

For his part, the great director believed that he was simply trying to cure Mary of her reliance on "the Pickford tricks," and bring her into his screen world of sexual cajolery, the coin of the Lubitsch realm. If he seemed more overbearing than absolutely necessary, it might have been because he spoke almost no English and something was being lost in translation.

"The first day he was on the set," remembered Mitchell Leisen, "they came to tell him his wife was on the telephone. He said, 'You mean I can have copulation with my wife here?'" Eventually, practically all of Lubitsch's instructions had to be relayed through assistant directors.

Despite the troubled production, Mary felt that the results were worth it. Her correspondence at the time reveals her to be quite enamored of Lubitsch and their collaboration, so much so that she tried to arrange a production deal for him at United Artists. On June 13, two weeks after *The Street Singer* had been completed, she wrote Cap O'Brien, her attorney, that "Lubitsch would be a great asset to our company if he could do spectacles. Personally, I still believe he is the greatest director in the world and would be willing to back him if I could afford it." Six days later, after O'Brien had gently urged her to title the film *Rosita* ("it is soft and sweet, and if it typifies the character, it ought to be a valuable title"), she reiterated to O'Brien that "I am very pleased with *Rosita* and think it will be well received."

Mary attempted to set up a deal whereby she, Douglas and Chaplin would each contribute an equal amount to finance two Lubitsch pictures a year, but "both Charlie and Douglas decided . . . they are both under very heavy expenses and feel they are shouldering all they can carry."

Lubitsch also wanted to continue with United Artists and direct Mary in another picture in the early part of 1924. Mary delegated O'Brien to negotiate with some Eastern bankers so the Lubitsch deal could be set up, and then closed her letter with an admonition about his salary: "I believe $3,500 a week is exorbitant, in fact anywhere from $2,500 to $3,000 is more like it." O'Brien began negotiations with the Guaranty Trust Company, but the deal fell through; Lubitsch signed a contract with Warner Brothers and never made a second picture with Mary.

The physical production of *Rosita* is stunning; huge, vaulted sets, lavish outdoor constructions of old Seville, populated by thousands of extras. (There's nothing like American money for foreign directors used to pinch-penny budgets. Like Murnau and Lang when they first arrived in America, Lubitsch turned a basically intimate story into something of a visual opera.)

Although *Rosita* is a fairly weighty nine reels long, it moves at a far steadier pace than the films that bookend it. In addition, Lubitsch gives the film a texture derived largely from a procession of carefully chosen, baroque faces that give *Rosita* a far more specific sense of realistic humanity than most other Pickford films. The compositions are precise, formal—there is only one tracking shot and one pan right in the entire picture—without being academic. It is among the most physically beautiful of all silent films.

The premise of *Rosita* is simplicity itself: Rosita is a street singer, the idol of the mobs. The King sees her and wishes to make her his mistress, despite his wife's disapproval, Rosita's love for the penniless nobleman Don Diego (George Walsh) and Rosita's penchant for singing satirical songs about royalty.

Rosita's situation is made more ticklish as a result of the support she gives her worthless family, which she moves wholesale into the King's (Holbrook Blinn) palace. The family proceeds to hang laundry on lines strung from priceless armoires, while Rosita attempts a balancing act between the good life on the one hand and her maidenhead on the other.

While *Rosita* is a recognizable half-way point between Lubitsch's Griffith-influenced German silents and the later, sly sexual comedies that were heavily influenced by Chaplin's *A Woman of Paris,* he does not entirely neglect the familiar Pickford turf.

There's a delightful scene when a hungry Rosita, a poor girl in a palace, is trying to fight off hunger pangs while alone in a room with a large bowl of fruit. The camera holds on a static shot of the fruit on top of a table, while Mary passes in back of it, giving it surreptitious glances. After a few practice cruises, her arm darts out and grabs an apple; another pass, yields up a banana.

But all of Lubitsch's skill can't hide the fact that Pickford's performance is external and obviously unfelt, with Mary uncomfortable with the Mediterranean gestures and displays of temperament. When Rosita believes her lover to be dead and is planning to kill the King for ordering it, Pickford flares her eyes and contorts her mouth with the evil avidity of a vampire for blood, rather than playing the scene with cold fury.

Rosita is a very good film but it is a very good film in spite of its star's performance rather than because of it. Mary's street singer lacks the emotional force she brings to the entertaining but often trivial material in which she usually appeared. Part of the problem might have been her innate insecurity; she may have felt that Lubitsch was too "arty" for her, too demanding of something she may not have been sure she could give. As an actress, security was everything to Mary; she freely admitted that "I freeze up if someone is critical of me. I can't laugh or cry; I'm devastated."

Yet, even though it isn't a particularly smooth meshing of talents, *Rosita* (along with *Stella Maris* and a few other films) is a clear harbinger of the kind of career that Mary could have had, a career of different kinds and styles of movies, a career that, had it not been managed by two people terrified of alienating the audience, might have lasted somewhat longer than it did.

Rosita was an experiment Pickford would never repeat. "I have to remind myself that there is a tremendous gap, a mighty difference between the traveled, sophisticated Mrs. Douglas Fairbanks and the Mary Pickford the public knows," she said a few years later, leaving unsaid that it was Mrs. Douglas Fairbanks who had employed Ernst Lubitsch.

"Mary wanted to be sophisticated in Douglas's eyes," said Frances Marion explaining the misalliance of star and director. "At the same time she didn't want to grow up. She was afraid people wouldn't love her [anymore]."

Of the finished picture, Mary thought that "He tried to be as moral as possible, and I tried to be slightly naughty. I've always felt the results were pretty terrible. I didn't like myself as Rosita. I think it was my fault, not Lubitsch's. We just didn't seem to get together, but I was very proud of the fact that I was able to bring him to the country with no bad effects.

"Lubitsch could understand Pola Negri or Gloria Swanson, but he didn't understand me. Just as John Ford, I don't think, could direct Negri." For his part, Lubitsch would occasionally joke to co-workers and friends about the vast gulf between Mary's dainty looks and her tough sensibility.

Rosita premiered September 14, 1923 at New York's Lyric Theater and received excellent reviews. The New York *Times* called it "exquisite," *Vanity Fair* referred to it as "that distinguished and lovely film," and *Photoplay* said that "there is no actress today who could portray the gay, graceful, coquettish little street singer of Seville . . . as she does," while Lubitsch again showed "why [he] holds his place among the leading directors of the world." The influential monthly concluded, "No, don't worry about Mary growing up."

Despite the praise, Mary always preferred to think of *Rosita* as a terrible film ("It's the worst picture I ever did, it's the worst picture I ever *saw*") and a financial failure to boot. Yet it grossed $940,872 in the United States, Canada and South America alone, $35,000 more than the next year's *Dorothy Vernon of Haddon Hall*, which she preferred to think of as a successful recovery from the Lubitsch debacle. The latter film, however, was directed by the laughing, amenable Marshall Neilan who provided an atmosphere much more to her liking and whom she coddled mercilessly.

The truth was that she was uncomfortable submitting to any-body's will but her own.

"I have always felt the need of a good director," she would claim in later years, "and I relied upon my directors. They weren't expected to 'yes' me, and I insisted they use their initiative and authority." Indeed, testimony of her studio technicians tends to support Pickford's claim, although Allan Dwan remembered things quite differently. "This is what we're gonna do today," he said to her one day, whereupon Mary, hands on hips, replied "Who says that's what we're gonna do today?" Taken aback, Dwan said, "Don't you think it would be a good idea?" Mollified, Mary let it drop with "Why didn't you ask in the first place?"

She allowed the director or film editor to choose what they felt were the best takes to make up a sequence, but, remembered Stuart Heisler, "When it was all finished, she might ask to see the other takes. I'd put the other takes together and show them to her. Once in a while she'd say, 'Well, I like that take better than the one that's in the picture,' so you'd take that one out and put the other one in."

Howard Hawks, who worked as Mary's prop man and helped direct a couple of scenes for *The Little Princess* when Mickey Neilan went off on a drunk, said that "You didn't really direct Mary. She was a very sure person in her own category." Charles "Buddy" Rogers, Pickford's co-star in her 1927 film *My Best Girl* and, much later, her third husband, asserted that "On the set, she was just one of the cast. . . . She would take direction. If she wanted to make changes, after the working day she would have a meeting, but you never would see her showing her determination, her authority on the set. Never."

But there are many ways of asserting control, and one of them is to hire people whom you know in advance will not engage in struggles for autonomy. Pickford would always assert that she was unhappiest working for Lubitsch and deMille—her two strongest directors. Although she would always regard 1929's *The Taming of the Shrew* as another disaster, she did not hesitate to hire its com-pliant director, Sam Taylor, to direct her next completed picture, *Kiki.*

She would always hire directors who were competent profes-sionals. Some were better (Frank Borzage) than others (William Beaudine) but all of them were used to working under autocratic studio bosses and none of them had a history of independent thought or were likely to create startlingly original images or characterizations. Like Chaplin, Pickford quickly learned that if she was to bear primary responsibility for her films, then there could be no question about who must be in charge.

Another way of asserting control is through choice of material; even poets like Griffith or Ford would have been hard-pressed to achieve excellence ploughing through stories like *Through the Back Door* and *The Love Light.* "I'd like to be artistic, but I see no pleasure in an empty theater," Mary said by way of explanation. "I think it's self-indulgence to go along and do something that just pleases ourselves. Of course, the combination, to be an artist and a commercial success, is a wonderful thing, but there are very few people who have been able to reach that goal. Of the two, I chose to be commercial. I don't know with what result . . ."

She only came close to overcoming her security-oriented instincts once more, in late 1925, when Chaplin showed Douglas and Mary a film he was raving about called *The Salvation Hunters.* The director was a young, intense, short man named Josef von Sternberg. All three of them were quite taken with this moody, obscure tone poem in which one of the primary characters was a San Pedro Bay dredge. Despite all the anxiety Lubitsch had caused her, Mary promptly asked von Sternberg to direct her next picture.

After some thought, von Sternberg came up with a story called *Backwash,* about a blind girl and a deaf mute living in the squalor of industrial Pittsburgh. It was a story that was heavily indebted to the work of Erich von Stroheim, who was in turn indebted to the work of Emile Zola.

Much of *Backwash* was to be subjective, picturing what the girl, in her imagination, thinks the world consists of, juxtaposed against the grime and ugliness that the world actually consists of. Once the picture was announced, there was a negative public reaction. "People didn't want to see Mary Pickford defective in any way," explained Meri von Sternberg, the director's widow. Mary stalled for time and told von Sternberg she wanted to think over the story. In the meantime, she would make a "normal film" for a "normal" director.

"Oh, what a fake!" exploded Mary when asked about von Sternberg in 1965. *"Mon dieu!* He proved to be a complete boiled egg. Not even a boiled egg. The business of *von* Sternberg, and carrying a cane, and that little moustache! I'm so glad I didn't do the film . . . It was a very sad story, and everything was covered in dust. I liked *The Salvation Hunters,* but you never know who was really the guiding hand."

Backwash would be the last time Mary would even think about getting involved with someone who aspired to the title of artist;

from now on, she would seek out competent pros like herself. Years later, when she instructed Matty Kemp to restore her pictures so they could be preserved, she expressly withheld *Rosita* from the list. "That film was a dirty word to Mary," remembered Kemp. "She told me, 'If you ever restore that film, I'll not only fire you, I'll sue you.' "

———— • ————

While both Mary and Douglas's films were consistently profitable, there was continuing trouble with United Artists, usually centering around insufficient product and what most of the producers regarded as bad salesmanship. While the corporation, anchored by the four great personalities that owned it, presented a fairly solid front to the industry and the world at large, United Artists was, in fact, in very tenuous straits for most of its first five years. As early as January 1920, while Mary was still editing *Pollyanna,* she had to wire a negative response to Griffith regarding his request for a production advance. *"Romance* losses (a film directed by Chet Withey, a Griffith assistant and that had been co-financed by the United Artists principals for $70,000 apiece) have so depleted . . . treasury that present funds insufficient to balance due Douglas and me . . . Your note [has] so far exhausted our personal credit that we have difficulty in financing present production on which we are working hard to complete in order to carry United burden . . ."

In July 1922, Mary wrote to O'Brien, decrying a raise for the company's directors. "This . . . corporation is very much of an experiment . . . and we don't know that it will be a success and we should not assume a dollar more expense than is absolutely necessary . . ."

Much of the problem was caused by the inability of the principals to get along with each other, a failing common among artists even when they are supposed to be united. For all of Mary's respect for Griffith, theirs was not a relationship of any intimacy whatever. For one thing, whenever he was with Mary and her mother, he would always pretend that he had no money on him and would say that since the Pickfords were so rich, their picking up the tab wouldn't matter. Although it was something of a running gag, it also served notice to Charlotte and Mary that Griffith saw through their particular quirks. Marshall Neilan recalled an exchange in the '30s, when Griffith turned on Mary and called her "a goddamn Hetty Green, with your millions . . ." Mary replied, "Yes, and if I'd have stayed with you, I'd have had nothing."

As far as United Artists was concerned, needed revenue was being diverted by the partners' habit of road-showing their pictures in Los Angeles, i.e. personally renting a theater, paying for all advertising and publicity and owning the proceeds 100 percent. By the time the picture was finished at the prestige downtown location and handed over to United Artists for exhibition in neighborhood theaters, it was basically played out.

Douglas and D.W. Griffith had first crossed swords over the issue when *Way Down East* had been released. The heavily mortgaged Griffith had a cash flow problem; although his independently exhibited road-shows of *Way Down East* were enormous hits, the money was slow in coming in, and he had insufficient funds to complete his film-in-progress, *Dream Street.* He asked United Artists for help, and they dreamed up a scheme whereby future Canadian receipts for *Way Down East* would be used to guarantee the advance. Not unreasonably, they then made plans to begin Canadian distribution of the film through United Artists.

Griffith, while taking their money, didn't want United Artists to handle his picture. He fired off a telegram to Douglas. On January, 12, 1921, Douglas sent back a scorcher: THIS RECENT ACTION OF YOURS WITH WAY DOWN EAST IS MOST UNFAIR. IT SEEMS TO ME THAT IF YOU HAD APPLIED A SENSE OF JUSTICE TO A MATTER WHERE HONOR HAD SOMETHING TO DO WITH IT, YOUR ASSOCIATES WOULD HAVE GOTTEN A BETTER DEAL. I SEND YOU THIS TO LET YOU KNOW HOW I FEEL AND THAT IT MIGHT HAVE SOME EFFECT ON YOUR FUTURE.

Mary quickly stepped in as a peacemaker, wiring Griffith on January 17 that the United Artists treasury had insufficient funds to pay her and Douglas monies that the company had collected from their films. Despite that, she argued, they were ASKING NO SPECIAL CONSIDERATION OR GUARANTEE FROM UNITED AND ARE LIVING UP TO THE SPIRIT AND LETTER OF OUR CONTRACTS. She added that they would be willing to advance the money for *Dream Street,* PROVIDED THAT IT BE REGULARLY SOLD BY UNITED AS SOON AS POSSIBLE AND WITHOUT OTHER CONDITIONS THAN THOSE SPECIFIED IN YOUR CONTRACT.

Griffith grabbed an out, saying in a return telegram that the whole idea had been floated by functionaries and flunkies and that he CAN SEE THE JUSTICE OF YOUR WIRE AND BELIEVE

YOU ARE ABSOLUTELY RIGHT SO HAVE NO HARD FEEL-
ING CONCERNING THIS . . .

Yet, later that year, Griffith tried to avoiding using United Artists
for *Orphans of the Storm,* which he felt sure would be an enormous hit for foreign markets. He wanted to engage a distributor
other than U.A., which would, he hoped, offer him better terms.

Mary pointed out to Griffith that he had voted to expand the
foreign operations of United Artists, but was now trying to divert
much-needed product that would support the overhead of what,
after all, was his own company. "If we are to succeed," she wrote
Griffith on June 24, 1922, "we must all work together for the good
of the organization."

She asked Chaplin to join with her and Douglas in opposing
Griffith's scheme, only to be told that he, Chaplin, thought it was a
fine idea and that he was also thinking of selling his films to some
other foreign distributor.

Mary wrote Cap O'Brien in July that she was "incensed" at this
response and that "if Mr. Griffith and Charlie are going to equivo-
cate about giving us their pictures for foreign release and when
they do get pictures like *Way Down East* and *The Kid,* sell them to
the highest bidder and leave us with their mediocre output such as
The Idle Class and *Dream Street,* then Douglas and I should insist
that they should be shown no favors but they should pay 40 percent instead of 30 percent [the going foreign distribution fee]. In
that event, they can pick and choose, leaving us the lesser lights."
Faced with Mary's wrath, Chaplin and Griffith both backed off.

People who knew Mary in later years would always comment on
the intense, emotional bond she felt for United Artists. It was, in
many respects, the baby she would never have, and she brought to
bear all the tongue-clucking attention to detail a mother feels for a
promising, but as yet undeveloped infant.

"Do you realize, Cap, that are are twelve key cities which have
not yet played *Fauntleroy?*" an irate Mary wrote on June 18, 1923.
"It is all right for Mr. Abrams (the managing director of United
Artists) to demand certain prices, but I think it is fatal for him to
keep me out of towns of that size for two years. An investigation
must be made before *Rosita* is released."

No detail seemed too small to escape her attention. In January
1923, she asked for an explanation of checks for $2.75 and $7.30 she
had received from United Artists for showings of her films.
O'Brien wrote back that one check represented the overage
above a guarantee of $62.50 in Ortonville, Minnesota, while the

other stemmed from a showing at an Army base in Texas. He added that *"Little Lord Fauntleroy* was not quite virile enough as an attraction for the troops on the border."

In April 1923, when an angry exhibitor in Washington complained to her that United Artists would not let him play a Pickford picture unless he took other pictures on the same basis—the very policy the avoidance of which was the primary reason for the existence of United Artists—she fired off a letter to Dennis O'Brien.

"I am sending you a copy of the . . . letter, which is very upsetting. I am sorry his feelings are hurt for my belief is that a friend is always better than an enemy. His letter sounds most convincing and sincere and I would like very much to pacify him if it is possible . . ."

Mary was continually dissatisfied with the pictures United Artists was releasing from outside producers. "Charlie, Douglas and I after months of consideration, have come to the conclusion that the United Artists would be far better off without these outside pictures," she wrote to Cap O'Brien on June 18, 1923. "The output should be cut to the four of us as soon as possible . . . I am quite sincere in what I said about withdrawing from the United Artists unless something is done. I am not satisfied and feel that I could do much better in the returns from my productions by waiting until they are completed and selling them to the highest bidder, which I intend doing unless a radical change is made immediately.

"Charlie is thoroughly frightened and realizes he has to get down to business if he hopes to keep in public favor and he needs the money, so I am looking forward to getting a picture from him very soon now."

Mary was doomed to be disappointed in Chaplin again. After taking what seemed like forever to work through his contract with First National, Chaplin's first film for United Artists was finally released in October 1923. But *A Woman of Paris* was a sly, subtle drama about sex and self-delusion in which the great comedian did only an unrecognizable walk-on. While *A Woman of Paris* earned Chaplin a sheaf of rave reviews and proved that he was a masterful director when he wanted to be, his first United Artists release was a financial failure, which could only have made Mary more impatient.

O'Brien tried to dissuade Mary by pointing out that the company's total gross from pictures other than those of the four founding partners was nearly $3.5 million dollars, with the company's distribution fee from those pictures amounting to $941,693.04. "Without this revenue, it would have been very difficult for our corporation to have carried on," he scolded.

In a letter dated October 20, 1923, a clearly worried O'Brien noted that the number of play dates on subsequent pictures had fallen far below the level established by early United Artists' releases like *Pollyanna* and *His Majesty, the American.* He suggested they hire somebody to go into each exchange district and get play dates for pictures that hadn't gotten the exposure they deserved. He closed his letter with a simple statement: "We have got to increase our business." He was right; by the end of the year, United Artists' deficit was $300,000.

Despite all the handwriting on the wall, Mary had stubbornly written to Griffith on June 18, explaining that United Artists would be able to cut labor costs if it got rid of outside product. She then told him that "there is a great possibility of our getting Harold Lloyd if we are willing to let him in on the ground floor, giving him representation on the board and the chance to buy stock . . . Chaplin and Lloyd should mean more in drawing power than ten [George] Arliss pictures.

"We hope that your vote will coincide with ours, making it unanimous. If we do not hear from you, we will know that you approve. Really, I should be very much offended as you have not answered any of my letters or wires. I appreciate the fact that you are busy, but so am I, and matters of this kind are quite as important as making pictures. Your contract [for the initial group of pictures each partner had promised to deliver] is nearly out and so are Douglas' and mine and if we are to continue, I think an absolutely new policy is necessary in the organization."

Harold Lloyd signed with Paramount; Griffith, uncomfortable facing what he regarded as the united front of Mary, Douglas and Chaplin, and increasingly short of cash, was convinced that the problem with his pictures was the United Artists sales team, not the pictures themselves. He therefore opened negotiations with Paramount.

Despite the fact that Griffith's United Artists pictures, which were being made at the rate of two per year, were grossing around $30,000 in an average week, he was growing increasingly desperate. ("One would think there must be bad management somewhere," sniffed Cap O'Brien.)

Griffith's always-chaotic business arrangements grew even more complicated when he agreed to a new contract with United Artists in March 1924. Yet, incomprehensibly, on June 10, Griffith also cut a deal with Adolph Zukor. His partners in United Artists were outraged and threatened suit. A compromise was reached whereby United Artists would distribute *Sally of the Sawdust,* Griffith's first picture made under Paramount's auspices, after which he would be free to leave the company.

But the fact was that Griffith had supplied nine pictures to United Artists, which had grossed a total of $8 million; the revenues he had produced had to be replaced, and quickly, for by 1924, the United Artists deficit was over half a million dollars.

At the same time Mary was stoutly resisting United Artists' involvement with marginal program pictures, she was exerting pressure on the board to undertake the distribution of pictures starring Jack; for the first picture, *Garrison's Finish,* she appealed to Griffith to approve a United Artists release. "Expect to lay off this summer after finishing *Fauntleroy,*" she had wired Griffith on April 26, 1921, "which would mean that Jack would have my organization and of course my supervision."

The telegram was clearly a (successful) attempt at an end-around Chaplin. As she explained to Griffith, "Douglas feels the same way [I do] . . . I haven't approached Charlie on this subject simply because I think our friendship has covered a greater period of years . . ."

Despite Mary's supervision, *Garrison's Finish* managed to gross only slightly more than $300,000. Nevertheless, Mary coerced her partners into handling two more of Jack's pictures. There was no opposition to this double standard; *The Hill Billy* and *Waking Up the Town* were distributed by United Artists.

Another vanity production was 1921's *They Shall Pay,* starring Lottie and Allan Forrest, her husband at the time. The writer/director was listed as "Martin Justine," a man without any other credits in either features or shorts in the silent era. Since monies from *They Shall Pay* were paid directly to Charlotte, there is a reasonable suspicion that she might have turned her hand to film production in addition to career management.

There has been much fervent exaggeration printed over the years about the earnings of silent movies, ranging from reputed grosses of $50 million for *The Birth of a Nation,* to $18 million for a modest little comedy like Mabel Normand's *Mickey.* Both of these pictures were sold on a states rights basis, in which the picture was bought for a flat fee for a given territory, after which all monies the picture earned in that territory were the sole property of the purchaser. This had the effect of, on the one hand, flattening out potential earnings for the picture's original producers, while, on the other, ensuring that investors would at least get their money back, plus a decent profit.

But it is wildly improbable that these pictures did anything remotely resembling such business. A more likely figure for *The Birth of a Nation* is around $5 million, the same gross that was earned ten years later by *The Big Parade,* another *bona fide* smash hit that ran for a year or more in many cities. The movie business of sixty and seventy years ago was only rarely like the boom-or-bust, all-or-nothing film economy of today. Very few individual pictures made enormous profits. Rather, individual pictures made modest but reliable profits which, cumulatively, over the course of the releasing year, added up to large aggregate profits for the releasing company.

The exaggerated grosses that were claimed were partially attributable to the puffery endemic to show business, partly to the psychological need of the early film pioneers to make themselves seem wealthier and their work seem more important—in the industrial and commercial sense—than it really was.

Mary and Douglas's own pictures returned solid, consistent profits, but they were not gold mines. *Pollyanna* of 1920 had cost $300,000 and 1924's *Dorothy Vernon of Haddon Hall* had cost considerably more. The increased costs could not really be justified in terms of box-office grosses; *Little Lord Fauntleroy* grossed slightly over $800,000 domestically, slightly less than the cheaper *Pollyanna.* Costume pictures made money for Mary, but not as much as she was used to and not as much as they made for Douglas.

——— ———

Underneath the pomp and pageantry that was the public's inevitable perception of Mary's marriage and career, one senses an intense desire for normalcy. A group of young starlets formed a group called "Our Club" and asked Mary to be honorary president. The likes of Billie Dove, Colleen Moore, Loretta Young, Ann Harding and, occasionally, Mary would take turns meeting at each other's homes, where they'd drink hot chocolate, eat cookies and talk about the movies as well as such nominal components of the

Jazz Age as the poetry of Edna St. Vincent Millay, the cartoons of John Held Jr. and the novels of F. Scott Fitzgerald.

Occasionally, Mary undertook a function designed for publicity purposes. She would, for example, invite the WAMPAS Baby Stars of 1928–29 over to Pickfair. Among them was Lina Basquette, just married to Sam Warner, one of the Warner Brothers. The star of deMille's *The Godless Girl* remembered that Mary "was a rather distant but charming hostess." Basquette went on to say that "I'm not sure that she had a great deal of warmth for anybody but her closest friends."

When it came to running the Pickford Corporation, Mary ceded most of the business decisions to her mother. When it was time to clip stock coupons, Charlotte would happily disappear into the bank while Mary stayed behind in the car, mulling over a problematic aspect of her latest picture, or mentally casting the next one.

"She'd come back and show me the marks the scissors had made on her hands from cutting all the coupons," Mary remembered. " 'You know, Mother, I'm not going to sympathize with you—you had a wonderful time cutting, and if your whole hand had been blistered, you would have been very pleased.' "

At times, the normalcy verged on the staid. Paul Lazarus Sr., who started working in the sales department at United Artists in 1919, would often complain that, while Doug was flexible and cooperative with the press and exhibitors, Mary was remote, unbending and seemed to be mentally casting herself as the Great Lady of Cinema.

Just after Douglas and Mary returned from their honeymoon, they met the usual crew of reporters and photographers at the Ritz-Carlton Hotel in New York. A reporter suggested calling up Charles Ray, who was also in town, and grouping the three of them for a shot. "Mary's nose went up, up, at the thought of sharing the publicity," reported one Delos Lovelace. " 'Do you,' she asked with a touch of her new French, 'really think that would be *au fait?*' " The room was suddenly enveloped in a thick silence, and the idea was dropped.

It was largely a case of insecurity. "I always thought that the public would catch up with me one day," Mary confessed when she was an old woman. "They'd find out that I wasn't really a good actress, that I was too little, too fat or too something. I wanted my family to have security. I wanted them to have the best of medical care and to have warm clothes in the wintertime.

"So I saved. I was a little miser. Even after I had the money, I'd always go down the price side of the menu to see what was twenty cents or twenty-five cents—could I eat that? I would compromise and take whatever I could eat that was the cheapest. It took me many years to get over that."

Because the operative word for Hollywood was and is fear—fear of competition, age, bad publicity, whatever—Mary threw herself into her work with the avidity of a nun for worship, seeking to overwhelm by force of will any and all outside forces that might get in her way.

The years of impoverishment and humiliation had bred in her a strong desire to be a cultured, well-read, sophisticated woman. At the same time, her view of the world was that it was a wonderful thing to hide from; the studio became her shelter, her surcease from pain. "She hated society, she hated strangers and she was, in truth, afraid of them," wrote Adela Rogers St. John.

But there was one way to cope, one way to survive: to work, and to be rigidly in control of every possible eventuality. Mary usually rose at 6:30, had breakfast at 7:00, was at the studio from 8:00A.M. to 7:30 P.M. Dinner would be at 8:00, her nightly French lesson at 8:30, perhaps a movie at 9:00 or 9:30 and then to bed, usually before 10:30 P.M.

"My pictures were my whole life, outside of my family. I never went any place, I never went to cafes, restaurants, never went dancing, I had no social life whatsoever. My whole life was wrapped up in the creative. The career is a very exacting thing. In fact, it's a monster. It possesses you, body and soul."

Years later, she realized the price she had paid, and regretted it. "The mistake I made as a young person [was in] being so inordinately ambitious that I didn't want to do anything if I couldn't succeed. Well, that's wrong."

Co-existing with this panicked little girl was a very unsentimental businesswoman who had learned her trade from very close up. "The businesswoman was her mother," said Stuart Heisler. "Mrs. Pickford knew the business inside and out, and nobody ever got the best of her. An awful lot of people didn't particularly like [Mary]. In that period, the entire world went for her kind of innocence—whether or not she was innocent."

Bruce "Lucky" Humberstone, Mary's assistant director on several pictures, asserted that Mary "was an extremely shrewd businesswoman, even to the extent that [she] was not only looking after her own [productions], but when Doug was in production on his own pictures and Mary was out of production, she would look after his costs . . . Doug never asked a question pertaining to costs. Mary questioned just about everything."

The hard years on the road and the example of her mother's business flint would never leave her, and they left her a slightly pinched, stunted woman. She would come to agree with Irving Thalberg that, although nobody can always be right, they can always be busy; that it isn't mistakes that destroy a career, it's inactivity. "She was always *alarmed,*" remembered Chaplin.

She would come to believe that exploitation and publicity amount to between 50 percent and 60 percent of a star's success, and that the most important thing about a movie was, first the story, then the direction, then the editing. In late 1923, Mary and Doug were planning the New York openings of *Rosita* and *The Thief of Bagdad,* when Herbert Howe caught a priceless exchange that perfectly summed up their respective characters.

"I have only 300 billboards for the New York showings of *Rosita,*" mused Mary. "Do you think that's enough? I wanted 500. I think billboards are very important in the advertising campaign. Douglas, how many billboards have you for *The Thief of Bagdad?*"

"I've got 50 billboards," said Fairbanks. "The first of the year is a long way off."

"But you need to reserve billboards a long time off," replied Mary.

As her stepson observed, "In business, Mary was very masculine-minded."

———— ——

Although her responsibilities had increased with the formation of United Artists, her manner remained mostly unchanged. Irving Sindler, a member of the production crew on *Rosita, Little Annie Rooney* and *Sparrows,* remembered her regular, considerate inquiries. "Good morning, Irv. Is it too warm? Would you like a cold drink?"

Nor was this attitude limited to those whom she knew on a personal level. In the silent days—and well beyond—extras were usually treated like cattle, herded around, given cheap, bad box lunches. Extras hated night scenes, because, as one remembered, "you froze your ass off." What did they expect for five dollars a day? Yet, Loyal Lucas, who worked as an extra on *Rosita* remembered that, for the flamboyant scenes of revelry and celebration that had to be photographed at night, Mary constructed little coops with benches and fires to keep the anonymous extras warm.

"On the last night all the extras worked, she made a little speech and thanked us for working with her," remembered Lucas. "She didn't have to do little things like that, and we all loved her for it."

The atmosphere was collegial; if a prop boy or makeup man had a suggestion, Mary and the director would talk it over and, if both were agreeable, would put it into action. Mary summarized her feelings about her co-workers when she said, "No one ever worked for me; we worked together." At lunchtime and quitting time, Douglas would come by and they would walk off hand in hand. "In those days, they were a very lovable couple," Sindler remembered. "They were very clearly a man and wife under the spell of love. In many ways, I felt that it was the best part of both our lives."

Douglas's productions were equally pleasant; at the end of a day's shooting, Douglas and his friend and trainer Chuck Lewis would organize a game of "Doug" with the other actors. "Doug" was similar to badminton, except the bird was heavier and, like a volleyball, it could be hit more than once. After that, everybody in the game was invited to take an ice-cold shower followed by a steambath. Fairbanks intimates like Chaplin or Sid Grauman would often drift into the steam bath at the end of their own busy days.

The relaxed atmosphere was, at least in part, due to Mary and Douglas's position on the top of the mountain. Now that they were their own bosses they were not about to churn out five pictures a year. Production schedules were leisurely; Mary's magnificent 1926 *Sparrows* took six months from the start of set-building until the last shot was taken. Douglas's *The Thief of Bagdad*, his masterpiece, took more than nine months.

Douglas' films had changed, too. His early films were light situation comedies that were partially satires of current events and fads, often laborious, partially acrobatic flights of exhilarating fancy from the star, invariably delightful. Where the stage had weighed Douglas down with mundane requirements such as plot and a three-act structure, Douglas' early films were usually content with a situation; they distilled the essence of his spirit: a ten-year-old who had unaccountably been placed in the superlatively conditioned body of a mature athlete and gymnast.

In the '20s, Douglas pursued a series of swashbuckling adventure films, long before such things existed as an entertainment staple. It was films such as *The Thief of Bagdad* (1924), *The Black Pirate* (1926) and *The Gaucho* (1927) that made Douglas more of a presence, an axiom, than a mere movie star. Even when making million-dollar productions, rife with sets, costumes and pageantry that threatened to become oppressive, the exuberant Douglas could lighten a scene, make it effervesce, simply by entering it. It was no accident that he was the only man the moody, somewhat depressive Chaplin ever loved.

The Hollywood mountain itself had grown immeasurably as well. Mary and Douglas were the cornerstones of a giant industry that fostered a good-sized city as well. By 1925, the city of Hollywood had 115,000 people, 13 grade schools, 30 auto agencies, 74 drugstores, 15 florists, 188 grocery stores, 34 restaurants, 25 photographers, 19 jewelers, 38 women's apparel stores . . . and precisely one department store.

The Pickford-Fairbanks studio was one of fifty-three movie companies operating in the town for which movies were the principal industry. The total value of the output of Hollywood's movie studios was estimated to be in excess of $75,000,000 yearly.

Pickfair itself had served as the leading edge of a gilt-edged population shift to Beverly Hills, as stars like Gloria Swanson, Chaplin and Tom Mix moved to within walking distance of Doug and Mary's hilltop home. Property values ascended accordingly; the price of a lot in Beverly Hills moved from $500 in 1920 to $30,000 five years later, when the city was incorporated.

After the misadventure of *Rosita* came 1924's *Dorothy Vernon of Haddon Hall*, Mary's response to the wave of successful costume pictures such as *When Knighthood was in Flower* and Douglas's *Robin Hood*. These films emphasized length, production values, and Lord and Ladies foiling plots against the King (or Queen), with a notable loss of exuberance and filmmaking flair. Seen today, they are killingly dull, and *Dorothy Vernon* is no exception.

For ten reels, beautifully costumed people enter a magnificently appointed room, have brief conversations in static, well-composed shots, and leave. It's a dull, de-personalized picture completely bereft of the antic comic spirit with which Neilan had imbued Mary's movies of six and seven years before. Just a few years later, Mary admitted that something was wrong with the picture when she said that perhaps she might have made a mistake in trying to compete with a flurry of other costume pictures, "and most of them done better than mine."

Costume pictures didn't seem to be the answer; neither did naughty sophistication. Increasingly, Mary would be torn between two opposing poles: The tight vise of the public's expectations vs. her own sense of what she could get away with. In a 1922 interview, when the inevitable question about adult roles came up, she replied, "There are plenty of other actresses to play those roles. . . . Perhaps in the very last picture I make I'll do something different. Perhaps!"

By 1925, Mary was in something of a quandary about scripts; as a promotion, she asked the readers of *Photoplay* to suggest possible screen roles for her, offering at the same time the reasons for her past choices. *"Stella Maris*—Because it offered my first opportunity of playing a dual role and doing character work, which is always a keen pleasure to me. Because I could end one of the characters unhappily *and not sacrifice the desired happy ending."* (italics added)

She closed with the admonition that "I do not want costume pictures nor foreign themes, but only those dealing with the problems of the average American girl." (Obviously, *Rosita* had begun its fifty-odd years of troubling her like a meal that wouldn't digest.) At the time, this "average American girl" was thirty-three years old.

If she was hoping for a mandate for change, Pickford must have been bitterly disappointed. The favored choices of her public were, in order, Cinderella, Anne of Green Gables, Alice in Wonderland, Heidi, and The Little Colonel.

The latter two were produced years later for Shirley Temple, at the time a child of nine. As for the others, *"Cinderella* I did years ago," Mary tartly commented. "It is possible I may do it again. *Anne of Green Gables* was done by Mary Miles Minter. *Sara Crewe* I did under the title of *The Little Princess."* Clearly, as far as her fans were concerned, Mary could play adolescents until senescence.

She was more than smart enough to realize that she had a problem. In fact, Mary was not above believing she had a problem when she didn't; unlike many insecure people, who compensate by adopting a pose of steely toughness, she didn't mind letting others know she was habitually scared. "She . . . lacks confidence in her own powers," wrote Herbert Howe, an accurate observer of the Hollywood scene. "She is the first to suspect that she's slipping. Indeed, Mary is something of a calamity howler where she, herself, is concerned."

But Herbert Howe was a friend; for those who didn't subscribe to the Pickford myth, it was already late in the day. In what was evidently supposed to be a fond portrait of the couple in 1927, the journalist Allene Talmey said of Mary that "[she] stands alone, unadorned, simple. She is dowdy, old-fashioned, her skirts too long and her hair still piled in those golden unconvincing curls which were so admired in 1915 . . . Compared to her showman husband, alive with jokes, Mary, always by his side, fades a little. But what woman could have competed with the ebullient plumage of a glorious peacock like Fairbanks?" Another editorialist compared Mary favorably to the voluptuously hyperkinetic Clara Bow and said that Mary "was as comfortable as an old shoe."

Although all this was her public image, her image within the Hollywood community was not much more flamboyant. That vaguely chilly dignity that Mary had alluded to when she noted that Charlotte would rough-house with Jack or Lottie but not with her was again asserting itself. A premiere at Grauman's Chinese would not start until Mary and Douglas were in their seats; once, when Mary arrived late at a tea where most of the screen's most glamorous women stars were attending, every woman in the room rose when she entered.

With friends like these, and a native insecurity ("No one is less sure of self, no one more open to criticism and advice" wrote James Quirk) that abided beneath an image that was seeming more and more dowdy, it is no wonder that Mary was headed for trouble in the midst of Jazz-age revelry.

George S. Kaufman often told the story about the moment he fell in love with Beatrice Bakrow, who would become his wife. They were walking up Broadway together when Kaufman saw a pair of salamanders on the sidewalk. As he moved to step on them, Beatrice exclaimed, "Don't! It might be Mary Pickford and her mother!"

Although the contempt of a pair of New York sophisticates would not seem to hold much danger for a woman who had virtually created, then defined the word "star," the truth was that, in the very near future, show business in general and the movies in particular would belong to Kaufman, his Algonquin friends, and the values they represented. The day of the country was fast being replaced by the day of the city.

She was still enormously popular; her films continued to gross large amounts, but the older she got, the less like Little Mary she became. Conversely, the less like Little Mary she became, the more fervently her public willed the fiction that Mary Pickford stay sixteen . . . forever.

Chapter Eight

———

"If you will read the story of Peter Pan and Wendy, you will know a great deal more about Mary and Doug than you do now."

—*Charlie Chaplin*

F O R a very long time, Mary and Douglas's marriage was in something of a perfect balance. Mary the quiet, determined anchor, Doug the mercurial Ariel, as fascinated by the possibilities of play as by the responsibilities of work. Douglas correctly appraised the situation when he said that "her feet were on the ground when we were married. I was just floating through space."

He called his wife "Hipper"; she called her husband "Duber." Mary and Douglas were usually up around dawn six days a week, breakfasting on fruit and coffee, lunching without butter or sweets. Mary maintained her figure by rarely eating any meat except chicken, and never eating candy or dessert. Douglas marked a day a success if he could knock off work at the studio by 4:00 P.M.

Douglas was an attentive, loving husband; Mary carefully preserved dozens of his gift cards and letters to her, and they are the mirror reflections of an ardent, adoring husband.

"Hipper darling. The duber's gone shopping. Will be back soon."

"I adore my beautiful wife."

"My Darling."

"For the world's finest woman."

"For my beautiful girl."

"For the sweetest girl in the world."

And there is one card that is sadly revealing of an aspect of Mary that was carefully kept hidden from the world, the little Canadian girl named Gladys Smith who was determined to achieve, and who her husband knew needed bolstering.

"Be happy dear," the card says. "Everybody admires you."

The flip side of Douglas's attentiveness was his passionate jealousy. If Douglas saw Mary laughing with an old friend, he was convinced they were discussing life pre-Douglas; if she went to the hairdresser's, he would telephone to make sure she was where she was supposed to be.

Doug hated drinking, which meant that he was not overly fond of Mary's family; in addition, Charlotte, Jack and Lottie rather reveled in their shanty-Irish background, while Douglas was something of a culture-vulture and a title-hound.

During the mid- and late-'20s, invitations to Pickfair were avidly desired and just as avidly controlled. Invitations were usually via telegram, with a phone number for replies. The evenings were rarely improvisational, but, rather, programmed. "There was always some little feature cooked up," remembered William Bakewell, a frequent guest in that period. "I remember one night the feature of the evening was *Steamboat Willie*, the Disney cartoon. And once there was a well-known psychic named Jean Dennis. We all went upstairs to the Oriental room, where she made predictions for each of us."

"Mary and Douglas were treated like royalty," remembered Lord Mountbatten, who honeymooned at Pickfair, "and in fact they behaved in the same sort of dignified way that royalty did. They also filled the role of running the very loose sort of society there would have been in Hollywood in those days. They were a great unifying force."

The fabled Pickfair was actually a comparatively modest house, offering only four bedrooms, even as it provided five reception rooms. The hallway at the entrance was of polished parquet, lined with eighteenth century chairs. The design of the house was unusual in that the actual entry hall was at the top of stairs that led off the portico. Once at the top of the stairway, a butler would greet arriving guests and show them into the living room, which was on the left. On the second floor were the bedrooms, while the third floor was a glorified attic that Mary had converted into her "Oriental" room.

The predominant color scheme was of a pale green. In the living room, goldenrod yellow curtains stretched from floor to ceiling and in the corner stood a white grand piano for the use of Mary's niece Gwynne. In the dining room there was a fireplace that didn't get much use, so Mary designed a sliding mirror to cover it.

Both Pickford and Fairbanks's bedrooms offered twin beds; Mary's was decorated with heavy Venetian furniture and a cabinet that was kept as a shrine to Charlotte. Doug's room concentrated on photographs of his wife. There was also a secret bar, installed during Prohibition, that could only be entered by pressing a button.

Pickfair offered a library, although Pickford preferred the less pretentious term "book room." There was only one wall of books, but the shelves were hinged, revealing two more walls of books behind them. "No vulgar display of bookish culture at Pickfair," crowed *Photoplay,* anxious that the silent idols should not seem distastefully intellectual. All of Douglas and Mary's library had bookplates saying "Douglas and Mary Fairbanks" over which was a rather attractive design showing Douglas in character as Zorro, flexing his sword over his head. At his right foot sits Zorro, their wire-haired terrier, and, at his left stands Mary, in costume from *Pollyanna.* Mary's taste in reading leaned towards the disciplinary rather than the narrative or intellectual; she read slowly, sometimes taking as long as twenty minutes a page.

In truth, Mary's taste was not that far removed from that of her audience; in 1924, she listed her favorite pictures of all time as *Robin Hood, The Birth of a Nation, Deception, A Woman of Paris, Tol'able David, Over the Hill, The Kid, Blood and Sand, Seventeen* and *Smilin' Through.* She called Chaplin the greatest director of the screen, saying "He knows women."

Of that list, only Lubitsch's *Deception,* Chaplin's *A Woman of Paris,* Griffith's *The Birth of a Nation,* and King's *Tol'able David* have retained their hold on film historians; the rest were stock favorites of the *Photoplay* sensibility. (To be fair, it should be noted that, a few years later, Mary expressed rapt admiration for Raoul Walsh's decidedly racy *What Price Glory,* calling it "the best picture ever made. Even its vulgarity enchants me.")

In fact, Mary and Doug were so beloved of their fans because, talent aside, they appeared to be so much like them. Their reading appears to have been the equivalent of the reading of their fans: self-help books like *The Mind Makes Men Giants,* and *Biography of an Attitude* were favorites, although Fairbanks had a weakness for crime and detective stories. (It should be noted that some people who knew Douglas very well, like Frank Case, were convinced that he had never been able to sit still long enough to ever read a book. His son, however, remembers him accurately quoting goodly amounts of Shakespeare and Byron from memory.)

Every night, dinner was set for fifteen, even though only two or three might actually sit down to it. Mary sat at the table's head, with Douglas at her side. "We'd go there all dressed up," recalled Miriam Cooper, the wife of director Raoul Walsh, "and sit down at this huge table with the lovely china and servants falling all over themselves serving you, and not even get one lousy drop of wine."

Once in a while Douglas might quietly disappear under the table to startle one of his guests by grabbing their ankles; invariably, one of the chairs would be wired so that the most prestigious VIP would get an electric shock when he sat down. On nights when a movie was shown, the after-dinner drink was a cup of Ovaltine or a dish of fruit, which did not always sit well with everybody. After the movie, people went home . . . but not always.

One night, Mary invited both Charlie Chaplin and John Barrymore to the house. She was nervous about the meeting; neither actor had met the other, both were accustomed to being the center of attention and both were at the apogee of their fame. She needn't have worried. The two of them began talking at dinner and kept talking after dinner.

By this time, everybody else was excluded from the conversation. As Mary had to work the next day, she excused herself and went off to bed. The next morning, when she came down for breakfast, Chaplin and Barrymore were still sitting there, and the conversation was still at flood tide.

"I wish I had been a fly on the wall," she said, and freely admitted to envy and curiosity about the kind of intellectual conversation the two great actors had had.

Mary ran the house, chose the colors, supervised the household staff, but Fairbanks paid for all of it, believing that it was the man's responsibility. As one of Douglas's nieces snidely observed, "Doug paid the bills, Mary bought corner lots." On the other hand, they split the upkeep for the studio.

Household salaries were on the modest side; the butler made $300 a month, with two subsidiary butlers drawing $150. The chief cook earned $200, two chauffeurs earned $150, with one of them doubling as a projectionist and earning an extra $50 for his trouble.

The head gardener earned $200, the laundress $80 a month. Add a governess, a personal maid for Mary, a watchman, a handyman, a kitchen maid, a scullery maid and a few other assorted household hands, and it can be seen that, even in the '20s, Doug Fairbanks was liable for a considerable outlay of what he casually regarded as petty cash. At times, he even helped carry Mary's studio expenses; when playwright Edward Knoblock was hired to work on two scripts, one for Mary (*Dorothy Vernon of Haddon Hall*) and one for Douglas (*Monsieur Beaucaire,* later sold to Paramount for Valentino), it was Douglas who paid Knoblock's £10,000 guarantee.

It did not, however, faze Douglas; money, as far as he was concerned, was good only if it was enjoyed. To that end, one day he took his brother Robert and Robert's wife Lorie to visit some friends in Laurel Canyon. No one was home, but Douglas walked in anyway, and asked Lorie what she thought of the house. "It's just what I'd like to have someday," she said, whereupon Douglas replied, "Then why don't you move in. It's yours!"

They could afford *beau gestes* like that. Financial records filed in 1928 reveal that the average after-tax annual net for the Pickford unit for the previous five years was $300,000; Fairbanks's, on the other hand, was $665,000. Both partners were making one picture a year; Mary's negative costs were in the $400,000-$500, 000 range, while Douglas's were, on the average, around a third higher, although some of his films actually cost as much as a million dollars, the rough equivalent of $6.8 million today.

Mary and Douglas looked upon their films with a minimum of sentimentality, as did, for that matter, everybody else. Every few years, they would ship all their used prints to Eastman Kodak, to be melted down so the silver content in the nitrate prints could be reclaimed. On September 11, 1925, seventeen prints of *Pollyanna* were burned and $28.04 of silver was reclaimed; twenty-one prints of *Rosita* brought $53.68 and so on. The total price for 130 prints of Mary's United Artists productions was $302.74. This wholesale destruction of all spare prints, which was the rule, not the exception, coupled with often indifferent storage conditions that exacerbated the volatile chemistry of the nitrate film itself, explains the tragic, lamentable gaps in the surviving films from the silent era.

Mary's library of old United Artists productions brought in around $5,000 every month from Europe alone; a new picture could be expected to earn an advance of $50,000 from a country the size of Germany. The Pickford Corporation prodded United Artists into aggressively selling her films to countries as far away as

South Africa *(Pollyanna* brought a flat fee of $3,500 and *Little Lord Fauntleroy* brought $5,000), while Russia bought the mysterious *They Shall Pay* for $1,500.

Douglas's first eight pictures for United Artists *(His Majesty, the American; When the Clouds Roll By, The Mollycoddle, The Mark of Zorro, The Nut, The Three Musketeers, Robin Hood,* and *The Thief of Bagdad)* had a cumulative domestic gross of $8 million, a million more than Mary's first eight pictures *(Pollyanna, Suds, The Love Light, Through the Back Door, Little Lord Fauntleroy, Tess of the Storm Country, Rosita,* and *Dorothy Vernon of Haddon Hall).*

Fairbanks's greater earning power indicates a slightly broader (presumably male) audience base, while Mary reigned supreme over the same audience that went to see Norma Talmadge, and, somewhat later, Greta Garbo.

The partners' net worth was wildly over-estimated about this time at $15 million to $20 million for Fairbanks and considerably more for Mary. A more rational figure came from Margaret Case Harriman, an old friend, in 1934. The daughter of the Algonquin's Frank Case, she estimated Mary's worth at between $2 million and $4 million.

Among Douglas's main assets was Rancho Zorro, 300 acres near Del Mar, near San Diego, for which Douglas paid $100,000 in October 1926. Rancho Zorro was to be a sort of country home, while their beach house at Santa Monica, built in 1927 and also costing $100,000, was more of a weekend getaway.

Their friends were few. Mary "loved" Mabel Normand, perhaps because that hoydenish free spirit had a similar personality, a similar Irish bloodline, and similar vices, but with fewer inhibitions. In March 1926, Mabel returned to Hollywood after her experience of being falsely implicated in the William Desmond Taylor murder led her to make a disastrous stab at a Broadway play; Mary bought a full page in *Motion Picture World* and filled it with an adulatory, supportive open letter: WELCOME BACK TO THE SCREEN, MABEL NORMAND.

But Mary and Mabel moved in different social circles. Mary was really only on intimate terms with Frances Marion and, of course, Lillian Gish. "Lillian and Dorothy Gish, and Jack and Lottie and I have always been friends," Mary remembered. "When Jack was a little fellow and we used to ask him who he was going to marry he'd always say 'Dorothy Gish.'" Besides them, there was only Charlotte, or "my world" as Mary called her.

Doug's closest friends were his brother Robert and Chaplin;

underneath them was a retinue of glorified flunkies. Chaplin defined Mary and Douglas's marriage thus: "If you will read the story of Peter Pan and Wendy, you will know a great deal more about Mary and Doug than you do now."

They were each other's most valued critic and best friend; they even made occasional invisible guest appearances in each other's pictures. In a love scene in *Dorothy Vernon of Haddon Hall*, Douglas pinch-hit for Allan Forrest, Mary's brother-in-law at the time, because she wanted a big, athletic back, which Forrest did not possess. In 1927, for his film *The Gaucho*, Doug drafted Mary to play the Virgin Mary in a vision—in two-color Technicolor—that appears to the people of an Andes mountain town. Mary regarded it as "as lovely compliment." She had already played a love scene with Douglas, with her back to the camera, in the previous year's *The Black Pirate*, when leading lady Billie Dove was called away on another picture.

For a long time, they were content this way, in hermetically sealed closeness, safe and secure in Pickfair and at the studio. There they ruled as uncontested bosses. "Nobody, and I mean *nobody*, ever told either one of them what to do," remembered H. Bruce Humberstone, who worked as an assistant director on both of their pictures at one time or another. While Humberstone respected and liked both of them, like most men, he seemed drawn more to Douglas's exuberance.

According to Allan Dwan, who directed them both, Douglas's grasp of film production was more profound, more creative, than Mary's. "[Douglas] liked to begin with no story, no location, no cast, no nothing and build from there," remembered Dwan. "He'd get some glimmer of an idea, turn loose all that enthusiasm and off we'd go on a new project." For Mary, such improvisational looseness would have been terrifying.

At the studio, Mary had her own bungalow, complete with dining room and chef, while Mary and Douglas's business offices were adjoining. Douglas didn't have a bungalow *per se*, but rather used about a third of the administration building as his personal headquarters. There he kept his office, dressing room, barber shop, make-up room, bar, gymnasium and salt water plunge.

Douglas loved to receive presents; one year, Mary gave him a gold cigarette case and a Remington painting (Douglas adored Remington and Charles Russell); another year, she had an authentic bar from a Nevada ghost town installed. For their fifth wedding anniversary in 1925, Mary bought Douglas a gym full of rolling pins, tennis rackets and athletic equipment.

For ten years following their wedding in March 1920, the couple were almost never separated, not even for one day. They began a ritual of taking a long vacation after they finished a picture. By 1931, they had amassed one world tour and six jaunts to Europe.

The destinations varied. In 1929, they went to Switzerland, journeying back to California through Egypt, India, China, Japan and back to Los Angeles via ocean liner across the Pacific. In April, 1926, they, along with Charlotte, sailed for Europe on the *Conte Biancamano*. They attended the premiere of *Little Annie Rooney* in Berlin on May 4, while a week later they had moved to Rome where they were received by Mussolini. While they were on vacation, Charlotte kept her nose to the grindstone; copies of Mary's deposit slips were forwarded to Charlotte at every stopping place. By July, they were in Russia, where 25,000 fans mobbed them at the Moscow train station. Although they had initially planned to continue on around the world, a recurrence of the cancer that would eventually kill Charlotte forced them to return home in August.

As a favor to the nascent Russian film industry, they consented to appear in a scene with a popular Soviet comedian, with the understanding that it would be used as the climax of one of his comedies. It became the centerpiece of a particularly enchanting film called *A Kiss for Mary Pickford*.

Goga (Igor Ilinsky) is a ticket taker at a movie theater that happens to be showing *The Mark of Zorro*. He's desperate to impress his girlfriend, who has eyes only for Douglas Fairbanks. "Boy, Doug can kiss," she moans at every closeup.

Ilinsky, who is more than slightly reminiscent of sad-sack comics like Lloyd Hamilton or Harry Langdon, decides to get into the real movie industry, and worms his way into a studio that Doug and Mary just happen to be visiting. The adoring throngs gaze at their idols as if Jesus was performing the parable of the loaves and the fishes.

Goga stumbles into his opportunity, and there is an impromptu scene with Mary that ends with her giving him a kiss on the cheek. He is promptly rushed by the crowd ("He was kissed by Mary!!!"), which nearly tears him apart attempting to touch Mary, if only by proxy.

"Are you O.K.?" he is asked after being pulled away.

"Could a man who's kissed by Mary *not* be O.K.?" is his reply.

A Kiss for Mary Pickford has no particular sense of Russian-ness about it; it could just as well be German or French. But it shows, with particular vivacity and charm, just how much Douglas and

Mary meant . . . not just to their country, but to their world. Russia, above all other countries, knew icons when it saw them.

———————

After the comparative financial and complete creative failure of *Dorothy Vernon of Haddon Hall,* whose increased production costs had failed to commensurately increase its returns, Mary was in something of a quandary. "People were grumbling," she recalled. "They" [read "I"] didn't like *Rosita,* they didn't like *Dorothy Vernon.* I thought, I have to go back to the little girl whether I like it or not." Searching for a story, Mary began wandering around the back lot, always a haunted, lonesome place, where she engaged in a Socratic dialogue with herself.

"What am I going to do?"

"Well, you're part Irish, right? Who else do you know that's Irish?"

"Well, Mabel Normand."

"All right, if you were producing Mabel Normand's next picture, what would you do?"

"Oh, something Irish, something like . . . *Little Annie Rooney.*"

And that was that. Mary remembered that the story was written quickly, with she and a bunch of gag writers sitting on the lawn for a week from 9:00 A.M. until 5:00 P.M. and another week in the studio, with the only break being lunch over sandwiches. In something of an in-joke, she gave screen credit for the story to "Catherine Hennessey": her grandmother.

Little Annie Rooney was shot from April 6 to June 11, 1925, and released in September. An examination of the production log for the film, apparently the only one to have survived from Mary's silent films, reveals that the filming averaged a fairly leisurely twelve set-ups a day, with most shots requiring no more than four or five takes. Mary did allow herself the luxury of, for the most part, shooting in sequence, which makes it considerably easier on the actors.

But not always. For Mary, acting was primarily an exercise in emotional tranference, not technique. On the day Mary was shooting the scene of Annie Rooney's breakdown upon learning her father has been shot, Rudolph Valentino unexpectedly walked onto the set. Mary liked Valentino and was glad to see him, but she found that when she tried to get back into the scene, it stubbornly resisted her efforts.

"Until he'd walked in, I was twelve years old. When he came in, I was Annie. After his visit, I was Mary, not Annie. I walked up and down outside in agony. I never got it back."

As always, Mary was too hard on herself. While no earth-shattering masterpiece, the what-the-hell, let's-make-a-movie spirit of its production rubbed off. *Little Annie Rooney* is spirited, charming, rambunctious fun, while the scene of her breakdown that, in her mind, she "never got back" is as good a scene as she ever played.

On the other hand, the film suffers from relentless ethnic stereotyping that, while typical of the period, seems antediluvian today, and it is needlessly padded out to ten reels when seven or eight would be a more comfortable fit for the story.

Little Annie Rooney grossed over $1.1 million domestically. In its premiere run in New York, it grossed a total of just over $70,000 at the 2,900 seat Strand Theater, compared to $78,000 for Douglas's *Don Q, Son of Zorro*, which also ran two weeks that same year. (The record run for 1925 at the Strand was Chaplin's *The Gold Rush*, which grossed $214,700 in just four weeks.)

For her next picture, Mary chose a story entitled *Scraps*, which was changed to *Sparrows* shortly before release. The film has often been compared to the work of Dickens and, in its basic plot of imprisoned children, the comparison is apt enough, but *Sparrows* is Dickens laced with a strong dose of Poe.

Mary plays Mama Molly, guardian of ten children imprisoned on a baby farm in what looks to be a mossy, backwoods Louisiana. Living in a shack surrounded by quicksand, presided over by the demonic Mr. Grimes (Gustav von Seyffertitz, in a makeup that owes a good deal to John Barrymore's Mr. Hyde), Molly and her charges make a dash for freedom across alligator-infested swamps, pursued by Grimes and his evil dog, in harrowing scenes that Charles Laughton obviously used as the inspiration for the latter portion of his masterly *Night of the Hunter.*

To buttress the efforts of Charles Rosher, Mary also hired Karl Struss and Hal Mohr and these three great camera artists produced images of dark Gothic splendor as convincing as anything in silent film.

The set designer Harry Oliver aged the tree stumps with blowtorches, and the entire picture has that netherworld quality of a slightly stylized environment that could only be created in a movie studio. *Sparrows* is by far the most densely textured of Mary's later films; although director William Beaudine's reputation was irrevocably tarnished by the endless series of programmers he ground out on Poverty Row during the '40s and '50s, his work on *Sparrows* shows dash as well as creativity.

Take, for example, a shot of Mary and her ten children waving goodbye to another child through cracks in a ragged wooden wall. The disembodied, waving hands and arms provide an image eerily reminiscent of the famous scene in Cocteau's *Beauty and the Beast,* where arms without bodies hold candelabras.

There is notably less comedy in *Sparrows* than was usually the case with Mary's films, but the production design and atmosphere of storybook evil are so strong that it hardly matters. *Sparrows* dates hardly at all, and has the perennial appeal, the Manichean conflicts and visual splendor of one of the great Disney animated features.

Working with so many children appealed to Mary's maternal side, and she developed a particularly strong bond with Mary Louise Miller, a cherubic two-year-old. "None of us were afraid [of the alligators] because we loved Miss Pickford so much," remembered Miller. "She was so beautiful and sweet." Mary particularly liked Mary Louise because she was sweet-tempered, a trouper, and didn't cry. In short, she was what Mary prided herself on being. Mary Louise carried on bravely even when Mary accidentally slipped and fell in the mud, with Mary Louise strapped to her. "She didn't worry about herself," said Miller. "My parents were both there when we filmed and they said all she cared about was whether I was hurt or scared."

At the end of shooting, Mary had become so enraptured by Mary Louise that she evidently talked Douglas into considering adoption. Although the newspapers heralded an offer of a million dollars for the baby, Miller said that "My mother said that she never really said anything about a million dollars. In any case, my parents were only poor people, but they wouldn't give their daughter away for any amount of money." In later years, Miller married a shower installer in Burbank and occasionally corresponded with Mary in her house on a hill. Mary's letters would usually be signed "Momma Molly."

As one of Mary's most unexpected films and her only Gothic melodrama, *Sparrows* might have proved too strong for audiences; although it did well, it did somewhat less so than *Little Annie Rooney*. Produced at a cost of $463,455, its domestic gross was $966,878. Factoring in distribution and advertising costs, Mary realized a clear profit of nearly $200,000 without even considering the money derived from the film's foreign release.

Mary invariably spoke of Douglas fondly, with a particular mixture of love and pride, for the rich and titled of the world knew Douglas and liked him, and, by extension, her. Still, by the late '20s, intimates could sense a strain around the edges of the marriage. Douglas was beginning to be distracted by the opulence of the world outside Hollywood. "You must understand, when you weren't working here, or didn't want to work here, there's nothing," said Phil Rhodes, a makeup man who began working in Hollywood in the early '30s. "In Switzerland, the challenge is to climb the mountain, but once you've done that a few times and gotten bored, there's nothing to do. Hollywood is a lonesome place; Europe has never been a lonesome place."

Conversely, Mary was frankly uninterested in the world outside Hollywood. As *Photoplay*'s James Quirk once wrote, "The only time I ever saw her tired or bored looking was the day after she had approved the final working print on *Little Annie Rooney*.

" 'You're going to take a rest now?' " I asked.

" 'Rest?' she said. 'I'm getting disgusted with loafing already. Do you know a good story?' "

Mary was often worried by Douglas's mania for stunts, for continually topping himself. "Charlie [Chaplin] and I used to sneak down to the set of *Robin Hood,*" she anxiously confided to a friend in later years. "We'd check the hand-holds on all those jumps Douglas used to do. And even though they seemed firm, sometimes I would just sit and cry. I'd talk to him about it and he'd try to convince me it was safe, but if he'd fallen from those heights . . .."

"If a friend comes to Pickfair on a Sunday," said a woman writer, "and peeks inside the gates . . . they will give him a welcome that will warm his heart. They will say, 'Come in, come in' to everyone. But if you try to say, 'Come out, come out' they will shake their heads at you."

It was a parochial, Crusoe-like ideal that jibed neatly with Douglas's view of a relationship; a friend of his once remembered that, coming out of a play dealing with marriage, Douglas had been unusually quiet. Then, suddenly, he said, "But marriage should be you and your wife—and the rest of the world outside."

Enraptured by each other's company, they neither sought nor needed anybody else. Once, when Prince George, the future King of England, asked Pickford to dance, she refused, saying she didn't dance.

"Well, I do and I don't," she added. "You see, I have never danced with anybody but my husband." In retrospect, it can be seen that their's was a relationship that contained the roots of its own destruction, for there was no room in it for anybody but Douglas and Mary. It depended on each of them being totally there for the other at all times, a practical impossibility in any two-career family, let alone one existing in the public eye at the highest reaches of show business. When either was distracted by the demands of career or internal pressures that could not be controlled, the other was bound to feel abandoned.

Charles Rogers was born in Olathe, Kansas, in 1904. From childhood, he had been known as "Buddy," a name bestowed on him by his sister. At the time, Olathe was a farming community of about 3,000, and Rogers' father, Probate Judge B.H. Rogers, also ran Olathe's weekly newspaper. Buddy was seduced by music at an early age, when the town mailman, one F.M. Ott, gave him a baritone horn. "I didn't like it, but that was it," remembered Buddy. "Later, I traded it off for a slide trombone."

Rogers's father was a homey type who knew the first name of everybody in the town, and Buddy quickly grew used to the steady stream of couples arriving to be married at the two-story white frame house on North Kansas Avenue.

When it came time for college, Rogers was sent to the University of Kansas at Lawrence. "When I started going to the University of Kansas I was playing in a little five-piece jazz band," Rogers recalled. "My favorite musicians were Red Nichols and Coon Saunders. They could play!" On good weeks, Buddy could make as much as twenty-five dollars playing one-man duets on the trombone and the drums.

Rogers was also taking journalism courses, but, as he admits, "I really couldn't write very well." Nor did he want to go back and live in Olathe. His long-term ambition involved honing his musical skills in the big city . . . *any* big city. In Rogers's third year of college, his father sent him a letter that said an Olathe exhibitor wanted to enter him in a talent hunt that Famous Players-Lasky was launching.

"I wrote him back and said that I didn't care to participate, as I was interested in music, not dramatics, and besides, I was living at the Phi Kappa Psi fraternity, with a lot of football players, and I thought they'd give me an awful hard time if they thought I wanted to be an actor."

Rogers's father promptly wrote him back. He'd always been a good son, Judge Rogers said, and he'd always tried to be a good father. Would Buddy please take the test as a personal favor? Buddy, always accommodating, said yes.

A few months later, a cameraman, a technician and a director arrived in Olathe and took young Rogers to a park. "It was hot and I was perspiring and they put some makeup on me and told me to smile . . . then laugh . . . then look angry. It was very bad and I photographed terribly. I know, I saw the film later. To this day, I don't know why Mr. Lasky hired me."

But hire him he did, for fifty dollars a week. Rogers and nineteen others were assigned to a nascent young talent program based at Paramount's Astoria studios. The ten boys lived in a hotel for men, the ten girls—among them Thelma Todd—lived in a hotel for girls. "We'd all meet on the subway and converge on the studio and learn how to act," said Rogers.

After a brief stint playing opposite W.C. Fields in *So's Your Old Man* ("He was a very affable man, as long as you didn't bother him when he was drinking"), Rogers appeared with the other talent school members in *Fascinating Youth,* then just missed getting cast in *Beau Geste* and *Old Ironsides.* Rogers was getting quite depressed when he met director William Wellman, who was putting a picture together that was to be called *Wings.* "Bill introduced me to Dick Arlen and we met Gary Cooper going down to San Antonio on the train. I don't think he said ten words all the way down."

The production of *Wings* took eight months and cost $800,000. Rogers's salary was seventy-five dollars a week, from which Paramount deducted ten dollars a week for some suits they'd bought him.

When *Wings* opened at New York's Criterion Theater in August 1927, it was the war film of that year, immediately launching Rogers and Arlen into careers as handsome juvenile leads. Paramount promptly bumped Rogers's salary to $200 a week, and did it out of the effusive goodness of their corporate hearts; Rogers had no agent and didn't want one, for Paramount "had been so nice to me."

This kind, naive Kansas boy was enthralled by the land in which he found himself. "What was nice about silent movies was that we had orchestras on the set for mood music," remembered Rogers.

"If you had to cry, you'd tell them the tune that made you sad—mine was 'Liebestraum'—and they'd sail into it."

While Rogers's looks, genuinely sweet personality and lack of driving ambition limited him to gee-whiz male ingenues, the fact was that he had a bedrock guttiness underneath the cornfed decency.

"I love Buddy," said *Wings* director William "Wild Bill" Wellman shortly before his death in 1975. "He's a tough son of a bitch. To show you how tough he is, he used to hate flying. It made him deathly sick. When we made *Wings,* he logged over ninety-eight hours of flying time and every time he got back down on the ground, he vomited. Yet, he never complained or gave me a hard time. That's a man with guts."

Around the Paramount lot, Buddy was shy but well-liked. "He was a very quiet guy," remembered Artie Jacobson, an assistant director at Paramount who first met Buddy in 1926. "If you wanted to get him to talk, you'd have to talk music. Then, he'd light up like a firecracker. He loved music. He was a whole band, actually; he could literally play every instrument in an average band.

"He was very much a family boy, and proficient in his work. Notice I don't say fantastic. Actors are as good as their script or directors. Occasionally, they're naturals. But Buddy was one of the nicest guys I've ever known."

Shortly after *Wings* finished production, Hope Loring, a writer friend of Rogers's who was working on the script of a story Mary had bought from Kathleen Norris, invited him to a dance, a monthly white-tie-and-tails social engagement called the Mayfair. There, she told Rogers to meet her for lunch the following Monday.

"We drove over to a studio that I didn't realize at the time was United Artists. We drove in front of a beautiful bungalow, and Hope let me out while she parked the car. I rang the bell and Mary opened the door. And that was it."

At the time of their meeting, Mary Pickford was thirty-five years old, more or less happily married, and the most famous woman in the world, while Buddy Rogers was twenty-three and single. During Rogers's screen test for the part, Rogers remembered that "Mary was warm. She was trying to help me. We made a close-up of our two heads together and she put her head against mine and I sort of pulled away and thought to myself, 'Hey, she really wants me to get this part.' She asked me who my favorite movie star was and I stupidly said 'Norma Shearer,' but she was very gracious and laughed."

For her part, Mary noticed "his blue-black hair . . . that lay in thick waves on his beautifully shaped head . . . the next thing I noticed was his dark brown eyes . . . I knew at once that this was a man who would put the idea out of his head if he ever thought the world was otherwise than good."

Buddy Rogers got the job—the actor who lost out to him was stage leading man Donald Cook—and spent six weeks playing opposite Mary; after the grueling production of *Wings*, it seemed like the easiest of jobs.

During production of *My Best Girl*, it very quickly became clear that Rogers had developed a crush on his co-star. There is no question that the attentions of such an attractive younger man as Buddy did much to assuage Mary's fears about the parade passing her by. Buddy was already on his way to earning a reputation as a genuinely kind, overwhelmingly decent man. As Douglas Fairbanks Jr. would say of him, "He's almost too nice; sometimes you wish he'd be a son of a bitch, just to break the monotony."

There is also no question that it was not merely a one-way attraction. There is a famous story about Doug Fairbanks visiting the set of *My Best Girl* on the day the film's charming love scene was shot, and turning away in quiet distress, saying "It's more than jealousy; I suddenly felt afraid." If so, he couldn't have felt too afraid, for Buddy (along with Charles Farrell, Big Boy Williams and Joel McCrea) was often called into service as an "extra man" at Pickfair gatherings.

Still, something, if only a mild flirtation, must have been evident on the *My Best Girl* set. "Her mother wanted Mary to leave Douglas for me while we were making *My Best Girl*," Buddy Rogers claimed after Mary's death. "Her mother brought me presents at Christmas that year.

"You see, Senior was rather a strict man; he had a lot of rules and regulations. Mary's mother was not that welcome at Pickfair when he was there, which was one of the tragedies of Mary's life. She adored her mother, but Doug didn't particularly want her around."

According to Mary's intimates, a woman whom Douglas wanted very much to be around about this time was Lupe Velez, his co-star in his 1927 film *The Gaucho*. Whatever the nature of the relationship, it didn't last long, although Mary was to brood about it for years, and about the insufficiency implied by Douglas's attraction to another woman.

But Mary didn't brood that deeply; a few months after *My Best Girl* wrapped production, Buddy was making *Get Your Man* back at Paramount, with the notoriously man-hungry Clara Bow. Studio workers were shocked to see Mary often showing up on the set, apparently to keep a proprietary eye on Buddy. Asked about it sixty years later, Buddy Rogers giggled slightly and didn't deny it.

Nobody had ever known Mary to do anything like that before, and it was then that, very quietly, people in Hollywood started to wonder about Mary and Douglas's marriage. In truth, Mary needn't have worried about Buddy and Clara. They had already worked together on *Wings,* and nothing had happened; at the time, Bow had been involved with director Victor Fleming.

"Women considered Buddy handsome," said Artie Jacobson, "but he wasn't the kind of guy they'd chase. He was on the shy side, not forthcoming. Temperamentally, Buddy wasn't really an actor."

———— ————

My Best Girl was to be Mary's last silent film, a beautifully produced effort about a poor shopgirl falling in love with the son of the owner of the department store where she works. It had the identical plot of Clara Bow's *It,* released eight months earlier, except that Mary, as in *Rosita,* did what she could not bring herself to do in real life and again portrayed her character's family as a worthless crew of loafers, leeches and hangers-on.

The critics were kind, if condescending; the New York *Times* said that *My Best Girl* would be all right for children but that "Miss Pickford would do better to employ her talent in a more intelligent type of picture." The *Times* also found space to bitchily remark on her eyes having too much makeup. The *World Telegram* said it was a pleasing example of the "simple, exquisite art of Mary Pickford."

And yet, seen today, free of contemporary associations that were tainted by the new breed of raw, sensual films like *What Price Glory,* or a work of art like *Sunrise, My Best Girl* shows an emotional richness and maturity, as well as an increased technical sophistication, that makes it a particularly charming example of Mary's filmmaking expertise. Some of the gags—Mary trying to kick off a pot that has gotten stuck on her foot, and doing it so vigorously that her bloomers drop around her ankles—were venerable wheezes even in 1927. Likewise, her final attempt at convincing the young man she loves that she's really a gold-digger is overplayed and overlong, but the film easily overcomes these minor handicaps.

In the film's most romantic scene, Mary and Buddy walk entranced amidst hordes of pedestrians, awash in the middle of a pouring rain, while streetcars and autos pass within a few feet of them. The enraptured couple pause in front of a furniture store, where the window displays an idyllic scene of domesticity, kids in front of the fire, Dad reading the paper, Mom sewing. "It must be wonderful to spend an evening like that after supper," says Maggie/Mary, with the same plaintive yearning and wistful wishing for just one fixed point in the otherwise chaotic universe of the traveling actor that Gladys/Mary must have expressed twenty-five years earlier.

In another scene, Mary comes out of the store at quitting time and fixes her hat in the reflection of a brass "Employees Entrance" sign. While the other employees hop on a streetcar, Mary hops on the back of a truck to get home, and the film briskly achieves nearly as effective a picture of the mean lives of the *lumpen* proletariat of the '20s as King Vidor's devastating *The Crowd*.

With the film's intrinsic, gentle romanticism, and with the elegant night photography of Charles Rosher emphasizing the vastness of the city (which oddly echoes the impersonal metropolis of Murnau's concurrently shooting *Sunrise*), *My Best Girl* moves quite beyond the realm of a shopgirl's romance. There are odd, unstressed behavioral details, like Maggie's father rubbing his head with liniment to stimulate hair growth, that are absent in other Pickford films.

As in *Rosita,* Mary plays the voice of sanity and the sole support of an otherwise frivolous, worthless family ("Where's Maggie—can't she do something about it?" says a title at a critical plot point). A few scenes later, Maggie promises her harridan mother "Don't worry Ma—I'll never leave you again as long as I live."

My Best Girl captures the homely myths of an America that was still poised awkwardly between rural values and urban lifestyles. In the mingling of shame, devotion and impatience that Maggie displays towards her family, and in Mary's smooth pairing with the youthfully ardent Buddy Rogers, which is, even without hindsight, far more emotional in nature than the nominal love interests her films usually displayed, it is clear that, in a way that Mary herself might not have understood, *My Best Girl* served as some sort of emotional autobiography.

The film had the solid success it deserved; in its premiere New York engagement, at the Rialto, *My Best Girl* grossed $81,000 in its three week run, recouping a sixth of its production cost of $483,103 at just one theater. It's total domestic gross amounted to $1,027,757.

While on a trip to New York on business, Mary had been met at the train station by Tess Michaels, who was working in the publicity department at United Artists. At first, Mary struck Michaels as "slightly aloof, but warm," but the employer/employee relationship soon evolved into close friendship. For years, Michaels had an open invitation to spend Christmases at Pickfair, a remarkable gesture from a woman who did not have a particular gift for making friends.

"If Mary liked you, then you had a true friend," remembered Michaels, who found her occasional eccentricities fascinating. Mary would, for instance, rarely carry a purse, which made it difficult for her to satisfy her charitable impulses. Panhandlers invariably got something, but it would have to come from whomever she was with. Once, when Tess Michaels was meeting her at Grand Central Station, they were approached by a panhandler. Michaels dug into her purse and gave him five dollars.

"Mary acted like I'd insulted her," remembered Michaels. "Tess, Darling, give him a little more than that," Mary said.

In *My Best Girl*, Maggie/Mary is saved from a life of family servitude by her Milquetoast father's last-reel declaration that "From now on, *I'll* be the father of the family." Mary was not as lucky as her character of Maggie, but the intermingled feelings of resentment and dependence about her mother and siblings were equally as strong.

Mary had bought Charlotte a house at 917 Beverly Canon Drive. Just before Prohibition, Charlotte bought out the entire stock of a neighborhood liquor store and had it stashed in her basement, so Jack and Lottie would have a safe place to drink. Charlotte also had something of a thirst, and regularly stationed Lottie's daughter Gwynne on the porch to warn her if Aunt Mary should happen to drive up unannounced, so Charlotte could stow the offending bootleg bottles.

Late in 1924, Charlotte had been foraging in an old trunk for some material for a costume for Mary. The trunk lid fell, striking her on the breast. Shortly thereafter, Charlotte felt a slight burning sensation and noticed a lump. In December, the lump was examined and the diagnosis came back: carcinoma of the breast. Charlotte refused to have the disfiguring operation that was called for.

The cancer began spreading, to the lungs, liver and finally, and most agonizingly, to the bones. Charlotte tried to keep her mind off the pain by taking up painting and managed to complete some oil still lifes that showed some modest talent. Alienated from her own religion, and feeling guilty that Charlotte's attentiveness to her career had been directly responsible for the cancer, Mary began to panic, dragging Christian Science practitioners to Charlotte's bedside. Nothing helped, although Charlotte did live more than three years after the diagnosis.

As soon as *My Best Girl* was completed in the fall of 1927, Mary moved into her mother's house to take care of her. Finally, Bebe Daniels and her mother brought a priest to Charlotte so she could have the last rites. When Charlotte finally died, on March 21, 1928, at the age of fifty-five, Mary exploded in grief, smashing Douglas in the face with her fists as he tried to comfort her. Later, when Jack and Lottie arrived, she screamed at them, for not being with her when their mother had died.

"I was completely out of my mind," remembered Mary. "I have a few fitful snapshots of sanity that come back through that maddening cloud of grief: being amazed, for example, at Douglas's lips being as white as they were."

In keeping with Charlotte's feelings about surgeon's knives, there was no autopsy. Charlotte was buried on March 24 at Forest Lawn. When her will was probated, it was found that she had left an estate valued at $1,144,972. Her will directed that three trust funds of $200,000 apiece be carved out of it, for Lottie, Jack and Gwynne. The rest went to Mary "because whatever property I am possessed at the time of my death has come to me through my association with my said beloved daughter in her business and through her most unusual generosity to me." As it happened, the estate was not settled until 1933, by which time Jack had died.

Charlotte's death also left the fate of Lottie's daughter up in the air. When Lottie's marriage to Albert Rupp had gone on the rocks, leading Lottie to the bottle, Charlotte had adopted the child, Mary Charlotte. On Charlotte's death, Mary was made guardian of Mary Charlotte, who, in 1930, had her name changed to Gwynne "because . . . the similarity of her name and that of her guardian caused much confusion."

For a long time, Charlotte's terminal illness had given Mary an alternative obsession to her career. By the time Charlotte died, however, sound had come in; although *The Jazz Singer* premiered in October 1927, the great, panicked changeover to talkies didn't occur for nine months or so, when it became apparent that even an awful movie with sound was grossing considerably more than the finest silent picture.

The normally astute Joe Schenck tried to stonewall the inevitable when, in August 1928, he announced that United Artists would not make talkies. "I do not believe the present talking picture craze is more than a public curiosity in a novelty," he said. "It is a novelty and a badly done one. I prophesy they will not last more than four or five months."

Mary's feelings were more ambivalent than Douglas's and Schenck's. "I would rather *do* talking pictures," she said, "but I would rather *see* silent pictures, because they lend themselves more to action and imagination." At the same time, she bewailed the loss of that stark, vivid immediacy, the strong, immutable way that silent pictures had of communicating often quite complicated emotions to an audience. Still, the future had to be faced.

On June 21, 1928, Mary chose to face it in a most surprising fashion. On that day, she walked into the Charles Bock salon on East 57th Street in New York and had her hair, which by that time extended halfway down her back, cut into a stylish bob. Just three years before, the subject had arisen as short hair became increasingly stylish. "Wouldn't it be a shame to bob that wonderful hair?" asked *Photoplay* in a 1925 caption underneath a portrait of Mary with her hair cascading down, covering her breasts.

Two years later, in a by-lined article in *Pictorial Review,* Mary claimed that "my curls have become so identified with me that they have become almost a trademark, and what old-established firm would change its trademark without giving considerable thought to the matter?" It was a rare public glimpse of Mary the hardheaded businesswoman.

She also admitted that she was by nature conservative and old-fashioned, but said that the biggest single reason she had kept her hair long was "fan mail." "Every day letters come in saying 'Please do not bob your hair.' . . . I should feel that I was failing them if I ignored such an insistent plea. I haven't the courage to fly in the face of their disapproval, nor have I the wish. If I am a slave, at least I am a willing slave. For their love and affection and loyalty, I owe them everything and if curls are the price I shall pay it."

Yet, slightly more than year after that article was published, the beloved curls were no more. "I wanted to be free of the shackles of playing little girls with curls," Mary said frankly in 1958. "I thought [cutting my hair] was one step towards it. I got the most indignant, insulting letters. I thought, 'If that's all it is, after a lifetime in the theater and motion pictures, if all it is is eighteen curls keeping me in pictures, it's about time I retired.' "

It was, of course, no accident that Mary had waited until Charlotte was dead. For Charlotte, Mary's screen character was the family franchise, and Charlotte's supreme object of contemplation. For Mary, it was the childhood she'd never had. As Adela Rogers St. Johns had noted, Mary and Charlotte's relation to each other was more than that of a loving mother and daughter, it was that of a sculptress and her masterpiece. To cut off her curls, to play something other than the well-defined Pickford screen character, would have been the equivalent of abandoning the child that Mary created on the screen, the child that Mary, in large part, was.

But now that Mary's mother was dead, she—and by extension, her character—was free to grow up . . . or attempt to. The absence of Mary's curls brought her up to date, made her look more modern, but it also had the presumably unintended effect of making her look older; where the long hair had softened and given her oval features a classical Madonna-like beauty, shorter hair made Mary look her age. Which is just what she wanted: to bury the little girl with the curls once and for all, to play women with husbands and lovers and children; women, in short, with a sexual identity and a sexual role to play.

But the truth—and a truth that was within the knowledge of even Mary's fans, if they chose to listen—was that Mary's cutting of her hair was in some measure a belated act marking the end of a time that had already passed.

It seemed like a typically independent act for Mary, but the world at large didn't know that Mary was far from independent; she was, in fact, secretly dependent, partially on Douglas, certainly on Charlotte. But Charlotte was dead. Now, without Charlotte to help her choose her scripts, without Charlotte to please, Mary had to fall back on her own judgment, which was largely predicated on pleasing her public. But that judgment was clouded by grief, by worry over her marriage, and by this new thing called "sound." In the fall of 1928, Mary Pickford had too much on her mind.

Chapter Nine

"There is no trouble between Douglas and me. We are devoted, as much in love with each other as ever."

—*Mary Pickford, 1929*

*I*N 1928, Helen Hayes had made a considerable hit on Broadway in the Jed Harris production of *Coquette.* Mary had seen
the play in New York and adored Hayes's performance, calling her "a superb actress, with . . . wonderful diction."
Norma Besant was precisely the kind of part Mary had been lust-
ing after: feminine, cute, but with a willful sensuality that destroys
the lives of all the other characters. She bought the play and
prepared to make her talkie debut.

Coquette went into production just after Christmas 1928, and the
cumbersome, inefficient method of shooting sound films made it a
difficult film for everyone. "Mary had been fine when her photographic tests were made," recalled Edward Bernds, a technician
at United Artists during the changeover to sound. "But she was a
little less confident when we did the sound tests. I recall the cameraman telling her of the difficulties that sound shooting entailed:
the use of incandescent lights instead of arc lights; the necessity of
shooting from a soundproof booth through a plate-glass window,
which, in effect, made mediocre lenses out of superb ones. Mary
understood the problems. It seemed to annoy her rather than
intimidate her."

Mary's memories jibed with Bernds's sense of her feelings. She did her initial voice test at Paramount, listened to the playback and was horrified. "That's not me! That's a pipsqueak voice. It's impossible. I sound like I'm twelve or thirteen. Oh, it's horrible!"

She was not the only star appalled at her own voice. "Over at Paramount, we'd been reading all about talkies and getting pretty nervous," remembered Buddy Rogers. "Dick Arlen had been on the stage once, [Gary] Cooper never had and I knew I had this corny Kansas accent. Dick and Coop and I made a pact to protect the one of us that we figured would turn out not to have a voice; the other two would give him a certain segment of our salaries until he could find something else to do.

"I'll never forget the time I was standing outside a stage, and the door burst open with some guy running out yelling 'Wally Beery has a voice, Wally Beery has a voice!' It was a strange time in Hollywood."

The pressure intensified; Mary couldn't help but unfavorably compare her voice to that of Helen Hayes. To make matters much worse, Pickford also lost the services of Charles Rosher. During an emotional scene, a shadow fell across Mary's face and Rosher yelled "cut." In addition to his own drive for perfection, Rosher had grown to feel a personal responsibility for Mary's appearance.

When she found out why Rosher had stopped the camera, Mary stalked off; once again, a highly emotional scene had been spoiled by a thoughtless intrusion. Rosher responded in kind. "He walked off and that was it," remembered Joan Marsh Morrill, Rosher's daughter. "He knew his business so thoroughly that he could become temperamental. He had a temper."

Mary was frankly embarrassed over firing Rosher. "He was so much of an artist," she complained years later to a friend. "And it was *my* scene." Explaining the incident to George Pratt of Eastman House, Mary said that "it nearly broke my heart. His devotion to me was such that it had to be perfect every moment. When it was time, I didn't have the backbone to face him. I left him a letter." Mary remembered the letter as saying "I am determined to give a performance and I have to cry a lot. Tragedy is an ugly mask; I don't care how I look. I'm going after the Oscar. I don't want to look like something on a candy box or a valentine. I can't do it unless I'm allowed full liberty."

When she returned to the bungalow, Mary found Rosher pacing back and forth, very upset. He told her that he didn't think she appreciated the devotion he had given to her career; he had never expected anything like that from her, of all people. Although Rosher and Mary eventually repaired their friendship, he never photographed another one of her pictures. Mary replaced Rosher with Karl Struss, who had worked with the older man on *Sparrows;* even though Rosher had shot a good deal of the film before his departure, Struss received sole screen credit.

(Edward Bernds remembered that Rosher's departure might just as easily have been partially due to an inability on his part to make the thirty-seven-year-old actress look seventeen; Rosher's considerable ego, would certainly not have permitted him to acknowledge such a failing.)

Mary's firings did not end with Rosher. At one point during the production, she wanted to see a test she had made. The head of sound at United Artists, Howard Campbell, had been dissatisfied with the sound quality and ordered the tests shown to no one, then had them taken away. "In those days," explained Ed Bernds, "sound recording was photographic, not magnetic as it became in just a few years. The sound had to be photographed correctly, and developed correctly. Likewise, the print had to be exposed correctly and developed correctly.

"When Mary came to the projection room and was told that there was neither sound nor picture available, Campbell was as dead as a man who has just been stabbed through the heart; he just hadn't fallen down yet."

Pickford did not scold, threaten or explode; a security man from the studio drove a car around to a fire exit on Santa Monica Boulevard and helped Campbell move his personal belongings out of the studio. Nobody in the United Artists sound department ever saw him again.

As if all this wasn't trouble enough, Mary and co-star Johnny Mack Brown became involved. "I was very good friends with Johnny and his wife, and Connie [Mack Brown's wife] came to me crying that this terrible woman was trying to break up her marriage," remembered Lina Basquette. "Johnny and Connie had a very good, decent, small-town kind of marriage, but Mary rattled him. He was never much of an actor, but, my, he was gorgeous! At the time, it was almost a scandal, but Mary had enough power to keep it quiet."

For over a half-century, it has been thought that Douglas's initial wanderlust led to a lessening of the bond between the marriage partners, which was followed by his infidelities, and that Mary was a blameless victim of her husband's male menopause. But it would seem that the instability may very well have co-existed in Mary as well. After the death of Charlotte, Mary felt terribly isolated. The most famous woman in the world, a role model of marital ballast,

Mary was really a frightened woman who was seeking out others, ever so discreetly of course, for reassurance.

All the accumulated tension inevitably lapped over onto the set. During the scene where Norma is informed of her lover's death, Mary began crying and couldn't stop. "Auntie cried steadily for twenty-four hours," remembered Gwynne. "They had to shut down production. I told her, 'You don't really know him; Michael doesn't really exist.' She'd say, 'I can't help it, it's so sad.' "

As with the story about Mary being yanked out of character by the inopportune appearance of Valentino on the set of *Little Annie Rooney,* the story reveals the intensely emotional conduit between acting and Mary's deepest feelings about the death of a loved one, the most final abandonment of all.

Whether or not the attraction between Mary and Brown assumed sexual status, Douglas must have been unaware of it; Brown and his wife were regular guests at Pickfair for several years after the filming of *Coquette.* Shortly after Brown starred in King Vidor's *Billy the Kid,* he and Douglas even went on a bachelor's jaunt to New Mexico together, touring the haunts of the character Brown had just played. It was on the trip that Douglas came across the mahogany bar that Mary later had installed at Pickfair as a gift for her husband.

———

Shooting *Coquette* was an enormously frustrating experience; Mary preserved dozens of reels of out-takes that show that, if the equipment wasn't nervously malfunctioning, the actors were. Two weeks were spent in rehearsals, with Karl Struss devising a method for shooting most sequences with four cameras, in a precursor of the system now commonly used to shoot TV sitcoms. The idea was to give Mary and the other actors more of a chance to get into the dramatic flow of the scene. Most scenes ran three or four hundred feet, about two or three minutes, but the climactic trial sequence, an intended dramatic tour de force, ran eleven minutes. For that, Struss used six cameras, and the resulting rush of footage and editing choices meant that director Sam Taylor was able to shoot the scene in only two days instead of the scheduled five. The film was finally completed for the reasonable cost of $489,106.

Coquette was released in April 1929, opening at New York's Rialto Theater. Since nothing else had gone smoothly, nobody should have expected the premiere to either. Two minutes into the picture, a fuse blew. The projectionist rewound the first reel and started again, but something was wrong with the sound system; all that could be heard were intermittent flashes of dialogue, accompanied by very faint music.

Mary's voice proved to be a small, piping thing, but with a certain piquant charm. In a way, it fitted her screen character more than a smoky, mysterious contralto would have, but it also was more ordinary, less distinctive than it might have been. Mary's voice, however, was not the main problem with *Coquette*. It is a fatal example of the dreaded disease of "early talkie-itis," a slavish transcription of a play so silly, so bereft of recognizable human behavior that David Belasco would have cheerfully committed murder for the opportunity to produce it.

The story involves Norma, the flighty daughter of a small town southern doctor with a terrible temper. After Norma spends the night with a well-meaning ne'er-do-well played by Johnny Mack Brown, the father shoots and kills him (inexplicably off-screen). At the trial, Norma perjures herself by claiming rape in order to save her father, whereupon his oddly dormant sense of honor is reawakened and he commits a public suicide with the murder weapon, which the court has conveniently kept loaded for just such an eventuality. Norma, now supposedly transformed from girlhood to womanliness by these twin tragedies, pulls herself together and announces that she's going home "to help [her brother] Jimmy with his algebra."

As cinema, *Coquette* is paralytic, a devastating falling-off from the fluid, entirely satisfying *My Best Girl* of just eighteen months earlier. (Clips from the two films could be juxtaposed as an example of the terrible toll that was exacted on the cinema by the coming of sound.) As a performance piece, the actors are trapped by the cornpone dramatics and the sexual hysteria. The performances are all redolent of barnstorming melodrama, which is to say resolutely artificial and slightly absurd. While pleasant enough, Johnny Mack Brown was rather obviously cast for his southern accent and his strong resemblance to Buddy Rogers.

Although designed by the superlative William Cameron Menzies, the sets are disappointingly pedantic and unrealistic. They are, in effect, stage sets, and the camera(s) of Karl Struss, helplessly enclosed in the big box that muffled the sound of the mechanism but forbade any kind of movement, is static, never breaking through the fourth wall.

Yet, any doubts about Mary's viability as a star in the Brave New World of sound were washed away by the commercial success of *Coquette*, which grossed over $1.4 million domestically, providing

Mary with her most successful picture ever. More importantly, it fulfilled the ambition she had revealed in her letter to Rosher by winning her the Academy Award for Best Actress. Considering the caliber of her performance, the Oscar would have been incomprehensible were it not for her social position within Hollywood. Mary's Oscar for her inferior work in *Coquette* surely qualifies as the first Life Achievement Award to be handed out by the Academy. Nevertheless, she was nearly as proud of the Oscar as she was of her credits for Belasco; for years, the Oscar resided in the guest house at Pickfair.

Despite the film's public success and Mary's recognition as Best Actress, many remained unconvinced. "It was a creditable first try," sniped *Photoplay,* heretofore a relentless Pickford booster, "but few could be found who would agree with the Academicians that it was last year's outstanding labor before the microphone."

"I never thought her voice was quite what it should have been," said Douglas Fairbanks, Jr. "It needed some loosening up, because it was a little small and tight. But she was always very self-confident about it. She always talked about her stage experience, but even though she'd only been a child actress, she always referred to it as if she'd had a very long career. Looking back on it, I don't think she wanted any advice."

Concurrently, Douglas was making *The Iron Mask,* a sequel to *The Three Musketeers.* It was predominantly a silent picture, and a fine one, but in a brief scene, the world at large heard Doug Fairbanks's voice for the first time . . . a barking, explosive tenor.

The prologue for the film's second half involved Douglas facing the camera and delivering a short speech. After numerous trial runs, a successful take was achieved, but on the playback, the machine spun out of control; Douglas's voice sped up until it was a prancing falsetto. He turned a ghastly green. Who could blame him? Rumors of disastrous sound tests were rampant throughout Hollywood, and even the biggest stars could not affect indifference.

Yet, both Mary and Douglas surmounted the threat of disaster, and rather triumphantly at that. Joe Schenck had partially financed Douglas's last two silent pictures, *The Gaucho* and *The Iron Mask.* Their combined negative costs were $2,522,000. Of that, $2,170,000 came from Schenck while $352,000 came from Fairbanks. After the returns were all in, Schenck's Art Cinema

Corporation made $130,000 profit while Doug received $370,000 from his profit participation, in addition to $100,000 salary per picture.

Everybody was making money, although everybody was assuredly not happy. Still, no one seemed to have any idea that the days of Douglas's—and everyone else's—carefree prankishness were coming to an end.

———————— ——

By the time *Coquette* was released, Mary was already forging ahead on her second talkie, a film that would prove to be a watershed in both her and Douglas's careers: *The Taming of the Shrew.* The impetus to make their first co-starring vehicle a Shakespeare adaptation came from the January 1929 appearance in Los Angeles of the Stratford-Upon-Avon players. Mary and Douglas saw the play and enjoyed the manner in which the knock-about aspects of the script were emphasized. They both agreed that this was the vehicle in which they should make their long-awaited co-starring effort.

By March, Sam Taylor, who had again been hired to direct (at $4,000 a week) was charged with collecting and collating the various stage adaptations that had been done over the years, from E.H. Sothern and Julia Marlowe's, to Augustin Daly's. On March 9, Taylor wired Laurence Irving, the nephew of Sir Henry Irving, who Douglas and Mary had met on their 1928 trip to Europe and who they wanted to supervise the film's art direction: CHEERIO. THE FOLLOWING IS MY IDEA OF PRODUCTION . . . WILL EMPHASIZE LIGHT AND WHIMSICAL FEELING OF PLAY AND MAINTAIN SPIRIT OF CHEERFUL FUN WHICH MUST BE REFLECTED IN SETTINGS. HAVE NO MASSIVE SETS, BUT KEEP EVERYTHING INTIMATE AND INTERESTING WITH TRUE FEELING OF PERIOD WITH SETS THAT ARE UNUSUAL AS AN ARTISTIC IMPRESSION RATHER THAN A MOUNTAIN OF WOOD AND PLASTER. HOPE TO HAVE MENZIES WORK WITH YOU . . . BEFORE LEAVING YOU BETTER DRINK ENOUGH TEA TO LAST SEVERAL MONTHS, AS YOU'LL GET NONE AT 5 O' CLOCK WHILE WORKING FOR ME, YOU LAZY, LANKY, LANGOUROUS LONG-LEGGED RACK FOR PONDEROUS OVERCOAT . . .

Daniel Frohman heard of Mary's ambitious new film and wrote her suggesting that at the end of the movie, Katherine should give a broad wink to her assembled friends to let them know that she had been in control of the situation all along.

Mary wrote Frohman back that she thought his suggestions "excellent and agree with you that it is Katherine who eventually tames Petruchio. I believe Ada Rehan had the same idea, for after delivering the famous speech to the wives she always gave a most meaning and knowing wink. She credited Katherine with the intelligence to know that both flies and husbands are better caught with syrup than with vinegar."

In mid-May, Constance Collier arrived to serve as Mary's acting coach. Rehearsals began on June 6. Although Mary in later years always insisted that the making of *The Taming of the Shrew* was a disastrous experience that irrevocably showed her the vast, irreconcilable differences between her husband's temperment and hers, no one who worked on the picture saw it that way.

"[Doug] was not difficult," insisted Karl Struss, the cameraman. "He was very exuberant, full of fun, and Mary was more concerned about the dollars and cents aspect of it all. One afternoon about three o'clock this man came in with a tray about three feet in diameter, loaded with sandwiches and drinks. The director called out 'Take ten,' meaning take a break.

"Well, Mary was horrified at stopping the production in the middle of the afternoon and taking a break. She was very serious, and Doug was very exuberant and full of fun, a great kidder, a lot off-screen like he was on." Struss also insisted that, contrary to Pickford's version, Fairbanks was never late in the morning and that he only had to play a few scenes using cue cards.

Edward Bernds, who was again working on the sound crew, remembered that "Mary was businesslike, professional and tolerant of Doug's pranks." A favorite on the set of *The Taming of the Shrew* was a director's chair that happened to be wired to a Ford spark coil. When the switch was thrown, the chair passed on a terrific jolt that stopped just short of manslaughter. A particularly prized variation on this joke was when the man whose job was to throw the switch was persuaded to sit in the hot seat, with the victim thus giving himself the jolt. It was this atmosphere of frat house exuberance that made movies an almost accidental by-product of the Fairbanks lot.

"Mary had a prop man," recalled Ed Bernds, "an earnest, loyal retainer, who happened to have a very sensitive sternum. Doug was expert in many things and among them was the ability to work with his back to his victim. One day on *The Taming of the Shrew,* the prop man passed Doug, carrying a valuable prop vase. Doug tipped the handle of his sword forward, which raised the scabbard and made a direct hit on the man's most sensitive spot. He screamed, and tossed the vase high in the air. It landed on the sound stage floor, smashing into the proverbial thousand pieces.

"Mary surveyed the damage and said, with just a touch of reproof, 'Oh, Duber!' "

Seeing *The Taming of the Shrew* today, it is hard to determine just what the objective reasons for Mary's unhappiness were. Although she complained in later years about Sam Taylor's condescension towards her, two years later she hired him again, which hardly indicates a burning dissatisfaction on the part of the producer/star. In any case, the technicians who worked on the picture remembered Taylor as a classically passive Hollywood director: set the camera up, make sure that the shot was composed, and then have the actors do what the script told them to do.

In later years, Mary's complaints about the film seemed to revolve around a slightly paranoid feeling that Douglas had taken advantage of her. "In the first place," she explained to George Pratt, "Shakespeare requires a great deal of study and control of breath. Also . . . thought. The more you think, the better your diction, the better you're able to project what, to the modern world, is almost a foreign language . . . On the other hand, Douglas gave a magnificent performance [but] he'd been studying it since he was seven . . . I wasn't fair to myself when I took Katherine on. I wasn't torn to pieces in London and I deserved to be."

In retrospect, Mary would refer to her Katherine as "a spitting kitten" instead of a whip-cracking harridan and, in her interview with Pratt, acted out how she would play the part with the advantages of thirty years of hindsight. The later interpretation is all chest and stomach tones; deeper, more menacing and noticeably malevolent. Because the all-important lyricism is absent, Mary's re-interpretation is more redolent of Lady Macbeth than of Lady Petruchio, and not that much of an improvement.

Mary and Douglas's *The Taming of the Shrew*, while a heavily cut version of the original play, is intelligent and is, in fact similar to a "tab" version of the play that David Garrick used—under the title of *Katherine and Petruchio*—for years. In essence, the rival lovers Lucentio and Hortensio are compressed into a single character named Hortensio, and Bianca barely exists. The adaptation concentrates instead on the crowd-pleasing hurly-burly between Petruchio and Katherine.

In his memoirs, Laurence Irving (who, along with William Cam-

eron Menzies, was responsible for the art direction) spoke disparagingly of Taylor, saying that "Day and night, he was attended by
two gagmen—rude nonsensicals after the Bard's own heart . . .
Whenever dialogue that could not be cut tended to lag, or was
reckoned incomprehensible to the ninepennies, they were called
upon for a diversion."

Earlier in Irving's book, he disapprovingly quotes a studio func-
tionary as admitting that, yes, Pickford and Fairbanks are producing *The Taming of the Shrew,* but they "were turning it into a
comedy."

But what else could it possibly have been? Taylor's decisions are,
for the most part, completely appropriate to the material and
would surely have been approved of by the original author, an
experienced theatrical professional.

The only alteration that might be said to change the play's
intent takes place during Petruchio's soliloquy wherein he ex-
pounds on just how he intends to curb Kate's "mad and head-
strong humor." Taylor has him explaining all this to his dog, Troi-
lus, but he also has Kate overhear Petruchio from a balcony, which
has the effect of letting her in on her own humiliation. Kate's
acquiescence to her taming is strongly suggested in the play, but
Taylor evidently felt the need to make that which was suggested
blatantly obvious.

Fairbanks does not particularly need to *act* Petruchio; there is
no need for a performance in the conventional sense simply because he was born to play the part as written. Pickford is not quite
as comfortable, and is more obviously "acting" while her husband
is more comfortable to just "be."

In any case, the picture was co-financed by its stars on a budget
of $504,000. Rehearsals began on June 6, 1929, production began
on June 24 and finished on August 5, an expeditious schedule of six
weeks. In spite of the quick schedule, there was no question of
making a "cheater." Mary and Douglas even shot a couple of reels
of tests in Technicolor, but decided not to use it in the finished
film. Sadly, that Technicolor footage, the only record of Mary's
Nordic coloring, appears to no longer be extant, save for a few
brief, greatly faded moments that indicate Mary's displeasure with
all about her.

When released in October 1929, the ads proclaimed TO-
GETHER FOR THE FIRST TIME! ALL TALKING ALL LAUGH-
ING COMEDY SENSATION! The critics were properly generous;
the New York *Times* named *The Taming of the Shrew* one of the
ten best pictures of the year.

For the first time, however, the partners' timing had deserted them. The stock-market crash had diverted attention from a long-hoped-for-pairing of what had for so long been the world's favorite lovers.

Whether because of that, or perhaps because they had begun to be perceived as an old married couple of nearly ten years standing who were both treading heavily on the thin ice of middle age, the world wasn't wildly interested.

The Taming of the Shrew grossed $1.1 million, doubling its negative cost, so it was far from a disaster. But, considering the expectations that the pairing of the two most famous actors in the world had aroused, it seemed an insufficient amount.

For years, the film lay unseen, the victim of a supercilious story that Sam Taylor had helped himself to the ludicrous credit title: "By William Shakespeare. With additional dialogue by Sam Taylor." It was a good story, repeated ad nauseum for years in various motion picture histories. Like the horror stories about John Gilbert's falsetto voice (a thoroughly imaginary tale, as even a cursory glance at any Gilbert talkie reveals), it was a handy club with which to lash the (supposedly) childishly naive early filmmakers.

There's only one problem: It's not true. As both the script, the pressbook and the print of the original version of the film preserved at the Museum of Modern Art attest, Taylor's credit was "Adapted and Directed by Sam Taylor."

Although Pickford always loathed the film, the release of the successful Franco Zeffirelli production of 1967 impelled her to allow a modest re-issue. Originally seventy-three minutes long, *The Taming of the Shrew* was cut by seven or eight minutes, mostly bits and pieces of footage involving the already limited other characters.

Matty Kemp, a former juvenile for Mack Sennett, by then the director of the Mary Pickford Company, took the liberty of re-dubbing all the actor's voices except those of the two stars, and added a reasonably efficient, if anachronistic, musical score, which had the unfortunate effect of banishing the lovely and appropriate Scarlatti that Sam Taylor had originally used. This slightly modified version of one of the few Pickford films that needs no context for a modern audience is the only one available today.

Pickford's unhappiness with her husband and their co-starring collaboration and her feelings of failure in attempting classical parts, seemed to be largely a case of hindsight; shortly after *The Taming of the Shrew* was shown in London, Mary and Douglas made inquiries to George Bernard Shaw about the rights to *Caesar and Cleopatra.* Shaw, although fond of Douglas, had not liked their adaptation of Shakespeare, and asked Ivor Montagu, a mutual acquaintance of his and Fairbanks, to discourage the idea.

Douglas told Montagu the dubious story that he and Mary had no intention of starring, but only wanted to produce the picture. When that failed to convince Shaw, Mary asked Montagu to lunch and told him that no one but she could do justice to the part. "Mr. Shaw is most insistent in the play that Cleopatra . . . is only a young girl just starting in her teens. Well, I am the only actress in Hollywood who is capable of playing a really young girl and also accustomed to acting as a Queen." Although Montagu, on reflection, thought she was probably quite right, Shaw still refused to sell.

In any case, Mary's apparent bravado was a very thin shell covering a larger disaffection. In her own mind, she still had not resolved the question of just what kind of actress Mary Pickford was going to be in the talkies. Of equal importance was the restlessness of Douglas's that could no longer be ignored. In that year of 1929, she was saying petulant things to the press like, "I will not give up making pictures!" when nobody had suggested she should. "Why should I [quit]" she continued. "I am young. The public still wants me."

". . . There is no trouble between Douglas and me. We are devoted, as much in love with each other as ever."

". . . If mother had only lived."

The defensiveness, and the pining for her mother and the only relationship in which she had ever felt completely secure, are startling. There is a sense that Mary, however much she loved her husband, was disturbed by his drive, his lust for new places, new experiences. It was a drive that would only increase as he aged and attempted to avoid confronting those parts of himself with which he was uncomfortable.

Once, while making one of his swashbucklers, Douglas was run through the lower thigh by a rapier. Later, Mary noticed the double scar and asked about it. Upset by his keeping the injury from her, she exclaimed "But you didn't even limp. You didn't say a word about it."

"It was over and done with," Fairbanks countered. "You couldn't have done anything about it, so I kept it to myself. I didn't want to upset you."

The story is fascinating for what it reveals about Douglas's inability to acknowledge a setback or pain, as well as for his inability to completely share himself with his wife.

Away from the faltering campfire, the wolves began to smell weakness. In February 1929, the *Women's Home Companion* ran a dual article speculating on Doug and Mary's eventual replacements at the box office and in the hearts and minds of their fans. It was a bold, preemptive strike that clearly implied Doug and Mary's day was nearly done, a judgment that would have been unthinkable even two years before.

The article mentioned Gary Cooper, as well as Charles Farrell, Richard Arlen, and other bland leading men who utterly lacked the *panache* of the older star. If that was as far as it had gone, the article would have only revealed an essential misreading of the Fairbanks persona. But there was another, far more intriguing replacement mentioned, supposedly by Fairbanks himself, more probably by a sarcastic editor who had heard just a breath of scandal.

"Buddy Rogers."

In 1929, Douglas Fairbanks Jr. had married Joan Crawford (née Lucille LeSueur), a working-class girl. Although born in San Antonio, she spent a good part of her childhood in Lawton, Oklahoma. The mother of the future novelist Gore Vidal had been warned about playing with Lucille because her mother was "light," or sexually promiscuous.

"Joan was a little bit on the wild side," remembered William Bakewell, who made several pictures with her before she met Doug Jr. "She was always dancing the Charleston all night long." She was frozen with terror at her first meeting with her stepmother-in-law, even wearing an extra pair of panties, just in case. "I didn't kiss her hand, did I?" she anxiously inquired of her husband on their way home.

During ritualized Sunday visits, Crawford, a sharp-eyed observer of the Fairbanks/Pickford marriage, reported that, "Exuberant Uncle Douglas would come whirling into a room, pick her up and hold her high in the air while she laughed her girlish laugh and cried, 'Now Douglas, put me down.' She was enchanting with him and he was obviously enchanted with her. She had the manner and bearing of a little queen."

Although Mary's background was no more exalted than Crawford's, there were no discussions of the diffulties of Making It in Hollywood. When Doug Sr. would take Doug Jr. off to the studio for a sauna, Pickford would simply retire to her room, rather ungraciously leaving Crawford alone to rattle around Pickfair as best she could.

Occasionally, Mary would allow Gwynne to bring Crawford into her room while she decided on her wardrobe. Crawford, deathly afraid of saying the wrong thing, felt it necessary to call her "Ma'am." It is a measure of the distance Pickford wanted to keep, a measure of her insecurity at having a younger, more vibrant personality under her roof, that it was not until Crawford and the younger Fairbanks had been divorced for years that she allowed Joan to call her "Mary."

When the men returned, Pickford, beautifully gowned, would descend. "During the time of that marriage," Crawford wrote about her step-mother-in-law, "we never had a word of conversation save in a group of people." (Her then-husband had a somewhat different memory of those times together; "Mary," he remembered, "is, in my memories, always the essence of gentle, hospitable charm. Whenever we were asked to the house she did all she could to make the clearly shaky young girl feel at home— just as she had with me.")

The reason for the steely forbearance was probably twofold; Pickford appears to have subtly disapproved of young Doug's choice of a bride—Crawford was unlettered and unsophisticated, with none of the satined *panache* Mary had grown to deem important—and there was the worry that this interloper might give her the entirely unwanted gift of a grandchild.

Yet, Mary had a more-or-less positive influence on her step-daughter-in-law. "Joan was always a strict disciplinarian with herself as well as her children," said William Bakewell. "She was determined to be as much of a lady as Mary. It's my feeling that the impetus to cross over and be a lady that began around this time was all wrapped up in Joan's desire to have Mary approve of her."

On one of the rare occasions when the two couples were together, Doug Sr. suggested a trip to a dance marathon on Santa Monica pier. "A couple have been dancing seventy-eight hours," he explained.

"Douglas, love, you know we can't be seen in such a place," Mary replied. Douglas Fairbanks looked at the woman that he loved and said, "Hipper, love, the steel hand is showing through your velvet glove."

A vague, creeping waspishness began seeping into the relationship. The crash had damaged Douglas's financial standing more than it had Mary's, and she was not above reminding him of the fact. "I told you to stay out of the market," Mary told Douglas in front of a reporter for the New York *Sun,* "but like all men, you knew it all." As if his stock-market losses—and his wife's supercilious attitude—weren't bad enough, Douglas in March, 1930, wrote a check to the government for $650,000 in back taxes, negotiated down from an original figure of $1,092,273. (Four months later, he got some of that back when he was credited with $109,768 for past overassessments.)

Douglas began spending more time away from home, and took up golf with a vengeance. Although newspapers, observing the occasional partings between a couple that had once been inseparable, thought there might be trouble on the way, the marriage appears to have still been in reparable condition.

William Bakewell, who had acted in *The Iron Mask* for Douglas, was a frequent visitor to both Pickfair and the Santa Monica beach house in this period. He observed nothing but warmth and hospitality . . . and Douglas's usual penchant for practical jokes.

"One day at the beach house," he remembered, "we were all standing around the pool. There was Johnny Mack Brown, his wife, Mary, Sonny Chalif (husband of Mary's cousin Verna) and Maurice Chevalier. Suddenly Doug came out of the house and whispered something to Sonny. Sonny protested, but Doug whispered to him again. Sonny went over and pushed a fully dressed Chevalier into the pool. You have never seen an angrier man in your life. Well, Doug was immediately chagrined, calmed him down and bought him a new suit. But that was Doug."

Increasingly, Douglas was obsessed by golf. "Douglas's only ambition now is to break 70," explained Mary. "I told him this morning that I wished he would hurry up and make 70, so he could live normally again." William Bakewell remembers Douglas arriving at the beach house one day obviously half-drunk. Everybody was startled because Douglas was a strict teetotaller. It seemed that he was fresh from a particularly triumphant win at golf, and had been talked into a celebratory drink. With no tolerance for alcohol, he was reeling. "He was very apologetic about his condition and went directly to bed," chuckled Bakewell.

For the last time, Mary and Douglas embarked on one of their fabled trips, accompanied by Albert Parker (Douglas's director on *The Black Pirate),* newspaper columnist and friend Karl Kitchen and Douglas's friend and trainer Chuck Lewis. It was, remembered Lewis, a happy trip. "Every day was an adventure," he remembered. "Doug loved humanity, he wanted to get out in the countryside, or on the streets of the city, be with the people, live the way they lived. Funny thing, though, Mary wanted to stay in the hotel."

After four months abroad, Douglas and Mary returned to Los Angeles on January 3, 1930. When they got back home, Douglas and Mary wrote a little book about their trip. Entitled *Our Trip Around the World*, it was printed and bound, but, for some reason, never released, although a single copy survives in the files of the Pickford Corporation at the Academy of Motion Picture Arts and Sciences. Each partner contributes alternating chapters, describing their journey from Lausanne to Athens to Cairo to Luxor to Port Said to Ceylon to Singapore to Shanghai to Japan (Kobe, Osaka, Kyoto and Tokyo) to Hawaii and then home, some 24,000 miles. *Our Trip Around the World* is an innocuous travelogue with writing that never rises above the awestuck and banal.

Later that year, Douglas left for England unaccompanied by Mary. He explained that the only reason he was going to England was to play golf, but that rather begged the fact that there were plenty of golf courses in California. The night before he left, Douglas dined with Mary in her bungalow at the studio. She was hurt, he was defensive, and neither bothered to conceal their feelings.

Douglas's brother Robert dropped in to wish his brother *bon voyage* but stayed only a few minutes because of the tense atmosphere. "I don't like it," he said, "I don't like it at all. Douglas is establishing a dangerous precedent."

Mary had made three consecutive successful pictures with director Sam Taylor, and both were anxious to continue the partnership. In late 1929, Taylor signed a lucrative contract with Schenck's Art Cinema corporation that guaranteed him 25 percent of the net profits of his films. Mary was perfectly willing to pay good money for the talent she wanted—on *Taming* she paid Taylor $4,000 a week, as opposed to the $2,500 weekly he was getting under his contract with Schenck—but a percentage was out of the question.

Under the title *Forever Yours*, Mary embarked on a remake of *Secrets*, a Norma Talmadge hit of 1924. Instead of Taylor, she hired Marshall Neilan to direct, even though his alcoholism had been seriously hindering his career for some time, and his assignments were growing increasingly marginal.

For her leading man, she hired Kenneth MacKenna. After a month or so, with, she said, the movie one quarter finished, she shut the picture down. There were rumors that she was distressed by the quality of the rushes, distressed by the fact that Kenneth MacKenna photographed far younger than she did—he was in fact only seven years younger—or distressed by a fight that she and Neilan had supposedly had on the set.

For the public, Mary mostly kept a diplomatic silence, first saying that the picture had lacked action, then hinting at her version of the disaster when she said "I knew it was wrong, yet I held on too long. A director, marvelous as he might be, can be miscast exactly as a good actor can be."

The between-the-lines fingering of Neilan as the problem ignored her own contribution to the alcoholic disequilibrium on the set. "If you had seen Mary Pickford before noon in those days," said Cap O'Brien's son Paul, "you would have thought her still the beautiful, intelligent, clear-minded woman she had been for so many years."

She felt so strongly about the irreparable quality of the footage that she always claimed to have burned the film, taking, she claimed, a dead loss of $300,000. In fact, she did no such thing. An inventory of Mary's vaults taken in 1946 clearly lists six edited reels of *Forever Yours*, which were donated to the Library of Congress. Evidently, Mary had assembled as much completed footage as she had, looked at it, then decided to pull the plug. If this is indeed what happened, then the six reels represent more like two-thirds of the picture than the one-quarter Mary remembered as having been completed, and the film's shelving really did represent a considerable financial loss.

In the stills that survive, Mary is quite beautiful, her face aglow with a very becoming womanliness, she was past the stage where she could play dewy ingenues.

"I have come to the conclusion," she said afterwards, "that a good picture is almost an accident. *[Forever Yours]* was not that kind of accident. It was the most stupid thing I ever saw—including myself. I looked all right. I really photographed younger and better than I did in *Kiki*. But it was all talk and no action." She went on to say that the script would have made a good picture for Ruth Chatterton and that talkies should not have more dialogue than silents had titles.

Now, needing to work, her self-confidence shaken by the *Forever Yours* debacle, she leaped at the first opportunity; Joe Schenck, as he had done that same year for Douglas, offered to finance a Pickford picture through his Art Cinema corporation. Schenck assumed all production duties and Mary worked for a straight salary for the first time since she had left Zukor. Mary received the same astronomical paycheck as Douglas: $300,000. Presumably as a courtesy in return for Schenck's financing, she acquiesced to his choice of material as well. *Kiki* was another story that had been done successfully by Schenck's soon-to-be ex-wife Norma Talmadge in 1926.

Before embarking on the picture, she admitted to some misgivings and said that she had a horror of doing anything that might shock the public. After some equivocation, nudged along by the fact that both she and Schenck thought a comedy might help her career, she made the picture.

In later years, Pickford would refer to *Kiki* as "a misadventure," which, like most of Mary's critical judgments, seemed to be predicated on the basis of vague, slowly percolating reminiscences of mood and ambience during production, and of success or failure afterwards. To learn a French accent, Mary studied with Fifi D'Orsay and the wife of Maurice Chevalier. The film did give Mary a chance to speak the semi-fluent French she had worked so hard to master, and it also gave her a chance to play her first daring, '30s woman. She looks just fine in shorts and a selection of dressing gowns.

The main plot line involves Kiki's ardent pursuit of the producer of her show, who is in turn interested only in his ex-wife, a famous star. With her French accent and her ardent pursuit of the considerably more passive Reginald Denny, *Kiki* often resembles a Pepe Le Pew cartoon with its genders flipped. While much-maligned at the time, *Kiki* seems to modern eyes an enjoyable romp in roughhouse courtship à la *The Taming of the Shrew*. There is some effective slapstick humor, as Kiki, a free-spirited, obstreperous chorus girl, clumsily devastates an important production number, losing her pants in the process and falling in the bass drum in the orchestra pit.

It's a pre-Production Code romp, thoroughly artificial in the best sense, with Mary flouncing around as a self-absorbed, self-dramatizing floozy, albeit a good-hearted one. While not a complete success, it's certainly a thoroughly good idea for a star who was increasingly considered to be a prim, pensive, dignified figure too proud to come out of her attic while the kids were dancing in the parlor. *Kiki* represents a correct attempt to try to sex up Mary's image. It was, unfortunately, too late.

Kiki was a nearly total financial disaster, costing $810,568 and domestically grossing, only $426,513. It was the first Pickford film to lose money since the formation of United Artists. Its failure seemed to signal that Mary's audience did not want to see her in a part like Kiki. But chilly, cutting winds buffeting the film industry were also a factor. Movie attendance had increased from 40 million attending weekly in 1922 to 110 million in 1930. But the Depression had devastated the business, cutting attendance first to 75 million weekly in 1931, then to 60 million in 1932.

The picture Schenck had concurrently financed for Douglas, *Reaching for the Moon*, also failed, if not quite so miserably as *Kiki*. The combined negative costs of the two films were $1,938,000; the loss to Art Cinema on the two was precisely $600,000. The films, besides serving as Mary and Douglas's first financial failures, also served as their first critical failures. *Reaching for the Moon* was termed "cheap and brashly vulgar" by Thornton Delehanty of the *New York Sun* who listed the talents it had taken to make the movie—Edmund Goulding, Elsie Janis, Irving Berlin—and concluded by wondering "My, what a lot of talent it takes to make a bad picture." Douglas must have known what the reaction would be, for, just after Christmas 1930, on the night *Reaching for the Moon* had its New York premiere, Douglas boarded the S.S. *Belgenland* on a trip to the Far East.

Douglas gave out interviews saying that talkies needed something quite different from silent films, and that that something probably involved the intensely rhythmic editing favored by Eisenstein or Lewis Milestone. But his next picture turned out to be nothing more than an embarassingly patchy travelogue of his wanderings called *Around the World in Eighty Minutes*, for which he insisted on a United Artists release despite Joe Schenck's objections. Initially, the travelogue idea seemed like a godsend to Douglas, a way to discharge his obligations to United Artists without the exhausting brouhaha of actual production.

Douglas was so sure that travelogues would be a comfortable niche for him that on November 17, 1931, he embarked for China with his brother Robert, Lewis Milestone and Robert Benchley to make a sequel, this before the first travelogue had even been released. But *Around the World in Eighty Minutes* opened a few days later, and quickly folded; a chastened Douglas cut the Chinese trip short and returned to America on December 23 with no mention of any film footage having been shot.

Around the World in Eighty Minutes grossed a measly $200,000. Since the picture had only cost $80,000, the failure was not so much of finances as of inspiration. For the first time, Douglas had made a cheater and, with that sixth sense that drives producers into early graves, the public had sensed it and stayed away.

Quite suddenly, their careers seemed to be simultaneously endangered. While the results may have been the same, the reasons were different. Douglas Fairbanks had simply lost interest; Douglas Fairbanks Jr. believed that his father "Didn't like sound pictures. He was fulfilling obligations to his partners in United Artists. He didn't really want to make those pictures but they gave him excuses to travel."

Later on in the '30s, Fairbanks and his son spoke of setting up a joint production company, with the older man to produce and the younger man to star, but only one project, *The Californian,* made it as far as first draft scenario stage.

"He didn't really want to do anything," says his son. "Those plans were temporary enthusiasms without any follow-through. He had a sense that his time of mime and ballet—and I use the phrase deliberately because he thought of silent films that way— were over. He liked telling a story visually, on the quite correct theory that the impact on the eye is greater than the impact on the ear."

At bottom, the elder Fairbanks was an extremely complicated man, forever prey to depressions that seemed to result, at least in part, from some sort of inherent knowledge that the superficial, aphoristic means by which he led his emotional life had proven insufficient.

"He had this one thing," remembered his son in wonderment nearly sixty years later. "I remember him telling John Barrymore that he should have been shot after he played *Hamlet.* That everybody should stop after they reached their peak. Unfortunately none of us know when our peak is. But when my father was 50, he told me that he'd done everything and seen everything he'd wanted to and it was all anti-climactic. He said he'd like to "cash in his chips." I remember being terribly shocked at such an attitude, because I've always eagerly looked forward to every day. I only wish I could live, in good health, for two or three hundred years.

"In 1939, when he finally became very ill, I think he just gave up."

In the early spring of 1931, right after Mary finished *Kiki,* Douglas convinced her to come to Europe with him. It was not a happy trip. As Chuck Lewis related it years later, one night in Paris Mary began drinking, yelled at Douglas and left the restaurant. Douglas sat there for a bit, then turned to Lewis, "Chuck, please follow her and make sure she gets back to the hotel all right." According to Lewis, it was not the only time he had to perform this particular duty. "All Doug ever wanted," he said, "was a sober Mary."

Douglas had entered an Easter week golf tournament in Rome, but Mary, sick of being a golf widow, decided to go back to Los Angeles. Douglas pleaded with her to accompany him, but she was obstinate. Douglas continued his European tour alone . . . most of the time. "It was when they began spending so much time apart, Doug traveling all over the place . . . that [he] began seeing other women," said Paul O'Brien.

That same spring, Gloria Swanson was in London for the premiere of her new film, *Indiscreet.* At a party for King Alfonso of Spain, she introduced Douglas to her friend Lady Sylvia Ashley, a former chorus girl with fair hair, and a rich husband.

Fairbanks was instantly attracted; she was tall, elegant, *très chic,* a quantum change from homebody Mary. That Christmas, Gloria dropped by Lady Ashley's Ritz Hotel suite. There were pictures of Douglas everywhere. "I thought you knew," said Sylvia to Gloria's questioning look. "After all, you introduced us, remember? It's frightfully complicated."

It was to get considerably more complicated.

Sylvia Hawkes was born in London, probably in 1904 (the birth certificate has never been traced). At any rate, she was a pubkeeper's daughter who had worked her way up to the status of lingerie model, then chorus girl, then small-part actress in plays like *The Whole Town's Talking.* In 1927, the woman who came to be known as "Silky" married Anthony Ashley-Cooper, Lord Ashley, the elder son of the ninth Earl of Shaftesbury, despite the Earl's strenuous attempts to stop the marriage. She told the newspapers that her father was deceased, but Arthur Hawkes promptly fired off a letter to the newspapers indicating he was very much alive.

The marriage faltered almost immediately; in July 1928, Lord Ashley put a notice in the papers saying that he would not be held responsible for any debts incurred by his wife. By that time, they were living under separate roofs; at one point, Sylvia was sued in High Court for $335 back rent. She had been married to Ashley for four years when she met Douglas; Sylvia was set to trade up yet again.

One wonders if part of the problem with the Pickford-Fairbanks marriage was the impossible expectations it brought along with it. No marriage is a non-stop day at the beach, but Doug and Mary's union was puffed and apotheosized to a ridiculous extent. Sam Goldwyn wrote that Douglas and Mary seemed like prisoners of their own images, even to themselves, but how could they help it? How could two human beings possibly live up to such lofty dreams of perfection, even if the dreams were their own?

It is hard, at this late date, to gauge what made Sylvia Ashley special enough to attract men as disparate as Douglas Fairbanks (her second husband) and Clark Gable (her fourth). Makeup man Phil Rhodes, who met her near the end of her life, when she possessed only remnants of her good looks, ascertained "a quality of recklessness about her. There was a very sexual quality about the way she looked at you."

Suffice it to say that Sylvia doesn't come across in stills like she must have in life. Sylvia had a long, slim, not particularly attractive face, but a palpable, compensating air of *dégagé* elegance. "She had sort of a Dietrich look about her," remembered Joan Marsh Morrill, "but without the eyes." She struck Doug Jr. as "witty, sharp, conniving but charming—a sort of English Scarlett O'Hara."

After years of marriage to a woman like Mary, in whom the signs of a proud dowdiness could already be seen and whose own problems made her an unlikely source of comfort to a man who was losing his youth, his career and his public, Doug's affair with a woman like Sylvia Ashley made a predictable, sad kind of sense.

She was a woman who could give a tired, aging man a return to passion. Although she was "rather a lightweight," according to Joan Marsh Morrill, that could well have been a point in her favor. She was much more likely to respond with a soothing "That sounds wonderful, Douglas" than was Mary. As one reporter put it, "On one hand as [Sylvia] talks, she dangles a tiny Scotty with a huge plaid bow. Mary's plaything is usually a contract to enrich the Pickford coffers by so much."

The affair appears to have been under way for less than a year when Mary found out, although, as far as the public was concerned, Mary pretended ignorance until after the release of *Secrets*, her last film, in March 1933. "He tried to bluff his way through," remembered Douglas Fairbanks Jr., who occasionally would be called into service as an intermediary for both Mary and Douglas. "He wanted to avoid a break if he could. At the same time, he was so carried away with the situation with Sylvia. The thing with Sylvia was very intense. It was more than an affair; it was a strong infatuation."

And yet, the relationship with Mary would seem to have been stronger than any infatuation, if the surviving letters and cables between the two are any indication. In an undated letter that would seem to be written before his European gallivanting made their separations common, Douglas wrote her, "My beautiful, you are so lovely dear. I just left you at the bungalow. So intelligent, so unselfish. I'm mad about you dear . . . I feel so very sad at times because I hope against hope that you are going to get aboard."

Yet, another undated letter shows that Fairbanks knew that whatever problems they were having basically stemmed from the male half of the relationship. "Wonderful girl, please know, dear, that I adore you, that my need for you is as great as ever, but that my low moments [illegible] I am so anxious that we get a lot of time to ourselves this spring. With no one around . . . I know I will be my old self again. Duber."

But the fact of the matter was that the Douglas Fairbanks of the '30s had no intention of being in any one spot for very long, especially if the spot was Beverly Hills.

On March 24, 1931, while in India hunting tigers for scenes from *Around the World in Eighty Minutes,* Douglas wired Mary: WILL YOU EXAMINE MY BUSINESS AFFAIRS GENERALLY WITH CLARENCE AND ROBERT AND ADVISE WITH ME. STRANGE DREAM LAST NIGHT. AM WORRIED. LOVE DUBER. Later that day, as if the first cable (and the panic that prompted it) had never existed, he dispatched banal news flashes: THREE LEOPARDS OVER SEVEN FEET; TIGER TOMORROW. Still later that day: SEVEN FOOT PANTHER SHOT FROM ELEPHANT. TERRIFIC.

The next day, Douglas sat down and, in his nearly illegible scrawl, tried to explain himself. "Am writing this on edge of jungle. Bad dreams last night . . . Cabled you to look into my affairs. Isn't it cute? Always come to the baby. Don't know what I would do without her."

These alternating currents of anxiety and childish glee had their own effect on Mary. On March 4, she wired him that she had had a very nasty dream of her own the night before, and was worried about him, was everything really all right?

While bad dreams might be smoothed over, the essential problem of missed connections and loneliness couldn't. On April 4, Mary cabled Easter greetings to Douglas in Delhi. Back came the response: I LOVE YOUR WIRES. ALSO YOU. DUBER.

A week later, Douglas was finally homeward bound. On April 12, Mary wired Douglas that she was excited by the prospect of seeing him. When no response came, she wired that she had had no cable and was worried.

Three days later, Douglas woke from his reverie. JUST HEARD ABOUT ACCIDENT YOU HAD TWO MONTHS AGO. CABLE BOAT IMMEDIATELY. DETAILS. WORRIED, CAN'T SLEEP. DUBER. Mary wired back that it was Jack who had had the accident, not her, and that it wasn't serious.

In March 1931, the same month *Kiki* was released, Pickford sat down for an extraordinary interview with *Photoplay* magazine. "I hope to make another picture, but I may never make it," she said. "Certainly, I will never make another bad picture." (Obviously, she had come to a quick conclusion about the merits of *Kiki.*)

"I have never been a happy woman; it is not my nature. For the first time, I am learning about contentment.

"Pictures have progressed. My pictures will soon be old-fashioned. My old pictures are already old-fashioned. It is marvelous for me to remember *Daddy Long-Legs.* I do not want to see it. I am more happy now in the memory of it than I was during the success of it." About her husband, and the marriage about which rumors were already flooding the popular press, she obliquely said "If I had a girl, I would not spank her. I would spank a boy. Boys need punishment.

"Separation? Not now, no. Douglas and I are two normal human beings who like each other very much. In six months or six years, how can I say in this peculiar, shifting, weird nightmare of a world what will happen? I cannot deny that there may be a separation. I can only say there is none now. Just a vacation.

"I realize I am not a baby. I don't want to play Pollyannas. But I must have pictures where I not only can show merit as an actress but can live up to the public's conception of personality. I must be able to move in them. Which is to say, if a really good picture comes along, I will probably make it but I will retire rather than make a bad one."

It would have been an impossible breach of the rules of the

Hollywood game for *Photoplay* to make up such inflammatory quotes. Nevertheless, Mary panicked when she saw her words in cold print. On April 16, she wired Douglas that an "unpleasant" article in *Photoplay* had misquoted her about the possibility of a separation and that it had made the London and New York papers. She advised him to pay no attention and just know that she loved him.

The next day, Douglas wired cryptically back: ADVISE STREN-UOUS ACTION AGAINST LIBELOUS ARTICLE. ALL LOVE.

Even when he was in Los Angeles, Douglas began shying away from home unless there was absolutely no place else to go. He grew frankly inattentive in matters concerning business or United Artists, and simple things like getting his signature or finding him in order to ask him a few questions about what his wishes were could take as long as several weeks. "He is perfectly agreeable to do whatever Mary decides" becomes a recurring refrain in business correspondence of the period. The man who had described himself as "floating through space" at the time of his marriage was wafting away all over again.

He introduced new friend Fred Astaire to his particular passion for riding in police cars, traveling to the morgue and to crime scenes. "He was an extraordinary man," remembered Astaire. "[By the time] I got to Hollywood, he was through in films; he simply had no more interest at all." When Astaire would worry aloud about how he could possibly keep topping himself in film after film, Fairbanks offered some simple fatherly advice: "The way I worked it," he told Astaire, "I just did the best I could, then I went away and got some fresh ideas and came back. I did that for so long that I can't remember how I did it, but that's what I did."

Douglas did more for Astaire than merely give him a subjectively wooly version of the innate perfectionism that, at his best, he had assuredly possessed; he also gave Astaire the idea of using a necktie as a belt, a stylish bit of *déshabillé* that Douglas had been using for years, but for which Astaire was to get all the credit.

———— ————

Douglas spent Christmas of 1931 at Pickfair, but by March 1932, he was in the South Seas shooting *Mr. Robinson Crusoe.* Beneath the bare informational bones of the cables and letters, one senses churning reservoirs of emotional loss.

On March 8, Mary cabled Douglas that Gwynne's birthday was on the tenth and not to forget to wire greetings to her. Two days later she cabled that she was talking and thinking of him all the time. Douglas responded on the eleventh with a grumpy SADIE THOMPSON RIGHT. RAIN, RAIN, RAIN. ALL MY LOVE.

Four days later, a worried Mary cabled Douglas's traveling companion Chuck Lewis that she had had no word in four days. Was Douglas all right? Douglas and Lewis explained that the lack of communication was because of radio problems and/or government regulations, an explanation that failed to assuage Mary's own faltering feelings. On March 23, she cabled Douglas that she had again been plagued by terrible nightmares about him. Five days later, on their wedding anniversary, Mary cabled TWELVE YEARS AGO TODAY DARLING, AND I STILL LOVE YOU AND ALWAYS WILL.

Douglas arrived back in America May 6, hurriedly cut *Mr. Robinson Crusoe* and attended the Los Angeles Olympics. As soon as they were over, he departed again. On August 26, a forlorn Mary wired Douglas, this time on his way to China, that Pickfair looked beautiful but empty. Douglas, accompanied by Chuck Lewis and a few other friends, spent most of his time in the Orient, moving through Japan, then China, "being royally entertained as usual" noted his son. From Shanghai he went to Canton, Nanking, Hankow. On the way back, he stopped at Biarritz, followed shortly thereafter by Sylvia, but they were not noticed by the press. Douglas did not return to America until December 21.

In the spring of 1933, Douglas managed to convince Mary to join him in Italy, where he had been since February. Mary returned after a few weeks, but Douglas didn't go back to California until May. In mid-June, he was off again for Europe.

Like most women brought up in the Victorian era, Mary was something of an apologist for men; within certain limits, it was considered more or less normal for a man to have an occasional affair, so long as his wife was not subjected to embarrassment. But the whispers were gradually filtering through to the newspapers, especially in London. "Mary would frequently talk about what she'd been subjected to," recalls a family intimate, "and that [Douglas] had gone too far. She remained devoted to him always, but it was a question of pride. Justifiably so." At Christmas 1932, Mary finally gave Douglas an ultimatum.

Even then he couldn't choose, couldn't decide. What was mostly private became quite public in July 1933, when Sylvia was hospitalized and Douglas rushed over to London to see her at Lady Carnarvon's nursing home near Regent's Park. Fleet Street reporters staked out the hospital and had the satisfaction of seeing a panicked Douglas duck out the servants entrance to avoid conversation, smashing his bowler hat as he went.

Douglas was a man in a hopeless situation; on the one hand devoted and dependent on Mary; on the other, bound by passion and a sense of rebirth to Sylvia. On June 2, 1933, from London, he wired Mary at the Sherry Netherlands: HOROSCOPE ALL WRONG. MORE DEPRESSED THAN EVER BEFORE. Three days later, he was making up excuses to stay with Sylvia: DECIDED TO SEE RYDER CUP MATCHES AND BUY A COUPLE OF SUITS CLARIDGES. ALL LOVE. A day later he wired her again, this time with a forced bonhomie: UP TO MY NECK IN TAILORS. MUCH, MUCH LOVE. DUBER.

Douglas's behavior forced Mary's hand; she could no longer keep silent. News of the separation hit the papers during the first week in July when Louella Parsons got the story during a lunch with Mary and Frances Marion at the Vendome. Mary always insisted that she told Louella the whole sad story with the strict understanding that it be off the record and that Parsons broke her word. Parsons' version was that Frances turned to an obviously distraught Mary and said, "Tell Louella, Mary. Confession is good for the soul," whereupon Mary blurted out "Douglas and I are separating. It's just—over." Parsons further claimed that she implored Mary not to do anything rash, that she'd sit on the story until Mary was absolutely sure. Mary, according to this version, told her to go ahead and run with it, possibly hoping that seeing the sordid story in print might force Douglas to his senses.

Frances Marion's version of the story was less throbbingly dramatic. "Mary was going to give the break to the Los Angeles *Times.* I said to her, 'If you're going to give it out, give it to Hearst. Make it a national story.' " Which Mary promptly did. As a means of getting some of the sympathy she undoubtedly felt she deserved, not to mention administering a much-needed dose of shock therapy to Douglas, Marion's version sounds the most like Mary, hence the most likely.

Parsons went with her story, and saw it splashed on front pages all over the world. On Monday, July 3, 1933, the banner headline on the front page of the New York *Daily News* (two cents a copy, daily circulation 1,400,000) proclaimed, in ninety point type: DOUG AND MARY PART.

"It is a very sad and distressing situation," wrote Loyd Wright, whom Mary had retained to represent her in the divorce, to Cap O'Brien. "She waited for over seven months, and finally decided that it was the only course she could pursue. I think Clarence [Ericksen] and Bob [Fairbanks] have the same feeling now . . . that any hope of reconciliation has been destroyed."

O'Brien promptly commissioned an investigation into Sylvia's background, which failed to sidetrack Douglas's growing obsession. It is almost certainly around this time that Mary accepted the attentions of Buddy Rogers and began using him, to goad Douglas. Buddy had established a relationship with starlet Sue Carol who "was madly in love with him," according to Lina Basquette. "He broke off with her to take up with Mary. Sue was devastated. Buddy was always considered such a nice, sweet young man."

As early as the last week in July 1932, Buddy had met Mary at the train in Harmon, New York, and brought her to New York City in a forty-five foot cabin cruiser for what was evidently supposed to be a quiet tryst lasting till August 1. Any hope of confidentiality was destroyed on July 25, when the boat, moored near 18th Street and the Hudson River, caught fire and exploded while Mary and Buddy were elsewhere. When reporters asked questions of the crew, the story made the papers, although quietly, with little uproar and no major headlines. Just a few weeks before Parsons broke the separation story, Mary had flown to Chicago to be with Buddy when he brought his orchestra to play at the World's Fair.

On December 8, 1933, Mary filed suit for divorce. The complaint was filed just before closing time at the Los Angeles County Clerk's office. The wire services and local press had been alerted that an important story involving Mary Pickford would be announced. Copies of the complaint were on hand for the reporters. A few days later, tracked down in New York, Mary was asked if her future plans included another marriage. Mary Pickford looked as if she had been slapped. "Aren't you a little premature?" she asked. As recently as nine months before, Douglas had still been sending his wife wires with the magical message: BY THE CLOCK.

The divorce petition stated that Douglas lacked consideration for his wife's feelings and sensibilities; that he publicly announced that he had no interest in life except traveling, which "destroyed the legitimate ends of matrimony"; that he absented himself from Pickfair for months at a time, and that this caused "much public criticism and unfair comment." There was no mention of infidelity.

Douglas's assistant Clarence Ericksen had the duty of breaking the news to Cap O'Brien. HERE IS THE SAD NEWS, he cabled. MARY FILED SUIT FOR DIVORCE AND . . . IS LEAVING

FOR NEW YORK . . . TONIGHT. Mary spent Christmas of 1933 in New York, while Douglas was in Europe. It was their first Christmas apart.

That Christmas, newspapers reported, she sent Buddy a pair of initialled silk pajamas. Mary refused to either confirm or deny the story, saying only that "The past is dead and I am going on to new things."

"Mary and I would telephone," Buddy says of this period. "We were friends. I was happy as a bachelor, but I wanted her and she wanted me."

He was kind, he was loving, and he was more than willing to devote his full time and attention to taking care of Mary. "I never thought about myself, particularly," Buddy would say. "I always wanted to build her up." It is a judgment with which everybody who knew the couple concurs. In an eerie way, Mary fell into the pattern of Charlie Chaplin, William Powell and other renowned men who often choose adoring younger spouses for their final (and successful) marriages. Certainly, by 1934, Buddy's movie career was in eclipse, although he had compensated by starting up a moderately successful swing band.

"I was doing very well; I was making $3,000 a week and I had five homes. That sounds good, but a home only cost $20,000 back then. I was on the road, having fun, but Mary was always in the background."

When word got out that Mary had filed for divorce, the reaction was one of bewilderment—and even malicious amusement, except on the part of Clark Gable, who had long lusted after the kind of class Mary represented. Gable, who had spent more time around oil rigs than he had women of quality, had heard all about Pickfair and Mary from Joan Crawford, with whom he had been carrying on a discreet affair for the last two years of her marriage to Douglas Fairbanks Jr.

He called her, and Mary resented his obvious intentions. "He didn't want to go out," she told intimates, "but rather to stay home, if you know what I mean. He called often, and I made myself unavailable." Although Mary's pride forbade her to meekly acquiesce to Gable's tomcat charms as easily as the waitresses and extras he preferred as sex partners, her hormones didn't give up without a fight.

"I regretted ignoring him," she confessed. "In fact, I must have been out of my mind." And, shortly before her death, she admitted that "my only regret is that I never made a film with Clark Gable. I loved him."

The proud owners showing off Pickfair, circa 1924.

Mary and Douglas pretending to plant a Douglas fir at Pickfair. "They are ardent promoters of all United States reforestation schemes," says the original caption.

Douglas and Mary. "They were very good together," remembered his son; looking at this picture, you can believe it.

Mary in "Little Annie Rooney," (1925) a charming return to teenagers after several adult roles.

Mary and Douglas amusing themselves during the simultaneous productions of "Little Annie Rooney" and "Don Q, Son of Zorro."

Mary and Douglas among the first
to be immortalized in the forecourt
of Grauman's Chinese Theater
in 1927, watched over by Sid
Grauman himself.

Mary and her brain-trust during the production of "Sparrows."
From left, director William Beaudine (kneeling), writers
Ed Newman and Tom McNamara.

By 1926, Mary was no longer afraid to appear overtly chic . . . offscreen.

"Sparrows," (1926) offered a few good scenes for Mary to play, but its most distinguishing feature was its wholehearted dive into Gothic story and art direction.

Charles "Buddy" Rogers and Mary in "My Best Girl," (1927).

Buddy Rogers, Mary and director Sam Taylor on the set of "My Best Girl."

A solemn Mary photographed at Pickfair in 1929.

The most famous couple in the world in 1929's "The Taming of the Shrew."

In addition to its stars, "The Taming of the Shrew" showcased the
invariably superb designs of William Cameron Menzies and
Laurence Irving.

Although "Coquette" (1929) was a paralyzing bore, a terrible fall-off from Mary's last, satisfying silent films, it was one of her greatest commercial triumphs . . .

. . . as attested to by both the lines at the box-office . . .

. . . and the 1929 Academy Award for Best Actress.

Although Mary was in the prime of her beauty by June, 1930, when she and Douglas attended the premiere of Marion Davies' "The Floradora Girl," strains in the marriage were beginning to be evident.

1931's "Kiki" was a radical change of pace in which Mary played a good-hearted floozie, a Gallic Clara Bow. Audiences weren't interested.

Good-luck visits to each other's productions were a nominal part of the marriage. Here, Mary visits the "Mr. Robinson Crusoe" set in 1932.

"Secrets," (1933) Mary's last film, offered some charming love
scenes with Leslie Howard . . .

. . . and the opportunity to wear some stunning gowns, as well as
play a character of some depth.

Although he was already deeply involved with Sylvia Ashley,
Douglas tried to keep up appearances. Here, dapper as ever, he
visits Mary, Leslie Howard and an unidentified actress on the set
of "Secrets."

Mary in one of the test stills for
"Alice in Wonderland," the pro-
posed collaboration with Walt
Disney. (*Robert S. Birchard
Collection*)

A George Hurrell portrait of Mary from 1935; no longer setting fashion, Mary was now following fashion.

Douglas and Sylvia Ashley Fairbanks, 1937.

Shirley Temple had remade several of Mary's past successes and was about to embark on "Since You Went Away" for David Selznick, Mary's U.A. partner, when this publicity picture was taken in October, 1943.

Christmas, 1948. Roxanne, Buddy, Mary and Ronnie.

Mary visiting Malcolm Boyd for his ordination at the Church Divinity School of the Pacific, Berkeley, California, 1954. (*Malcolm Boyd Collection*)

Mary and Arthur Krim in 1954, on the occasion of the 35th anniversary of United Artists.

During the '50's, Mary began to venture out into the world. Here, in 1955, she and Buddy embark for Europe. . .

. . . where they visited the Brandenburg Gate in Berlin.

Buddy and Mary visit actress Mary Howes during a January, 1955
visit to Palm Beach.

By March, 1961, the little girl with
the curls seemed very far away
indeed.

Mary was still canny enough to
favor her left side in her last public
appearance, receiving her honorary
Oscar at the 1977 Academy Awards.

Perhaps because nothing better had presented itself, but more probably because there was something deep within the story of *Secrets* that appealed to her, Mary began circling around it again. For a while, she vacillated between *Secrets* and an original script by Frances Marion called *Shantytown*, a romantic comedy set against the tuna fishing industry.

Shantytown seemed like it would be Mary's next film; she even announced that Karl Dane, the gangling comic who had made a big hit in *The Big Parade* but had seen his career slide into oblivion because talkies had revealed his heavy Swedish accent, would appear as a supporting player.

But she couldn't make up her mind. On October 12, 1932, she wired Douglas, in Shanghai, that she was confused and discouraged by differing opinions regarding her next film and needed his advice. There is no record of a response.

She decided to forge ahead with *Secrets*, hiring the graceful romanticist Frank Borzage to direct and, when Gary Cooper proved unavailable, Leslie Howard to co-star. On November 29, 1932, Mary began filming *Secrets*. On the second day of shooting, Mary wired Douglas that all was well. Once again, Joe Schenck was providing most of the financing; of the picture's $531,641 cost (one internal United Artists memo claims $400,000, which seems low), Art Cinema put up $347,500. Nervous and unsure as she was, Mary still found time on December 3 to wire Douglas in London not to forget to bring presents from London for his son and Joe Schenck.

In *Secrets*, Pickford plays the daughter of a New England shipbuilder who is adamantly opposed to her romance with the penniless young clerk played by Howard. The film's first third is played —very adeptly—as social comedy. "You insolent young scoundrel!" rages C. Aubrey Smith, as Pickford's father, to Howard. "You ungrateful whippersnapper!! *You badly dressed young man!!!*"

To escape her family, the couple head west; although Leslie Howard is nobody's idea of a two-fisted empire builder, with Pickford's help and steadfast support, he hangs rustlers, is elected governor, and gets seduced by the siren call of the madding crowd and a flashing-eyed senorita named Lolita (!).

Pickford, playing a genteel Mother Courage, stands by her man. As the film ends, they are elderly people returning from Washington to California, ignoring the pleas of their grown children, eager to talk of the "secrets" of their marriage and, at long last, ready to live for themselves. It is all idealized wish fulfillment, with Mary pining for a husband who would be satisfied to stay home and savor the fruits of years of arduous labor, instead of forever leap-frogging off in pursuit of some new country . . . or girl.

While *Secrets* is somewhat under-written, lunging from its characters youthful crises to their middle-aged crises without ever quite explaining the basis for Pickford's adamant trust and love for her husband, it is well-produced, makes effective use of montage in the manner of Slavko Vorkapich, and betrays absolutely no trace of the nervousness its star/producer must have felt during its making.

The only marked change from the silent version—and an interesting change it is—was Pickford's decision to alter the flashback structure of the film. In the original, the film opens at the deathbed of John Carlton, the wayward but adoring husband. The story proper thus unfolds as the loyal wife keeps a watch over her dying husband.

At the end, rather than the optimistic foxy grandpa and grandma finish of the Pickford version, the dying husband calls for his wife and, as she comes through the door, the husband and wife are reunited.

In spite of Mary's alteration of the structure, the 1933 *Secrets* is a very good film—if anything it's too short—for which no apologies need be made. Certainly it's Pickford's best late performance. It is also notably free of what critic Edward Wagenknecht, one of her biggest fans, once described as Pickford's tendency to "a certain stock 'cuteness' . . . a tendency to apply, at times, just a shade too much pressure."

Secrets comparative excellence didn't help; it seemed that nothing would. Opening the week Franklin Roosevelt declared a bank holiday, it went on to amass a worldwide gross of $697,432. Deducting United Artists' distribution fee of 25 percent and adding in the usual costs for prints and advertising (between $50,000 and $100,000) the net loss on the picture came to around $100,000.

Compared to *Kiki, Secrets* was only a very modest failure, but Mary decided not to fight it. It was quite clear that, while she still had an audience of a sort, it was half of what it had been only five years before. Mary Pickford had had two financial failures in a row, and was an astute enough businesswoman to realize that her starring days were over. She tried to put the best possible face on it. "I wanted to make my own pictures and I did," she said. "But it was too hard for me being the producer and the actress. When everybody else went home, I stayed there and signed checks. I couldn't take it." But she, as well as all of Hollywood, knew the truth.

She was precisely forty-one years old; her life was less than half over. Yet, the day she stopped acting was the day that, in the largest sense, her life lost its meaning. Now, the only thing to hold onto was Douglas. But he was in England . . . with Sylvia.

Chapter Ten

"I've always thought that Mary Pickford was a victim. She had no background, no education. And within a few years, she was the toast of the entire world, with all the money and the glory and the fame that went with it. It's pretty hard for anybody, even if they have a strong character, to be able to withstand all that."

—Lina Basquette

PARTIALLY to provide product for United Artists, but mostly to be near his lover, Douglas agreed to star in *The Private Life of Don Juan* for Alex Korda. He rented a vast medieval house about forty-five minutes from London called North Mimms Park, with enough room for fifty houseguests. Here he entertained Sylvia's friends, the bright young things of London society. He should have been happy, for he had what he thought he wanted: a film was the best possible excuse to concentrate all his attentions on Sylvia. If his permanent flat at the Ritz wasn't enough, and the account at Cartier's for lavish gifts for her seemed even slightly insufficient, then maybe the old manor house would cement his place in the eyes of Sylvia and her friends.

Douglas steadfastly refused to allow his son to visit him at North Mimms, perhaps out of some subliminal sense of shame and impropriety. On February 25, 1934, as production of *Don Juan* was about to begin, he wired Mary: HIPPER DEAR, PASSING THROUGH WORST PERIOD I'VE EVER KNOWN. TRYING TO PULL MYSELF TOGETHER TO START PICTURE. LOVE DUBER.

A few months later, Mary was in Philadelphia for a personal appearance in a one-act play called *The Country Mouse* at the Earle Theatre. She told reporters that she liked making personal appearances because she couldn't find a picture to do and "I get tired of staying at home—alone." Naturally, the reporters jumped at the bait. When they asked if she was still in love with Douglas, she responded with "Oh, now, really, I won't answer that," saying her personal life was too sacred to have it kicked around like a football. She complained about "dirty pictures" like Raoul Walsh's *The Cock-Eyed World*, (a sequel to *What Price Glory*, which she had loved) and, in response to a question about the good old silent days, said that she "couldn't imagine any worse Hades than to have to go and look at ten-year-old pictures of myself. When they say to me, 'Step this way, you've got to see a picture you made in 1918,' I'll know where I am."

On that same tour, in May, Mary returned to Toronto for the first time in years. It was nearly a state occasion. Although Mary stayed at the Royal York Hotel, crowds gathered everywhere she might be. There was a massive parade on Bay Street, and she told the crowd "I love all of you, my fellow Torontonians." Police said that far more people came to see Mary than had come to see the Prince of Wales (the future Edward VIII) when he had come to Toronto a few years earlier.

Although Douglas had allied himself with the conservative Republicanism of Louis B. Mayer in fighting Upton Sinclair's 1932 Socialist campaign for the California governorship, he was, for the most part, apolitical. Mary, on the other hand, was growing vociferously conservative. Her politics were publically exhibited when she attended a celebration at the Hotel Ambassador celebrating the fifteenth anniversary of Fascism. Surrounded by Primo Carnera and a host of dignitaries and politicians, Mary addressed the 300 people, saying "The last time I visited Italy I found a different spirit there than on my earlier trip. That was because Mussolini had taken it over. I congratulate you upon having produced *Il Duce*. Italy has always produced great men and when she needed one most Mussolini was there." She then gave the Fascist salute, cried *"Viva Fascismo! Viva Il Duce!"* and got a bigger hand than Primo Carnera.

Although her endorsement of Mussolini appears to be, at the best, criminal naivete and, at the worst, an indication of a stone-age mindset, it was actually nothing new. Years previously, on one of their jaunts through Europe, both Douglas and Mary had been cheered as they visited the Fascist Labor Organization in Florence, where they had been presented with membership cards in the cinema workers' union.

Mary was by no means alone in the Hollywood community in her enthusiasm for Mussolini. D.W. Griffith was also an early fan of Fascism, and Hal Roach, producer of the Our Gang and Laurel and Hardy comedies, kept an autographed picture of Mussolini in his den as late as the early 1980s. In 1933, Columbia released a feature-length documentary entitled *Mussolini Speaks* that was little but blatant glorification, while, three years later, producer Walter Wanger came to a producing agreement with the dictator that involved the newly constructed Cinecitta studios.

In the depths of the Depression, Fascism, in the guise of a single charismatic leader, seemed to many a viable, even necessary answer to America's political and social needs; in any case, for those accustomed to the authoritarian rule of Louis B. Mayer, Harry Cohn, or the rigid demands of mobs of movie fans, Mussolini might have seemed like business as usual.

Mary's politics would always remain staunchly conservative. As late as May 1937, she was saying that "I think Mussolini is a wonderful man" and "Hitler has been marvelous for Germany. Certainly the country looks better and everyone there thinks he is simply wonderful."

In 1944, she wrote notes to all of her friends, even people she hadn't seen in years, urging them to vote against a third term for Franklin Roosevelt, a longstanding *bête noire*. When that failed to derail his easy re-election, she contented herself by writing to the Roosevelt-hating columnist Westbrook Pegler: "After the defeat of yesterday, I wakened in the lowest possible spirits this morning, ready to give up the struggle for good government. But when I turned to the Los Angeles *Examiner* and found that you were still there, battling away, it gave me fresh courage and hope. Keep up the good work. Sincerely, Mary Pickford.

"P.S. I do believe I have written my first fan letter."

On February 5, 1934, Douglas was named as co-respondent in Lord Ashley's divorce petition against his wife. The news was the journalistic equivalent of a declaration of war, a public acknowledgment of what had, in the American papers at least, only been hinted at. Mary went to ground; from the monied hideaway of Palm Beach, she gave out a quiet "No comment."

Lord Ashley's divorce action went uncontested. When it came

to court in November of that year, Lord Ashley put Douglas's private secretary on the stand, who testified that Douglas and Lady Ashley had lived in adjoining bedrooms at North Mimms Park for several months. The divorce was granted, and Douglas was assessed $10,000 in court costs.

It was one thing to have an affair, as Mary well knew. But to be so obviously enslaved by the third party, and to subject a loyal wife to public humiliation, went far beyond the rules of the game. Mary would always love Douglas but she would not be able to forgive him until after he was dead; by that time it would be too late.

Still, Mary and Douglas remained in touch and, quite obviously, in love. In March 1934, while Mary was at the Sherry Netherlands in New York, Douglas was at the racetrack in Aintree, England. He placed a bet on a horse called Lone Eagle II "because Mary once gave me a horse by that name." Ominously, Lone Eagle II did not finish in the money.

On April 13, he arrived in Dublin via mail boat under the pseudonym of "Smith" for a weekend with Sylvia. When the press discovered his presence, he panicked and left early. Hounded by the press on one hand and feelings of guilt and passion on the other, Douglas's nerves were very frayed. On August 12, 1934, after another story had broken about Douglas's continuing involvement with Sylvia, a desperate Douglas wired Mary IS THERE ANYTHING I CAN SAY TO PRESS TO CORRECT . . . SITUATION. LOVE DUBER.

A day later, Mary wired back that the less that was said the better. On August 8, after a night-long talk with Joe Schenck, Douglas made a sudden decision to return to California and talk to Mary. Typically, he could not bring himself to tell Sylvia the truth and misled her by saying he was only taking a pleasure cruise to Gibraltar. He had been in Europe for fourteen consecutive months.

During his confrontation with Mary, he seemed unwilling to face his predicament, preferring to dwell on his travels during his fourteen months in Europe, telling her of how he had met and become friends with a Chinese warlord who controlled the opium trade. He had actually gone so far as to attend an opium party and sample the goods. There were, he insisted, no ill effects, although Mary must have wondered if, given his increasing self-indulgence, Douglas might not have ingested more than a sampling of the narcotic. Again, they parted without a decision.

But Douglas refused to go away. Sylvia was fire, but Mary was comfort, security and old lace. On November 22, 1934, he wired

Mary at the Sherry Netherlands: HIPPER, DEAR LOUELLA IS AT IT AGAIN. THINK IT IS TERRIBLE. ABSOLUTELY UN-FOUNDED. MAY COME TO NEW YORK. LOVE YOU. DUBER.

By this time, their cables were being intercepted and sold to the tabloids that were eager for scandalous news of the world's most famous couple. Pseudonyms were in order; Douglas began using the name of his valet, Lucien Rocher, so Mary could wire him. On November 27, she wired Lucien/Douglas that she was sorry to upset him, but that a warning was in order, if only because she loved him. A follow-up telegram said simply that the entire sorry business was too bad. On December 8, Mary filed for divorce. On December 30, Douglas sailed for Europe.

On January 10, 1935, Mary received her interlocutory decree of divorce, which would become final in one year. Douglas spent most of 1935 in Europe, squiring Sylvia around Rome, Naples and on a world cruise to St. Thomas, Hawaii, Tahiti and other South Sea islands accompanied by Fred Astaire, Donald Ogden Stewart and Benita Hume. He was far from the carefree, glistening figure that he had always presented to the world. On February 15, before they all boarded the boat train that launched the tour, Douglas was frantic, continually threatening to punch reporters if they got too close and dodging behind pillars in an effort to keep from being photographed with Sylvia.

In November of that year, in response to an announcement by Douglas that he was thinking of remaking some of his old successes as a producer in London, Mary cabled him that she believed him to be making a mistake; that the industry needed American pictures more than it needed English ones. In any case, remaking old hits rarely worked and a new story, maybe George Armstrong Custer, would be a better idea.

By December, with the divorce showdown approaching, Douglas began making overtures of reconciliation to Mary, with his brother Robert acting as intermediary. "I've never loved anyone but Mary and I never will," Douglas told his brother. Mary responded . . . again in code.

Douglas must have been disturbed by snide cracks in the press that subtly characterized him—not necessarily inaccurately—as a jaded roué. One article in October 1934 characterized him as "the world-traveler/actor." In the midst of an interview promoting the November release of *The Private Life of Don Juan,* one reporter disparagingly asked, "Your latest picture shows a libertine growing old, losing his power over other women and finally returning to his own wife. Does this parallel your own life?"

Douglas laughed nervously. "Well, that's a good one, isn't it?" he said. "Nothing to say," he added.

———— ————

On December 9, Mary cabled "Betterson" that she was concerned about him, that "McLaren" (obviously Sylvia's code name) was, in the opinion of those in America, the aggressor, and that he should terminate the entire matter as soon as possible.

She told him that she agreed with him that he had to get back to America, and that whatever negative public feelings existed would be offset by a successful picture. I KNOW YOU CAN BE COURAGEOUS. TAKE YOUR FUTURE INTO YOUR OWN HANDS. DON'T LISTEN TO OTHERS, WHICH ONLY RE-SULTS IN CONFUSION. THE COMPANY NEEDS YOU, THE INDUSTRY NEEDS YOU. SO COME BACK. IF HOLLYWOOD DISTASTEFUL, MAKE YOUR HEADQUARTERS NEW YORK, BUT I FEEL YOU NEED THE STIMULATION OF THE SPIRIT OF HOLLYWOOD TODAY.

HOWEVER, ALL IS WITHIN YOU. BEAR ONLY UPON YOUR OWN EXCELLENT INSTINCT AND JUDGMENT.

Mary had told him that movies needed him and that United Artists needed him; she had pointedly not told him that she needed him, which, at that point, was the only thing Douglas wanted to hear. Neither person would capitulate.

Finally, however, Mary relented. On December 9, she cabled "Betterson" in London that she had decided against canceling their contract in January and was instructing both their attorneys to this effect.

Yet, something changed Mary's mind for her. Mary's divorce from Douglas became final on January 10, 1936. Douglas was distraught; that night, he was at a New York nightclub with Adele Astaire and a few others when the bandleader dedicated the next number to "Douglas Fairbanks and Lady Ashley." But Sylvia was in England; Douglas stormed out of the club.

The divorce settlement was simplicity itself: Mary was deeded Pickfair, while Douglas kept the Santa Monica beach house. Shortly afterwards, Fairbanks began a concerted attempt to win his ex-wife back. She was, he told his brother Robert, his "one true love." He began frantically haunting Pickfair, taking her for long drives, trying to convince her that they could never be happy apart. While acknowledging that possibility, Mary adamantly refused to allow herself to be so vulnerable ever again. On the off-chance that she might change her mind, Douglas told her that if she ever decided she wanted him back, all she would have to do would be to say "Come home for Christmas dinner."

Frustrated, Fairbanks took a train to New York with his son, pausing at every stop to send long, impassioned telegrams to his ex-wife. Between messages, he sat alone, brooding. Arriving in New York, Fairbanks found no messages awaiting him. He and his son attended the premiere of *The Postman Always Rings Twice* with Richard Barthelmess, which failed to halt his deepening depression. The day after the premiere, without telling his son, Douglas left for Europe.

A few hours later, a cable arrived at the hotel from Mary. She had relented, saying, in so many words, all was forgiven, come back. Doug Jr. got his father on a ship-to-shore telephone and told him the good news, but the distraught older man exploded in anger. He accused his son of lying, of not approving of Sylvia—that part was true enough—and bellowed that everybody was on Mary's side. He refused to call Mary himself for confirmation, and hung up. Doug Jr. called Mary; she agreed to call his father.

Once the connection was made, Douglas asked her what it was she wanted to tell him. "I wanted to ask you for Christmas dinner, Douglas," she replied.

"It's too late," he replied. "It's just too late." The craven capitulation had curdled inside him; he had already asked Sylvia Hawkes Ashley to marry him. Two weeks after Fairbanks arrived in London, on March 7, 1936, he and Sylvia were married in Paris, at the gold-leafed marriage salon of the Eighth Ward City Hall. Although French law required thirty days residence and an eleven-day publication of bans, Douglas and Sylvia got a special dispensation from city officials. After the ceremony, they honeymooned in Belgium, Holland and Spain, where their car was burgled of a $660 fur wrap that had been one of Sylvia's wedding presents. In New York, Mary declined to offer any comment.

When they arrived back in America on April 30, Douglas remained on the defensive about Sylvia, refusing to let her speak to reporters, except to deny that her hair color was a dirty blonde. "It's English mouse," she insisted.

Now, finally, Mary knew it was over, knew that Douglas had freely chosen another woman when he might have had her. In Hollywood, Charles Rosher read the news of the wedding and turned to his wife. "She will carry this to her grave," he said. Mary's niece Gwynne said that Mary "was never the same after the divorce from Douglas. A certain sense of direction went out of her life. They never should have divorced; neither of them survived it, they both lost heart."

Among the surviving artifacts of this most agonizingly public of marriages, there is one of particular poignance. It is an undated note, but it is in Douglas's hand, and surely from this period: "Wish hard," it says. "Pray for Duber."

The mysterious alchemy that nurtures solid careers (and solid marriages) had irrevocably altered. What happened? What soured two extraordinary careers in such a short time?

Douglas Fairbanks's pictures never really changed because they were an authentic projection of a large part of his personality; they demonstrated his instinctive flair for beauty, both in art direction and in movement. Mary's relationship with her screen character was a good deal more ambiguous, not to mention objective. As she told the historian Kevin Brownlow, "I left the screen because I didn't want what happened to Chaplin to happen to me. When he discarded the little tramp, the little tramp turned around and killed him. The little girl made me. I wasn't waiting for the little girl to kill me . . . I was typed."

But there is more than a trace of self-justification in her remark; besides, two of Chaplin's post-tramp films (*Monsieur Verdoux* and *Limelight*) are among his finest achievements. No, Pickford's problem was less of intellectual and emotional burnout than one of story sensitivity, and, beyond that, of an inability to cope with a changing of the rules.

Mary's was a career without compare and nearly without imitators. For a time, in the late '20s and early '30s, Janet Gaynor played Pickford-type parts, and even re-made some of Mary's silent screen successes, but Gaynor's career burned out quickly. In truth, the closest thing Mary had to a successor was Shirley Temple: the pre-sexual screen character, the never-say-die spirit, etc. But, chronologically co-existing with Temple was Mae West, an incredible apparition of voracious sexuality that would have been impossible in the era of Mary Pickford's years of greatest influence.

In an eerie simulacrum of Pickford's career, once Temple became too old to even attempt playing adolescent roles, once she hit puberty, her career also became one of diminishing returns. By that time, World War II was erupting, and any possibility of innocence was buried; the great mass audience would no longer be able—or willing—to invest emotional energy in such innocent icons.

Mary and Douglas's qualities as stars were wrapped up in silent films, their special demands and illusions. Silent films, at their best, were more than just movies and their stars were more than just actors. In silent films, the specific identity of the actors was somewhat nebulous. The audience, swayed by the continuum of the story, guided by the music of the orchestra in the pit that underlined the acting and photography, projected their own feelings onto the actors, and thus participated in a kind of communal dream state. To paraphrase the critic Alexander Walker, silent films gave emotions a human shape.

Talkies were less romantic than silents, more real; less utopian, more democratic; less behavioral, more psychological. Because silent films were such an anomalous hybrid, and closer to ballet than anything else in the arts, actors who had an aptitude for them often seemed comparatively ordinary, if not inadequate, in the more plebeian talkies.

Similar things were happening to the great comedian Harold Lloyd. Like Mary, his first talkie, an otherwise unremarkable pastiche called *Welcome Danger,* had been extremely successful, grossing just under $2 million. Like Pickford, this success was apparently due to the public's curiosity about the voice of a beloved figure; his second talkie (*Feet First*) grossed just over a million, while his third, *Movie Crazy,* although a far better picture than *Kiki,* Pickford's third talkie, grossed only $675,000, a quarter million dollars more than Mary's film.

Great silent stars like Lloyd and Pickford had lost that which made them unique: an empathetic ability to communicate with an audience with their eyes and their body. Sound made their singular gifts less important and left them struggling to maintain their position in a Hollywood newly overrun with lighter but more *au courant* talents drawn from Broadway and vaudeville.

Mary's problems were compounded by the fact that, as the English critic Caroline Lejeune cruelly but not inaccurately said, she "never [came] to grips with real movies . . . never created a part of first-rate importance nor contributed anything by her productions to the pioneer development of the screen . . . The Pickford productions have never created either a director or a player [but] by leading consistently a quiet, hard-working and unspectacular life, by playing consistently in decent, simple unostentatious pictures with a certain wistful emotional note, she has achieved for herself a position unique among stars and producers."

And then Lejeune encapsulated the problem when she referred to Mary's rigorous conservatism and said of Mary's pictures that, although she "never denied herself to an audience, never stinted measure, never supplied us with inferior goods," the reality of the majority of her pictures was that they were "competent but conventional, made yesterday for today rather than today for tomorrow."

Lejeune's comments are borne out by the opinion of Mary's contemporaries; in the *Film Daily Yearbook*'s annual list of the ten best pictures, Douglas placed five pictures on the list from 1922 to 1928, while Mary placed precisely one: the despised *Rosita*, which tied for seventh (with *Safety Last*) in 1923.

In addition to everything else, an actress who had traditionally appeared in films tailor-made for her, or in parts that had not been successfully traversed by anybody else, had finally succumbed to her insecurity by doing remakes of material associated with other actresses; material, moreover, that was utterly out of step with the tastes of Depression audiences.

It was a predicament from which there was no real escape. If she attempted something more attuned to the tastes of the '30s (which would have been out of character), she risked alienating her die-hard fans whose approval she needed, the ones who looked to her as a reassuring constant in the "loose" moral climate signaled by the likes of Mae West.

At the same time, younger audiences thought of her as a relic of their parents' generation. Although she was only thirty-nine by the time she released *Kiki*, Mary's stardom was nearly twenty years old, and new audiences—and the new realism of the talkies —were demanding new idols.

As Alexander Walker wrote, "The powers of inventive imagination which enabled her to remain within the mind as well as the body of a child also helped her play such parts better than any other actress of her generation . . . But the price she had to pay for it petrified her artistry . . . the loving public simply would not allow her to grow up and play mature parts until it was . . . too late for her to make the adjustment."

She had had a reign unparalleled in cinema, but the key to its ending was in something Charlotte Smith had said to her daughter nearly thirty years before: *"A child has charm only when she is sweet."* Mary had adopted it as a kind of unofficial psychological motto; it had created a worldwide fame for her greater than that of any woman who had ever lived. And now it rendered her as old-fashioned as whalebone stays, as quaint as a worn, yellowed lace valentine.

Nearly ten years before, Mary had correctly judged her greatest strength which, like most great strengths, was also her great weakness. "I've worked all my life," she had said. "Work has become life to me. I can think of nothing to fill the void. Douglas talks of travel and study. I could enjoy a few months of travel every year, but . . ."

Her need for an isolation in which she could find a semblance of security was about to snap back in her face. "You never quite felt that Mary Pickford was human," said Adela Rogers St. Johns. "There was a psychological wall around her and her circle, if not a concrete one."

Originally, that wall had been constructed to keep the world out; increasingly, it would now be utilized to keep Mary in. The day would soon come when the world would cease to care what went on behind the high walls around Pickfair and would begin to forget about the woman who lived there.

Chapter Eleven

"Marion [Davies] couldn't drink . . . no Irishwoman can."
—*Adela Rogers St. Johns*

O N January 3, 1932, Jack Pickford, aged thirty-six, died in Paris, of what was euphemistically termed "progressive multiple neuritis which attacked all the nerve centers." It was really just chronic alcoholism. Four years later, on December 9, 1936—the same year Mary received her divorce decree from Douglas—Lottie would also die, aged forty-one, from chronic myocarditis and coronary sclerosis that had begun four years earlier, at least partially as a result of her drinking. Although Lottie had been married four times, her own valedictory seems to have been something she told her daughter shortly before she died: "At least I married them all. I didn't have round heels."

In a strange way, Jack and Lottie's fate in the Pickford family matched that of the outsider Owen Moore; both brother and sister were rendered powerless, psychologically excluded by the force of the love between Charlotte and Mary, and by the subtly demoralizing effects of Mary's own fame. Lottie's daughter Gwynne remembered her mother's last stab at show business, a children's radio program that went on the air at the same time as Mary's own brief series in 1934. "One Pickford on the radio at a time is enough," Mary had screamed at her sister, practically ordering her off the air. "Auntie broke my mother's heart," Gwynne said.

In the eight disastrous years bookended by Charlotte's death in 1928 and Lottie's in 1936, Mary lost everything meaningful to her: career, husband and family. She never really stopped grieving over Charlotte and Jack, and, after Lottie died, she refused to ever go past her mother's or sister's houses. This was difficult—both were on Benedict Canon, the street Summit Drive, the location of Pickfair, wends off of—and entailed circuitous detours for the next forty-odd years.

Mary began casting around for something to fill up her days, and there were things—United Artists, the gentle pursuit of Buddy Rogers—but there was nothing all-consuming. "Mary didn't care about traveling," remembered Douglas Fairbanks Jr., "and she wasn't all that interested in anything outside of her profession. She wasn't particularly social and wasn't a great reader, for instance."

So Mary began to do what all the Pickfords did. She began to drink.

It wasn't much of a secret, really, because Mary didn't seem to care whether anybody knew or not. To one reporter who interviewed her in 1934 while she was sipping a rum cocktail, she said the drink made her feel "naughty, very naughty." In a perceptive *New Yorker* profile published in April, 1934, Margaret Case Harriman, an old family friend, observed simply that "She likes to drink a little port at home, these days, and, when she goes out, occasionally gets very funny on a couple of cocktails or—in another mood —volubly indignant about something or other."

For a long time, only intimates really noticed. "It wasn't something that people could see at the studio or office," said Douglas Fairbanks Jr. "She was something of a secret drinker when she was married to my father, but it was nothing serious at all; a glass of sherry sneaked at dinner, something like that. He was a teetotaller, although he didn't mind other people having a drink and in fact kept quite a good cellar. But she didn't want to drink in front of him because she thought it would upset him.

"It was after the divorce that it really stepped up. If the truth were known, the Pickford family was the reverse of the genie that comes out of the bottle; they all disappeared into it."

For years, Mary's drinking was something of an open secret in Hollywood. In later years, the anesthesia of choice tended to be vodka or gin, in a waterglass, sipped on a regular basis. By then, if you wanted to do business with her, you had to call before a certain time, no later than lunch. Afterwards, she would be "indisposed."

Only close friends knew about it, for Hollywood was a town adept at keeping secrets. "Hollywood was a feudal system," re-

membered Lina Basquette, "a dictatorship really, with centralized government. And there was a caste system, which was utterly
ridiculous, because it was usually based on how much money you
were making or who you were sleeping with."

"There were no free souls here," said Phil Rhodes. "Everyone,
you see, was accountable to the head of the studio. Everybody
knew who was a drunk, who was a homosexual, a lesbian, whatever, but if you told—If you were an extra, or If you were a producer—you were *out*. And I don't mean out of a job, but out of the
industry.

"Mary wasn't accountable to anyone, but she was definitely part
of the system, and it protected her . . . just like Buddy did." And
Buddy would not be the only one. Frances Marion, ever loyal,
bristled when the question of Mary's drinking was brought up.
"What's that got to do with the happiness Mary Pickford brought
the world?" she charged.

———— ————

There is no question that Mary did not mean for her retirement to
be a hard-and-fast thing. As late as as July 1936, in a releasing
agreement she signed with United Artists, she inserted a clause
saying that "Pickford shall be the star, director or the actual producer" of the prospective pictures. Indeed, concurrently with the
release of *Secrets*, she was engaged in trying to set up a film that
would have been fully fifty years ahead of its time.

In 1932, United Artists had signed up Walt Disney to be its sole
supplier of shorts. The carrot they had dangled in front of him was
60 percent of the gross as well as ownership of his negatives. The
favorable terms may well have been because of Mary's long-standing admiration for Disney's work.

In June 1930, she had written to thank Disney for his gift of a
replica of Mickey Mouse, saying that, for the first time Douglas had
a rival. She went on to complain about Mickey's infrequent appearances, and asked Disney to speak to the Mouse and see if he'd
be willing to step up his schedule.

Mary's business relationship with Disney nearly broadened out
to a full-fledged co-production in the early part of 1933, when an
acquaintance named Frank Reilly suggested she make *Alice in
Wonderland* with Mary as Alice and Disney animating the world
and the characters around her. Despite the reservations of some of
her associates in the Pickford Company, who may well have been

leary of such an obviously expensive production in the darkest days of the Depression, Mary approached Disney.

It seemed like a natural project for both parties. The first films Disney had made in Hollywood after moving from his native Kansas City had been a series based on the same story, in which a live-action little girl lives in a cartoon world. At the same time, Mary's expertise in playing children was a phenomenon to which the entire world had paid tribute.

During the initial discussion in Disney's Spanish-style studio on Hyperion Avenue, the subject of a Disney project-in-the-works came up. After talking with story man Ted Sears, and listening to a little ditty that composer Frank Churchill had devised, Mary turned to Walt and said "If you don't make this cartoon about the pigs, I'll never speak to you again."

Disney overcame his doubts about the "cartoon about the pigs," but he had some problems with Mary's idea; to her disappointment, he did not immediately embrace the project. Stung, she wrote to Disney on April 26, 1933 and told him that the doleful predictions for *Alice* did not faze her. She was, however, disturbed about Disney's own apparent lack of enthusiasm, and, realizing that the project was impossible without Disney's complete commitment, embarked on a pep talk.

She tried to assuage Disney's fears about money, guaranteeing him an amount of profit from *Alice* equal to Disney's average profit from shorts that would total a similar amount of footage. She even offered to pay Disney this guarantee over the period of the production, with the guarantee to be applied against Disney's percentage of the profits. Mary proposed that, after the cost of production was recouped, the amount she had advanced to Disney would go to her, and she even offered to finance the picture herself, charging the same interest required if the monies came from a bank.

There can be no question about the seriousness of Mary's intentions at this point. She even went to the trouble of posing at her studio for some costume tests as Alice, posing in storybook sets with a stuffed Mickey Mouse, probably the same one Disney had presented her with three years before. The stills, which survive, prove that the forty-year-old Pickford could still get away with playing an adolescent child.

A puzzled, hesitant Disney responded to her letter eight days later. "As I tried to explain to you on our last meeting, the apparent lack of interest on my part was due to my reluctance to work myself up into an enthusiasm which would lead to great disappointment should the deal fall through."

After reiterating his unwillingness to emotionally commit to anything in such a speculative stage, Disney came to the heart of the matter. "My business representatives have been awaiting word from you. They have been perfectly willing to get together with your representative at any time. But nothing has been done from your end which would indicate you seriously intended going ahead with this production. The tentative proposition which you outlined in your letter is the first definite step that you've made towards working on our business proposition.

"I would suggest that you immediately delegate someone from your organization to get together with our business representatives and work out a mutual business arrangement. Until this is done, I do not feel justified in spending any time or thought on Alice or working myself up into any enthusiasm over it.

"In closing, I should like to say that I sincerely believe that a Pickford-Disney production of Alice would be a sensation."

The dance went on for one more month before Paramount, getting wind of the proposed project, made a preemptive strike. On May 24, Mary wrote Disney from the Super Chief train that she had hoped to straighten out the complications that had arisen from the copyrights Paramount had bought in England. Unable to do so, she abandoned the project.

After thanking Disney for his time, trouble and hospitality, Mary chattily told him that she and Douglas were on their way to New York, he to work on a new script, she to search for new material.

Three days later, *The Three Little Pigs* premiered and was an immediate sensation, going on to gross $250,000, unheard of for a short subject, while its theme song, "Who's Afraid of the Big Bad Wolf" became a national rallying cry during the Depression. More than anything else, it vindicated and justified Disney's nascent animation empire in the years before *Snow White and the Seven Dwarfs*.

Paramount's version of *Alice in Wonderland* was released late in 1933. The film was live-action, with most of their contract actors emoting behind giant masks meant to simulate the Tenniel illustrations. With the exception of W.C. Fields' Humpty Dumpty and Gary Cooper's The White Knight, it was an ignominious creative failure that met an equivalent fate at the box office. Nor was Disney's own fully animated version of 1951 entirely successful; by that time, the producer's style had become the animated equivalent of petrified maple syrup, and his homogenized versions of Lewis Carroll's characters lacked the necessary dangerous edge.

Mary's relationship with Disney remained outwardly friendly, yet, only two years later, Mary allowed him to leave United Artists over a minor business detail. Disney wanted his distribution fee lowered to 27$\frac{1}{2}$ percent. Mary and the United Artists board agreed, but the deal collapsed when Disney also demanded television rights during the distribution period. Both Mary and Sam Goldwyn objected. Disney promptly went to RKO, which offered him a $43,500 guarantee on each negative, plus a $12,000 advance for prints and advertising, with a 50-50 split of the profits after the advance was recouped. Taken all in all, the RKO deal was richer by far, and the fact that they were eager to have Disney undoubtedly meant that the unpleasant haggling that had destroyed the Disney/United Artists partnership could be avoided in the future.

Had Mary and Goldwyn been less adamant, United Artists would have had the coup of distributing—and taking the distribution fee on—*Snow White and the Seven Dwarfs,* among others.

In truth, the completely successful amalgam of live-action and animation that Mary had in mind did not happen until 1988 when *Who Framed Roger Rabbit* was made, in a pricelessly ironic touch, by the Disney studio.

———— • ————

Increasingly, Mary began to devote more time to United Artists, which, increasingly, needed it. When the separation between Mary and Doug was first announced in *Photoplay*, it was explained that the rift had begun with the making of *The Taming of the Shrew* and that both Mary and Doug were selling their shares in United Artists to Joseph Schenck and Sam Goldwyn. It is likely that the item was a trial balloon floated by Mary to see if Schenck and Goldwyn would be interested in buying . . . at her price, of course. They weren't.

Joseph Schenck had done yeoman work in providing the company with product as its original founders slowed down their production activities and, in the case of Mary and Douglas, ground to a complete halt. In 1924, United Artists had released only three pictures, but Schenck, who came on board in November, quickly upped production; United Artists released eleven pictures in each of the next three years, with fifteen and seventeen pictures being released in 1928 and 1929, respectively.

Schenck's own company, Art Cinema, had produced a number

of mostly successful United Artists pictures, as well as co-producing Mary's last two films. He had talked Sam Goldwyn into joining as a partner, and enticed Disney, Howard Hughes and others into releasing through United Artists.

Equally importantly, he snagged Darryl Zanuck's new company, Twentieth Century. Zanuck had resigned as production head at Warner Brothers in early 1933. By April, Twentieth Century was a reality, with the surreptitious backing of Louis B. Mayer. The MGM mogul wanted his son-in-law William Goetz to have a producer's job without the tacky trial of working his way up the ladder, and was willing to loan-out valuable MGM stars to ensure it. Schenck was president of Twentieth Century, Zanuck first vice-president in charge of production and Goetz second vice-president. Schenck and Goetz put up $1.2 million, the Bank of America came through with $3 million, and Consolidated Film Industries tossed in $750,000.

In its first year of operation, Twentieth Century produced twelve pictures; nine were successes, three failures. The profit was considerable. Zanuck had thought that his contract offered him a $5,000 salary per week plus 10 percent of the gross profits of the Twentieth Century pictures. At the end of the first year, he discovered that United Artists believed that his contract gave him 10 percent of the *net* profits, after the distribution fee of United Artists was taken off the top, considerably lessening Zanuck's share.

The deal was amended in Zanuck's favor, but not without a good deal of wrangling, which Zanuck found demoralizing. Zanuck was also informed that, although he was contributing a goodly share of the profits to the company, he was not to be allowed to buy stock.

As Zanuck later remembered it, "The pictures I was working on had to carry the entire United Artists distributing organization; I had to carry the whole goddamn load. While Chaplin was still brooding over the future of talking films . . . and King Fairbanks was worrying about how best to dump Queen Pickford . . . they were helping themselves to our profits and socking us for their expenses."

Although that was an oversimplification, it was not a gross oversimplification. Zanuck *was* carrying a great deal of the load. To be precise, United Artists released twenty pictures in 1934, of which nine came from Twentieth Century. Those same nine pictures accounted for more than half the $23 million corporate gross. On top of that, Zanuck was fuming because he believed the United

Artists studio charges were exorbitant, that he could make pictures cheaper someplace else.

Although Twentieth Century was thriving, Schenck's Art Cinema Corporation was staggering. Besides the $600,000 loss on *Reaching for the Moon* and *Kiki,* Schenck had poured money into such disasters as *Putting on the Ritz* with Harry Richman, *DuBarry, Woman of Passion,* and *New York Nights,* both with his soon to be ex-wife Norma Talmadge, *Rain,* with Joan Crawford, and the Al Jolson vehicle *Hallelujah, I'm a Bum,* which had to be expensively re-shot.

As early as January 1932, Clarence Ericksen, Fairbanks's general manager, was telling Cap O'Brien that "the financial condition of Art Cinema is none too sound, and inasmuch as they hold the majority of the stock of the . . . Studio Corporation, to whom [Mary and Douglas's] studio property is leased, we are wondering if some special action should be taken to protect our lease." Art Cinema was liquidated the following year, with stockholders receiving about forty cents on the dollar. Among the disgruntled investors was Lee Shubert, who, Cap O'Brien wryly noted, "does not lose money well."

The Depression hit United Artists hard. On February 20, 1934, Twentieth Century was in debt to the studio for rental and other services to the tune of $231,550, while Goldwyn owed $95,460. Cash on hand was slightly more than $16,000.

Zanuck and Schenck began looking around for greener, cheaper pastures and spotted the moribund Fox film corporation, an effective sales organization saddled with inferior product. After slightly less than two years of releasing through United Artists, Twentieth Century merged with Fox; on May 21, 1935, Joe Schenck resigned from United Artists to join his young protégé.

United Artists could afford to lose Zanuck, although barely; it could not afford to lose Schenck at all, for he was not only a fine moviemaker—albeit a fine moviemaker going through a bad slump—but he was also a conciliator who could mediate between people otherwise at each other's throats. Unfortunately, the reasons for the defection of Zanuck would come to be repeated over and over again in varying degrees. United Artists had been deliberately structured by Mary, Douglas, Chaplin and Griffith as a passive, break-even convenience company intentionally bereft of a centralized, profit-oriented management. That other producers, who were actively engaged in competitive production, could not reasonably be expected to be as solipsistic and *laissez-faire* as the founding members never seemed to dawn on them.

The defection of Zanuck and Schenck left Douglas, Mary and United Artists with an empty studio lot and not enough pictures being made on it, a situation worsened by the effects of the Depression. Robert Fairbanks, who was in charge of the lot at the time, complained in a letter to an associate that he had made Harold Lloyd an offer that was "considerably better than the prices which both the Goldwyn and the Twentieth Century Company are paying." But, after what Robert described as "cut-throat competition," Lloyd signed a contract with another rental studio for a price that was 25 percent less than United Artists' best offer.

———— ————

Away from the boardroom, Mary seems to have been in a particularly vulnerable state at this time. She had been going to fortune tellers for some time, assiduously writing down their predictions so as to check their accuracy later. She was also following numerology and astrology, and began to consult mediums, so that she might maintain contact with Charlotte. She began to dabble in mysticism; "Whenever I'm making some sort of contract or deal or planning a trip," she confided to an interviewer, "if I dream of a half-empty or empty theater, it's a bad omen." At the same time she was engaging in those classically vaporous activities, she idly contemplated the rock-hard vicissitudes of politics, with the ultimate goal of becoming a Congresswoman from California by the time she was fifty.

She was in a dangerously pliable emotional condition; even in business, she seemed unsure of herself. When there was some wrangling with Joe Schenck over a new studio lease, Mary wired specific instructions to Cap O'Brien, then finished by saying, BELIEVE YOU ARE LOGICAL ONE TO BE ADAMANT ESPECIALLY IN DOUGLAS ABSENCE. It all seemed to be too much for her.

Talking to one reporter who seemed to expect a sad, benighted creature, devastated by the collapse of her stardom and her deteriorating marriage, Pickford would enact a veritable pathetic slavery, albeit one with assets in the vicinity of $3 million. Should another reporter suggest that he expected to find a never-say-die, spunky female out of one of her movies, Mary would pick up on the suggestion and enact Spartan gaiety.

"She does this unconsciously, almost automatically, because she has tried for so long to be what she thinks the public wants her to be," wrote Margaret Harriman, in an accurate analysis of the essential psychology of the actors and actresses. But the public did not really want her anymore, and Mary Pickford implicitly believed in giving the audience what it wanted. As Harriman observed, what had sustained Mary through the trials of early poverty, a marriage with an alcoholic, the ultimate failure of her relationship with Douglas and everything else, had not been an inherent optimism derived from her screen character, but, rather, a passion for work. Without that blessed surcease from her own passive psychological makeup, trouble was bound to happen. Someone was gradually reduced to no one.

At least she didn't need the money. Under the guidance of, first, Charlotte, and later Cap O'Brien, Mary's investment strategy was strictly blue chip. Among Charlotte's early investments had been bonds for the city of Los Angeles, some $80,000 worth, which brought in a perfectly respectable $4^{1/2}$ percent. "Our principals speculate all that they should in the motion picture business," wrote Cap O'Brien, "and all other transactions ought to be on as stable a basis as we can find for them."

In 1923, Charlotte had set up Mary's finances in the manner they would be kept for years. Income from securities, real estate, and other investments was kept separate from income from pictures. The Mary Pickford Company was set up as the repository for all film returns, while a joint account carrying Mary and Charlotte's names held the rest.

A 1932 Los Angeles county tax assessment showed Mary personally to own stocks worth $2,316,940, a remarkable achievement given the economic climate of the times. The assessment also listed foreign trusts of $176,190 and real estate worth $ 192,260. Douglas had stocks valued at $1,384,690, foreign trusts of $75,480 and real estate worth $75,480, not counting Pickfair, which was assessed at $70,170. Neither of them had wealth to compare with their friend Chaplin, whose 1932 tax assessment showed he had stocks and bonds worth $7,687,570.

Two years later, Mary's wealth had dropped to $1,950,770, partially because she had extensively increased her real estate holdings, the total of which was now assessed at $340,750, a sum far below market value. By 1939, the assets of the Pickford Company were valued as in excess of $2,500,000; the company's sole stockholder was Mary.

In early 1934, just past the deepest point of the Depression, the bank balance of the Pickford Company fluctuated between $45,267 and $4,653. Mary paid her bills once a week, and an examination of her account books reveals that she was spending $200 a week for groceries.

She owned bonds that were returning between 5 percent and 6 percent and dozens of pieces of real estate, mostly commercial, that ranged from Pacific Palisades to a miniature golf course on the corner of Wilshire and La Cieneaga. "She became very rich buying tracts of land, and buildings," remembered Lillian Gish. "I was always respectful of her talent for knowing what to buy, and apologetic for my own lack of interest."

Among the pieces of land that Mary owned was the corner of Wilshire and Hamilton in Beverly Hills, for which, in 1935, she paid $66,500. Another piece of property, the corner of Third and Catalina in Los Angeles, was rented for years by the Citizens National Trust and Savings Bank for around $400 a month. To take an average month, January 1934, the revenue from Mary's real estate holdings totalled $1,498.25, which covered about half her monthly payroll.

Yet, Mary's legendary wariness in money matters was not entirely predicated on unfounded paranoia. In May 1927, she and Douglas had formed part of a syndicate that purchased 627 feet of beach footage, a pier, and eight lots across the street in Playa del Rey, California. The other investors included Louis B. Mayer, Joseph Schenck, and John Considine Jr. among others. Mary's investment in the syndicate was $39,930.02.

In the late fall of 1942, Mary and her business manager were approached by a nephew of Louis B. Mayer, who, on behalf of Mayer, wanted to dissolve the syndicate because of damage the beach and pier had sustained during a series of storms. Mary's business manager advised against the dissolution, mostly for tax reasons, but also because he felt that, with time, the land would recover its value.

Nevertheless, the other members of the syndicate over-rode the Pickford interests and arranged for the dissolution. A few months later, it was decided to sell the property outright, thus creating capital losses. The entire property was sold for $1,000 to a tenant operating a sandwich shop.

Later, Mary's business manager was chagrined to find that the sandwich shop operator was really a front for Louis B. Mayer's nephew, who had effected a world-class real estate killing, presumably with his uncle's advice and blessing. Mary's share in the sale was $123.47; her net loss on the property was listed as $39,806.55.

Because of deals like these, Mary's business sense was on the same level as Chaplin's, who, in the words of Sam Goldwyn, "just knew he couldn't take anything less." She could be a steely landlord, often refusing rent reductions to struggling tenants, such as one Edward Hubner, who ran a gas station on Mary's property at Wilshire and Hamilton.

However, even initially classic Scrooge-like responses were often resolved in something of a happy ending; Mary ultimately agreed to cut the beleaguered Hubner's rent by $25, to $125 a month.

She was less accommodating to a local merchants' organization, which sent her letters of complaint about a four-foot space she owned at 5535½ Santa Monica Boulevard. Mary rented it out, usually as a costume jewelry stand, and studiously ignored protests that it was lowering rental values and attracting an undesirable clientele.

Although it was Chaplin who earned a reputation for remarkable frugality, Mary's own habits were far from spendthrift. In the late '30s, when John Hay ("Jock") Whitney solicited funds from within the film industry to establish the film library at the Museum of Modern Art, Mary was persuaded to hold a reception at Pickfair. Some time later, Whitney was stunned to receive an itemized bill, in pencil, "that . . . included the cost of the wood burned in Mary's fireplace."

Charlotte had taught her little girl well.

——— —

In New York in June 1933, smarting from the fast failure of *Secrets,* and casting about for something to do, she desultorily interviewed prospective playwrights. Among them was Edmund Wilson, then an aspiring author, not yet the critic who would become the literary conscience of America. Wilson found her "businesslike, practical, clear in her mind, fairly intelligent—an American small-town girl, probably Irish, who by dint of her peculiar position had become something of a woman of the world. I liked her."

He was, however, appalled by Mary's recent face-lift, which had had the effect of immobilizing the lower half of her face. "Only the upper part of her face was alive," noted Wilson, "the eyes, dark, agatelike blue which glowed, even flashed from time to time, with a slate-blue power of energy and will . . . human and very attractive, while the lower part of her face remained immobile." What had no doubt been intended to make Mary look younger for whatever was left of her public—or for her own vanity—had the unintended effect of making her look older and more rigid.

Looking back on the encounter, which bore no dramatic fruit, it seemed to Wilson that "when she first came into the room, and for a moment when I was leaving, there was a little despiteful look . . . as of resentment and disappointment against a world to which she was no longer irresistibly winning."

She scratched the old *Alice in Wonderland* itch by mounting a theatrical production that she tried out on the road and brought into New York's Paramount theater on December 22, 1933. She was guaranteed $10,000 a week against 50 percent of the profits over a gross of $60,000, but she had to work for it with five shows a day.

Alice in Wonderland did well, if only because it gave Mary's fans a chance to see her in person, but there was no future in it. By September 1934, she was back in New York, playing around with producing and directing a movie about a woman psychiatrist who cures a male alcoholic. "The great drawback to most of the talking pictures made today is that they are chiefly talk," she told her old friend Karl Kitchen.

She backed off on the psychiatrist story, and tried radio instead, beginning a series on the Hollywood station WEAF Wednesday nights in October 1934. After considering adaptations of *Seventh Heaven* and *Coquette,* Mary decided to place herself in the hands of the advertisers, who, she reasoned, knew more about the new medium than she did.

She expressed the need for an audience, believing in the validity of their reactions. "I believe they'll help me to know whether or not they like the material I have to offer. I really believe that the material is 65 percent of the battle, and that an actor is no better than his material." After a month of doing the radio show in Hollywood, Mary transferred production to New York in November. She apparently had some trouble concentrating amidst the hurly-burly of a radio broadcast; she had the studio partitioned off with black walls, with Mary and the other actors huddled around the microphone inside, while the orchestra was left outside.

The weekly plays did not do that well and they were replaced by a show called "Party at Pickfair," a variation on the popular "Hollywood Hotel" program hosted by Louella Parsons. "Party at Pickfair" offered Mary as mistress of ceremonies, chatting with celebrities, encouraging songwriters to sing.

After three weeks, it was clear that the program was not drawing an audience, so the sponsors decided to spice it up by adding gossip columnist Sidney Skolsky to the mix. Skolsky's items—"You'd be surprised at who was at Sylvia Sidney's house last night. I saw Gary Cooper's car parked outside, and he lives miles and miles away"—helped, but not enough.

"It didn't make a dent in the audience that tuned in 'Hollywood Hotel,'" remembered Skolsky with the brutal matter-of-factness of one used to the law of the jungle. "One reason was that Mary couldn't attract as many big-name guests for her show; her film career had declined, and with it her power." Louella Parsons, on the other hand, still had her column, which gave her enormous leverage. After thirteen weeks, Mary's option was dropped and "Party at Pickfair" went off the air.

She continued to dabble in radio through the '40s and occasionally into the '50s, her appearances often coinciding with an appeal for one of her favorite charities: the Motion Picture Relief Fund or the March of Dimes. Occasionally, though, she'd do a show just for fun, as in a 1948 broadcast with Edgar Bergen and Charlie McCarthy.

"Won't you sit down, Miss Pickford?" helpfully asks Charlie.

"Thank you . . . but where?"

"Oh, Bergen's other knee?"

Other appearances were less fruitful, notably a 1940 appearance as the Virgin Mary (with Ronald Colman as Joseph) that plays like a vicious parody of bad radio, complete with a droning organ for music and dialogue like "The Prince of Peace . . . see how sweetly he sleeps."

Concurrently with her activities in radio, she tried her hand at writing, or, rather, dictating. *Why Not Try God?* was ghosted by Hearst's favorite sob sister Adela Rogers St. Johns, and landed on the bestseller list in 1934. Trouble, it explained, is only bad thoughts. "God is a 24-hour station; all you have to do is plug in. You plug in with your thinking."

This philosophy of optimism was by no means only for public consumption. Once, when Gwynne was sulking, Mary told her not to scowl. "Why shouldn't I scowl? Everything is wrong and my feelings have been hurt."

"In the first place, distorting your face won't help the situation . . . In the second, it's unbecoming. You're much prettier when you're thinking beauty and living it!" The Glad Girl lived.

The success of *Why Not Try God,* an early version of a gospel that might have resulted if Mary Baker Eddy had united in unholy union with Norman Vincent Peale, led to *My Rendezvous with Life,* a followup of sorts a year later. These excursions into *echt*-religion impelled Adela Rogers St. Johns to give full vent to the throbbing emotional hysteria that she usually kept slightly veiled. "It is my belief," she wrote around this time, "that Mary Pickford . . . will within our time become one of the great religious leaders of our century."

The success of *Why Not Try God?* encouraged Mary to think she might have a writing career. She embarked on a novel that was eventually entitled *The Demi-Widow*. Mary enlisted the services of another ghostwriter, one Belle Burns Gromer, to whom Mary gave a $500 advance, the same amount she got from the publisher. Bobbs-Merrill gave Mary a contract paying a 10 percent royalty on the first 5,000 copies and 15 percent thereafter, with Mary cutting her ghostwriter in for 25 percent of her royalties.

Work with Gromer went smoothly enough, although Mary occasionally took a day off, wiring Gromer that she felt guilty about being so lazy but promising to show up for work tomorrow.

The Demi-Widow was published in 1935, to fairly good reviews. It is essentially a scenario for a silent movie, with a widowed young mother finding riches and True Love as a theater star. It had an indifferent success; after January 31, 1936, the publishers reported to Mary that it was not earning any more royalties (the total for 1936 added up to just $1,294.49). Given the indifferent state of publishing in the pit of the Depression, it seems highly likely that Mary did the book in the expectation that she would make more out of an eventual movie sale than from royalties.

In an apparent attempt to test the market shortly after *The Demi-Widow* was published, she paid Noel Langley, later to be one of the writers on The *Wizard of Oz,* a thousand dollars a week to do a treatment. Mary evidently thought so little of the treatment she never bothered to commission a full screenplay, and the property was neither sold nor produced. At around the same time, she also commissioned new treatments of several of her old films, among them *Suds* and *Heart of the Hills.* Whether this was done in an attempt to interest other producers in buying the properties or whether she was considering them as possible projects for her own production activities is unknown.

She was finding out, in the most brutal way possible, that her fame, prestige, even most of her friendships, depended on her career as an actress. Once, a friend asked Harry Cohn if he was going to sell Columbia Pictures, as was being rumored. "Are you crazy?" replied Cohn. "If I sell the company, who's going to call me on the telephone?" Cohn, a smart streetfighter, *knew.* Mary, smart, but no streetfighter, didn't. Her years of exile and anguish were beginning.

———— ————

Buddy Rogers and Mary had been spending a great deal of time together ever since Mary's separation from Douglas. They had traveled together to Santa Cruz in April 1935 for a vacation at the Pasatiempo Golf Club, and Buddy had spent Christmas of 1936 at Pickfair. A week after that, Mary announced they would be married in June.

The ceremony took place on June 26, 1937, at the home of producer Louis Lighton and his wife, Hope Loring, who had introduced the couple more than ten years before. The bride's party was small, thirteen people, mostly family, and Frances Marion. Mary's niece Gwynne remembered that Mary was extremely agitated that day. "The dress didn't fit right and had to be pinned," Gwynne told Robert Windeler. "She delayed upstairs in the bedroom at Pickfair and would not come down. She kept stamping her foot and squealing—almost crying—'I don't wanna' like one of the little girls in her films." Mary was ten minutes late for her own wedding.

Despite Mary's anxiety—was she afraid of finally cutting off Douglas, or was she just afflicted with buyer's remorse?—newsreels of the wedding reception show Mary looking slim, vivacious and quite beautiful. As they were cutting the cake, Mary leaned over and whispered in Buddy's ear, "Who's your favorite actress?" He whispered back, "Mrs. Charles Buddy Rogers." After a reception at Pickfair—where Buddy, self-conscious about being in what he regarded as another man's house, refused to allow pictures of him to be taken—they were off to Hawaii via the S.S. *Lurline* for their honeymoon, on the same cruise as newlyweds Jeanette MacDonald and Gene Raymond.

It had all gone smoothly enough, except for one change that Mary had mandated in the ceremony. Instead of saying "Love, honor and obey," she vowed to "Love, honor and cherish" her new husband. It seems a startlingly contemporary alteration, as well as being an accurate approximation of Mary and Buddy's relationship. Now, Mary Pickford would obey no one but herself.

———— ————

Why marry Buddy Rogers, this gentle, passive man whose career was already on the downhill slide?

"They had known each other for a long time," said Kemp Niver, a friend of the couple in later years, "and there was an explicit trust between them. She knew she could trust him absolutely, and she liked the idea that she was protected at all times. And, let's face it, he was handsome."

"Buddy was a sweet, handsome lad," said Vitalis Chalif, one of Mary's lawyers during the '40s. "I think she was fond of him. But there was no question who was the boss."

Buddy was also a non-threatening, reassuring presence for a woman in need of one. As an old man, Buddy would speak of his habit of "giving in" to the wishes of others and it was true. He gave in to his father's wishes about the movie contest, he gave in to Paramount when he made the movies they told him to, and, finally, he would invariably give in to Mary.

All of Mary's friends liked Buddy. Indeed, in all of Hollywood, it is nearly impossible to find anybody who doesn't like Buddy. Even fiery rebels like Lina Basquette said that "I think it was serious love affair, on both ends. Mary probably had more love and fidelity from him than from Douglas Fairbanks."

The only negative opinion came from Clark Gable, who, in an uncharacteristic fit of pique, snarled that it wouldn't last six months. In fact, it lasted forty-two years, and Buddy Rogers always took a quiet pride in the fact that he had beaten Clark Gable's time.

Despite the new marriage and Mary's glow of happiness at the ceremony, there was never any question among her intimates as to with whom she was really in love. In fact, on December 28, 1936, while Buddy was still in residence at Pickfair, she had sent a wire to Douglas on board the S.S. *Aquatania.* Mary's copy of her message was kept in a private shorthand that is only partially decipherable. But the sense of it is that she will do whatever he needs her to do, and that if he can manage to pull himself together, "I shall again love you."

"In all the years I knew her," recalled Tess Michaels, "I never heard her say a bad word about Douglas. Did she regret the failure of the reconciliation? Yes . . . in a small way."

Douglas Fairbanks was not to be expelled from her consciousness then, or ever, or she from his. Until his death, whenever he ran into a mutual friend from the old days, he would invariably ask "Have you seen Mary lately? How is she?" Mary continued to use the Fairbanks name in business matters for at least a year after her marriage to Buddy. And, years later at Pickfair, sitting with a friend, she would sip a beer and say "It was never the same after he left here. Neither were our lives."

At first, Mary and Buddy lived in his house near the Riviera Country Club, where he played polo. "Her help had to come down to help her with United Artists," remembered Buddy, "and she wasn't happy there. Finally she said, 'Come on darling.' So we moved to Pickfair." Buddy's loyalty and steadfastness had finally been rewarded. A few years after he married Mary, they met the Duke and Duchess of Windsor, and the former Wallis Simpson said to him, "I am married to the best-known man in the world and you to the best-known woman." It was a distinction each consort would cling to, even when it was no longer true.

In 1937, after over forty years of living with domineering personalities, first her mother, then her second husband, Mary Pickford was, for the first time, in total control of her own life, with no one to answer to but herself. The question was, what would she do with it?

Chapter Twelve

"I've worked and fought my way through since I was twelve, and I know business."

—*Mary Pickford*

*I*N 1928, *Variety* estimated that Jesse Lasky, vice-president of production at Paramount since 1916, was the eighth richest man in show business, worth about $20 million. In 1932, Jesse Lasky was fired from a Paramount reeling from the effects of the Depression. Paramount stock for which Lasky had paid $1,550,000 brought exactly $37,500 when it was sold by Harry Warner to cover a loan he had made to Lasky. Basically, Lasky was broke.

But the bouncy, ebullient producer recovered after a fashion, with a $3,000-a-week contract at a pre-Darryl Zanuck Fox. While there, he made a few notable pictures like *Zoo in Budapest* and *The Power and the Glory,* in addition to forgotten programmers like *I am Suzanne,* and *The Warrior's Husband.* On balance, his three years at Fox were financially indifferent. It was at that point that Lasky and Mary, two longtime insiders fighting to avoid becoming outsiders, banded together and formed Pickford-Lasky Productions.

The schedule for the first year was four pictures, none of them remotely like an old Mary Pickford picture. "To produce one type of picture was irksome enough when I was playing them," she explained. It was her first attempt at fulfilling a prophecy she had made twelve years earlier: "If I ever retire from the screen, I will become a producer . . . unless I am forced into retirement."

The plans for the company involved none of what Mary believed to be a wave of lubricity overwhelming Hollywood. There was no question in her mind about who the ringleader was: Mae West. "There will be no salaciousness in our films," she said. "Not one little bit. We will consider only those stories which will ensure wholesome, healthy, yet vital entertainment. Be a guardian, not an usher, at the portal of your thought."

Luckily, the first Pickford-Lasky Production was considerably more interesting than Mary's twee philosophizing. Mary and Lasky bought the rights to a 1935 French film entitled *Monsieur Sans-Gene* and re-made it under the title *One Rainy Afternoon*. The film is a voyage deep into Lubitsch country; there is the happy-go-lucky young man about town (Francis Lederer); a slightly hesitant sweet young thing (Ida Lupino, before she found her niche at Warner Brothers as a tormented proletarian heroine), officious bureaucrats and creamily lit, expansive sets . . . all taking place in Paris, of course.

Although Mary and Jesse Lasky tried to cover themselves by hiring most of the best character actors in Hollywood (Roland Young, Mischa Auer, Donald Meek, Erik Rhodes, Hugh Herbert, Billy Gilbert) as well as a considerable array of behind-the-screen talent, including Preston Sturges for the song lyrics and for the script Emeric Pressburger, (a few years before Pressburger would team up with Michael Powell), the film is undone by the lightweight leads. Francis Lederer was no Chevalier, and the entire picture lacks the necessary effervescence.

The story is certainly serviceable. A young blade is having an affair with a married woman. They go to movies after the lights go down so none of her friends will see her. In the darkened theater, he kisses the wrong girl, is arrested and becomes a national *cause célèbre*. The girl he kisses by mistake is, of course, The Right One.

One Rainy Afternoon is the sort of material that, unless directed by a genius like Lubitsch, seems like the book for a weak musical, and Rowland V. Lee, while gifted, was no Lubitsch. As there is only one song, the film is a strained, becalmed affair that seems far longer than its eighty minutes.

"*One Rainy Afternoon* was not very successful," remembered Jesse Lasky. Indeed. The film's negative cost was $511,383, and its worldwide gross was $603,903. Deducting United Artists' distribution percentage and a nominal prints and advertising budget puts the loss at around $150,000. Its failure spelled a quick end for

Pickford-Lasky Productions; the dissolution of the partnership was announced while the second production, *The Gay Desperado,* was still being made.

For *The Gay Desperado,* the partners hired the innovative Rouben Mamoulian to direct a young tenor named Nino Martini, whom Lasky had used at Fox, and whose singing sounded a great deal like Mario Lanza bereft of chest tones. A comedy operetta about a small-time Mexican bandit who reorganizes his outlaw band into a Chicago-style mob after seeing a gangster movie, *The Gay Desperado* is notable mainly for Mamoulian's lavishly picturesque visuals.

Sadly, the film regularly stops dead every time Martini breaks into song, as if to compensate for the lack of music in *One Rainy Afternoon.* (The mid-'30s were bad times for operettas; Lubitsch's exquisite *The Merry Widow* had been a failure for MGM only a year before, and that was followed by *The Gay Desperado,* which includes a malevolently awful "Celeste Aida" and is no *Merry Widow.*)

Ironically, *The Gay Desperado* did considerably better than *One Rainy Afternoon,* with a worldwide gross of $922,878 against a cost of $649,160, but not well enough. It still lost about $30,000, putting the total bath of red ink for Pickford-Lasky Productions at nearly $200,000.

After one year, with two unsuccessful pictures released, Pickford-Lasky Productions was disbanded. Although Jesse Lasky tried to put the best public face on it, saying "it was a very pleasant [association]" Lasky felt that Mary was unsettlingly tough.

"Her attitude was 'I know as much about making movies as you do,'" says Kemp Niver. "'I was out here at the same time you were,'" she told him. "And that was true; the difference was that she hadn't been producing for as long as Lasky had. She would have been difficult to work with; as a businesswoman, she was a spoiled, indulged brat."

The Pickford-Lasky films are most interesting for the glimpses they afford into the kind of material Mary was attracted to when not burdened by her screen character or the expectations of her public: gay, effervescent romps in continental settings, much like *The Demi-Widow.* They make it clear just why she had been attracted to the great gifts of Lubitsch even before they had fully matured.

Mary began thumbing through her files of story properties; Irving Thalberg offered her $110,000 for rights to *Coquette* and *Kiki* (which she had picked up for the fire-sale price of $1,000 apiece when Joe Schenck dissolved Art Cinema Corporation), but Mary wanted $130,000 and stood firm. No deal. There was some interest in the rights to *Little Annie Rooney* and *My Best Girl,* but Mary demanded $25,000 ("net to us") for the former and $30,000 for the latter. No deal.

In August 1938, Mary was thinking of moving to New York, to be nearer Buddy and his touring, but nothing came of it. They seemed to be a happy couple; Mary would often come out to cheer when Buddy played polo. And, despite Mary's preference for staying at home, they would occasionally venture out.

And, of course, there was Buddy's band. In September 1938, while touring through the midwest, Buddy was involved in an auto accident near Delaware, Ohio, and was taken to University Hospital in Columbus. Although his injuries weren't serious, Mary flew in from Los Angeles and arrived in the early afternoon.

The reporters asked for some comment, even if only about her flight. "Soon," she said, "as soon as I see Buddy." Within a half-hour, she invited the half-dozen reporters into the hospital room so they could talk to her and Buddy.

"When it was about time to break up," remembered Sidney Elsner, one of the reporters, "she interjected, 'You boys have been here a long time. Did you get any lunch?' We hadn't. We didn't dare leave the hall vigil. 'I'll ask for something to be sent up.' " She called the hospital kitchen, precisely as if it was hotel room service, and continued chatting with the reporters while they ate their sandwiches, fruit and coffee.

In early December 1938, Mary and Buddy were in Mexico City. Although they were noticed, there was nothing like the attention, the clamor, that would have greeted an appearance by Mary just ten years earlier. Slowly, the public was beginning to forget, and even supposed friends occasionally let slip the fact that Mary was no longer to be taken completely seriously. Elaine Barrymore, the young wife of John Barrymore, attended a luncheon with Mary and Hedda Hopper. Mary gave her scheduled speech, which ended with her asking "Why not try God?" At that point, Hedda Hopper leaned over to Barrymore and said, "Why not? She's tried everyone else."

On June 12, 1939, Owen Moore was found dead in his home of a cerebral hemorrhage. He had been lying on his kitchen floor for two days. Mary was saddened but did not cry.

The passing of the years had been no kinder to Douglas than to Mary. To many of his old friends, it seemed that the marriage to Sylvia put more stress on him than his tiring body could withstand. The once maniacally maintained, svelte figure gradually added an unmistakable spare tire, and the man who had once prided himself on getting to bed by ten or eleven was now up at all hours dutifully following Sylvia from club to club, chain-smoking the whole time.

Hedda Hopper ran into an obviously exhausted Douglas at a nightclub and asked him why he didn't go home. "I can't," he replied. "I have to wait for Sylvia."

"Someone will see she gets home. She always does. This is killing you."

"I know, but she's my wife."

On December 9, 1939, Douglas attended his son's thirtieth birthday party. His niece Mary Margaret saw him lean his head against a chair and close his eyes. "Are you all right?" she asked. "I'm tired," he said, "so tired."

On the morning of December 11, Douglas had pains in his wrist and a feeling of tightness in his chest. He couldn't get comfortable, nor could he quite get his breath. His accountant, Art Fenn, noticed him acting strangely and called Douglas's brother Robert. When Robert arrived at the beach house, he called a doctor, who quickly diagnosed a heart attack and prescribed weeks, possibly months of bed rest.

Doug Jr. arrived to find his father weak but glad to see him. He'd rather die, he told his son, than be an invalid, and Doug Jr. could tell he meant it. For a while, the son read to his father from the works of his favorite writers, Byron and Shakespeare. Finally, Doug Sr. fell asleep. Then, for the first time in their relationship, Doug Jr. leaned over and kissed his father on the forehead. Later that afternoon, a despondent Douglas asked his brother, "If anything happens to me, I want you to give Mary a message. Tell her, *By the Clock.*"

That night, around midnight, Douglas roused himself from his sleep. His bull mastiff Polo lay at the foot of the bed, looking worried. "Please open the window and let me hear the sea," Douglas asked his nurse. The nurse did so, then asked him how he was feeling. "I've never felt better," he said, smiling. On December 12, 1939, at 12:45 in the morning, the nurse heard Polo growl softly. He checked his patient and found that Douglas had, very quietly, died. Sylvia, in hysterics, called Doug Jr., who rushed over to find his father looking much the same as the last time he'd seen him. Then, for the second and last time, he kissed his father.

Mary was in Chicago, traveling with Buddy and his band. Gwynne dreaded calling her, but did, at four in the morning. "But when I got through I didn't even have to tell her why I'd called. She was psychic, and there was something in my voice when I said, 'Oh, Auntie.' She said 'Don't tell me, my darling is gone.' " Shortly afterwards, Robert Fairbanks fulfilled his promise to his brother, calling Mary and relaying Douglas's message: "By the Clock." Mary said nothing, seemed frozen. The next day, on a train bound for New York, the tears finally came in floods. Douglas was gone, and she felt alone.

———— — ·

Gladys Cooper wrote from California to her daughter in England: "Doug Fairbanks died here very suddenly this week and the papers are full of funeral pictures of Sylvia draped in heavy black, but with her red painted toe-nails sticking through the end of her sandals, which rather spoils the effect."

Two years after Douglas's death, Sylvia commissioned a tomb for Douglas, next to the mausoleum of the Hollywood Memorial Cemetery, at a cost of $40,000. Stately columns surround a bas relief of Douglas; the inscription quotes from *Hamlet:* "Good Night Sweet Prince; May flights of angels sing thee to thy rest."

Even though his lifestyle had been lavish and he had not had much money coming in for the last several years of his life, Douglas left an estate valued at $4 million; his half-interest in the Goldwyn studio land was valued at $240,000. Sylvia, after living in luxury off her dead husband's estate for a number of years, delayed its final settlement until the early '50s, by which time it had been drained of a good deal of its assets.

In 1944, she married Edward John Lord Stanley of Alderly. The marriage broke up quickly, Lord Stanley charging her with adultery; Sylvia returned to the beach house Douglas had left her. In December 1949, after the proverbial whirlwind courtship, Sylvia married Mary's one-time suitor Clark Gable. The speedy courtship was abetted by the fact that Gable, still grieving for Carole Lombard, was drinking very heavily at the time. The marriage lasted less than a year and a half; Sylvia collected $150,000 in alimony, payable over five years.

In 1954, she married Prince Dimitri Djorjadze, but this too failed. In 1967, she moved to Los Angeles to live with her sister.

She died on June 30, 1977, of cancer. Mary's reaction went unre-corded.

In retrospect, Mary blamed Douglas for straying as early as the Lupe Velez incident, but she also blamed herself for not being able to overlook it. No, there was no shortage of blame, but Mary never honestly blamed Sylvia for the break-up of her marriage.

Douglas's death impelled Mary to maintain even closer ties to Douglas Jr., whom she began addressing as "Jayar," a corruption of Jr., and his father's nickname for him. He was, tangibly, his father's son, and Mary always made sure that he regarded Pickfair as his second home. Most revealingly, in some of her correspondence to him, she would sign herself "Mama Fairbanks."

At Pickfair, life went on as before. Buddy quickly took to his stunningly trivial role as the adoring prince consort and was usu-ally in transit to the golf course or from the polo field. Occasionally, Mary would have little parties at Pickfair, and she would always be sure to invite old-timers from the Biograph or Famous Players days. She remained fiercely loyal to old compatriots. When Billy Bitzer, the Biograph cameraman and Griffith's good right arm, had a heart attack and fell on hard times, Mary removed Bitzer from the public hospital where he had been taken and had him admitted to a private hospital. Later, she arranged for the Motion Picture Relief Fund to pick up the bill and help Bitzer out with a modest pension.

Until that came through, she personally helped out. On Febru-ary 10, 1940, from her suite at the Sherry Netherlands, she sent him a check for thirty-five dollars, instructing him that it was to be used to buy both a suit and a coat, even specifying that a good place to go would be Barney's, on Seventh Avenue and 17th Street, where there was a sale on until Monday. They were, she told him (sound-ing a good deal like Charlotte at her hectoring best) open until 10:00 P.M. on Mondays.

Other friends from the old days weren't as desperate for aid. On one occasion in 1940, James Kirkwood Jr. was accompanied by his mother, Lila Lee, on a visit to Pickfair. "Occasionally, we would all go on tours in the attic where Mary kept her costumes," remem-bered Kirkwood. "Every costume that she had ever worn was in big garment bags. Mary also kept her furs and shoes up there. It was all air-conditioned and immaculately preserved.

"Anyway, at about 8:00 that evening, someone said, 'Let's go look at Mary's costumes.' To get to the attic, there was a stairway, a landing, a window seat and another stairway. Well, my mother and I went up the first stairway, made the turn and there, on the window seat, banging a girl, pants down around his ankles, was Errol Flynn.

"Of course, I looked, and my mother said 'Don't look,' and I peeked around her to get a better look and she really started yelling 'Don't look, don't look!' It was my introduction to sex; I've always had a warm spot in my heart for Errol Flynn because of that."

Mary's reaction to Flynn's creative—if unauthorized—use of her window seat went unrecorded.

In March 1942, Buddy entered the Navy Air Corps as a flying instructor, and served with distinction. Life at Pickfair became even lonelier for Mary, so she was more than willing to welcome family and friends like Arthur Loew Jr. "She was totally informal around the house," remembered Loew. "She made you feel very much at ease and comfortable. There was a lot of joking and clowning." On one occasion in 1944, while Loew Jr. was in the army, he was sitting in his uniform out by the pool when a bus pulled up and about thirty soldiers got out for a guided tour. After the tour was over, they got back on the bus, whereupon the sergeant in charge came up to Loew and said "C'mon, buddy, back on the bus." Loew stared at him in disbelief. "Don't be a wise guy, get on the bus!" the sergeant reiterated.

After thirty minutes of pleading, Loew managed to hold on to his chaise lounge. "If it hadn't been for the driver honking on the horn and the other guys on the bus yelling at the sergeant, I just might have been intimidated enough to get on the bus," Loew remembered.

"I went into the house and asked Fenton, the butler, what the hell that had all been about. 'Oh, every Wednesday they have tours of the place for the soldiers,' he said. So from then on, I just made a point of it to stay away from Pickfair on Wednesdays. Or make sure I wasn't in uniform."

Loew, and other Pickfair guests of these years, noticed that, unlike many stars, Mary never ran any of her old pictures. (She would, on very rare occasions, make an exception for someone from her peer group.) At bottom, Mary sensed that many of her pictures, and the values they represented, hadn't held up. She was not about to open herself up to the possibility of ridicule, saying "I'm not going to ask the Mary of yesteryear to compete with the actresses of today. I look upon her as my daughter. She worked hard that I might retire and live in security, and I have to protect her memory."

There had always been a creative tension between Mary and Charlie Chaplin that accompanied their admiration for each other's professional skills. "Charlie thought she was a marvelous actress, with remarkable charm," remembered Jerome Epstein, Chaplin's assistant on his last three pictures. As early as 1917, Chaplin had his brother Syd approach Mary when she was shooting *Rebecca of Sunnybrook Farm.* Charlie, Syd explained, had an idea for a picture to co-star the two of them, called *Bread.* Chaplin would direct and pay her the same amount Zukor was paying her, $10,000 a week, with a four-week guarantee. Mary managed to conceal her irritation. "I said I was sorry, that I [wasn't] a comedienne. 'Tell your brother I don't think I could get out of my contract.'" In fact, as she later confessed, the idea of working with "that pie-throwing individual" appalled her.

A few years later, after they had become good social friends through their mutual adoration of Douglas, Chaplin attacked her fabled reputation for business acumen, about which Mary was extremely proud.

"Where do you get this idea that you're such a fine business woman?" Chaplin had asked. "I can't see it. You have something the public wants and you get the market price for it." Chaplin saw that the remark hit home; he also saw that Douglas was furious with him for slighting Mary, however mildly.

There had been business dissension between Mary and Chaplin as early as 1922, over whether or not United Artists would distribute Chaplin and Griffith's pictures in foreign markets.

But in those early years, their differences could be mediated by a man they both respected, like Joe Schenck, or a man they both loved, like Douglas. But by 1940, Douglas was dead, Schenck was at Fox, . . . and the relationship was suffering, partially over their very different politics, partially over their very different personalities. More importantly, United Artists began to founder as a direct result of disputes between Mary and Charlie. For over ten years "they fought like Kilkenny cats," as Vitalis Chalif, one of Mary's lawyers and her representative on the United Artists board, put it. "Fundamentally, it was a love-hate relationship."

Not surprisingly, it was mostly over money, specifically Chaplin's extraordinary (even for an artist) solipsism in the matter of United Artists. The great comedian's view of the world was largely one in which he was the axis around which everything else spun;

United Artists was, to him, a convenient outlet for the distribution of the films of Charles Chaplin. It freed him from having to contend with the onus of block booking, and it offered him a lower distribution fee than he could have gotten anywhere else in the industry.

But Chaplin's productivity had slowed to the point where he was only making a film every five years, hardly sufficient to support a major distribution mechanism, especially one whose other major partners were inactive. This gaping product vacuum had been filled for over a decade by Sam Goldwyn, Mary's other major nemesis of the period.

In the fifteen years of his association with United Artists Goldwyn had made forty pictures, most of them solid commercial money-makers. Goldwyn had long felt that, because Mary and Douglas were drawing profits from a company to which they were not contributing in any material fashion, he was being unfairly treated, in spite of the fact that he owned 1/5 of the company. Goldwyn was particularly incensed that Alexander Korda had been given a 17 1/2 percent distribution fee in England for some of his quota quickies. Goldwyn began a strong lobbying campaign to have a man of his choice, Murray Silverstone, appointed president of United Artists.

A compromise was reached when Dr. Attilio Henry Giannini was elected president, which failed to ameliorate Goldwyn's paranoid rage. "All my life I've been an adventurer, and have been in a lot of tough situations," said Dr. Giannini, "but let me tell you, I never saw fights like the ones at United Artists board meetings in my life. Screaming was the least of it; personal attacks and imminent physical violence were always a possibility."

Loyd Wright, one of the United Artists attorneys, was appalled at Goldwyn's petulance and constant threats to cancel his agreement with United Artists. On March 23, 1937, he wrote company counsel Edward Raftery, "Keeping in mind that the contract is Goldwyn's child more than any one else's, that he practically dictated all of the terms and conditions . . . and personally knowing of no breach . . . that he could claim . . . I am at a loss to understand how any lawyer could think that such a procedure would be successful."

Joe Schenck, although now the chairman of the board of the successful Twentieth Century Fox, tried to function as an intermediary. "A producer who spends between eight and nine million dollars a year (a gross exaggeration of Goldwyn's yearly outlay) has a perfect right and good reason to be apprehensive if he thinks the company through which he distributes is not properly managed," he wrote Mary on March 16, 1938.

"Knowing United Artists as well as I do and knowing Sam as I do, I am convinced that he has no ulterior motive in what he wants to bring about. . . . Please do not think that I have any ulterior motive in writing you this letter. . . . I am doing it purely out of my desire to see the United Artists Company a success and my desire to help you, Sam, Douglas and Charlie, who are the owners of the company . . .

"I think you, Sam and Douglas, who have a great stake in the United Artists Company, should pull together. The reason I don't mention Charlie is not because I disregard him but simply because I know Charlie and I know how little interest he takes in the management of the company. Furthermore, I know how bitter Charlie can get to be and he wouldn't hesitate to destroy the company rather than do something constructive that may be of some benefit to Sam, whom at the present time he despises."

But other, more objective outsiders were none too sure of Goldwyn. Neil McCarthy, Cecil B. deMille's attorney and a widely respected figure of probity in Hollywood, told Douglas in a confidential letter that "I am more convinced than ever that Sam is a ruthlessly destructive force against everything except his own selfish interests. He will ingratiate himself with anyone to accomplish his purpose and, when he has done that, he will turn on them . . .

"If Sam gets control of this company, he will use it for his own personal selfish interests, regardless of the returns to the company. He resents the fact that you and Mary and Charlie receive earnings from the distribution of his pictures and . . . if you permit him to get in charge of the company . . . he will work unceasingly to reduce the amount United Artists shall retain and increase the amount that he gets from his product . . .

"My advice to you is . . . do not agree to any action unless it is also agreeable to Mary and Charlie, even though you differ with them or they may differ with you. A united front between the three of you in my opinion is essential to the preservation of your interests."

Silverstone was indeed elected president, and the partners discussed a further attempt to placate Goldwyn. They devised a scheme of producer's rebates that would kick back percentages of the gross for particularly successful movies. Pictures that grossed more than $750,000 domestically would return 2 percent, while on receipts in excess of $1,000,000 the rebate would be 3 percent. Although this would have had the effect of diverting a quarter of a million dollars a year from a company that needed it, it was still being actively considered by Mary, Douglas and Chaplin.

But, at a meeting on November 30, 1938, Goldwyn suddenly felt Mary was about to renege on the rebates that he thought had already been agreed to. (Company documents indicate the matter had *not* been agreed to.) A livid Goldwyn called Clarence Ericksen, Fairbanks's general manager, and told him that he would "never trust Pickford again," that he was through trying to reorganize United Artists and was going to turn the entire situation over to his attorneys.

Board meetings began to deteriorate noticeably; at one, Goldwyn referred to Pickford, Chaplin and Fairbanks as "parasites"; at another, he called Douglas "a crook," whereupon Fairbanks went for him, seizing him by the throat. Giannini separated them, and took Goldwyn outside to calm down. When he re-entered the room he said to Fairbanks, "I apologize for calling you a crook. I can't prove it."

Finally, Goldwyn offered to buy the other partners out for $500,000 each. They conferred among themselves and made a counter-offer of $2 million each. Goldwyn, in league with Alexander Korda, tried to raise the $6 million but couldn't. Even the fact that Murray Silverstone, Goldwyn's candidate, was president failed to calm him down. Goldwyn continued to have doubts about the company's sales ability, and harassed Silverstone unremittingly. The beleaguered president responded by sending off tearsheets of recent publicity coups: "Full page of Sunday [Portland] *Oregonian* . . . on Alexander Korda's *Thief of Bagdad* . . .

"Full page of the Atlanta *Constitution* . . . in rotogravure, on Alexander Korda's *Lady Hamilton* . . .

"Thought you would like to see these as they are a barometer of the kind of important publicity we are getting for our producers free of charge." (italics Silverstone's)

On January 16, 1939, Goldwyn demanded to be made the sole voting trustee, voting the stock of the other three members. Failing that, he would refuse to deliver any more pictures to United Artists. Charles Schwartz, Chaplin's attorney, offered to let Goldwyn out of his United Artists contract, which had three years to run, if he would pay $500,000. He refused.

The meeting tried to move on to other business. Douglas Fairbanks wanted to set up a new company with outside financing, and release the resulting pictures through United Artists. Goldwyn said he would vote against it unless Fairbanks ceded his voting rights.

"Sam," said Fairbanks, "I've been your friend for many years, and now that I ask this thing, you attach this condition. Surely you don't mean it?"

"Yes, I do," said Goldwyn. Struggling to control himself, Fairbanks left the room. The meeting's last words were delivered by Charles Schwartz, who screamed at Goldwyn, "Get out, you punk."

By 1940, Goldwyn was desperate to get out of United Artists; in February 1941, Frances Goldwyn, a paranoid with an overwhelming fear of poverty, terrified by her husband's involvement in a war of attrition that could beggar him, ended the stand-off. She drove to Pickfair and threw herself at Mary's feet, begging her to let Sam out of his contract, "for my husband and child." Mary was appalled. "I'll settle," she said, "but for God's sake, get up, Frances."

The next month, United Artists let Goldwyn out of his contract. They paid him $300,000 for his stock—half its book value. Goldwyn cadged another $200,000 from the Silverstone Plan, then validated what Neil McCarthy had said about him by enticing an RKO that was desperate for prestige product to distribute his films for the fire-sale fee of 17 1/2 percent of the gross. In effect, this meant that RKO lost money on every Goldwyn picture it distributed—$137,000 on *The Little Foxes,* $147,000 on *Ball of Fire* and so forth. It was a completely insupportable deal for RKO, except for the fact that the studio used the Goldwyn pictures as loss leaders; if exhibitors wanted the Goldwyns, they'd have to take four or five RKO programmers bracketed with them. It was precisely the same system that had driven Mary and Douglas to distraction when they were working for Zukor; the fact that Goldwyn had accomplished a beautiful end-around on RKO—and on United Artists—galled Mary no end.

As the Goldwyn debacle was ending, the Selznick debacle was just beginning. David O. Selznick had signed an eight-picture contract with United Artists in July 1935, and, except for *Gone With the Wind,* all the Selznick-International Pictures had been United Artists releases. In October 1941, Selznick had bought into United Artists as a full partner, paying $300,000, which was not due for five years. At the same time, United Artists advanced Selznick $300,000 to buy story properties, and he was given *de facto* recognition as the leader of United Artists. Selznick's contract set

United Artists distribution fee as 25 percent up to $800,000 gross, and only 10 percent after that.

For Selznick, it was a sweetheart of a deal, a tacit admission of the value United Artists placed on him and his pictures. But the firestorm success of *Gone With the Wind* and *Rebecca* had brought on something of a mid-life crisis; although he became a partner in 1941, his next United Artists picture, *Since You Went Away*, wasn't released until mid-1944.

In the meantime, Selznick had repaid the company's trust by using the advance money to buy *The Keys of the Kingdom*, *Claudia* and *Jane Eyre*, and develop screenplays and casts for all three pictures. He then promptly turned around and sold them all as ready-to-shoot "packages" to Twentieth Century Fox for a large personal profit.

Although what Selznick had done was blatantly unethical and, as the English would say "dodgy," under the terms of his contract it was quite legal. Nevertheless, Chaplin was enraged and instigated a lawsuit. Predictably, Selznick was offended; equally predictably, Mary was caught in the middle.

Her business acumen told her what must be done. "Despite the fact that never before in history have motion pictures known such prosperity," Pickford wrote to Chaplin in October 1943, "United limps along with barely enough to meet its heavy obligations. Why? Because there has been nothing but dissension for the past fifteen years among owners of the company . . . And now your lawsuit against David is not the least of these costly and public wrangles . . .

"It is said that you claim I have deserted you and am now in David Selznick's camp. Nothing could be more untrue or unfair. I am in neither his camp nor in yours, but am first and foremost for the company's best interests and for protecting my rights as a fourth owner of this potentially powerful organization . . .

"I am perfectly willing to go on record in saying David was wrong morally and ethically in not producing and delivering pictures to us, but I believe legally under his contract he had the right . . . to part with the assets he sold to Twentieth Century.

"Does it not strike you as being incongruous Charlie, that you are suing David for not having produced a picture for three years, and yet Douglas and I waited six years for the first Chaplin picture? [Mary was intentionally overlooking *A Woman of Paris*]. And twenty-odd years ago your picture was certainly as important, if not more so, than David's is to the organization today. Undoubtedly you, too, had reason for not seeing fit to deliver the much-needed product and I would think this fact would give you a more tolerant attitude toward David . . .

"I am confident that you and David, without the interference of attorneys and those persons motivated by selfish interests, could get together and settle this lawsuit. The three of us could then formulate some plan whereby the partners vote as a unit thus forming a sound basis for our future policy . . .

"Surely you can take no pride in the truck that we are now forced to lend our name to and permit to pass through United Artists channels. For myself, I am deeply embarrassed for there is neither profit nor pride in the United Artists of today.

"You are the last person in the motion picture industry who should ever question my good faith and loyalty to you. But if after twenty-five years of such close partnership, you still don't know me, Charlie, it is useless for me to set forth the innumerable times I have stood loyally by you and have closed my eyes to the many hurts, rebuffs and humiliations I have endured at your hand."

It is an extraordinary letter, making its points lucidly and well, until veering off into the paranoia of its closing. Mary waited two weeks for a response from Chaplin. It never came.

At a stockholder's meeting on October 28, 1943, the friends became former friends.

Chaplin: You are doing very well. So am I.

Pickford: Thank you.

Chaplin: I think we have done very well in the past. I think your credit shows so.

Pickford: My credit is nothing to the United Artists. If my credit was run like that of the United Artists I would be penniless today, and that is why I am going to get relief from the courts. If we can't sit down and discuss our business like any other modern organization, then it is too bad.

Chaplin: I don't think this was ever intended to be a modern organization. We never intended it.

The meeting continued; the relationship did not. On November 9, 1943, Pickford wrote to United Artists president Edward Raftery: "In the future, any business dealings I may be forced to have with him will be done as though with a total stranger." Chaplin began referring to her as "The Iron Butterfly," while Mary contented herself with the blanket term "Dirty old man."

For his part, Selznick was invariably unhappy with what he believed to be the lack of aggressive selling on the part of the United Artists sales department, even though United Artists' modest distribution fee was a bargain. In fact, every Selznick picture

United Artists distributed cost the company money, which meant that, as a stockholder, Selznick was losing the money he was making as a producer.

With all the sniping and counter-sniping going on, Selznick was still planning for his super-western *Duel in the Sun* to go out as a United Artists picture; preliminary advertising material was issued, announcing it as such. But in early 1946, Selznick did it again; he sold RKO the scripts, actors and directors for *Notorious, The Spiral Staircase, The Bachelor and the Bobbysoxer* and *The Farmer's Daughter.* Chaplin re-activated his lawsuit and, at the end of the year, as *Duel in the Sun* was nearing release, United Artists struck back by refusing to release the picture.

With over $5 million of his own money tied up in the picture, Selznick was financially stretched to the breaking point. His nervousness manifested itself as outrage, and he filed a countersuit for $13.5 million for "willfull mishandling" of his productions. After the usual amounts of lawyerly haggling, the suits were settled by United Artists' repurchase of Selznick's stock for $2 million.

It was another debacle for United Artists, as well as another drain on the already paltry United Artists cash surplus, which had been seriously diminished by the $950,000 purchase of Alexander Korda's stock in 1943.

With Selznick out of the company, United Artists now settled down to a long, enervating point/counterpoint between Mary and Chaplin. There was an unhealthy element of hostile, outrageously petty tit-for-tat in their running of the company; whatever concessions Chaplin bargained for in relation to United Artists' release of *Monsieur Verdoux,* for example, were automatically written into Mary's contracts.

A distribution executive named Bill Roach, exhausted by running back and forth between the two camps as they compared distribution contracts, fired off a plea to Mary's lawyer, Paul D. O'Brien. "Would it be feasible to draft an amendment to both the Chaplin and Pickford contracts to the effect that unless otherwise notified by Producer, United will distribute any picture delivered to it [by Chaplin or Pickford] in any year under the most favorable terms, providing not more than two per year shall be so distributed, etc? That would make it automatic and would probably cover most situations, since Pickford and Chaplin may let many years go by without delivering up to two pictures per year."

Although both Pickford and Chaplin insisted that their antagonism was a classic business disagreement, onlookers disagreed. "It was *very* personal," said Vitalis Chalif. "They were both strong-willed, spoiled, physically little people. And when they became angry, they became actors. They would storm, rave and rant, although no matter how heated the argument might become, [Mary] never used vulgar language. She was Irish and very emotional and, like Charlie, never could forget her early poverty."

Mary's growing antipathy was increased by the fact that her cat had taken to ambling down Summit Drive to Chaplin's house. Chaplin, who liked cats, fed it, which only made the cat more determined to visit, which in turn fed Mary's sense of betrayal. She would call Chaplin's house and furiously demand that her cat be sent back.

Mary managed to put a good public face on her relationship with Charlie; in 1947, she attended the New York premiere of Chaplin's *Monsieur Verdoux* and provided moral support when his brave black comedy was pilloried by the critics,although privately she said she loathed the picture. For Chaplin's part, the debacle of *Monsieur Verdoux* killed off whatever lingering feelings of good will he might have had toward United Artists. The domestic gross of *Verdoux* was only $325,000. Although the foreign take of more than $1.5 million put the picture into the black, Chaplin felt he could have done much better by distributing it independently.

"[Psychologically] Chaplin wrote his percentage of United Artists down to $1," remembered Paul Lazarus Jr., head of advertising and publicity at United Artists from 1942 to 1950. "He just didn't care about the company anymore; he was indifferent."

Yet, in some private way, Mary still cared about Chaplin, even though she would derogatorily compare him to "a solid citizen of Beverly Hills" like Harold Lloyd. When the witch-hunters made it impossible for him to live in America, Mary spoke up and defended him, saying on a New York radio show in July 1955 that the Chaplin of the Peglers and Hoppers was not "the Charlie Chaplin I've known for years . . . I've told you before he told me he was not a Communist . . . I am no Communist, but I don't think anybody, including Chaplin, should be condemned without his day in court.

"And let anybody try to say that I'm a Red or even slightly pink and he'll answer to me in court. I'll sue them for every last penny they have."

One of the main raps against Chaplin was that he never became an American citizen; what Mary failed to broadcast was that she hadn't either; although her Canadian citizenship had lapsed when she married an American—which, technically, made her an American as well—for years Mary traveled with a Canadian passport, and in fact, remained proudly Canadian to her dying day.

Mary's libertarian statements and the fact that, in terms of citizenship, she had no firmer ground to stand on than Chaplin, did not stop her from volunteering as an informant to the F.B.I. about her old partner. According to a declassified government document dated March 22, 1948, F.B.I. agent L.B. Nichols called on her on March 16 of that year, after Mary had made repeated calls ("stating that she wanted to speak to Mr. Hoover personally . . .") and sent telegrams to J. Edgar Hoover for at least a week before that.

Finally, Hoover delegated an agent to talk to her. "She impressed me very favorably," wrote Nichols in his report to Hoover's assistant Clyde Tolson. Mary outlined to Nichols the history of United Artists, of how the other founding partners had gradually dropped away until "gradually she has acquired 50% of the stock and Charlie Chaplin has acquired 50% of the stock."

The rest of the document is censored. Given the date, Mary could not have been passing information to Hoover about Joan Barry, Chaplin's inamorata of some years before and the woman who brought a successful 1944 paternity trial against the actor, even though blood tests proved he could not possibly have been the father of the child. Given Mary's own erratic feelings about Charlie, it is highly likely that Pickford was informing on the actor's politics, cooperating with the Bureau's scurrilous persecution of a great artist.

What Mary did not know was that the F.B.I. was also keeping tabs on her. When, in the latter part of 1944, she attended a banquet to raise money for the Free French that was, according to the F.B.I., "sponsored by several Communist front organizations" among them the Screen Director's Guild and the Screen Actor's Guild, her presence was duly noted, along with that of Edward G. Robinson, Robert Montgomery and Irene Dunne, the latter two stalwart Republicans.

In the midst of this round-robin of surveillance, Mary and her circle had been actively funneling information about Chaplin to the F.B.I. for some time. Mary's business manager had told F.B.I. agents that United Artists was going to release a picture produced by Chaplin's friend Tim Durant as a payoff for services rendered during the comedian's involvement with Joan Barry. No such picture was ever released.

In April 1944, Buddy told an F.B.I. informant that Hedda Hopper had told him the jury in the first Joan Barry trial had been bought off. When he asked her how she knew that, Hopper replied that a woman, claiming to be a Christian Scientist, had told the columnist that she had a vision in which members of the jury had discussed receiving payoffs from Chaplin. Buddy asked her why she hadn't told the F.B.I. Hopper said she was waiting to see if the woman's "vision" returned, so she could identify specific members of the jury. Although Hopper was a frequent F.B.I. informant on the Red Menace, she never did pass the story on.

Chaplin was particularly vulnerable to these kinds of grotesque whispers because he lacked the instinct—or the interest—to protect himself or, failing that, to deflect the charges by responding in kind. "Charlie never gossiped about people's private lives; he wasn't that kind of person," remembered Jerome Epstein. "He had a deaf ear about that sort of thing. He never spread gossip and he wasn't interested in hearing it."

Mary may very well have been under pressure from Hopper, the Madame DeFarge of the Red Scare. In April 1947, Hopper wrote to J. Edgar Hoover thanking him for a copy of his book *The Story of the F.B.I.* and went on to proclaim her sympathies: "I loved what you said about the Commies in the motion picture industry. But I would like it even more if you could name names and print more facts . . . I'd like to run every one of those rats out of the country, starting with Charlie Chaplin. In no other country in the world would he have been allowed to do what he's done. And now he's finished another picture and Miss Mary Pickford is back in New York helping him sell it."

To a great extent, Mary's feelings about Chaplin seemed to depend on her mood, or, possibly, on her alcoholic intake. In February 1954, once he was safely out of the country, Mary was saying that "he's a wacky, mixed-up guy, but he's no Communist. He's just a damned fool. He's a great artist and genius and he wasn't treated properly. By heck and by Lord, he should have a chance to tell his story and not be told on the high seas not to come back." (Chaplin, a British citizen, had his re-entry visa revoked by the Attorney General after he had sailed for England to attend the premiere of his film *Limelight*.) Chaplin, she said, was "just a crackpot. And, while all Communists are crackpots, all crackpots aren't Communists."

By 1955 when she wrote her memoirs, Chaplin was in exile in Switzerland and almost universally—and exceedingly strangely—regarded as a dangerous radical. "Obstinate, suspicious, egocentric, maddening, and lovable genius of a problem child" is how

Mary summed him up in her memoirs, which seems eminently fair. At the same time, in conversation, she could be much harsher.

"I never liked any of his pictures when he wasn't in the tramp character," she said. "To tell the truth, I never saw most of his pictures. A lot of people shared my opinion that he was a cheap, hamfat comedian, throwing pies and acting in a very undignified manner." She took great pride in the fact that she had won a competitive Oscar and Chaplin had not.

Years later, in 1972, shortly before Chaplin's triumphant return to America to accept a long overdue special Oscar, a mutual friend, after visiting Chaplin in Europe, reported that he had mellowed considerably and had inquired about Mary in a friendly way.

"That's all very well," she replied, "but I still say he's a son of a bitch."

"Underneath everything, I think she was terribly fond of Chaplin . . . in a way," says Malcolm Boyd, a business partner of Mary's in the late '40s "If only because once, long before, they had been children together in a Golden Age."

Chapter Thirteen

"I'm grateful that the world is beginning to look upon alcoholism as a disease."

—*Mary Pickford, 1955*

S HORTLY after the Selznick settlement, Mary became embroiled in another matter with Sam Goldwyn that was less business, more personal.

When Goldwyn had been voted his one-fifth ownership in United Artists, he had also been deeded a one-fifth share of the former Pickford-Fairbanks studios, eighteen acres at the corner of Formosa and Santa Monica boulevards. Over the years, the studio had been a small but steady source of income. Douglas and Mary had paid $150,000 for the land, and had leased the property out to Schenck's United Artists Studio Company for ten years, with rental to start at $24,000 per year, rising to $36,000 over the life of the lease. In addition, Schenck paid all the costs of refitting the studio for sound: $1,108,000.

From 1926 to 1933, Mary and Douglas had received $200,000 in rent for the studio. After Schenck left to join Twentieth Century Fox, Goldwyn had gradually taken over the lot for his own uses, adding buildings and paying $2,000 a month to the other members for the use of that portion of the property that was not his. At the same time, he quietly began buying up the holdings of whatever partners he could find who were willing to sell, among them Alex Korda and Sylvia Ashley Fairbanks, Douglas's widow.

By January 1949, Goldwyn owned 39/80 of the property, Mary 40/80. She had control and the $2,000 a month rent. Knowing Goldwyn wanted to own the lot, but not particularly wanting to sell, Pickford put it on the market with a price tag of $3 million. Goldwyn passed, whereupon Pickford upped his rent to $30,000 a year. Goldwyn went to court to get permission to take down improvements he had made; Mary countersued to stop Goldwyn from "malicious and wanton destruction of studio property."

Goldwyn then petitioned the Superior Court of Los Angeles to have the lot legally partitioned; the court decided to put the property up for sale at a public auction, with the money to be split between the two owners in accordance with their percentages of ownership.

The lot where Mary and Douglas had made their most elaborate pictures went up for sale. The studio property involved 9.58 acres of land, on which rested forty-seven buildings and eight sound stages. As each of them had expected, the only bidders were Mary Pickford and Samuel Goldwyn. Mary's opening bid was $1,525,000, Goldwyn's $1,501,000. The two bidders went back and forth until Mary finally dropped out at $1,900,000; Goldwyn's winning bid was $20,000 higher. As the gavel dropped, announcing that the lot was, in fact, Sam Goldwyn's, Mary began to cry.

It was never easy for these two people to do business. It was, in fact, never easy to do business with Mary at all. In the late '40s, Goldwyn wanted to buy some story properties from Mary. She asked for $100,000, and Goldwyn responded with a succinct "You're crazy."

"So I'm crazy," she said.

A few months later, Goldwyn came back and said he would pay the $100,000, whereupon Mary informed him that the price was now $150,000. This time, Goldwyn really did walk away for good.

"Mary was not an easy one to buy anything from," remembered Vitalis Chalif, her representative on the United Artists board from 1948 to 1951. "She felt that if it was worth a given amount to you, it was worth more to her. Her reasoning was that, no matter how much you paid, it was worth more than that because you were going to make money from it, right?"

Unlike her embittering battles with Chaplin, Mary bore Goldwyn no personal grudge, and, in fact, testified on his behalf in a 1957 anti-trust suit against Twentieth Century Fox. Goldwyn, she testified, "was one of the finest producers—a man of great courage and vision."

Although Sam Goldwyn certainly had more use for a movie

studio than Mary did, it was more than a real estate transaction. The studio was where she and Douglas had made their pictures, where she had been the happiest; Pickfair aside, it was the property that meant the most to her. And now that, too, was gone.

———— ————

Children had undoubtedly been on Mary's mind for years, as had a considerable amount of guilt over her abortion. Adoption while she was married to Douglas had been out of the question; he was jealous of anybody that made demands on Mary but himself and had trouble enough relating to one child. That reality hadn't altered her idealistic, unrealistic maternal yearnings. "The mother lives her youth over again in the youth of her children," Mary said in 1925. "An old age without children about would be horrible." In 1934 she said that "If I had my life to live all over again, I'd exchange all the glory for children of my own. I'd rather be the mother of a son of whom I could be proud than the greatest movie actress that ever lived."

So, in an effort to make Pickfair a more balanced home environment, Mary adopted a child in 1943 at the age of fifty-one. The six-year-old she and Buddy chose was re-named Ronald Charles Rogers. Ten months later, in June 1944, they were sufficiently encouraged to adopt a two-year-old girl. They named her Roxanne.

"Mary went the whole nine yards," as one friend put it, complete with full-time nurse, and her letters of the period are full of a delight in having children. But, as with almost everything she attempted in her later years, it did not work out as planned. The trouble began with Mary's own ideas of child-raising, which owed a good deal to the Victorian era in which she had been raised. "I believe in discipline in children," she proudly announced in 1958, "with none of this impertinence and backtalk. My own mother passed on when I was in my thirties, but I was never allowed to use an impatient tone. I feel that motherhood is next to God; if a child does not respect its parents, I don't feel that they can possibly become a great, or even good citizen. That is the law set down in the Bible for us and we should follow it."

Mixing this sanctimonious, forbidding view with the reality of her own alcoholism must have struck Ronnie and Roxie as the essence of hypocrisy, and could not have made for a smooth environment for children.

"I was around Pickfair when those kids were there," remembered Arthur Loew Jr. "They would be brought in, the nurse would be with them, they'd curtsy, bow and say 'How do you do.' They'd ask 'Can I have an *hors d'oeuvre?*' and then they'd be gone. They were children in a palace.

"Obviously, Mary not having had children until comparatively late, her motherly instincts might not have quite been in place. It was like they were being raised in the '20s, the old-fashioned way that the rich raised their children. Very much at arm's length. Later, of course, there was a lot of rebellion. Disastrous results, really. But how could you have a normal life as a child at Pickfair? It would have taken a lot of work on everybody's part, including the childrens'."

――――― ――

Mary's native Irish resilience was no small part of her character. In a letter to Tess Michaels, she gaily talked about her plans for an upcoming trip to Las Vegas where she would be accompanied by old friends from the Biograph days. She might, she said, buy the Flamingo, so she could witness at first hand Bugsy Siegel's Waterloo.

And she was still dabbling in the movies. In 1945, Mary, in partnership with Ralph Cohn, formed an outfit called Comet Pictures. The results were an unimpressive roster of *B* pictures with titles like *The Adventures of Don Coyote, Stork Bites Man,* and *Susie Steps Out,* made for bargain basement prices of little more than $100,000 each. Revealingly, the United Artists contracts for these cheaters specified that the maximum amount to be spent on advertising was $25,000, a piddling amount even then. A short time later, she formed an equally short-lived company called Artists Alliance with Lester Cowan, best known for producing William Wellman's *The Story of G.I. Joe.* Within the industry, neither producer was considered to be even remotely comparable to the Selznick/Korda/United Artists tradition.

The alliance with Cowan proved particularly embarrassing. Cowan had negotiated a pre-production loan of $50,000 from Deluxe Laboratories in return for their making the release prints for four pictures, among them a prospective Marx Brothers picture and *One Touch of Venus,* both of which Mary was co-producing.

However, the money for the Marx Brothers picture, a debacle entitled *Love Happy,* ran out before production was completed, which was rather odd, as Harpo, Chico and Groucho had all worked for no salary in return for a more generous percentage of the profits. In fact, Harpo, Chico and Ben Hecht, the author of the original story, owned 50 percent of the film. During production, Cowan had so enraged the normally placid, benevolent Harpo that the comedian had called him "the vilest man in the world" and spit in his face.

"What did he do?" asked Harpo's wife.

"Nothing special," replied Harpo.

Smelling disaster, Mary took her name off the picture as co-producer. The lawyers for the Marx Brothers got into the act, complaining that the picture had not been aggressively sold, despite United Artists' promises, thereby cheating the brothers out of their rightful share of the profits.

Paul O'Brien, having succeeded to Mary's legal affairs from his father, Cap, explained that United Artists couldn't very well sell the picture effectively because they only had four prints and couldn't get the laboratory to make any more "because of . . . indebtedness . . . Also, Lester has been talking of making a new ending."

Cowan did indeed make a new ending, and financed it—Mary having long since abandoned the financial ship—by selling advertising space to major corporations. The climax of the picture took Harpo across rooftops wherein he passed signs for Bulova watches, Kool cigarettes, etc. The off-screen comedy that was so much funnier than anything that went on in the movie climaxed when, in November 1950, Groucho Marx sued Mary and Cowan for his share of the profits, or $35,000 in salary. Groucho wasn't the only one.

In 1952, Artists Alliance, the company Mary had formed with Cowan, was sued for $27,741.71 by the C.L. Miller Company in the matter of *Love Happy*. Paul O'Brien was put in the embarrassing position of having to explain to the Miller Company that there were some people ahead of them in line, among them the Bank of America, Standard Capital, Walter E. Heller and Company, and the Chemical Bank and Trust Company. The total liens placed against *Love Happy* amounted to $765,000, plus interest.

"I think that in a half-hearted way, she wanted to keep her finger in the business even though she was no longer performing," said Arthur Loew Jr. of this period. "A lot of people have trouble giving it up, you know. They dabble in it. And the people she was tying herself in with could use her. Where Zanuck or Jack Warner would have thought her passé, the lesser lights thought an affiliation with Pickford could enhance them."

Early in 1947, Mary geared up to produce *Sleep My Love,* her first *bona fide* picture in years, and signed a new releasing agreement with United Artists. Ironically, she made it a point to include a clause specifically allowing her the right to road-show the picture anywhere in America or Canada if she chose. It was the same revenue-diverting maneuver that, when practiced by Griffith twenty-four year earlier, had enraged Mary and led her to threaten to leave United Artists.

Later that year, Mary and Buddy were worried over the serious illness of Buddy's mother, and over the usual array of production problems on *Sleep My Love,* a variation on *Gaslight* that starred Claudette Colbert and Don Ameche. To drum up publicity for the picture, Paul Lazarus Jr. got the idea of holding the world premiere in Mary's native Canada. She was game, so the premiere was set for January 1948, in Ottawa.

Her homecoming was a sentimental occasion. She told reporters that it made her unutterably sad to drive by University Avenue and see her old home gone, the land now a part of the grounds of the Hospital for Sick Children. "She was just great in interviews," remembered Lazarus, "but after a couple of hours she'd begin to fade. So I'd let her go to her room for a while and she'd come out incredibly bright-eyed and ready to go."

On the night of the premiere, while Lazarus was occupied with preparations at the theater, Mary was invited to dinner with the Governor General of Ontario and Canadian Prime Minister William Lyon MacKenzie King. Just before the curtain was due to go up, the Governor General's party arrived in sleighs. Lazarus noticed, with a sinking heart, that Mary was wearing the Governor's hat. "I knew at that point that he'd served wine," says Lazarus.

Mary made her way to the stage and dropped a curtsy, except she couldn't quite get back up again. She began to make a short speech of appreciation but started rambling. She was in the middle of offering the befuddled crowd some of her favorite recipes when Lazarus cut the connection to the microphone and began the picture.

It was one of the few times that Mary let her guard slip publicly. She was, in fact, gradually withdrawing from public appearances of any kind; despite her financial involvement, she made no appearances on the set of either *Sleep My Love* or *Love Happy,* not even to introduce herself to the actors, let alone to keep a watchful eye on her investment. *Sleep My Love* was one of the few things that Mary turned her hand to in these years that was not a disaster. Its worldwide gross was over $1.8 million, a very respectable amount for a movie with slightly venerable stars in the years of the post-war attendance slump.

The picture's success failed to do anything to halt her drinking, which was generally confined to Pickfair, as in an informal meeting among her, Paul Lazarus Jr., and United Artists president Gradwell Sears.

"I'm terribly thirsty," she said after they had been talking awhile, and rang for the butler. He brought her what seemed to be a glass of ice water. By the time she was on her second glass, Mary was beginning to slur her words and Lazarus realized with a start that she wasn't drinking water, but gin.

Another time, at a dinner with Vitalis Chalif, she had a couple of drinks and began to talk about Douglas, going on and on about what a glorious man he had been. "It got to the point where it was quite embarrassing," remembered Chalif, "because Buddy was sitting at the table, pretending that none of it was being said. It was very clear that she had never gotten over Fairbanks."

Jim Kirkwood Jr., who saw Mary occasionally throughout the '50s and '60s, said that her drinking surrounded her with a "giddy, unrealistic, surrealistic aura. I rarely saw her cold sober. She was never falling down drunk, but she was in that hazy state, that fuzzy state. She always remained very sweet, very concerned, and always gracious and kind. And she would get very emotional about the old days at Biograph and at Famous Players."

"Drinking was a private thing with Mary," said Lazarus. "You never saw her drunk and disorderly, and, with her marvelous recuperative powers, she got away with a lot." Despite the inherent dangers of mixing a quiet case of alcoholism with the managing of a major entertainment corporation, Lazarus believed that Mary's drinking never affected her business judgment. "Her drinking was recreational, not compulsive."

Vitalis Chalif agreed, and believed that she was, simply, "allergic to alcohol. It didn't matter whether it was one drink or five, she just couldn't handle it. And if she got set off on alcohol, she could be very nasty."

In the latter part of 1949, at the suggestion of Norma Shearer, Mary extended help to Merle Oberon, who had been devastated by witnessing a flaming plane crash that had killed her lover and fiancé, Count Cini. Mary introduced Merle to Lilian Bailey, who had, Mary believed, enabled her to talk with Douglas after his death. Bailey, who served as a medium to members of the British royal family, also made Oberon a believer in spiritualism.

Living with a woman who increasingly felt the need to anesthetize herself with alcohol, it is no wonder that Buddy Rogers had developed an apparently unbreachable wall of gregariousness and charm. "It is difficult being a kept man," notes Phil Rhodes. "You . . . have to behave, you have to watch for signs of disagreement before they arise." Always passive, Buddy deferred to Mary about most things. As she liked to put it, "My husband is a musician and doesn't understand business." And that was that.

Her friends at this time centered on the Old Guard Elite Republicans of Summit Drive: Irene Dunne, Jeanette MacDonald, Claudette Colbert, occasionally Ronald Colman and his wife Benita Hume (Chaplin's next-door neighbors) and the Harold Lloyds. And there was always time for Lillian and Dorothy Gish; when they got together they invariably talked of the old days by Eighth Avenue, of catching streetcars to get to the Biograph studio, of Jack and Charlotte, of the times when they had all been young.

She tried to maintain contact with those who had been stars when she was and were now considered has-beens—as, increasingly, she was. "Constance Collier used to go up to Pickfair all the time," remembered Arthur Loew Jr., "and D.W. Griffith, when he couldn't get a job and people were brushing him aside. She had room for sentiment, room for loyalty, and would throw parties for these people. It was like a scene from *Sunset Boulevard.*" At these parties, Mary would offer an after-dinner turn, a scene between Elizabeth I and Mary Queen of Scots, with Mary playing both parts.

Malcolm Boyd, later to become an Episcopal priest and the best-selling author of *Are You Running With Me Jesus?*, was a frequent visitor to Pickfair in the post-war period. He and Mary had become acquainted when Boyd had handled some publicity chores on *Sleep, My Love.* As Claudette Colbert wasn't available, Boyd found that Buddy's glibness was a more-than-acceptable substitute and began booking him on a variety of radio shows.

Boyd found that he and Mary had a good deal in common; both were vaguely dissatisfied with their current lives, both were searching for something. Mary took Boyd under her wing and formed a radio and television production company called P.R.B. Inc. (Pickford-Rogers-Boyd) with offices in the penthouse of the Scripps Building in New York. During the company's three-year run, P.R.B.'s main success was in landing a hosting job for Buddy, from February to September 1951, on the Dumont network's "Cavalcade of Bands."

"With Mary, everything was image," recalled Boyd. "There was a gap between the public Mary and the private Mary and they

didn't meet." Boyd managed to interest NBC in a proposed program called "Mary Pickford's Theater of Valor." The guest for the
pilot episode was Lillian Gish, who, Boyd remembers, "just took
the show over. She had to; Mary couldn't handle the show. She was
all flouncy on the air. 'This . . . is . . . *Mary . . . Pickford!*' was
the way she talked. It was so bad I had the engineer wipe the tape;
I didn't want (David) Sarnoff to hear it."

Boyd noticed that Mary usually took advantage of the star's
prerogative of being late, and that the frugality that Gladys Smith
had had to observe all those years ago was still with her. In Boyd's
words, "she was paranoid about money. She put up very little
money for anything; P.R.B. generated most of its own income."

One night, when Boyd was visiting her in her suite at the Hotel
Pierre, Mary ordered finnan haddie and a boiled potato, then
turned to Boyd and asked that, as she wasn't very hungry, would
he mind sharing hers? He thought it was particularly strange behavior, as she was spending thousands a week on her basic expenses, including her suite. At any rate, a few hours later he
arrived at his own room at the Gotham, and was preparing for bed
when the phone rang.

"It was Mary. With no preamble at all, she began screaming at
me. 'I'll destroy you, you son of a bitch! I'll ruin you.' I went into
total shock. Sometime between when I'd left the room and gotten
back to mine she had gotten drunk. I had no idea. Nobody had told
me that she drank!"

Around Boyd, whom she called her "spiritual son," Mary drank
secretly, excusing herself from the table and coming back notably
the worse for wear . . . when she came back at all. Her covert
attitude towards her own drinking made it that much harder to
approach her about it, although the fact that she tried to keep it a
secret indicated that she knew very well that she had a problem.

The rare hostile outburst aside, Boyd found that, when Mary was
drunk, she was far more in touch with the reality of her life and its
failures than she ever was when she was sober. He found her, at
those times, to be utterly, bewilderingly vulnerable, a desperately
lonely woman without solace. At these times, they would talk far
into the night about life, mortality, even existential despair. What
came through at these moments was an emotional and spiritual
passion that the world never knew Mary possessed. Deeply into
alcohol, she became deeply into the truth.

During these talks, she would invariably refer to Buddy as
Douglas and refer to Douglas often. "As far as she was concerned,
Douglas was still her husband," said Boyd. "She talked about him

very possessively. All I could think of was Mary Tyrone in *Long Day's Journey Into Night;* both women had the same haunted quality."

These were the only times Boyd would see her this exposed. "That's when she had her intelligence, her awareness and her sensitivity," he said. "There was no anger, no recriminations about anyone else. She did desperately wish that she'd had a baby."

"But the next day," he recalled in wonderment, "there was no bridge, no recollection whatsoever of what had gone on the night before. At bottom, she never really understood what had happened, where it had all gone. That was where the frustration and confusion came in; that's where her self-confidence began eroding. By the time I met her, she was a woman on the run."

Boyd noted, rather incredulously, that the sober Mary was still intensely jealous of Buddy. When Boyd, his mother, Mary and Buddy attended a function at the University of Southern California, Buddy was seated next to someone pretty, and Mary responded by developing an angry, flushed face and displaying blatantly rude behavior.

"Buddy had looks, charm, and he had Mary Pickford," said Boyd. "And that was it. Fairbanks was an A-list person; she had hob-nobbed with Einstein and Chaplin, the cultural and intellectual elite. But now she was in socially with people she couldn't talk to. I think [Douglas] would have protected her from that. Ultimately, I think that might have been one of the reasons she withdrew, to maintain control over what was left of her own world."

The operations of P.R.B. Inc. were hampered by what Boyd called "the Alice in Wonderland thing." One Friday at two in the afternoon, he got a phone call from Mary's secretary to get Mary and Buddy tickets for a flight that night to Bermuda, as well as $4,000 in cash. The banks had all closed by that time, but Boyd remembered that the Plaza Hotel kept a large supply of cash on hand for the convenience of its guests. He called them, pleaded, and got the $4,000. He then made the reservations on four different flights, so Mary would have her choice of flight times, a necessity.

At the last minute, he got a call telling him that they'd changed their minds; they weren't going after all. "This happened *all* the time," he said with exasperation. "You could never count on anything; it was always a disaster waiting to happen. It was World War I in the shadows, a dysfunctional life. Buddy and Mary would occasionally shout at each other and be very cruel, like something out of [*Who's Afraid of*] *Virginia Woolf.*"

He also found Mary increasingly obsessed by Communism and its supposed threat. When he was a guest at Pickfair, Mary was tape recording some reminiscences and drinking at the same time. She began to have trouble operating the tape recorder and it began unspooling all over Mary's lap, which she loudly took as a personal attack by the forces of Godless Marxism. Another time, at a dinner party at Chaplin's, she found that the host had waggishly seated her next to Paul Robeson. Outraged at being in such close proximity to a man with prominent left-wing sympathies, she promptly got up and left.

"It wasn't a racial thing," remarked Boyd. "Personally I feel that she was remarkably open to anyone, as a person. She didn't have prejudices or biases." (Other observers noted an occasional anti-Semitism that tended to erupt when Mary had been drinking.) It was around this time that she began to record her phone calls.

"What she did have," said Boyd, "was this terrible problem with her image. It was, 'What would 'Mary Pickford' think about Jews?' 'What would 'Mary Pickford' think about Communists?' One of the few photographs of someone else she had at Pickfair was of Elsie de Wolfe (Lady Mendl), because she represented chic and elegance. Mary was very concerned about what people like Lady Mendl thought of her."

And yet, Boyd noticed and was drawn to the sweet, attractive little girl who furtively peeked out from behind the palpably unhappy human being. When she and Boyd went to San Francisco, Mary wouldn't do anything until she had ridden in a cable car. In March, 1948, on the day Vitalis Chalif and his wife were moving into their new home in Larchmont, New York, there was a knock at the door. Chalif opened it, and Mary bustled in and sat down amidst the crates and movers. She just happened to be in the neighborhood, she explained, and was in the mood for a happy visit. Which is just what they proceeded to have. "Free of pressure, she was a lot of fun," remembered Chalif. "And when she smiled, it was the sun coming up in the morning."

On July 24, 1948, D.W. Griffith died of a cerebral hemorrhage he had sustained the day before. Mary's statement read, "To the men and women who were fortunate enough to work with him, he will always be cherished as the man who produced and directed great motion pictures straight from the heart. A flame of perfectionism burned within him and made him refuse to accept the second-rate from himself or his co-workers. A poet who sang his song in celluloid . . . he had visions of great accomplishments for the medium and he imparted his faith to others."

Griffith's body was flown home to Kentucky; in May 1950, the Director's Guild donated money for a 7-foot slab of Georgia marble to cover the great director. Mary, Richard Barthelmess and Lillian Gish still cared enough to fly in for the dedication.

Despite his presence in the besieged foxhole that was P.R.B. Inc., Mal Boyd thought that "Mary had perfect taste and poise. She could have handled Buckingham Palace very easily. She made you feel that you were the only person in the world while she was talking to you. And she had a sense of humor about herself; she particularly liked telling a story about a woman who was supposed to be her biggest fan. This woman had begged and cajoled and bribed people on a train in order to be introduced to Mary, and when she was finally shown into her compartment, she blurted out, 'Mary Miles Minter, I love you!' " Boyd would come to believe that Mary should have taken Franklin Roosevelt's advice and gone into politics; there, building on the love and respect people had for her, she might have been able to build an alternative career, an alternative life.

Boyd found that Mary still had a canny eye for publicity. Once she took him aside and explained that the best kind of publicity was the cover of *Life*, eight pages inside, and a one-hour interview on CBS; if one could get that, nothing else mattered. "Of course, she was right," said Boyd.

Yet, the reality of these years that marked Mary's final stabs at being creative was that Mary was failing at everything she turned her hand to: parenthood, *B* movies that she put out through Comet, even radio, all were failing. At the same time, she was living, as Mal Boyd observed, a life of meaningless pretense.

One night at the Stork Club, Mary was nursing a drink when a photographer began to take her picture. "Wait a minute," she said, sliding the glass over to the far corner of the table, out of camera range. "Now you may take the picture. You see, essentially, I'm a hypocrite." The extent to which Mary was, at the age of fifty-nine, a prisoner of an image that at least one generation had never even witnessed first-hand, is chilling.

"Nothing was going to work," said Mal Boyd. "She was sick; the energy was all wrong. She was in control but she didn't want to be; on the emotional level, she very much wanted to be taken care of."

By 1951, Boyd had had enough. In September, he entered the

seminary, which fascinated Mary, whom he found to be deeply and sincerely religious. (For a year or two, Boyd had even attended Mary's favorite Christian Science church with her.)

"We were both looking for something. For Mary, religion was not a callow, controlled thing; at this point in her life, she didn't have that kind of discipline. For this driven, haunted human being, it was a raw element, like the wind."

Mary had been thinking about writing her memoirs for some years. On New Year's Day, 1950, she decided it was time to act, not ponder. For the next eighteen months, she dictated what would become *Sunshine and Shadow*, which was published in 1955 in fairly heavily edited form (Mary recalled having to cut 59,000 words in one long session, just to get the manuscript down to a publishable 100,000 words). Basically a case of too little too late, *Sunshine and Shadow* is a genteel, laundered version of Mary's personal history that drained much of the vitality out of her remarkable life and career and helped cement her public image as something of a prig. Nevertheless, the book was a fair success.

By 1950, United Artists was in dire condition. The loss for 1948 had been $517,000 and the loss for the six months ending June 1949 was an additional $400,000. United Artists president Gradwell Sears wrote to Pickford and Chaplin, "Your company is in a most perilous predicament. The company finds itself without credit, working capital or any guarantee of forthcoming production. Theatre receipts are declining and . . . will continue to do so due to inferior pictures and the competition offered by television . . . It is true the corporation has a sizeable backlog which, with the exception of one picture, *Red River*, will be slow liquidation due to [their] inferior quality. Without capital credit or proper production [United Artists] cannot now long continue to meet its obligations."

Selmer Chalif, who had married Mary's cousin, told Grad Sears that Pickford was "very depressed about the situation."

In August, Chalif reported that Pickford "seems to still be playing around with mysterious plans. She now says there are two situations that might mean something but she always ends up with a little touch of discouragement. I don't know what her ultimate goal is . . . but I have a distinct feeling that both she and Chaplin are waiting for a miracle."

By mid-1950, Pickford and Chaplin had negotiated a deal with Paul McNutt, former governor of Indiana, to act as a sort of regent until July 1952, during which time McNutt and his group could exercise an option to buy out the two owners for $5.4 million. Mary was optimistic; on June 25, 1950, she wrote Douglas Fairbanks Jr. that McNutt was determined to restore the company to its prestigious pedestal.

But when McNutt and company couldn't raise the necessary funds, the deal fell through, as did another possibility, the Nasser brothers. By the end of the year, the United Artists deficit was $871,000 and only two disposable *B* movies had been put into distribution since August. A group headed by lawyer Arthur Krim, a partner in the firm of Phillips, Benjamin, Nizer and Krim, and former president and production chief at Eagle-Lion studios, began examining the corporation. By the beginning of 1951, United Artists was hemorrhaging money at the rate of $100,000 a week. Whatever money was coming in from films in release was being diverted to pay basic operating costs.

"All this talk with [people like] Eva Peron and Jacques Grinieff," remembered Arthur Krim, "kept allowing Mary to think she had something to sell. These people would talk of $10 million, $15 million . . . and each time she had to be given a dash of cold water to realize that this was pie in the sky and while she was delaying in coming to grips with the reality of the situation . . . the company was getting sicker and sicker. If she and Charlie hadn't made the deal with us the day they did, there would have been a receiver in within three or four days."

Krim and his team took an option on buying the company with the proviso that, if the company made a profit in any of the next three years, they would be allowed to buy the 8,000 outstanding shares of stock for one dollar per share. Mary signed over effective control of the company in February 1951. An exuberant Mary, relieved at the load that had just been taken off her shoulders, scribbled a note to Tess Michaels, who had agreed to stay on with United Artists under the new owners. "Tessie!!! I just love you and I guess that's all I can say. M.P. of U.A.C. 1919–1951"

By aggressively searching out product that included *High Noon* and *The African Queen,* Krim and his group turned a profit of $313,000 by the end of the year. Within another year, the financial story of United Artists was even rosier, as Arthur Krim and his team accomplished one of the most prodigious leaps of creative legerdemain in movie history.

In February 1955, Chaplin phoned Krim from his home in Switzerland and asked for $1.1 million in cash within two days for his 25 percent share of the company. "If you have a certified check in Vevey tomorrow, you have my stock," said Chaplin. Krim quickly closed the deal, paying Chaplin $1,113,287.35. The reason for Chaplin's rush? The day after the certified check reached Switzerland, the U.S. government slapped a lien on all of Chaplin's American possessions until some outstanding tax claims were settled; somehow, Chaplin had heard of the stop order and gotten as much out of the country as fast as he could.

Shortly thereafter, Mary's old business paranoia asserted itself and she became convinced that the new management team of United Artists (whom she had once praised by saying "God will reward you for adding twenty years to my life") were cheating her. Calling Arthur Krim and Robert Benjamin to her suite at the Pierre, Mary told them that she wanted the company to declare dividends and give her a blank check for her productions.

Krim and Benjamin finessed the issue. Mary departed for London and Paris, and gave interviews suggesting United Artists was in the hands of chiselers. Richard Condon, a press agent who was later to become the best-selling author of *The Manchurian Candidate* and *Prizzi's Honor,* set up a Paris press conference for her. "She spoke absolutely flawless French," recalled Condon. "It really knocked me out, and knocked out all the Paris reporters, too. She explained that she had always liked the sound of French and had hired a woman to just be around her and speak French. Over a period of six or seven years, her French just got better and better."

Mary hired William Shea (later to lend his name to Shea Stadium) to press her charges that the Krim team had violated the terms of the trust agreement and had, moreover, fraudulently taken control of United Artists. Krim and company acceded to a full audit; shortly thereafter, Shea realized that Mary's claim was weak, if not entirely nonexistent.

After ominous threats and much haggling, which served the dual purpose of satisfying her own psychological needs and driving the price up, Mary sold her shares of United Artists in February 1956 for $3 million, $2 million in cash, the rest in debenture. The extra money Pickford earned by hanging on to her shares a full year longer than Chaplin was due to the skyrocketing success of United Artists under Krim and company. By the mid-'50s, the earnings of United Artists were up $45 million from 1950.

Mary issued a statement after the sale saying, in part, that "United Artists has been my pride and joy and also, at times, my despair. Upon the sale of United Artists stock I do not feel that I am parting with the company forever, and I will always take a prideful interest in its welfare." They were brave but empty words; Mary's severing of her ties with United Artists brought to an effective end a motion picture career that had begun forty-seven years before. Now more than ever, she would be an anchorite at Pickfair, an *éminence grise* without even a shaky bridge to the industry she had done so much to create.

During the nearly annual Christmas visits of Tess Michaels, she and Mary would often visit wholesale houses. Mary was fascinated by the concept of wholesale; although she clearly didn't need to economize, she allowed herself the guilty pleasure of shopping for bargains. "She'd buy the place out," remembered Michaels.

In the late '40s, Mary began to consider a return to the screen. "There was one picture that she really wanted to do," remembered Buddy Rogers. *"Life With Father.* She didn't test for it, but she was definitely up for it. But they decided on Irene Dunne, and that really hurt Mary."

In 1949, Mary was approached by writer/director Billy Wilder about a script entitled *Sunset Boulevard.* Wilder planned to cast this story of a faded silent film star embroiled with a screenwriter/gigolo with an actress whose own career would embody some of the same mythic resonance as Norma Desmond's.

During an initial meeting at Pickfair, Pickford said she adored the script, as did, surprisingly, Buddy, but she demanded a major structural alteration: The screenwriter/gigolo (to be played, hopefully, by Montgomery Clift) must be made completely subordinate to Norma Desmond; there must be no question about who was to be the star of the picture.

Wilder, leery of hiring someone whose ability to take direction might be in doubt, declined to alter his script; in any case, it is doubtful if Mary, one of whose strongest assets as an actress was her demure femininity, would have been able to dive into the role of Norma Desmond with the astonishing *brio* displayed by Gloria Swanson. Still, there was no question about a bond between Mary and the glorious, mad, self-destructive, but authentically great star Norma Desmond. Mal Boyd reports that, when he and Mary went to see the finished picture, Mary wept.

Still, the idea of *Sunset Boulevard* had aroused her competitive instinct and, once the Hollywood grapevine knew she might be interested, word began to circulate. By 1951, a young writer named Daniel Taradash had completed a script he called *The Library*, about a librarian whose commitment to keeping all manner of books on the shelves leads her to be accused of dangerous liberalism.

"I got the bright idea that it might be a fascinating casting idea," recalled Taradash. "We had a 2¹/2 hour meeting at Pickfair and she seemed perfectly normal, pleasant and open. She offered no particular criticisms of the script. One of the things she particularly liked about the script was that it was a role of enormous scope, the centerpiece of the film.

"She committed to the project. I think she seriously wanted to make the movie. I know [producer] Stanley Kramer took her seriously, and Columbia, which hadn't wanted to do the script, was also suddenly very interested."

Pickford announced that she would come out of her retirement of nearly twenty years to do *The Library* because "this is a picture which stands for everything we Americans hold dear. It is the most important subject in the world today and the one nearest my heart."

Mary took a screen test and attended some readings and rehearsals at Columbia studios. According to Taradash, who attended, "With a first-rate job of direction, she could have played the part." Yet, on September 18, three weeks before production was to begin, Pickford withdrew from the project, citing her desire to make her comeback in Technicolor rather than black-and-white. It was a fairly desperate attempt at saving face, for, according to Taradash, her announced excuse was "simply not true. She backed out because of McCarthy era Red-baiting. Kramer had just been labeled a Red, and Hedda Hopper started to work on Pickford. She couldn't take the pressure. The Technicolor excuse was a story concocted because she didn't want it about that she hadn't the guts to make the picture."

The Library would be Mary's last fling with acting. The project went on to be attached to Irene Dunne, whose conservative Republican politics also led her to back away, then Barbara Stanwyck, before finally ending up with Bette Davis. Taradash's script for *From Here to Eternity* had made him a hot property in Hollywood, so, in 1956, he elected to make his directing debut with *The Library*, retitled *Storm Center*. It was a financial and critical disaster.

Mary would never seriously consider acting again, but she never stopped thinking about it either. For a while, she circled around the idea of playing the lead role in a version of her mother's life, which she planned to end, presumably on a note of triumph, on the April day in 1909 when Mary had walked into the Biograph studio and got her first job.

"Let no one tell you they don't miss their career," she said in 1956. "I miss it terribly. It's a constant ache with me, but I had to do it, just as I had to say goodbye to my beloved family. Life goes on."

Chapter Fourteen

"I've been loved."

—*Mary Pickford*

I N April, 1953, Mary and Mamie Eisenhower went on a coast-to-coast tour selling Savings Bonds. Accompanied only by another woman with a long-rumored secret penchant for alcohol, the potential for disaster was immense, but Mary was on her best behavior and didn't drink at all. If the bond tour required the professional, then the professional would appear.

Her essential generosity remained intact. During one of Tess Michaels's annual Christmas visits, Mary tried to present her with a jade figurine that Tess had casually admired. "I can't take that, Mary; it's too nice," said Michaels. Mary was insistent, but Michaels managed to leave without it. A week later, it arrived in the mail. A strong-willed woman herself, Michaels knew when she had met her match. She kept and treasured the figurine for the rest of her life.

Beatrice Boyd, Mal Boyd's mother, also became close to Mary, at least partially because they both loved dogs. On one of her visits, Beatrice bought her dog Mickey, who liked to play with Mary's Labrador mix Baron. One morning Beatrice woke up to find Mickey sleeping on a beautiful, obviously expensive quilt. She shushed him off, and at breakfast apologized for the dog's bad manners. "Oh, I gave him that quilt," said Mary. "I'd gone to your room and seen him sleeping there on the cold floor, so I put it there for him."

"She was a very caring person," remembered Mrs. Boyd, who was later given the pick of Baron's litter, and who always treasured gifts of purses and a robe that Mary had picked out herself. But she also witnessed at least one unnerving bout with Mary in her cups, when, at the Plaza Hotel with Buddy and Mal, Mary suddenly dropped underneath the table and began playing peek-a-boo with the tablecloth.

By this time, Mary's drinking could incite bursts of wild paranoia; around this time, she wrote a confidential memo to her secretary Bess Lewis expressing fear of the "common" men and women that Buddy had to associate with in his nightclub engagements, and who, she was afraid, were capable of duping Buddy out of both his wife and her estate. She asked Lewis to be sure to investigate any accidental or strange circumstances that might surround her death. The memo then drifts off into a salute to the glorious American republic.

In another letter, dated June 14, 1952, she carefully instructs Buddy about what he should do in the event of her death, i.e. listen to the trustees, create trust funds for himself and the children. In the event of his remarriage, she thought the second wife was entitled to a third of his estate. The tone is that of a fond mother worried about sending her none-too-bright child off to college alone.

Beatrice Boyd was never able to work up much enthusiasm for Buddy, whom she found lightheaded, without depth. "Mal used to send Buddy off to play his music, and I know for a fact that Mary didn't miss him when he was gone." Beatrice found herself drawn to Roxanne, with whom she would go on long walks around the Pickfair grounds. "She wasn't happy," said Beatrice. "She wanted to get out. Neither one of those children belonged at Pickfair, if you know what I mean."

At long last, Mary began to make provisions for the survival of her films. In 1943, Howard Walls, an assistant in charge of the motion picture collection at the Library of Congress, had suggested to head librarian Archibald MacLeish that Pickford might be ripe for a donation of her films. Mary had always been unsympathetic to the film program at the Museum of Modern Art, partially because of curator Iris Barry's pronounced bias towards European art movies and partially because one of the first collections Barry had successfully gone after was Douglas's, a transaction that was completed the year he died. To add insult to injury, Mary had made a tentative move to donate her films to the National Archives, but the curator refused, on the grounds that the Archives could accept only American historical films.

Walls was right; Mary was immediately interested in the idea, and the donation, "for research and reference" purposes in perpetuity, was officially made on August 4, 1945. The Library's John Bradley, who negotiated the terms of the donation, reported that Mary was "deeply moved at the honor the Library was bestowing on her." For insurance and tax purposes, Mary's archives were valued at $150 a reel for 2,000 reels: $300,000.

The Library hired Carl Gregory to inventory and pack the collection, stored in the vaults at the Goldwyn studio. He found that although the nitrate films were in predominantly good condition, with only a few reaching the state of gumminess that precedes complete decomposition, they were chaotically disorganized. "Many subjects have been removed," he reported, "and in most cases no entry has been made to tell whether they have been returned or not. Many receipt slip carbons for removals have been clipped into the pages or illegible notations made in pencil. Also, when this inventory was made the collection took up three vaults whereas it is now in two vaults."

Gregory inventoried 286 titles spread over 2,000 reels, including the Biograph films and the Artcraft titles she had produced and traded for Paramount's interest. Mary withheld some titles from the Library donation, mostly films she owned but did not appear in; some films of Jack's; the Gloria Swanson silent film *Sadie Thompson* and the Joan Crawford sound version of the same story. There were, however, some Pickford films that she did not want included in the "research and reference" mandate given the Library: she held back the loathed *Rosita*, 283 reels of material from *Secrets,* and much miscellaneous material, including the two reels of Technicolor tests for *The Taming of the Shrew.*

Among the donated films there were many "that are beginning to smell [i.e. deteriorate] but are still in reproducible condition," wrote Gregory. "A crew of inspector editors should go to work on them as soon as possible."

Alas, it was not to be. The shipment arrived at the Library of Congress on December 26, 1946, but the following year the budget for the film program at the Library was eviscerated by Congress. It was not until the '50s that the delicate preservation work began;

by that time some of the films had deteriorated. In 1956, Mary donated $10,000 for a joint effort on the part of the Library of Congress and the George Eastman House in Rochester to copy her films on 16mm. In 1970, she donated to the American Film Institute original negatives of fifty of the Biograph productions she had bought in the late teens. Also, Matty Kemp did some preservation work.

Unfortunately, some pictures were beyond help. Others, like *Dorothy Vernon of Haddon Hall,* had to be cobbled together from inferior scraps of film, which effectively reduced the photographic quality of the original, thereby negating the only real quality the work had ever had.

The memory of Douglas refused to go away. Once, Doug Jr.'s wife and Mary were shopping in New York City when someone behind them called out "Oh, Mrs. Fairbanks?" Both Mary and Mary Lee Fairbanks turned around; at this point, Douglas Fairbanks Sr. had been dead for fifteen years.

Mal Boyd had emerged from the seminary an Episcopal priest and he and Mary stayed in fairly close touch. In New York, Boyd went to see a Tennessee Williams play that involved a weak, impotent clergyman. Soon thereafter, he had lunch at the Pierre with Mary. She proceeded to get ignobly drunk and ended the meal by falling face forward into her food.

Mary was bundled up and put on the elevator to go up to her room. As the door was closing, Boyd reflexively blurted out, "God Bless You." He suddenly realized that he had become the silly minister in the Tennessee Williams play, mouthing empty words to someone he couldn't possibly help. More than ever, he felt sorry for Mary, felt her to be a tragic figure, a true victim of celebrity.

In early 1955, three hundred ballots were sent out to stars of the silent cinema such as Mary, Lillian Gish, Harold Lloyd *et al,* by the George Eastman House in Rochester, New York. The purpose was to honor those premier artists of the silent screen that were still alive. As chosen by their peers, the winning actors were Charlie Chaplin, Richard Barthelmess, Harold Lloyd, Ronald Colman and Buster Keaton; the leading directors were Cecil B. deMille, Frank Borzage, John Ford, Henry King and Mickey Neilan; the leading actresses Mary Pickford, Gloria Swanson, Norma Talmadge, Lillian Gish and Mae Marsh.

In November, the winners gathered in Rochester for something of a class reunion of immortals. Mary held down the principal speaker's spot, and spoke extemporaneously, telling hilarious stories about everybody else on the platform. She closed by saying, "My life is a part of theirs and their life is a part of mine."

"Buddy was devastatingly charming," remembered Eastman House curator James Card, "especially to the women. Mary was not drinking and seemed fine; I would characterize her as 'professionally charming.'" Card's weekend was not problem-free; if Mary was cold sober, Buster Keaton was trying hard not to be; Card remembered that Keaton's wife was doing her best to keep her husband on the shortest possible leash.

Lillian Gish was still close to Mary. Her attitude toward Mary's loss of personal definition and resulting alcoholism was sympathetic but subtly disappointed as well. "Lillian is an incredibly disciplined woman," said Malcolm Boyd, who was often with the two women. "There was a tremendous sadness and a certain Spartan impatience in Lillian's attitude. It was unstated, but you could tell she was thinking that Mary was throwing her life away. I remember her telling us a story about how Dorothy was in terrible pain from cancer, but would always pull herself together and get on stage and give a perfect performance; the implication was very clear."

In April 1956, Mary and Buddy hosted a party at Pickfair. The guest list was entirely made up of silent film stars, directors, technicians and supporting players. "It was like a waxworks," remembered invitee William Bakewell. *Life* magazine covered the event and, although their praise was fulsome, there were at least some discordant notes. Mary had invited her old prop man and makeup artist Irving Sindler to the party, and it seemed to him that Mary had "all of a sudden become like an old lady. There was something bitter in her life and it was showing."

And now Mary had to begin to deal with the inevitable, what Mary referred to as "going across the border," the death of her coworkers and friends, many of whom were older than she.

Mickey Neilan had been deeply mired in alcoholism for over twenty years, subsisting on handouts and charity work from people like Darryl F. Zanuck. Finally, he had landed a good supporting part in Elia Kazan's *A Face in the Crowd*, courtesy of Budd Schulberg, who had met him on David Selznick's *A Star is Born*. Neilan cannily portrayed a wily, corrupt old politician, but he had already contracted throat cancer. Checking into the Motion Picture Country Home that Mary had helped found, Neilan sat down to put his fragments of a house in order . . . and in the process demonstrated the fighting heart that Mary loved.

"I have two possible things left," he wrote to friend and drinking buddy Gene Fowler at 3:00 A.M. one day. "They may give me next some radium isotopes, but they can't make that decision until my throat cools off from the radiation . . . My idea of this outcome and Gene, it has happened to others with this affliction, will be to have Our God Almighty toss a miracle my way and heal me. That is exactly what I am praying for.

"I'm facing this Gene, the only way I should. Jack Murphy— Harold Lloyd's [production] manager and Robert Peyton, an old school chum, are handling my will, with Mary Pickford sort of supervising."

After a recommendation on a new book he thought Fowler would enjoy, Neilan closed the letter with "Well, I'll close shop now and say good night, so me lad 'Vaya con Dios' . . . Yours as ever, The 'Mick' Neilan."

When Mary visited him, Neilan told her "I'll beat it yet." A few weeks later, Neilan took the opportunity to reminisce. "Those were the days . . . We had fun, loved to go to the studio, and hated to go home. Today they hate to go to the studio, they have no laughs and are tickled to duck home."

By early April, Neilan was down to 110 pounds and telling Fowler "whatever the Guy upstairs decides is good enough for me . . . giving me friends like you on my little jaunt through life is a wealth few men enjoy so why should I kick if he blows the whistle on me now." He signed his last letter "Mickey, The Neilan."

He died on October 27, 1958; his funeral was paid for by his first wife and his long-estranged film editor son, Marshall Jr. As per his instructions, no one accompanied his body to the cemetery. Instead, fifteen of his closest friends were to hold a private wake at the Hollywood Knickerbocker Hotel.

Pickford tried to ignore his wishes and see her old friend to his interment, but her Rolls-Royce broke down on Sunset Boulevard. Figuring it was a sign, Mary and Buddy gave up, caught a taxi, and went to the Knickerbocker Hotel, as per Neilan's wishes. At the end of the bar, where Neilan had always sat, there was a card on his chair that said "Reserved for Mickey Neilan." On the bar in front of his chair was an empty glass and an open bottle of beer.

"I could almost hear him," Mary said later, "saying to himself in glee, 'Look at the Tad—thought she was so elegant in her Rolls-

Royce, but I outfoxed her.' " A few days later, Mary invited Marshall Jr. up to Pickfair, where she gave him mementos of his father and talked about old times.

———— • ————

A month before Neilan had died, Mary and Buddy had sailed for Europe on the *Empress of England*. Free of the burden of United Artists, Mary and Buddy began to spend an increasing amount of time traveling, at least one major trip every year, often accompanied by Gwynne and her husband Bud Ornstein, and their children. In the summer of 1956, it had been Spain and the south of France, where they found that they were not immune from the perils that plagued less-renowned travelers.

They were marooned by engine trouble in the harbor of Antibes. A disgruntled Mary wrote Tess Michaels that they had had nothing but trouble with the ship from the very beginning of the voyage.

On the second night of their voyage, a storm blew up, forcing Gwynne and her four children to put on their life preservers in the middle of the night. The furniture flew from one side of the salon to the other. A horrified Mary swore off yachts for all time.

Bud Ornstein pulled his wife and children off the boat and went on to Monte Carlo by car, then rejoined the boat when it was fixed for a return trip to Majorca. For several days, Mary and Buddy just hovered in the Monaco harbor, where a star-struck Mary enjoyed gazing up at the palace of Rainier and Princess Grace. The area was one of her favorites, for a year later, at the tail end of a three-month trip to Europe, Mary and Buddy were in Nice, to visit Yvonne Vallee, Maurice Chevalier's ex-wife.

———— • ————

In 1957, Mary financed *The Parson and the Outlaw*, an odd little western with strong religious overtones in which Buddy, as a preacher, co-starred with Marie Windsor. The rehearsals, such as they were, were held in the western bar at Pickfair. Every once in a while, a quiet Mary would come in and watch. Marie Windsor noted the odd, patronizing way Mary treated Buddy, more like a child than a husband. "My Buddy," she'd say, patting his cheek, "he's going to make a picture." *The Parson and the Outlaw* went out as a second feature through Columbia and drew no notice whatever.

Around this time, Mary welcomed the young novelist and

screenwriter Gore Vidal to Pickfair. He was surprised by how small the house seemed, not at all the baronial mansion that its reputation led him to expect. He also noted that, although she seemed very sweet, Mary was always sipping at a glass that contained a dark liquid.

In the early part of 1959, Mary had Pickfair and its contents appraised by Robert Scott. He found a house in very good order that had last been redecorated—by Katherine Crawford—shortly after World War II. Nevertheless, the house had a pleasant, up-to-date air about it.

In the four months Scott spent at Pickfair he grew to appreciate Mary as "a lovely person, but sad in some respects. Hollywood had sort of passed her by, she knew it and didn't like it. What impressed me most was how bright she was." He noted that she was very easy to talk to, had none of the airs of some of the other Hollywood stars for whom he had done appraisals, but seemed older than sixty-six.

He was most fascinated by the third floor at Pickfair, which was completely given over to storage and memorabilia. There were trunks full of Japanese scrolls and an Oriental room filled with furniture and knickknacks that Douglas and Mary had accumulated on their trip through the Far East after the completion of *The Taming of the Shrew*. He also found the racks of old costumes, each of which Mary had cleaned and pressed every year, and, something that struck him as curious, boxes and boxes of old Christmas cards, at least twenty years worth.

"At Pickfair, *nothing* got thrown away," he remembered.

——— ——

Mary had always maintained a staunch interest in the operations of the Motion Picture Relief Fund and Home. Mary—and Douglas —had been activists in the industry's fight for recognition and its ability to take care of its own. The Motion Picture Home itself had been started with $27,000 left over from $40,000 Mary had raised for World War I ambulances.

Ann Doran, the little girl Mary had found work for in *Robin Hood*, was on the board of the Relief Fund in this period. She remembered that Mary "was *the* Dowager. She was gentle, quiet, never raised her voice. You could tell very quickly whether she approved of something or not. On the board, they deferred to her. She had a very sage outlook on things, and if she liked something, it tended to get done. Conversely, if she didn't, an attempt was made to change a proposal to where it would earn her approval."

One day in 1958, at a board of trustees meeting, the case committee was convened to decide on which applicants for assistance would get it. As always, no names were ever used in the meeting. It seemed that a prominent producer had died broke and his widow was asking for help. Mary listened to the case history then said, "Well, all I can say is, he was very foolish not to have handled his money any better. I can't be very sympathetic."

Another member of the committee, who believed he knew who the dead producer was, asked to have the name revealed. Otto Kruger, who was presiding, took a vote and got the necessary two-thirds majority. "It's Jesse Lasky, isn't it?" asked the committee member.

Mary flushed with embarrassment. "I cannot tell you how sorry I am," she said. "Jesse was my producer, my partner, my friend." Mary changed her vote; Bessie Lasky got some help.

Except for occasional meetings, she began retiring more and more from view, citing cataracts and "health problems." The truth was that her "health problems" were almost entirely the result of her drinking, which now began when she got up in the morning and continued throughout the day.

Mary's deterioration became increasingly noticeable. In 1959, her old sound technician Edward Bernds had been appointed to the board of the Relief Fund. Bernds was shocked when Pickford attended a meeting of the board in what was clearly an alcoholic stupor.

"She had been a great star, a great lady," he recalled, "but she was frail, silent and frozen. I reminded her that I'd worked for her on two pictures, but she just looked at me with a blank stare. It was a very embarrassing, tragic encounter." At another meeting, Mary walked up to William Bakewell, who was also serving on a committee and, apropos of absolutely nothing, said "Billy, Douglas loved you like a son." The puzzled Bakewell could only make appropriate sounds and wonder what had brought that up.

The woman who had once contemplated playing Norma Desmond had become Norma Desmond, a grotesque, semi-alcoholic anchorite increasingly hesitant to venture out of Pickfair. Even within Pickfair, things were not always safe; in November 1959, she fractured a collarbone when she caught her heel in a dressing room rug and took a fall.

Earlier that year, she had been testifying in a civil suit regarding the purchase of a TV station in 1953, when the opposing attorney asked her in cross-examination if, by chance, she might have been intoxicated when she made the original deal.

"Definitely not," she snapped, "and I want to say I'm not intoxicated today. I think it's a terrible thing that you take a woman of my prominence and ask a question like that of her. I resent it very much. I've lived a long and I think clean and decent life. The people who've followed my career know I've been kind and charitable. Once again, I resent that very much." She turned to the judge and asked why the attorney had asked such a question. Judge John J. Ford replied that the attorney was probably just being "overly cautious."

"And underly polite," snapped Mary.

She began to display imperious behavior that would have been unthinkable for the Mary who had been so considerate to her co-workers thirty years before. In the latter part of 1964, film technician William Ault was hired to make duplicate negatives for some of Mary's films, so they could be used for a documentary Matty Kemp was planning. Ault had previously met Mary when he had serviced Pickfair's Navy surplus DeVry projectors, and had shown Mary some of the Biograph films that were being restored by Kemp Niver. Mary, easily sentimental by then, would get upset at seeing Lottie or Jack and begin to weep.

On Christmas Eve, Ault, Buddy and Matty Kemp were kicking around the idea of whether there was any commercial potential in theatrical re-issues of some of Mary's pictures. They asked Ault what he thought. "Well, Chaplin has re-issued a lot of his pictures and done very well with them," he said.

Matty Kemp immediately called Mary back at Pickfair to mention this fact. Over the phone line, Ault could hear the sounds of angry squawking. Matty Kemps' face fell. He hung up the phone and turned to Ault. "You're through," he said. The mere mention of Chaplin's name in a context suggesting he was somehow more popular than Mary was reason enough to banish the technician.

(A few years later, Charlie Chaplin announced that his friend Jerome Epstein was representing him in the matter of negotiating a re-issue deal for the Chaplin library. Shortly after the announcement appeared, someone in the Pickford Company called Epstein to inquire if he would be interested in handling Mary's films as well. "I knew enough not to get involved," remembered Epstein. "I knew Charlie wouldn't have liked it. And I was very frank with the man; I told him that I didn't think her old pictures had the same re-issue value that Charlie's had.")

Ault's friend Kemp Niver had met Mary when he was a private

investigator. Sol Lesser had asked him to accompany Mary to a meeting at the office of the Los Angeles Supervisors. "I thought I was going to have a drunk on my hands," remembered Niver. "It was around ten in the morning, we were coming out Olympic Boulevard, and Mary said, 'Go to the rear door of the Beverly Hills Hotel; I want a drink.' I got her a double vodka martini, and this was at ten in the morning.

"She never tried to justify the drinking. She drank and she didn't care if you thought badly of it or not." Clearly, she had considerably less pride than she had had ten years before, when Mal Boyd could honestly say that he never saw her take a drink.

She was also less coy about admitting to a sense of disappointment over other things. She confessed to George Pratt that the ulterior motive behind her learning fluent French had been a secret desire to appear at the *Comédie Française*, a desire she had never pursued. "They might turn me down," she said, "and I'd be terribly embarrassed. My French accent isn't all I probably think it is."

Her attitude about the sudden end of her acting career varied with the telling. To reporters she tended to emphasize how busy she had been over the years, what with running United Artists, and charitable Good Works. But with friends, or sympathetic listeners, she told quite another story. "I would rather be in the studio working than anywhere on earth," she told George Pratt. "I have missed my work."

She became very involved in the formation of the abortive Hollywood Museum, and would invite Kemp Niver, who had by then been appointed administrative curator of the project, over to Pickfair to look through scrapbooks and stills. Once, they came across a publicity still of Mary sitting on a bench, complete with Mary Jane dress. "Look at that," she marvelled. "I was thirty-two years old when this picture was taken and they expected me to continue. I couldn't. *I couldn't!* So I shut myself away in this house. Even Douglas couldn't think of a way for me to continue."

Niver turned over a picture of Lillian Gish and Mary snapped "I hate her." Niver was shocked. "How can you say that? She's your oldest and dearest friend."

"Yes, but she still acts and she's too old to act. When I got to be forty, I couldn't play a teenager anymore and I had to quit. Any fool could see I wasn't a teenager by the way I swung my hips. But that didn't matter; I didn't want to quit but I had to quit."

Niver didn't know what to say and turned over the still of Gish.

Meekly, as if in apology for her outburst, he heard Mary say, "But I've been loved."

Buddy coped with Mary's drinking and general deterioration with resolute denial. "We had liquor in the house, of course," he said some years after Mary's death, "but Mary never had more than two or three drinks. Never. Never. It was said that I had a bed over in the corner somewere. We slept together for forty-five years. Frankly, the extent of Mary's withdrawal was exaggerated. Lillian would come, lots of friends would come. She was only withdrawn to the public and the press."

There was undoubtedly an element of truth in some of Buddy's explanations, particularly of vanity on Mary's part. "She wanted people to remember her the way she was," Buddy explained. "She thought everybody still expected her to be the girl with the curls. She knew she was only dealing in illusion."

Occasionally, there would be some talk of showing some of her films on television, but she circled warily around the idea. "The reason I'm [staying] at the Hotel Pierre today and not the Hotel Mills is because of that little girl I used to be, and I'm not going to do anything that will get her laughed at. You see, I really was that little girl." Nevertheless, she authorized spending a quarter million dollars to have preservation negatives made for her old films —often from badly deteriorated prints rather than negatives.

Some of Mary's better early films, like *The Pride of the Clan*, were preserved only in scrappy condition; *Daddy Long-Legs* had one of its best scenes snipped out for inclusion in a documentary, but the scene was never put back. As a result, the only available copy of the film, at the Library of Congress, lacks a particularly delightful comedy scene of Mary and Wesley Barry getting drunk and knocking a little girl down a well. Many of the Artcraft pictures that were owned by Paramount were lost entirely.

After Matty Kemp assumed control of the Pickford archives, it became difficult to see many of Mary's best films . . . at least those films that had not been allowed to fall into the public domain, as was the case with many of them: *Sparrows, Dorothy Vernon of Haddon Hall, Rosita* and *The Taming of the Shrew* (the only one of her talkies she still owned), among others.

Kemp, whether with Mary's tacit approval or not, made obtaining the films extraordinarily difficult. In May 1973, Mary's native city of Toronto held a tribute to her, and Gerald Pratley, director of the Ontario Film Institute, inquired about the possibility of getting some prints of Mary's films for the Toronto archives. Promises were made, but somehow, the prints never arrived.

"Kemp simply didn't want to part with them," remembered Pratley.

In 1972, the renowned theater organist Gaylor Carter was hired by the Pickford Corporation to record scores for seven Pickford films for a possible theatrical re-issue, among them *Little Lord Fauntleroy, Rebecca of Sunnybrook Farm, Sparrows* and *My Best Girl.* As per his usual routine, Carter watched each film two or three times, then spent a week compiling a score for it. Mary, through Kemp and Buddy, gave Carter guidelines about what she believed was needed musically.

"In *Rebecca,*" remembered Carter, "in the scene with the aunt on her deathbed, Mary said that she didn't want me to do anything 'funny' with the music, even though there were some gags in the scene. She wanted it kept somber. In *Sparrows,* she wanted me to be sure again not to try any funny business, that I would keep it serenely ominous. I would have anyway—the picture usually tells you what to do musically—but she obviously wanted very discreet music for the films."

The re-issues, as a package, were abortive, although *My Best Girl* and Matty Kemp's revised version of *The Taming of the Shrew* did get some showings over the years.

The obvious question arises: Why didn't anyone ever take the responsibility and try to dry her out? Kemp Niver had a simple answer. "If that woman did not want something done, it wasn't done. As she used to say, 'I'm a footstomper.' And she was." Arthur Loew Jr. said that, "When she told a story, it was like it was happening right then. When she told a story that involved her getting mad, then she got mad, and she got this particular set to her jaw than I can only think of as Irish. At those times, I used to think, 'God, I hope I never incur her wrath.' " Buddy remained eternally permissive, perhaps out of love, perhaps out of an unwillingness to disturb the status quo. "That little devil," he told director Eddie Sutherland, "she gets to drinking and she just can't stop."

Despite her alcohol intake, she was rarely completely incapacitated. "She didn't just tell the cook there would be five for dinner," recalled Niver, "she would order it all, specifically. One time I was there for lunch and she wanted some peanut butter. Her help couldn't find it, so she went into the pantry and got it out from behind another jar. She knew exactly where everything was."

In October 1961, Mary and Buddy journeyed to Cleveland, where Mary received the American Nursing Home Association's Humanitarian Award. A year later, in November, they returned, this time to preside over the opening of a nursing home in the Cleveland suburb of Lakewood. "I believe that we shouldn't record ages," she told nearly 500 senior citizens who came to hear her speak. "Dismiss it from your mind." She continued harping on the need for basic human interaction when she told the crowd that they should "Drop by and take an older person for a ride or to the movies. Remember birthdays, send cards. The greatest need today is for love and affection."

After her speech, Edward Campbell, a pipefitter, came up to Mary and asked to shake her hand. "I used to see your old Biograph movies," he told her. "I'm just your age. I looked you up in the encyclopedia." In response to a reporter's question, Mary admitted that her figure wasn't what it had been. "I'm a size twelve," she said, "but I'm aiming at a ten." From Cleveland, Mary and Buddy journeyed to Boston, where she was awarded an honorary doctor of humanities degree by Emerson College.

In 1963, her old friend Tess Michaels telephoned to tell her that she was going to get married.

"Married? Why?"

"Well, I met this very wonderful man."

"But," said Mary, "I love you more than he does."

Nevertheless, Tess Michaels became Tess Michaels Pook and brought her husband to Pickfair to meet her best friend. "Mary wouldn't even look at him for two days," she remembered, "but she came around later. We ended up having a very nice visit."

That same year her old director and lover James Kirkwood died at the age of eighty. Kirkwood's terrible temper had alienated nearly everybody that could have given him a job. If the person that upset him was Jewish, he was a "kike." If he was Irish, he'd be "a Mick bastard." There was nothing personal in all this, but it did tend to limit the number of people who wanted to see Jim Kirkwood to those who had known him forty years ago.

For some time, Mary had been trying to convince him to enter the Motion Picture Home, but Kirkwood adamantly refused, proudly existing in near-destitution, supported by his son, an occasional handout from Mary, or the more generous support of Marion Davies.

When Kirkwood Jr. arrived in Hollywood for his father's funeral after cutting short a theatrical tour in the East, he found the body in an open casket at the Blessed Sacrament Church, "which I didn't want." Suddenly, he became aware of the unmistakable sound of flashbulbs going off in the rear of the church. "This little lady came in, all dressed up, supported by two men. It was Mary. She was sobbing and carrying a rather large bouquet of flowers in her hands.

" 'Jimmy, Jimmy,' she cried.

" 'I know, darling.' I kissed her.

" 'Where's Jim,' she asked. These two men took Mary over and she said, 'Let me alone, let me alone.' She looked down at my father, said 'Oh Jim, Jim,' and threw the bouquet right at his face. She threw it *hard*. It hit him squarely in the face and bounced over to the side. I thought to myself, 'Ouch!' It was so comic, yet so sad. She didn't mean it the way it looked; it was a gesture of 'Here, my darling, I brought these flowers for you . . .' "

Two days later, Kemp Niver called her to mention that he had just restored one of her Biograph films in which she had played the part of James Kirkwood's daughter. She remembered making it but couldn't place the title. After Niver supplied it, she said "If you've got it to show me, I'll be right over." A surprised Niver said of course, but wondered why she was so anxious. "Well, last night was the first night Jimmy Kirkwood spent in his grave," responded Mary.

Her Irish sentimentality had by now worked its way to the forefront of her personality, and she began to pine for her dead pets, which ranged from Zorro, a wire-haired terrier that bit anything that moved, to Pearl, a horse. "I wish I could put my arms around [Pearl] and tell her that I love her, but our animals don't live as long as we do," she told George Pratt. "Don't you think there's some possibility we'll see them again? I had canaries, several dogs; I'd love to see them flying towards me, galloping towards me. That's one of my ambitions. Kind of a silly ambition, isn't it?"

In October 1965, she and Buddy journeyed to Paris for a month-long tribute from the *Cinémathèque Français*, encompassing more than fifty of her films. At the opening night on October 9, a compilation of bits and pieces from her career was presented, preceded by a short talk from Mary in her fluent French. She said she was touched by the attention and she asked for a little understanding because the films had been made so long ago.

The French were astonished by the vivacity of Mary's acting;

the retrospective served as both shock and revelation, for it clearly showed why the idols of silence had often been somehow truer, greater stars than those that had succeeded them. Silent film called for talents that could express not only mood and feeling but needs and wants, an elusive inner life, an emotional reality that talkies replaced with the easy alternative of indicative words.

At the conclusion of the compilation, the audience erupted in cheers, and, for the last time, Mary accepted the applause of an audience. "My heart sings," she said. She seemed gratified by the typically adulatory attentions of the Paris audience. "The French never forget an artist who has pleased them," she said the next day, "I have received many honors in my life and have had audiences with kings and queens and the world's greats. But this tribute touches me most of all."

It seemed unutterably sad to her that some of her contemporaries, as well as actresses who had come after her, had not had the same opportunities to savor their critical popularity. Among those she thought especially deserving were Marilyn Monroe, Jeanette MacDonald and Clara Bow.

Although she had made her best-loved films over forty years before, she still remembered every plot detail, a mark of how intensely she lived her parts. "Each one of those characters seemed like my children or my brothers and sisters," she said. "I began to look like the characters after a week or two. And I took them home with me. Today, when I think of them, my heart goes out to them; I wish I could meet them in real life."

Although a few years earlier she had freely admitted that, among her films, she "loved *Rebecca, Daddy Long-Legs, Little Lord Fauntleroy* ("it would embarrass me the least in revival") and *Coquette,*" now she was inclined to the view that she had no personal favorites among her films, "because I've never been completely satisfied with anything I did."

"Frankly," she said, "I have never liked myself too well. I don't know why. It's not a very happy nature, to tell you the truth, because I have standards for myself that I fall short of all the time."

Once again she flogged Lubitsch, said that without question her moment of deepest despair was the death of her mother in 1928, and then touched on the reason why the films of the United Artists represented a kind of filmmaking paradigm of their time.

"Douglas and I strove to perfect our films in every way. I scrapped the first version of *Secrets* at enormous expense, to do a second." And after *Secrets?*

"I knew it was time to retire. I wanted to stop before I was asked to stop. I think I'm a fairly good actress—I don't say great, but fairly good. I could have gone on and done more mature parts, but . . . I think it was the public that wouldn't accept it."

She was now listing her favorite movies as *Gone With the Wind, It Happened One Night, High Noon, All Quiet on the Western Front, The Informer, The Ten Commandments* (1956 version), and *The Birth of a Nation.* Her taste in films had improved markedly in thirty years, and there were two interesting addenda to her list of movie greats: "Any Charlie Chaplin film of his silent period. Chaplin is the greatest comedian in the world. It was too bad he decided to combine his movies with politics. He was above politics. He should never have stooped to politics. He stooped and he was conquered."

And Douglas's *The Thief of Bagdad.* "Douglas had the style and the wonderful rhythm of motion to make this one of the greatest of adventure movies . . . Watching him move was like watching the greatest of Russian dancers."

Her appearance at the *Cinémathèque* was among her last times out in public. Occasionally, she would give an interview to one of the wire services in a slow week, and rail about "dirty" movies, women's liberation and television.

She enjoyed watching "Bonanza" because she thought that Lorne Greene looked like Buddy. Once, she even talked idly of a comeback. "I'm getting ready," she said. "I'm looking for something. But it won't be a role for an old lady. I don't look like an old lady and I don't feel like it."

She journeyed to New York for the last time, and set up a pre-theater dinner at Sardi's with Mildred Loew, Arthur Loew Jr., Stewart Stern, and Jim Kirkwood Jr., who had made the transition from actor to successful novelist.

"Buddy was off with his cronies," remembered Kirkwood, "and Mary suddenly turned to me and said 'I don't know why your father didn't want to go to the Motion Picture Home. Have you seen it?'

" 'Well, no I haven't . . .'

" 'Well, it's beautiful! They all have their own separate little cottages and they're very well taken care of, but your father didn't want to go. He wanted to have his own apartment.'

"So she looked at Mildred and Stewart and she'd had quite a bit to drink by this time and she said, 'Now darling, don't you be stupid like that bastard father of yours. Darling, anytime you want to go to the home, you call up Aunt Mary.'

"I guess I must have looked like I wasn't doing very well. Anyway, everybody absolutely roared with laughter." Later, after dinner, Mary turned to Kirkwood and said, "Aunt Mary doesn't want to go to the theater tonight." Needless to say, they didn't.

She contributed to Richard Nixon's 1972 re-election campaign, read mysteries and newspapers (that were often clipped to spare her bad news that could upset her for days), handled her business affairs with a largely undiminished acumen, listened to records, watched television, and helped herself to gin from the glass at her bedside. Now, her parameters were defined by her bedroom walls, with Buddy serving, as Stewart Stern observed, as "her footman."

"She just sort of gave up, surrendered," said Arthur Loew Jr., who occasionally visited Mary after she banished the world. "She wasn't an invalid at all when she began retreating; in the beginning, she seemed fine, like she'd decided to take a couple of days off. She could still get around. But then she was in her bed for so long that she did get sick. She turned herself into a recluse and became an invalid."

Mildred (Mickey) Zukor Loew tried to rally her out of it, as did Lillian Gish, but nothing seemed to work. "It was like she'd done everything, seen everything, had everything and just decided 'the hell with all of it,' " said Arthur Loew Jr. Mary became an unseen presence around Pickfair. In the guest room, the photo of Lord and Lady Mountbatten still stood, inscribed "To Doug and Mary, with grateful thanks for a delightful day in Hollywood, October 1922." Although Pickfair was well maintained, inevitably it began to seem underpopulated. By the '70s, it seemed merely empty, and about as lived in as Mount Vernon.

In January 1972, Mary wrote to Douglas Jr. and reported that Christmas had been busy and happy, if only because of the arrival of Gwynne and Bud Ornstein on Christmas Eve (they had replaced Ronnie, by then an aircraft mechanic in San Diego, and Roxanne, a housewife in Portland, as surrogate children). Although Mary still stayed in her room, she did enjoy having them drop in during the course of the day.

A year later, in May, a plaque was unveiled on the site of the house where Mary had been born. Buddy attended the unveiling in Mary's stead. "Mary Pickford," it began. "Born in 1893 [sic] in a house which stood near this site, Gladys Marie [sic] Smith appeared on stage in Toronto at the age of five. Her theatrical career took her to Broadway in 1907 where she adopted the name Mary Pickford. The actress's earliest film, *Her First Biscuits*, was released by the Biograph Company in 1909 and she soon established herself as the international cinema's first great star. Her golden curls and children's roles endeared her to millions as 'America's Sweetheart.' She was instrumental in founding and directing a major film production company and starred in over fifty feature length films . . ."

Mary began to be troubled by the onset of chronic heart disease, but occasionally, she'd say something that showed the old, sharp Mary hadn't deteriorated entirely. "Hollywood now is like the rest of the world. It's disturbed and frightened. In the old days, Hollywood was young and the country was young. They are both mature now. Making movies was fun. There is not much fun today when one mistake can be fatal. In the old days, a star was loved through good, bad and indifferent pictures. Today, three bad pictures and a star is finished.

"But I don't know that they were really good old days. Perhaps they only seem that way because we forget our troubles and, as wine improves with age, so do memories. You only remember the good things.

"Looking back, there's nothing I would change in my life, except maybe I'd work harder. People no longer work hard. They do as little as possible for the most money. It's just money, money, money. Grab all the money you can and run."

Talking to a film historian she said, "I think illusions are so important. That's why I haven't gone back to pictures. I could handle a part as well as the next fellow—maybe not better—but I could if I felt it, loved it and wanted to do it. But I don't think that I could ever recapture what I once enjoyed and what other people seemed to enjoy."

So the exile went on and the good things she remembered all seemed so long ago. When a Canadian reporter came to Pickfair, she talked to him on the phone and told him she loved his accent, the way he pronounced "house" as "hoose," "out" as "oot." While talking on the phone, she was given to little coughs, which she would fix by sipping something. Occasionally she would say things like "Do you love me? Buddy says you do," and completely disconcert the reporters.

Buddy, long used to satisfying the needs of his Best Girl, went along with it. With so much time on his hands, Buddy had achieved competence as a golfer. One partner called him "a decent, fussy player, an infectious little butterfly." On walks around Tower Road, he would occasionally run into Norma Shearer, who had also been retired by a couple of flops and a forty-ish demeanor, but had managed to avoid being driven into hiding. "Mary's fine," he'd call out, waving. "She's just not seeing anybody. She's Howard Hughes." The last time he performed as a bandleader was in 1971, when he took over for Fred Waring when Waring fell ill.

———— ——

Although Mary's sense of direction had long since deteriorated, her competitive spirit never failed her, and neither did her mind. When Chaplin was knighted in March 1975, Pickford, still nursing her grudge, was irritated and put out some feelers through Douglas Fairbanks Jr. to see if she might be entitled to be "Damed."

Discreet inquiries were also made about whether or not she might be entitled to receiving the Order of Canada, given by the government to "distinguished citizens."

But it was pointed out that she had left the country at the age of eight and had come back no more than five or six times. She had to settle for having her Canadian citizenship renewed by Secretary of State John Roberts.

When it was announced that she would be given an honorary Oscar in the 1976 Academy Awards, there was a flurry of interest. "I could still be on the screen you know," she told one reporter on the phone. "I'm far from being elderly. And I'm sturdy. I'm ready to go back to work, yes I am."

Sitting nearby, Buddy couldn't help laughing at her wistful suggestion, and Mary adopted a hurt tone. "Buddy's laughing at me" she said, and then, her Irish up, "He'd better not be laughing at me." Inevitably, questions would be asked about her unwillingness to venture out in public any more. Why remain hidden behind the walls of Pickfair?

"Because I'm so happy here," she would say.

When she thought of the old days with her trusted crew and handpicked directors, she remembered the warmth of the lights on her face. "Those days were fun," she would say. "And hard work. I miss them very much."

She posed for a few pictures with Buddy, sitting carefully posed in a high-backed chair with strong arms, a blonde wig sitting precariously on her head, her face nearly as unlined as Buddy insisted it was. She looked eerily like the little porcelain doll Belasco had given her seventy years before and which she still cherished.

Her bad days were now outnumbering her good days; her weight was less than ninety pounds, and on those occasions when she got out of bed, a cane was necessary. Once in a great while, usually in the evening, she would go out for a short ride around

Beverly Hills. Whenever anybody but Lillian Gish or Douglas Fairbanks Jr. wanted to see her, she was "unavailable" or sleeping, being taken care of by Pickfair's six servants. On several occasions, she wrote to Mary Louise Miller, the little girl in *Sparrows* she had wanted to adopt, inviting her to come for a visit. But when Mary Louise would telephone, she could never get through to Mary.

Occasionally, Buddy would invite a reporter to Pickfair, where they would get the grand tour of the downstairs, especially Douglas's western bar, complete with the Frederic Remington paintings. Then, if Mary was having one of her good days, the reporter might be able to talk to her on the house phone. If not, Buddy might play a little tape recording of her, welcoming the journalists to her house. "She's a million times better than that," he'd say, switching the recorder off. "She's been sick, you know. She was 'My Best Girl' in 1927 and she's still my best girl."

But all of Buddy's wishful thinking, and the pervasive unreality of Mary's environment, could not hide her physical deterioration. She grew terribly thin, "like a skeleton" according to her stepson. The cook at Pickfair dutifully sent up her meals, but they usually came back untouched. Her hair grew sparse and wispy, and her eyesight began to fail. Her stepson spent many days sitting by her bedside or talking to her on the Pickfair intercom.

"By this time she looked like something out of Buchenwald," remembered Douglas Fairbanks Jr. "There was nothing left to her. But, most amazingly, she still had her bawdy Irish sense of humor and she was still mentally sharp." He noticed that the maple leaf insignia was prominently displayed in her bedroom; she was still proud of being Canadian.

"But sometimes her mind would wander," he continued, "either from medicine or drink or just illness, and she would be talking and I would suddenly realize that she thought I was my father. And I would have to pull her back very gently; 'No, dear, it's not him, it's me.' It was very touching. Embarrassing, but very touching. It was at those times that I realized that she always remained in love with him."

In one of the last letters she wrote to Douglas Jr., she thanked him for a recent photograph of himself he had inscribed for her: "To My Darling Mary. With all love—now as ever. Douglas. Jayar."

She thanked him for everything, told him she would keep it near her always and called him "a wonderful son." She signed the letter, "Devotedly, Mama Mary."

And now it was time for farewells. She had Buddy call Tess Michaels Pook to come out for one last visit. When Tess walked into Mary's room, she raised herself up and threw her arms around her old friend. Tess stayed for five days; Mary was weak, but could still rouse herself into a fury over the fate of United Artists. "It was Chaplin that did it," she would grumble.

When it was time for Tess to leave, Mary looked up from her bed and said the same thing she always said at the end of their visits: "Darling, I can't see you off; you know I don't like to get up in the morning. So I'll say goodbye tonight. You'll take care of yourself? And you'll come back?"

In 1978, Mary and Buddy's last year together, their Christmas card showed a picture of the two of them in close-up, facing each other with their noses just touching. Mary has a blonde wig on, with curls at the back; she looks elderly but her neck and jawline are firm and unmistakably those of Mary Pickford.

In March 1979 she began to fail and Douglas Jr. came by for a last visit. Sitting by her bed, holding her tiny, withered hand, he listened to her tell the story of the first time they met, of how she pointed to his toy trains and asked if she could play with them too. It was exactly the way he remembered it.

Malcolm Boyd came to see her. Although he had been prepared for the worst, he couldn't believe how wasted she was physically, completely emaciated. She tried to explain away her condition by telling him she had hurt her back. He held her and she traced the lines on his face with her fingers. "There's Mama and Papa," she said, pointing to pictures of her parents on the wall. "And there's Jesus." Boyd looked over and noticed a Byzantine icon of Christ. He left feeling utterly exhausted, terribly distressed at her driven, restless emotional state, and her physical condition— "like a derelict, without a mind" according to Boyd.

On Friday, May 25, 1979, she became disoriented; Buddy and Matty Kemp rushed her to Santa Monica Hospital, but her condition continued to deteriorate. On Sunday she slipped into a coma and on Tuesday, May 29, with Buddy at her side, at two o'clock in the afternoon, she died. "She wasn't in pain," said Matty Kemp, "she just went to sleep."

Although there was no autopsy, Dr. Lester Laurion, who had been attending Mary since 1942, listed the cause of death as "cerebral vascular hemorrhage," and her age as eighty-five, shaving two full years off the correct total. Two days later she was cremated, and shortly thereafter all that was left of the woman who had been born Gladys Louise Smith and had seen her image conquer the world was interred in the family vault at Forest Lawn, alongside her mother, brother and sister. Services were private.

There were few of her contemporaries still alive to mourn this remarkable woman. Howard W. Koch, president of the Academy of Motion Picture Arts and Sciences correctly said of her that "she was the only living legend of what we're really about. I wish we could make the kind of movies she used to make—innocent love stories."

On October 8, 1979, the Academy held a tribute to Mary. Young Doug was there, as were Biograph co-star Blanche Sweet, and Karl Struss, the cinematographer of *Coquette*, *The Taming of the Shrew* and *Kiki*. Lillian Gish sent a brief message that ended, "We always said that when Mary smiled you could hear the angels sing. Listen . . ." Buddy Rogers made a brief appearance, then excused himself by saying, "It's very difficult for me, but those years that I had, it was like a dream come true."

Before a screening of *My Best Girl*, there was a panel discussion during which Blanche Sweet, who started in films in 1909, the same year as Mary, recalled that "People all over the world loved her—except me. All I heard at Biograph was 'Mary this, Mary that.' No wonder I was fed up."

Proper notice was paid to Mary's spearheading of both the Academy itself and the Motion Picture Country House and Hospital in Woodland Hills. But mainly, it was left to Douglas Fairbanks Jr. to sum up the accomplishments of his stepmother. "It was her idea that artists who created their own works from the beginning; who invented the stories; who defined, authorized, approved and indicated the kind of settings they wanted; who chose their directors, the kind of effects they wished to achieve . . . in other words, they were not only producers who just packaged films but actually created films, and so should indeed have the rewards due to them —rather than [have them] be paid to the middleman, in other words, the big distributors . . . who were taking an undue amount of the profits."

He pointed out that "Mary Pickford was the best known and most widely loved woman who has ever lived, more than Queen Elizabeth II, who's on every stamp in the Commonwealth." And then Young Doug closed by saying something that all could agree on. "We are not here tonight in the form of a memorial, I hope. Rather, we're here in the combination of a tribute, a form of obeisance, an act of pride, of remembrance—but also to remind ourselves of her, to indicate our respect, our admiration and, of course, our love."

Mary's will, dated June 7, 1971, requested a gentle memorial service. "I gently admonish all loved ones and friends that there should be no weeping. Let there be a memorial service with beautiful music. Let no one be turned away . . . Perhaps my family will feel, as I do, that they should cause a blanket of flowers to be draped upon the casket." The bequests were numerous; a star sapphire, her costumes and some pistols, daggers and guns which once belonged to Valentino went to the Smithsonian, as did a set of Japanese swords Douglas had given her. Ronnie and Roxie were left $15,000, and a trust was set up for Gwynne amounting to $200,000, with another $150,000 set aside for a trust for Gwynne's children. Tess Michaels was left $25,000.

Buddy was left $25,000 in cash, a group of Rodin watercolors, a piece of property on the grounds of Pickfair, and numerous pieces of real estate. The remainder of the estate ("at least $10,300,000") was to be funneled into a newly created Mary Pickford Foundation ("to benefit religious, charitable, scientific, literary or educational purposes") overseen by Buddy and two other trustees. The value of personal property was estimated at $3.3 million, while real property was about $7 million.

In the years before her death, Mary turned out five codicils to the original will, which fine-tuned her original bequests, adding $5,000 for Douglas Jr., increasing Buddy's monthly allotment, set up a $125,000 trust to pay for the education of Mary's grandchildren and Gwynne's grandchildren as well, and jumped Ronnie and Roxie's bequests to $50,000 each. In the last codicil, dated November 28, 1978, Mary's signature is tiny and indistinct, noticeably deteriorated from her previously definitive, almost imperious signature.

Mary's trustees set up a trust for Buddy consisting of stocks in companies such as Exxon, Procter and Gamble, Revlon and Tenneco, in the amount of $99,825, and a piece of property on Van Nuys Boulevard appraised at $700,000. The total value of the trust amounted to $800,000, on which Buddy was to draw $4,000 monthly.

Malcolm Boyd, who had always had affection for Roxanne, called her after Mary's death when he happened to be passing through Las Vegas. Boyd was overjoyed to find that, after more than her share of mistakes and tragedy, at least one person in the Pickford family had not only survived, but thrived. Roxanne had married an Italian chef in an unfancy restaurant, where she worked as the cashier. She was happy. Beyond that, she didn't care about Mary's money; she had forgiven everything. For Roxanne, at least, life had worked out. Boyd left feeling exhilarated, with a sense of closure.

———————

Ten months after Mary died, Pickfair was put up for sale. The asking price was $10 million for the 12,000 square feet of the house, separate servants quarters, 2.7 acres of land, a 100-foot swimming pool, and, on increasingly rare clear days, a superlative view of the Pacific Ocean. Before she died, Mary had made efforts to donate the property to a charity, university or hospital after her death, but the $300,000–$400,000 yearly upkeep dissuaded those who were approached.

Pickfair had changed little over the years. The predominant motifs were still French and English antiques, giving it an unpretentious but slightly "heavy" tone. There was still an adobe-walled replica of a wild west saloon, with Douglas's collection of cowboy chaps and the Frederic Remington paintings he had left behind. In many ways, it was still Douglas's house. Although the mistress of the house had mostly kept to her third-floor bedroom for the last fifteen years of her life, she was still omnipresent; in nearly every room, there were oil paintings of Mary, most of them representing her as she looked in the heyday of her career, most of them painted from photographs taken in the '30s and '40s.

After a while, it became clear that the asking price for Pickfair was an impossible goal; for one thing, by May 1980, the home loan mortgage rate had peaked at more than 17 percent. In all, about twenty-five people qualified to see the house, with the normal tour for prospective buyers taking about an hour. "I think I'll cry when Pickfair is sold," said realtor Dorothy Barish. "This is the most exciting home I've ever had. There will never be another one like this."

The final purchase price was $5,362,000; the buyer was Jerry Buss, owner of the Los Angeles Lakers. Buss did modestly well on his investment. In January 1988, he sold the house to Pia Zadora and Meshulam Riklis, her industrialist husband, for just under $7 million. They hired architect Peter Marino to renovate it. Marino called Pickfair "total, split-level ranchburger, terrible and appalling" and Riklis "my crazed, wonderful, mad billionaire." He would, he announced, attempt to turn Mary and Douglas's dream-home into "the maximum 1930s Wallace Neff statement."

Later, however, Zadora and her husband announced plans for a more massive project that was more reconstruction than remodeling. Riklis was going to spend another $2 million to turn Pickfair into a Renaissance-style Venetian palazzo that would be more redolent of The Strip in Las Vegas than Summit Drive in Beverly Hills.

Malcolm Boyd, who remembered Pickfair in the days when Mary had wandered through it in a vain search for a reason to get up in the morning, would often think of that house, the history and grandeur it had contained, the secrets it held, the way it had been shorn of its dignity and sense of mystery by the slow process of vulgarization that had overtaken all of Hollywood.

"The whole concept of ghosts is that they come back to places where they had unfinished business, isn't it?" asked Boyd, thoughtfully. "Well, if you believe in ghosts, then Mary should be haunting Pickfair."

L'Envoi

MARY'S will had said that Buddy could have "such household furnishings as he may designate as necessary to properly furnish his home." But Buddy's new house, built on the grounds of Pickfair, was about 7,500 square feet; to furnish it, he claimed virtually every piece of furniture in the house. Mary's attorney Sull Lawrence was one of the trustees of the estate and admitted that "we were in an awkward position. Both Mary and we assumed that Buddy would want to furnish a much more modest house . . . She wanted him to be comfortable but she wanted the foundation to benefit as well."

William Abbey, the deputy attorney general of California, was called in to watchdog the negotiations because the remainder of the estate had been left to a charitable corporation.

Finally, Buddy was awarded $1,000,000 out of the estate for his part in helping Mary sell her share of what became the Goldwyn studios, and her share of United Artists, apparently in lieu of his share of the community property. Buddy also took about half of Pickfair's furnishings, including Douglas's Remington paintings and some Rodin drawings that were later found to be fakes and, as Sull Lawrence admitted, "of no great value."

In 1983, the Pickford Foundation donated $500,000 ($50,000 a year for ten years) to the Library of Congress to support screenings and symposiums. A sixty-four seat film theater in the Library complex was named after Mary, and over the years many silent film screenings have been held there.

In May 1983, a bronze bust of Mary that looks nothing like her was unveiled in a small, park-like little square on the grounds of Toronto's Hospital for Sick Children, on the corner of University Avenue and Gerrard Street, near the memorial plaque which tells passers-by that Mary's birthplace was on this spot. At the same time, Buddy presented the hospital with a check from the Pickford Foundation for $25,000, as recompense for the support Mary had always promised to the Hospital but had neglected to specify in her will.

In March 1981, in an effort to clear out some of the detritus from Pickfair, and to raise additional monies for the Pickford Foundation, a public auction was held. C.B. Charles, an auctioneer who specialized in movie star estates, was disappointed by the quality of the Pickfair furnishings. "Pickford didn't have anywhere near the classy taste of Mae West or Rosalind Russell," he remembered. Bidding was brisk; at one point, fever hit the bidders and autographed portraits were going for as much as $400 . . . around three to four times their worth at the time.

Certainly, Buddy could not have been accused of excess sentimentality. He put up for sale some of Mary's most cherished possessions: the makeup kit she had used in her Belasco days, the German doll that Belasco had given her in 1907, the satin dress in which she had married Douglas, the medallion that had accompanied her 1976 Academy Award.

There was the costume, beige corduroy with lace embroidery, from *Little Lord Fauntleroy,* a gown from *Rosita,* and even a dress from the abortive *Forever Yours.* Buddy also put up for sale a lot of Douglas's clothing: the black cape from *The Mark of Zorro,* his costumes from *Mr. Robinson Crusoe,* and *The Taming of the Shrew.*

There was a Chinese carved bed in lacquers of red and gold intended for opium smoking; there were six silver vanity sets, with each item monogrammed; there were seven paintings of Mary; there was an autograph book signed by, among others, Amelia Earhart and Charles Lindbergh; there was Doug's itinerary book from his Far Eastern tour of 1931; there was Rudolph Valentino's gun collection; there were William Cameron Menzies' set sketches for *The Taming of the Shrew.* And there were three undated admission cards to a party at Pickfair, each saying "Admit One Only."

There was also the usual detritus; miscellaneous awards that Mary had collected over the years, French road maps from her and Douglas's honeymoon trip, over 1,000 items in all.

Charlene Tilton, of "Dallas," bought a fourteen carat gold vanity set for $3,750; and Bette Midler spent $2,000 for a Pickford oil portrait. A Luis Vuitton leather trunk, complete with many destination labels and Mary's name, which Charles had figured would bring a maximum of $300, went for an astounding $7,000. Other, more interesting items, went begging; the ornately carved red and gold lacquer opium bed sold for just $800. When a silver bowl from Thailand drew a bid of only $40, Charles snapped, "Listen folks, you understand you're not renting these things, you're buying them." When a tortoise shell box brought only $75 he said, "Forget Mary Pickford. What if we were selling Rosa Schwartz' estate? What we're selling these things for is ridiculous."

The auction took three days and brought in over a million dollars. It would have brought in more, except that some of the more valuable items—some exquisite jade pieces—were apparently stolen by domestics working in the house; the executors believed that many items were hidden in shrubbery and picked up later.

As it turned out, some of the buyers at the auction did not take the same care with the merchandise as Mary had; some of Mary's costumes, by now in very fragile condition, went to two men from Seattle. A few weeks later, C.B. Charles was informed that their check had bounced. When he called them, they explained that the costumes had been dirty, so they had put them in the washing machine. When the costumes had come out in shreds, they had stopped payment on the check. Charles sued for his money and won.

———   ———

With Mary's films out of circulation for so long and most of the people that remembered her and her pictures being either dead or in their dotage, memories of Mary and her place in film history began to slowly recede. But there was still Buddy Rogers, who had loved her.

He was, as always, tall, trim, manicured, exceedingly well turned-out and a trifle embarrassed about a man of his years still being known as "Buddy." He had a residual, entirely sincere interest in people, and would often ask as many questions of them as

they did of him. He always expressed an exuberant sense of wonder at first sight of anything fresh or unfamiliar. More than anything else, he seemed frankly proud, not of his successive careers
as a light leading man and bandleader, but simply, of being the
husband of the woman he adored.

"I could never quite figure out why she loved me. She was a
romantic, and she carried around this image of a college boy for
years. I was it, I guess. Oh God, we'd have fights sometimes, and I'd
walk out. But ten minutes later, I always wanted to call her up and
she was the same way. There was a strong, wonderful feeling
between us; Pickfair was always a happy house."

After Mary died, Buddy waited nearly two years and married
fifty-year-old real estate agent Beverly Ricono, a woman he had
known for some time. Although he would acknowledge his second
marriage when asked, he seemed hesitant to discuss it, almost as
though he was being vaguely disloyal to Mary's memory. He did
not, at least at first, wear a wedding ring.

His new house on the grounds of Pickfair was filled with the
portraits and photographs of Mary that had decorated the old
house, often transposed to the equivalent walls in the equivalent
rooms where they had hung before.

He realized that, for better or worse, his name would always be
inextricably linked with that of Mary Pickford, and he felt a sense
of responsibility to keep her memory as evergreen for others as it
was for him.

Thus, he would occasionally take time out from his golf—a nine
handicap—and make a personal appearance with *Wings* or *My
Best Girl.* His bubbling insouciance would then triumph over the
impediments of old age and the sad reality of the last years of the
woman he loved.

"Did the show go well?" he would ask afterwards, with that
hungry, eager vulnerability that never truly leaves any actor. "It's
always hard for me to tell, because I don't watch the movie; it
brings back many memories . . . too many memories.

"I don't consider myself a sophisticated man," he would say.
"I'm a hick and I know my way around Kansas better than I do
Beverly Hills. I could have been a banker, but I don't think I was
bright enough to be a lawyer. *Wings* was good, and I'm proud of it,
but mostly there was no creativity, just a certain amount of days to
do it and that was it. Mainly, I should have worked harder. Maybe I
couldn't have done what Cary Grant did, but I could have done
my own thing. I should have trained a little bit and worked a little

bit. But having a band was more important to me. I'd get a script, do it, the critics would blast me and I'd go back on the road.

"I'm an old-timer to people, you know. These films are all over sixty-years-old and . . . Well, the days that make up a life are so short. People should live every day, be happy and do the best they can all the time. Hell, I'm over and done with and it seems like I've only been at it about ten or fifteen years. And I had such a beautiful life, you know, family, relatives, Mary, the movies, the band. I'd do it all again, day by day."

And then Buddy Rogers would lean forward conspiratorially, as if to impart a secret he was not comfortable with. "It's very strange for me now," he would say. "I'll be talking to someone and I'll overhear people saying, 'He was married to Mary Pickford.' And then someone else will say, 'Who was Mary Pickford?'

"And that hurts me."

Acknowledgments

ANYBODY who writes a biography ends up feeling a good deal like Blanche Dubois. Although the strangers weren't always kind, they usually were, so I hereby express my gratitude to all the people who knew Mary and kindly granted me interviews, and to the keepers of the archives in which I found so much invaluable information.

I early on resolved to approach this book as if no one had ever written about Mary Pickford before. (Her own volume of memoirs, *Sunshine and Shadow,* is cranky and subjective even by the limited standards of movie star autobiographies.)

To that end, I sought out as much primary source material as possible, either documentary or, in increasingly rare instances, people who knew her, relying on previous biographers almost exclusively for the remarks of intimates who have since died and whose comments have the ring of truth.

My goal was to achieve what Leon Edel has called "the portrait within," to answer the questions of Mary Pickford's doubts, failures and struggles, as well as the reasons for her successes, which were written so large in yellowing public prints.

In that pursuit, I encountered several remarkable people to whom I owe a special debt. First, David Pierce, my intrepid research assistant and compiler of the filmography, who found goodies at the Library of Congress even they didn't know they had, and who sat with me, hunched over a Steenbeck editor, as we watched dozens of Mary Pickford movies with reactions ranging from rapture to dismay. Thanks, pal.

To Kevin Brownlow, who responded to my hesitant inquiry at the beginning of this three-year journey with the original reel-to-reel tapes of his own interview with Mary. Although his own work serves as the yardstick by which all film historians measure their efforts, Kevin has never let his accomplishments nudge him towards arrogance. He is the kindest, most generous of men, and everybody who cares about silent movies is in his permanent debt.

And to Douglas Fairbanks Jr., who not only made himself available to me for several lengthy interviews, but gave me full access to the correspondence between him and his beloved stepmother. I hope the result is worthy of the great trust he demonstrated. (Although Buddy Rogers chose to withhold his cooperation, he had been gracious enough to grant me a lengthy interview in 1981, from which I have freely quoted.)

Will Fowler gave me the full benefit of the knowledge that comes from a lifetime of living in and around the film industry, as well as coming through with some invaluable research material from his own files. David Stenn generously shared sources and gave me some good ideas as well, as did Miles Kreuger (Jerome Kern lives!). The amazing Herbert Goldman helped me nail down the details of Mary's touring days and her time with Belasco.

Lou Giannetti, Sheldon Wigod and Bill Kelley read early chapters and gave me helpful criticism and, equally as important, encouragement, and Jeff Heise threw himself into the mysteries of probate with admirable alacrity.

More nominal, but no less sincere thanks, are due to the following persons and institutions.

For the viewing of films: The Library of Congress (Pat Loughney, Madeline Matz, David Parker) and the Museum of Modern Art (Eileen Bowser, Charles Silver). Doug Moore lent me rare titles from his vast and splendid collection of Biographs, and Christopher Stager came through with some valuable films as well. In England, Eileen Burrows and Jackie Morris of the National Film Archive were enormously helpful in arranging screenings for me on very short notice.

Libraries and Archives: The Library of Congress, Manuscripts Division (John Knowlton); the Metropolitan Toronto Reference Library (Lee Ramsey); Office of the Registrar General in Toronto (a deep bow of thanks to Mark Matthews); the New Jersey State Department of Health; the New York *Post* (Pat Wilks-Battle); the Toronto *Star;* the Toronto *Globe and Mail;* the University of Southern California (Leith Adams); the Director's Guild of America (Deac Russell); the State Historical Society of Wisconsin (Harry Miller); the Princeton University Library (Mary Ann Jensen); and the Disney Studio Archives (David Smith).

For the Freedom of Information files, the Federal Bureau of Investigation (Emil P. Moschella); the Wiener Oral History Program at the American Jewish Committee (Carol Goldner); The George Eastman House (Jan-Christopher Horak, Mari Howard); the Mugar Memorial Library at Boston University (Dr. Howard Gotlieb); the Harold B. Lee Library at Brigham Young University (James V. D'Arc); The Columbia University Oral History Program; and the inter-library loan department of the Broward County Library.

Motion Picture Historians: Rudy Behlmer, Robert S. Birchard, James Card, Dennis Doros, Luther Hathcock, Ron Haver, Stephen Higgins, Timothy Lyons, Gerald Pratley, Jack Spears, George Turner, and Marc Wanamaker. Personal Interviews: Don Ameche, William Ault, William Bakewell, Elaine Barrymore, Lina Basquette, Aaron Beckwith, Edward Bernds, Beatrice Boyd, Malcolm Boyd, C.B. Charles, Gaylord Carter, Vitalis Chalif, David Chasman, Richard Condon, Ann Doran, Jerome Epstein, Curtis Harrington, James Wong Howe, Artie Jacobsen, James Kirkwood Jr., Betty Lasky, Paul Lazarus II, Paul Lazarus III, Arthur Loew Jr., Loyal Lucas, David Miller, Joan Marsh Morrill, Mrs. Marshall Neilan Jr., Kemp Niver, Tess Michaels Pook, Howard Ralston, Phil Rhodes, Charles "Buddy" Rogers, Robert Scott, Daniel Selznick, Irving Sindler, Stewart Stern, Karl Struss, Daniel Taradash, Gore Vidal, Meri von Sternberg, William A. Wellman, Marie Windsor.

I owe an enormous debt to Fran Collin, a great lady and a great agent with a superior recipe for borscht. Finally, I would be remiss if I did not express my love and appreciation to Jim Hensel, without whom I would never have begun, and to Lynn Kalber Eyman, without whom I would never have finished.

—Scott Eyman
Fort Lauderdale, Florida
August 27, 1989

Bibliography

Adamson, Joe. *Groucho, Harpo, Chico and Sometimes Zeppo*. New York: Simon and Schuster, 1973.

Atkinson, Brooks. *Broadway*. New York: Macmillan, 1970.

Balio, Tino. *United Artists: The Company Built by the Stars*. Madison: University of Wisconsin Press, 1976.

Baxter, John. *The Cinema of Josef von Sternberg*. New York: A.S. Barnes, 1971.

Berg, A. Scott. *Goldwyn*. New York: Alfred A. Knopf, 1989.

Bergan, Ronald. *The United Artists Story*. New York: Crown Publishers, 1986.

Bitzer, G.W. *Billy Bitzer: His Story*. New York: Farrar, Straus and Giroux, 1973.

Bogdanovich, Peter. *Allan Dwan: The Last Pioneer*. New York: Praeger. 1971.

Brownlow, Kevin. *The Parade's Gone By*. New York: Alfred A. Knopf, 1968.

Brownlow, Kevin. *Hollywood: The Pioneers*. London: William Collins Sons, 1979.

Chaplin, Charles, *My Autobiography*. New York: Simon and Schuster, 1964.

deMilles, William. *Hollywood Saga*. New York: E.P. Dutton, 1939.

Drinkwater, John. *The Life and Adventures of Carl Laemmle*. New York: G.P. Putnam, 1931.

Edwards, Anne. *The deMille's: An American Family*. New York: Harry N. Abrams, 1988.

Eells, George. *Hedda and Louella*. New York: G.P. Putnam, 1972.

Epstein, Jerry. *Remembering Charlie*. New York: Doubleday, 1989.

Fairbanks, Jr., Douglas. *The Salad Days*. New York: Doubleday, 1988.

Forslund, Bengt. *Victor Sjostrom, His Life and Work.* New York: New York Zoetrope, 1988.

Fowler, Gene. *Father Goose.* New York: Covici-Friede, 1934.

Frohman, Daniel. *Daniel Frohman Presents.* New York: Claude Kendall and Willoughby Sharp, Inc., 1935.

Fussell, Betty Harper. *Mabel.* New Haven: Ticknor & Fields, 1982.

Gabler, Neal. *An Empire of Their Own.* New York: Crown Publishers, 1988.

Geduld, Harry (Editor). *Focus on D.W. Griffith.* Englewood Cliffs: Prentice-Hall, Inc., 1971.

Gish, Lillian, with Ann Pinchot. *The Movies, Mr. Griffith and Me.* Englewood Cliffs: Prentice-Hall, 1969.

Goldwyn, Samuel. *Behind the Screen.* New York: George H. Doran Company, 1923.

Gomery, Douglas. *The Hollywood Studio System.* New York: St. Martin's Press, 1986.

Graham, Cooper; Higgins, Steven; Mancini, Elaine; Vieira, Joao Luiz. *D.W. Griffith and the Biograph Company.* Metuchen: Scarecrow Press, 1985.

Griffith, David Wark (Editor, James Hart). *The Man Who Invented Hollywood.* Louisville: Touchstone Publishing Company, 1972.

Griffith, Linda Arvidson. *When The Movies Were Young.* New York: Benjamin Blom, Inc., 1925.

Gussow, Mel. *Don't Say Yes Until I Finish Talking.* New York: Doubleday, 1971.

Henderson, Robert M. *D.W. Griffith: The Years at Biograph.* New York: Farrar, Straus and Giroux, 1970.

Herndon, Booton. *Mary Pickford and Douglas Fairbanks.* New York: W.W. Norton, 1977.

Higham, Charles and Moseley, Roy. *Princess Merle: The Romantic Life of Merle Oberon.* New York: Coward-McCann, 1983.

Hopper, Hedda. *From Under My Hat.* Garden City: Doubleday, 1952.

Irwin, Will. *The House That Shadows Built.* Garden City: Doubleday, Doran & Co., 1928.

Janis, Elsie. *So Far, So Good.* New York: E.P. Dutton, 1932.

Jewell, Richard. *A History of RKO Radio Pictures, Incorporated,* a dissertation for doctoral degree at the University of Southern California. (Unpublished.) 1978.

Kahn Jr., E.J. *Jock: The Life and Times of John Hay Whitney.* New York: Doubleday, 1981.

Kirkpatrick, Sidney D. *A Cast of Killers.* New York: E.P. Dutton, 1986.

Lasky, Jesse. *I Blow My Own Horn.* New York: Doubleday, 1957.

Laurie, Jr., Joe. *Vaudeville: From the Honky-Tonks to the Palace.* New York, Henry Holt, 1953.

Lejeune, C.A. *Cinema.* London: Alexander Maclehose and Co., 1931.

Mantle, Burns and Sherwood, Garrison. *The Best Plays of 1899–1909.* New York: Dodd, Mead, 1944.

Mantle, Burns and Sherwood, Garrison. *The Best Plays of 1909–1919.* New York: Dodd, Mead, 1933.

McBride, Joseph. *Hawks on Hawks.* Berkeley: University of California Press, 1982.

Milne, Tom. *Rouben Mamoulian.* Bloomington: Indiana University Press, 1970.

Montagu, Ivor. *With Eisenstein in Hollywood.* New York: International Publishers, 1969.

Mosley, Leonard. *Zanuck: The Rise and Fall of Hollywood's Last Tycoon.* Boston: Little Brown, 1984.

Niver, Kemp. *Mary Pickford, Comedienne.* Los Angeles: Locare Research Group, 1969.

Niver, Kemp. *D.W. Griffith: His Biograph Films in Perspective.* Los Angeles: John D. Roche, Inc., 1974.

O'Dell, Paul. *Griffith and the Rise of Hollywood.* New York: A.S. Barnes and Co., 1970.

Paine, Albert Bigelow. *Life and Lillian Gish.* New York: Macmillan, 1932.

Pickford, Mary. *Sunshine and Shadow.* New York: Doubleday and Co., 1955.

Pratt, George. *Spellbound in Darkness.* Greenwich: New York Graphic Society, 1973.

Schickel, Richard. *The Disney Version.* New York: Simon and Schuster, 1968.

Schickel, Richard. *D.W. Griffith: An American Life.* New York: Simon and Schuster, 1984.

Shipman, Nell. *The Silent Screen and My Talking Heart.* Boise: Hemingway Western Studies Series, Boise State University, 1987.

Skolsky, Sidney. *Don't Get Me Wrong—I Love Hollywood.* New York: G.P. Putnam, 1975.

Slide, Anthony. *The Griffith Actresses.* South Brunsweick and New York: A.S. Barnes and Company, 1973.

St. Johns, Adela Rogers. *The Honeycomb.* New York: Doubleday and Co., 1969.

Stenn, David. *Clara Bow: Runnin' Wild.* New York: Doubleday, 1988.

Sterling, Anna Kate (Ed.) *Cinematographers on the Art and Craft of Cinematography.* Metuchen: The Scarecrow Press, 1987.

Sterling, Anna Kate (Ed.) *The Best of Shadowland.* Metuchen: The Scarecrow Press, 1987.

von Sternberg, Josef. *Fun in a Chinese Laundry.* New York: Macmillan, 1965.

Thomas, Bob. *Astaire: The Man, the Dancer.* New York: St. Martin's Press, 1984.

Thomas, Bob. *Joan Crawford.* New York: Simon and Schuster, 1978.

Wagenknecht, Edward and Slide, Anthony. *The Films of D.W. Griffith.* New York: Crown Publishers, 1975.

Wagner, Walter. *You Must Remember This.* New York: G.P. Putnam, 1975.

Walker, Alexander. *Stardom.* New York: Stein and Day, 1970.

Weinberg, Herman. *The Lubitsch Touch.* New York: Dover, 1977.

Weinberg, Herman. *Josef von Sternberg.* New York: E.P. Dutton, 1967.

Wilson, Edmund. *The Thirties.* ed. by Leon Edel. New York: Farrar, Straus, Giroux, 1980.

Windeler, Robert. *Sweetheart: The Story of Mary Pickford.* New York: Praeger, 1974.

Winter, William. *The Life of David Belasco.* New York: Moffat, Yard and Co., 1918.

Westmore, Frank and Davidson, Muriel. *The Westmores of Hollywood.* Philadelphia and New York: J.B. Lippincott, 1976.

Yurka, Blanche. *Bohemian Girl.* Athens: Ohio University Press, 1970.

Zukor, Adolph (with Dale Kramer). *The Public is Never Wrong.* New York: G.P. Putnam, 1953.

Filmography

Compiled by David Pierce.

Films are listed in order of release.

This filmography is based on Robert B. Cushman's checklist in *Tribute to Mary Pickford*.

More detailed information on many of these films may be found in *D.W. Griffith: The Years at Biograph*, by Robert M. Henderson, *D.W. Griffith: and the Biograph Company*, by C. Cooper Graham, Steven Higgins, Elaine Mancini and Joao Luiz Vieira, and The American Film Institute Catalog: Feature Films: 1911–1920, and 1921–1930.

American Biograph

1909:

TWO MEMORIES
IIIS DUTY
THE LONELY VILLA
THE VIOLIN MAKER OF CREMONA
THE SON'S RETURN
HER FIRST BISCUITS
THE FADED LILIES
THE PEACH-BASKET HAT
THE WAY OF MAN
THE NECKLACE
THE COUNTRY DOCTOR
THE CARDINAL'S CONSPIRACY
TENDER HEARTS
THE RENUNCIATION

SWEET AND TWENTY
THE SLAVE
THEY WOULD ELOPE
HIS WIFE'S VISITOR
THE INDIAN RUNNER'S ROMANCE
THE SEVENTH DAY
THE HEART OF AN OUTLAW
OH, UNCLE!
THE SEALED ROOM
THE LITTLE DARLING
1776, OR THE HESSIAN RENEGADES
GETTING EVEN
THE BROKEN LOCKET
IN OLD KENTUCKY
THE AWAKENING
THE LITTLE TEACHER
HIS LOST LOVE
LINES OF WHITE ON A SULLEN SEA
THE GIBSON GODDESS
WHAT'S YOUR HURRY?
THE RESTORATION
THE LIGHT THAT CAME
A MIDNIGHT ADVENTURE
IN THE WATCHES OF THE NIGHT
THE MOUNTAINEER'S HONOR
THE TRICK THAT FAILED
THE TEST
TO SAVE HER SOUL

1910:

ALL ON ACCOUNT OF THE MILK
THE WOMAN FROM MELLON'S
THE ENGLISHMAN AND THE GIRL
THE NEWLYWEDS
THE THREAD OF DESTINY
THE SMOKER
THE TWISTED TRAIL
AS IT IS IN LIFE
A RICH REVENGE
A ROMANCE OF THE WESTERN HILLS
NEVER AGAIN
MAY AND DECEMBER
THE UNCHANGING SEA

LOVE AMONG THE ROSES
THE TWO BROTHERS
RAMONA
IN THE SEASON OF BUDS
A VICTIM OF JEALOUSY
A CHILD'S IMPULSE
MUGGSY'S FIRST SWEETHEART
WHAT THE DAISY SAID
THE CALL TO ARMS
AN ARCADIAN MAID
THE SORROWS OF THE UNFAITHFUL
WHEN WE WERE IN OUR 'TEENS
WILFUL PEGGY
MUGGSY BECOMES A HERO
A GOLD NECKLACE
A LUCKY TOOTHACHE
WAITER NO. 5
SIMPLE CHARITY
THE SONG OF THE WILDWOOD FLUTE
A PLAIN SONG

1911:

WHEN A MAN LOVES
WHITE ROSES
THE ITALIAN BARBER
THREE SISTERS
A DECREE OF DESTINY

Independent Motion Picture Company (IMP)

THEIR FIRST MISUNDERSTANDING
THE DREAM
MAID OR MAN
AT THE DUKE'S COMMAND
THE MIRROR
WHILE THE CAT'S AWAY
HER DARKEST HOUR
ARTFUL KATE
A MANLY MAN
THE MESSAGE IN THE BOTTLE
THE FISHER-MAID
IN OLD MADRID
SWEET MEMORIES

THE STAMPEDE
SECOND SIGHT
THE FAIR DENTIST
FOR HER BROTHER'S SAKE
THE MASTER AND THE MAN
THE LIGHTHOUSE KEEPER
BACK TO THE SOIL
IN THE SULTAN'S GARDEN
FOR THE QUEEN'S HONOR
A GASOLINE ENGAGEMENT
AT A QUARTER OF TWO
SCIENCE
THE SKATING BUG
THE CALL OF THE SONG
THE TOSS OF A COIN
'TWEEN TWO LOVES
THE ROSE'S STORY
THE SENTINEL ASLEEP
THE BETTER WAY
HIS DRESS SHIRT
FROM THE BOTTOM OF THE SEA

Majestic

THE COURTING OF MARY
LOVE HEEDS NOT THE SHOWERS
LITTLE RED RIDING HOOD
THE DADDY'S DREAM
HONOR THY FATHER

American Biograph

1912:

IOLA'S PROMISE
FATE'S INTERCEPTION
THE FEMALE OF THE SPECIES
JUST LIKE A WOMAN
THE OLD ACTOR
WON BY A FISH
A LODGING FOR THE NIGHT
A BEAST AT BAY
HOME FOLKS
LENA AND THE GEESE

THE SCHOOL TEACHER AND THE WAIF

AN INDIAN SUMMER

WITH THE ENEMY'S HELP

THE NARROW ROAD

THE INNER CIRCLE

A PUEBLO LEGEND

FRIENDS

SO NEAR, YET SO FAR

A FEUD IN THE KENTUCKY HILLS

THE ONE SHE LOVED

MY BABY

THE INFORMER

1913:

THE UNWELCOME GUEST

THE NEW YORK HAT

Famous Players Film Company/States Rights

IN THE BISHOP'S CARRIAGE (1913)

Directed by Edwin S. Porter and J. Searle Dawley. Scenario by Ben Schulberg. Photographed by H. Lyman Broening. 4 reels.

CAST: David W. Hall, House Peters, Grace Henderson, George Moss.

CAPRICE (1913)

Directed by J. Searle Dawley. Photographed by H. Lyman Broening. 4 reels.

CAST: Owen Moore, Ernest Truex, Ogden Crane.

HEARTS ADRIFT (1914)

Directed by Edwin S. Porter. Photographed by Edwin S. Porter. 4-5 reels.

CAST: Harold Lockwood.

A GOOD LITTLE DEVIL (1914)

Directed by Edwin S. Porter. Based on the play by Austin Strong. Photographed by Edwin S. Porter. 5 reels.

CAST: Ernest Truex, William Norris, Iva Merlin, Wilda Bennett.

TESS OF THE STORM COUNTRY (1914)

Directed by Edwin S. Porter. Scenario by B.P. Schulberg. Based on the novel by Grace Miller White. Photographed by Edwin S. Porter. 5 reels.

CAST: Harold Lockwood, Olive Golden, David Hartford.

Famous Players Film Company/Paramount Pictures Corp.

THE EAGLE'S MATE (1914)

Directed by James Kirkwood. Based on the novel by Anna Alice Chapin. Photographed by Emmett A. Williams. 5 reels.

CAST: James Kirkwood, Ida Waterman, Robert Broderick.

SUCH A LITTLE QUEEN (1914)

Directed by Edwin S. Porter and Hugh Ford. Based on the play by Channing Pollock. 5 reels.

CAST: Carlyle Blackwell, Russell Bassett, Arthur Hoops, Harold Lockwood.

BEHIND THE SCENES (1914)

Directed by James Kirkwood. Based on the story by Margaret Mayo. Photographed by Emmett A. Williams. 5 reels.

CAST: James Kirkwood, Lowell Sherman, Ida Waterman, Russell Bassett.

CINDERELLA (1914)

Directed by James Kirkwood. Based on the fairy tale by Charles Perrault. 4 reels.

CAST: Owen Moore, Isabel Vernon, Georgia Wilson, Lucille Carney.

MISTRESS NELL (1915)

Directed by James Kirkwood. Based on the play by George Cochran Hazelton. 5 reels.

CAST: Owen Moore, Arthur Hoops, Ruby Hoffman, Amelia Rose.

FANCHON, THE CRICKET (1915)

Directed by James Kirkwood. Scenario by James Kirkwood and Frances Marion. 5 reels.

CAST: Jack Standing, Lottie Pickford, Gertrude Norman, Russell Bassett, Jack Pickford.

THE DAWN OF A TOMORROW (1915)

Directed by James Kirkwood. Scenario by Eve Unsell. Based on the play by Frances Hodgson Burnett. 5 reels.

CAST: David Powell, Forrest Robinson, Robert Cain, Margaret Seddon, Blanche Craig.

LITTLE PAL (1915)

Directed by James Kirkwood. Story by Marshall Neilan. Photographed by Emmett A. Williams. 5 reels.

CAST: Russell Bassett, George Anderson, William Lloyd, Constance Johnson.

RAGS (1915)

Directed by James Kirkwood. Photographed by Emmett A. Williams. Story and scenario by Edith Bernard Delano. 5 reels.

CAST: Marshall Neilan, Joseph Manning, J. Farrell MacDonald.

ESMERALDA (1915)

Directed by James Kirkwood. Based on the story by Frances Hodgson Burnett and the play by Burnett and William Gillette. Photographed by Emmett A. Williams. 4 reels.

CAST: Ida Waterman, Fuller Mellish, Arthur Hoops, William Buckley, Charles Waldron.

A GIRL OF YESTERDAY (1915)

Directed by Allan Dwan. 5 reels.

CAST: Jack Pickford, Gertrude Norman, Donald Crisp, Marshall Neilan, Frances Marion, Lillian Langdon.

THE FOUNDLING (1915)

Directed by Allan Dwan. Scenario by Frances Marion. Photographed by H.J. Siddons. 5 reels.

CAST: Frank Mills, Harry Ham, Gertrude Norman, Donald Crisp.

Completed in August, 1915, the negative for THE FOUNDLING was destroyed in the Famous Players studio fire in New York City on September 11, 1915. It was remade with John B. O'Brien as director.

Famous Players-Lasky Film Co./Paramount Pictures Corp.

MADAME BUTTERFLY (1915)

Directed by Sidney Olcott. Based on the novel by John Luther Long. Photographed by Hal Young. 5 reels.

CAST: Marshall Neilan, Olive West, Jane Hall, Lawrence Wood, Caroline Harris. M.W. Rale, W.T. Carleton, Cesare Gravina.

THE FOUNDLING (1916)

Directed by John B. O'Brien. Scenario by Frances Marion. 5 reels.

CAST: Edward Martindale, Maggie Weston, Mildred Morris, Marcia Harris, Tammany Young.

POOR LITTLE PEPPINA (1916)

Directed by Sidney Olcott. Story by Kate Jordan. 6 reels.

CAST: Eugene O'Brien, Antonio Maiori, Ernest Torti, Edwin Mordant, Jack Pickford, Edith Shayne, Cesare Gravina, W.T. Carleton.

THE ETERNAL GRIND (1916)

Directed by John B. O'Brien. Scenario by William H. Clifford. Photographed by Emmett A. Williams. 5 reels.

CAST: Loretta Blake, Dorothy West, John Bowers, Robert Cain, J. Albert Hall.

On July 1, 1916, Famous Players Film Co. and the Jesse L. Lasky Feature Play Company combined under the name of Famous Players-Lasky Corporation.

HULDA FROM HOLLAND (1916)

Directed by John B. O'Brien. Scenario by Edith Bernard Delano. Photographed by Emmett A. Williams. 5 reels.

CAST: Frank Losee, John Bowers, Russell Bassett, Harold Hollacher, Charles E. Vernon.

LESS THAN THE DUST (1916)

Directed by John Emerson. Scenario by Hector Turnbull. Photographed by George Hill. 7 reels.

CAST: David Powell, Frank Losee, Mary Alden, Mario Majeroni, Cesare Gravina, Russell Bassett.

In October, 1916, the Artcraft Pictures Corporation was created to distribute productions of Mary Pickford and other stars and producers.

Artcraft Pictures Corp.

THE PRIDE OF THE CLAN (1917)

Directed by Maurice Tourneur. Scenario by Frances Marion. Based on the play by Eleanor Gates. Photographed by John Van Der Broek and Lucien Andriot. 7 reels.

> CAST: Matt Moore, Warren Cook, Kathryn Browne Decker, Ed Roseman, Joel Day.

THE POOR LITTLE RICH GIRL (1917)

Directed by Maurice Tourneur. Photographed by John Van Der Broek and Lucien Andriot. 6 reels.

> CAST: Madeline Traverse, Charles Wellesley, Gladys Fairbanks, Frank McGlynn, Emile LaCroix, Marcia Harris.

A ROMANCE OF THE REDWOODS (1917)

Directed by Cecil B. DeMille. Scenario by Jeanie Macpherson. Photographed by Alvin Wyckoff. 7 reels.

> CAST: Elliot Dexter, Charles Ogle, Tully Marshall, Raymond Hatton, Walter Lang, Winter Hall.

THE LITTLE AMERICAN (1917)

Directed by Cecil B. DeMille. Story and scenario by Jeanie Macpherson. Photographed by Alvin Wyckoff. 7 reels.

> CAST: Jack Holt, Raymond Hatton, Hobart Bosworth, Walter Long, James Neil, Ben Alexander, Guy Oliver.

On April 15, 1917, Artcraft Pictures Corporation was absorbed by the Famous Players-Lasky Corporation. In January, 1918, the sales and executive departments of Artcraft and Paramount were coordinated and the corporate names of these concerns were discontinued, but the trademarks were retained and all sales made through Famous Players-Lasky Corporation.

REBECCA OF SUNNYBROOK FARM (1917)

Directed by Marshall Neilan. Scenario by Frances Marion. Based on the novel by Kate Douglas Wiggin and the play by Wiggin and Charlotte Thompson. Photographed by Walter Stradling. 6 reels.

> CAST: Eugene O'Brien, Helen Jerome Eddy, Charles Ogle, Marjorie Daw, Josephine Crowell.

A LITTLE PRINCESS (1917)

Directed by Marshall Neilan. Scenario by Frances Marion. Based on the novel by Frances Hodgson Burnett. Photographed by Walter Stradling. 5 reels.

> CAST: Norman Kerry, Katherine Griffith, Ann Schaefer, Zasu Pitts, Theodore Roberts, Gertrude Short, Gustav von Seyffertitz.

STELLA MARIS (1918)

Directed by Marshall Neilan. Scenario by Frances Marion. Based on the novel by William J. Locke. Photographed by Walter Stradling. 6 reels.

> CAST: Conway Tearle, Marcia Manon, Ida Waterman, Herbert Standing, Josephine Crowell.

AMARILLY OF CLOTHES-LINE ALLEY (1918)

Directed by Marshall Neilan. Scenario by Frances Marion. Based on the novel by Belle K. Maniates. Photographed by Walter Stradling. 5 reels.

CAST: Norman Kerry, Herbert Standing, William Scott, Ida Waterman, Wesley Barry, Kate Price.

M'LISS (1918)

Directed by Marshall Neilan. Scenario by Frances Marion. Based on the novel by Bret Harte. Photographed by Walter Stradling. 5 reels.

CAST: Theodore Roberts, Thomas Meighan, Tully Marshall, Charles Ogle, Monte Blue.

HOW COULD YOU, JEAN? (1918)

Directed by William D. Tayor. Scenario by Frances Marion. Based on the novel by Eleanor Hoyt Brainerd. Photographed by Charles Rosher. 5 reels.

CAST: Casson Ferguson, Spottiswoode Aitken, Herbert Standing, Fanny Midgley, Larry Peyton, Zasu Pitts.

JOHANNA ENLISTS (1918)

Directed by William D. Taylor. Scenario by Frances Marion. Based on the story by Rupert Hughes. Photographed by Charles Rosher. 5 reels.

CAST: Anne Schaefer, Fred Huntley, Monte Blue, Douglas MacLean, Emory Johnson, Wallace Beery.

CAPTAIN KIDD, JR. (1919)

Directed by William D. Taylor. Scenario by Frances Marion. Based on the play by Rita Johnson Young. Photographed by Charles Rosher. 5 reels.

CAST: Douglas MacLean, Spottiswoode Aiken, Robert Gordon, Winter Hall, Marcia Manon, Victor Potel.

Mary Pickford Co./First National Exhibitor's Circuit

DADDY LONG LEGS (1919)

Directed by Marshall A. Neilan. Scenario by Agnes C. Johnston. Based on the novel and play by Jean Webster. Photographed by Charles Rosher and Henry Cronjager. 7 reels.

CAST: Mahlon Hamilton, Marshall Neilan, Wesley Barry.

THE HOODLUM (1919)

Directed by Sidney A. Franklin. Based on a novel by Julie Mathilde Lippman. Photographed by Charles Rosher. 6 reels.

CAST: Ralph Lewis, Kenneth Harlan, Melvin Messenger, Dwight Crittenden, Aggie Herring, Andrew Arbuckle, Max Davidson.

HEART O' THE HILLS (1919)

Directed by Sidney A. Franklin. Scenario by Bernard McConville. Based on the novel by John Fox, Jr. Photographed by Charles Rosher. 6 reels.

CAST: Allan Sears, Claire McDowell, Fred W. Huntley, Sam De Grasse, William Bainbridge, Jack Gilbert.

On January 15, 1919, Mary Pickford, Douglas Fairbanks, Charles Chaplin, D. W. Griffith and William S. Hart signed the documents establishing the United Artists Corporation to release their own productions.

United Artists

POLLYANNA (1920)

Directed by Paul Powell. Scenario by Frances Marion. Based on the novel by Eleanor H. Porter and the play by Catherine Chrisholm Cushing. Photographed by Charles Rosher. 6 reels.

CAST: J. Wharton James, Katherine Griffith, William Courtleigh, Herbert Prior, Helen Jerome Eddy.

SUDS (1920)

Directed by Jack Dillon. Scenario by Waldemar Young. Based on a play by Frederick Fenn and Richard Pryce. Photographed by Charles Rosher. 6 reels.

CAST: Albert Austin, Harold Goodwin, Rose Dione.

THE LOVE LIGHT (1921)

Directed by Frances Marion. Photographed by Charles Rosher and Henry Cronjager. 7 reels.

CAST: Fred Thomson, Evelyn Dumo, Edward Phillips, Albert Prisco, Raymond Bloomer.

THROUGH THE BACK DOOR (1921)

Directed by Alfred E. Green and Jack Pickford. Scenario by Marion Fairfax. Photographed by Charles Rosher. 6-7 reels.

CAST: John Harron, Adolphe Menjou, Peaches Jackson, Gertrude Astor, Elinor Fair, Wilfred Lucas.

LITTLE LORD FAUNTLEROY (1921)

Directed by Alfred E. Green and Jack Pickford. Scenario by Bernard McConville. Based on the story by Frances Hodgson Burnett. Photographed by Charles Rosher. 10 reels.

CAST: Claude Gillingwater, Joseph Dowling, James Marcus, Kate Price.

TESS OF THE STORM COUNTRY (1922)

Directed by John S. Robertson. Adapted by Elmer Harris. Based on the novel by Grace Miller White. Photographed by Charles Rosher. 10 reels.

CAST: Lloyd Hughes, Gloria Hope, Jean Hersholt.

In June, 1923, Pickford bought the rights and negatives to 75 of the Biograph shorts in which she appeared. They had been reissued by Nathan Hirsh, who had re-edited the films and added new, often inappropriate titles. By buying them, Pickford was able to take them out of competition with her new releases.

ROSITA (1923)

Directed by Ernst Lubitsch. Adaptation and scenario by Edward Knoblock. Photographed by Charles Rosher. 9 reels.

CAST: George Walsh, Holbrook Blinn, Irene Rich, George Periolat.

DOROTHY VERNON OF HADDON HALL (1924)

Directed by Marshall Neilan. Scenario by Waldemar Young. Photographed by Charles Rosher. 10 reels.

CAST: Allan Forrest, Clare Eames, Lottie Pickford, Marc MacDermott, Estelle Taylor, Anders Randolf.

In July, 1925, Mary Pickford and Paramount settled the rights on the last 15 titles she produced at Famous Players, Famous Players-Lasky Corporation and Artcraft Pictures Corp. As Pickford and Paramount each shared fifty percent of the profits on each title, they decided to split the films, so that each would own a certain number of titles outright.

Choosing titles alternately, selections were based on remake and reissue value. Pickford chose REBECCA OF SUNNYBROOK FARM, THE PRIDE OF THE CLAN, LESS THAN THE DUST, THE POOR LITTLE RICH GIRL, THE FOUNDLING, RAGS, MADAME BUTTERFLY, JOHANNA ENLISTS, THE LITTLE AMERICAN, M'LISS and POOR LITTLE PEPPINA.

Paramount kept STELLA MARIS, HULDA FROM HOLLAND, AMARILLY OF CLOTHES-LINE ALLEY, THE LITTLE PRINCESS, LITTLE PAL, A ROMANCE OF THE REDWOODS, CAPTAIN KIDD, JR., A GIRL OF YESTERDAY, THE ETERNAL GRIND, and HOW COULD YOU, JEAN?

LITTLE ANNIE ROONEY (1925)

Directed by William Beaudine. Adaptation by Hope Loring and Louis D. Lighton. From a story by Catherine Hennessey. Photographed by Charles Rosher and Hal Mohr. 10 reels.

CAST: William Haines, Walter James, Gordon Griffith, Carlo Schipa, Vola Vale.

SPARROWS (1926)

Directed by William Beaudine. Adaptation by C. Gardner Sullivan. From a story by Winifred Dunn. Photographed by Charles Rosher, Karl Struss and Hal Mohr. 9 reels.

CAST: Roy Stewart, Mary Louise Miller, Gustav von Seyffertitz.

MY BEST GIRL (1927)

Directed by Sam Taylor. Adapted by Allen McNeil and Tim Whelan. From the novel by Kathleen Norris. Photographed by Charles Rosher. 9 reels.

COQUETTE (1929)

Directed by Sam Taylor. Adapted by John Grey and Allen McNeil. From the play by George Abbott and Anne P. Bridgers. Photographed by Karl Struss. 9 reels.

CAST: John Mack Brown, George Irving, Louise Beavers, Matt Moore, William Janney, John St. Polis.

THE TAMING OF THE SHREW (1929)

Directed by Sam Taylor. Adapted by Sam Taylor. From the play by William Shakespeare. Photographed by Karl Struss. 8 reels.

CAST: Douglas Fairbanks, Edwin Maxwell, Joseph Cawthorn, Clyde Cook, Geoffrey Wardswell, Dorothy Jordan.

FOREVER YOURS (1930)

Directed by Marshall Neilan. Screenplay by Frances Marion.

CAST: Kenneth MacKenna.

FOREVER YOURS not released, although a six-reel rough cut was prepared.

KIKI (1931)

Art Cinema. Directed by Sam Taylor. From the David Belasco play. Photographed by Karl Struss. 8 reels.

CAST: Reginald Denny, Margaret Livingston, Joseph Cawthorn.

SECRETS (1933)

Directed by Frank Borzage. Adapted by Frances Marion. From the play by Rudolf Besier and May Edginton. Photographed by Ray June. 9 reels.

CAST: Leslie Howard, C. Aubrey Smith, Blanche Frederici, Ned Sparks, Ethel Clayton, Bessie Barriscale.

Mary Pickford was producer only on the following films.

Pickford-Lasky Productions/United Artists

ONE RAINY AFTERNOON (1936)

Directed by Rowland V. Lee. Screenplay by Stephen Morehouse and Maurice Hanline. Photographed by Peverall Marley. 80 mins.

CAST: Francis Lederer, Ida Lupino, Hugh Herbert, Roland Young, Erik Rhodes, Joseph Cawthorn.

THE GAY DESPERADO (1936)

Directed by Rouben Mamoulian. Screenplay by Wallace Smith. Photographed by Lucien Andriot. 85 mins.

CAST: Nino Martini, Ida Lupino, Leo Carrillo, Harold Huber, Mischa Auer, James Blakely.

In September of 1936, Art Cinema, the Joseph Schenck-supervised production company releasing through United Artists, was dissolved. The films were split between Mary Pickford and Emil Jensen. Pickford got the best properties, including her version of "Kiki," which had been produced for Art Cinema, not her own company.

The titles Pickford received were a mix of silent and sound films. They included "The Bat," "The Bat Whispers," "Eternal Love," "Evangeline," "Hallelujah, I'm a Bum," "The Locked Door," "Rain," "Secrets," "Sorrell and Son," "Topsy and Eva," two D.W. Griffith-directed titles: "Drums of Love," "Lady of the Pavements." Also included were "Tonight or Never," the 1926 Norma Talmadge original and the 1931 Pickford remake of "Kiki," and two films produced by Samuel Goldwyn for Art Cinema: "The Greeks Had a Word For Them" and "Street Scene."

Many of these films were reissued, often in shortened versions, by Atlantic Pictures, and were licensed to television in the 1950s. Over the years Pickford disposed of many of the properties for their remake value.

Comet Productions, Inc./United Artists

LITTLE IODINE (1946)

Produced by Buddy Rogers and Ralph Cohn. Directed by Reginald Le Borg. Original screenplay by Richard Landau. Based on Jimmy Hatlo's comic strip. Photographed by Robert Pittack. 57 mins.

CAST: Jo Ann Marlowe, Hobart Cavanaugh, Marc Cramer, Eve Whitney.

SUSIE STEPS OUT (1946)

Produced by Buddy Rogers and Ralph Cohn. Directed by Reginald Le Borg. Screenplay by Elwood Ullman. Original story by Reginald Le Borg and Kurt Neumann. Photographed by Robert Pittack. 65 mins.

CAST: David Bruce, Cleatus Caldwell, Nita Hunter.

THE ADVENTURES OF DON COYOTE (1947)

Produced by Buddy Rogers and Ralph Cohn. Directed by Reginald Le Borg. Screenplay by Bob Williams and Harold Tarshis. Original story by Bob Williams. Photographed by Fred Jackman. 65 mins. color.

CAST: Richard Martin, Frances Rafferty, Val Carlo, Benny Bartlett, Marc Cramer.

STORK BITES MAN (1947)

Produced by Buddy Rogers and Ralph Cohn. Direction and screenplay by Cyril Endfield. Adaptation by Fred Frieberger. From the book by Louis Pollock. Photographed by Vincent Farrar. 75 mins.

CAST: Jackie Cooper, Gene Roberts, Gus Schilling, Emory Parnell.

HIGH FURY (1948)

British title: WHITE CRADLE INN.

Produced by Peak Films. Presented by Charles "Buddy" Rogers and Ralph Cohn. Produced by Ivor McLaren and A.E. Hardman. Directed by Harold French. Screenplay by Harold French, Lesley Storm and Basil Mason. Original story by Harold French and Lesley Storm. Photographed by Derek Williams. 71 mins.

CAST: Madeleine Carroll, Ian Hunter, Michael Rennie, Anna Marie Blanc, Michael McKeag.

Triangle Productions, Inc.

SLEEP MY LOVE (1948)

Presented by Mary Pickford. Produced by Charles "Buddy" Rogers and Ralph Cohn. Directed by Robert Siodmak. Screenplay by St. Clair McKelway and Leo Rosten. Based on a novel by Leo Rosten. 96 mins.

CAST: Claudette Colbert, Robert Cummings, Don Ameche, Rita Johnson, George Coulouris.

Artists Alliance, Inc.

LOVE HAPPY (1949)

Produced by Lester Cowan and Mary Pickford. Directed by David Miller. Story by Harpo Marx. Screenplay by Frank Tashlin and Mac Benoff. Photographed by William C. Mellor. 85 mins.

CAST: Harpo, Chico and Groucho Marx, Ilona Massey, Vera-Ellen, Marion Hutton, Raymond Burr, Bruce Gordon.

Other appearances

ALL-STAR PRODUCTION OF PATRIOTIC EPISODES FOR THE SECOND LIBERTY LOAN (1917)

(also known as WAR RELIEF)

National Association of the Motion Picture Industry. Distributed by Paramount.

CAST: Raymond Hitchcock, Theodore Roberts, Julian Eltinge, Douglas Fairbanks, William S. Hart.

ONE HUNDRED PER CENT AMERICAN (1918)

Famous Players-Lasky. Directed by Arthur Rosson. Photographed by Hugh McClung and Glen MacWilliams.

CAST: Monte Blue and Henry Bergman.

Mary Pickford also made a brief, unbilled appearance in the Virgin Mary in Douglas Fairbanks' production "The Gaucho," directed by F. Richard Jones in 1927.

Index